Lecture Notes in Artificial Intelligence 1634

Subseries of Lecture Notes in Computer Science
Edited by J. G. Carbonell and J. Siekmann

Lecture Notes in Computer Science

Edited by G. Goos, J. Hartmanis and J. van Leeuwen

Springer

Berlin
Heidelberg
New York
Barcelona
Hong Kong
London
Milan
Paris
Singapore
Tokyo

Sašo Džeroski   Peter Flach (Eds.)

Inductive
Logic Programming

9th International Workshop, ILP-99
Bled, Slovenia, June 24-27, 1999
Proceedings

 Springer

Series Editors

Jaime G. Carbonell, Carnegie Mellon University, Pittsburgh, PA, USA
Jörg Siekmann, University of Saarland, Saarbrücken, Germany

Volume Editors

Sašo Džeroski
Jožef Stefan Institute, Department of Intelligent Systems
Jamova 39, SI-1000 Ljubljana, Slovenia
E-mail: Saso.Dzeroski@ijs.si

Peter Flach
University of Bristol, Department of Computer Science
Merchant Venturers Building, Woodland Road, Bristol BS8 1UB, UK
E-mail: Peter.Flach@bristol.ac.uk

Cataloging-in-Publication data applied for

Die Deutsche Bibliothek - CIP-Einheitsaufnahme

Inductive logic programming : 9th international workshop ;
proceedings / ILP-99, Bled, Slovenia, June 24 - 27, 1999. Sašo
Džeroski ; Peter Flach (ed.). - Berlin ; Heidelberg ; New York ;
Barcelona ; Budapest ; Hong Kong ; London ; Milan ; Paris ;
Singapore ; Tokyo : Springer, 1999
    (Lecture notes in computer science ; Vol. 1634 : Lecture notes in
    artificial intelligence)
    ISBN 3-540-66109-3

CR Subject Classification (1998): I.2, D.1.6

ISBN 3-540-66109-3 Springer-Verlag Berlin Heidelberg New York

© Springer-Verlag Berlin Heidelberg 1999
Printed in Germany

Typesetting: Camera-ready by author
SPIN 10703406   06/3142 – 5 4 3 2 1 0   Printed on acid-free paper

Foreword

This volume contains 3 invited and 24 submitted papers presented at the Ninth International Workshop on Inductive Logic Programming, ILP-99. The 24 accepted papers were selected by the program committee from the 40 papers submitted to ILP-99. Each paper was reviewed by three referees, applying high reviewing standards.

ILP-99 was held in Bled, Slovenia, 24–27 June 1999. It was collocated with the Sixteenth International Conference on Machine Learning, ICML-99, held 27–30 June 1999. On 27 June, ILP-99 and ICML-99 were given a joint invited talk by J. Ross Quinlan and a joint poster session where all the papers accepted at ILP-99 and ICML-99 were presented. The proceedings of ICML-99 (edited by Ivan Bratko and Sašo Džeroski) are published by Morgan Kaufmann.

We wish to thank all the authors who submitted their papers to ILP-99, the program committee members and other reviewers for their help in selecting a high-quality program, and the invited speakers: Daphne Koller, Heikki Mannila, and J. Ross Quinlan. Thanks are due to Tanja Urbančič and her team and Majda Zidanski and her team for the organizational support provided. We wish to thank Alfred Hofmann and Anna Kramer of Springer-Verlag for their cooperation in publishing these proceedings. Finally, we gratefully acknowledge the financial support provided by the sponsors of ILP-99.

April 1999

Sašo Džeroski
Peter Flach

ILP-99 Program Committee

Francesco Bergadano (University of Torino)
Henrik Boström (University of Stockholm)
Ivan Bratko (University of Ljubljana)
William Cohen (AT&T Research Labs)
James Cussens (University of York)
Luc De Raedt (University of Leuven)
Sašo Džeroski (Jožef Stefan Institute, co-chair)
Peter Flach (University of Bristol, co-chair)
Alan Frisch (University of York)
Koichi Furukawa (Keio University)
Roni Khardon (University of Edinburgh)
Nada Lavrač (Jožef Stefan Institute)
John Lloyd (Australian National University)
Stan Matwin (University of Ottawa)
Raymond Mooney (University of Texas)
Stephen Muggleton (University of York)
Shan-Hwei Nienhuys-Cheng (University of Rotterdam)
David Page (University of Louisville)
Bernhard Pfahringer (Austrian Research Institute for AI)
Celine Rouveirol (University of Paris)
Claude Sammut (University of New South Wales)
Michele Sebag (Ecole Polytechnique)
Ashwin Srinivasan (University of Oxford)
Prasad Tadepalli (Oregon State University)
Stefan Wrobel (GMD Research Center for Information Technology)

Organizational Support

• The Albatross Congress Tourist Agency, Bled
• Center for Knowledge Transfer in Information Technologies, Jožef Stefan Institute, Ljubljana

Sponsors of ILP-99

• *ILPnet2*, Network of Excellence in Inductive Logic Programming
• *COMPULOG Net*, European Network of Excellence in Computational Logic
• Jožef Stefan Institute, Ljubljana
• LPA Software, Inc.
• University of Bristol

Table of Contents

I Invited Papers

II Contributed Papers

Part I

Invited Papers

Probabilistic Relational Models

Daphne Koller

Computer Science Department, Stanford University, Stanford, CA 94305-9010
http://robotics.stanford.edu/~koller
koller@cs.stanford.edu

Abstract. Probabilistic models provide a sound and coherent foundation for dealing with the noise and uncertainty encountered in most real-
world domains. Bayesian networks are a language for representing complex probabilistic models in a compact and natural way. A Bayesian
network can be used to reason about any attribute in the domain, given
any set of observations. It can thus be used for a variety tasks, including
prediction, explanation, and decision making. The probabilistic semantics also gives a strong foundation for the task of learning models from
data. Techniques currently exist for learning both the structure and the
parameters, for dealing with missing data and hidden variables, and for
discovering causal structure.

One of the main limitations of Bayesian networks is that they represent
the world in terms of a fixed set of "attributes". Like propositional logic,
they are incapable of reasoning explicitly about entities, and thus cannot
represent models over domains where the set of entities and the relations
between them are not fixed in advance. As a consequence, Bayesian networks are limited in their ability to model large and complex domains.
Probabilistic relational models are a language for describing probabilistic models based on the significantly more expressive basis of relational
logic. They allow the domain to be represented in terms of entities, their
properties, and the relations between them. These models represent the
uncertainty over the properties of an entity, representing its probabilistic
dependence both on other properties of that entity and on properties of
related entities. They can even represent uncertainty over the relational
structure itself. Some of the techniques for Bayesian network learning
can be generalized to this setting, but the learning problem is far from
solved. Probabilistic relational models provide a new framework, and new
challenges, for the endeavor of learning relational models for real-world
domains.

1 Relational logic

Relational logic has traditionally formed the basis for most large-scale knowledge
representation systems. The advantages of relational logic in this context are
obvious: the notions of "individuals", their properties, and the relations between
them provide an elegant and expressive framework for reasoning about many
diverse domains. The use of quantification allows us to compactly represent
general rules, that can be applied in many different situations. For example,

when reasoning about genetic transmission of certain properties (e.g., genetically transmitted diseases), we can write down general rules that hold for all people and many properties.

One of the most significant gaps in the expressive power of the logical framework, and one of the most significant barriers to its use in many real-world applications, is its inability to represent and reason with uncertain and noisy information. Uncertainty is unavoidable in the real world: our information is often inaccurate and always incomplete, and only a few of the "rules" that we use for reasoning are true in all (or even most) of the possible cases.

2   Probabilistic models

This limitation, which is crucial in many domains (e.g., medical diagnosis), has led over the last decade to the resurgence of probabilistic reasoning in AI. Probability theory models uncertainty by assigning a probability to each of the states of the world that the agent considers possible. Most commonly, these states are the set of possible assignments of values to a set of *attributes* or *random variables*. For example, in a medical expert system, the random variables could be diseases, symptoms, and predisposing factors. A probabilistic model specifies a joint distribution over all possible assignments of values to these variables. Thus, it specifies implicitly the probability of any event.

As a consequence, unlike standard predictive models, a probability distribution is a model of the domain as a whole, and can be used to deal with a much richer range of problems. It is not limited to conclusions about a prespecified set of attributes, but rather can be used to answer queries about any variable or subset of variables. Nor does it require that the values of all other variables be given; it applies in the presence of any evidence. For example, a probabilistic model can be used to predict the probability that a patient with a history of smoking will get cancer. As new evidence about symptoms and test results is obtained, Bayesian conditioning can be used to update this probability, so that the probability of cancer will go up if we observe heavy coughing. The same model is used to do the predictive and the evidential reasoning. Most impressively, a probabilistic model can perform *explaining away*, a reasoning pattern that is very common in human reasoning, but very difficult to obtain in other formal frameworks. Explaining away uses evidence supporting one cause to decrease the probability in another, not because the two are incompatible, but simply because the one cause explains away the evidence, removing the support for the other cause. For example, the probability of cancer will go down if we observe high fever, which suggests bronchitis as an alternative explanation for the cough. The same probabilistic model supports all of these reasoning patterns, allowing it to be used in many different tasks.

The traditional objection to probabilistic models has been their computational cost. A complete joint probability distribution over a set of random variables must specify a probability for each of the exponentially many different instantiations of the set. Thus, a naive representation is infeasible for all but the simplest domains. *Bayesian networks* [11] use the underlying structure of the domain to overcome this problem. The key insight is the locality of influence present in many real-world domains: a variable is directly influenced by only a few others. For example, smoking causes lung cancer, which can be detected by an X-ray. But the effect of smoking on the X-ray is an indirect one: if we know whether the patient has cancer, the outcome of the X-ray no longer depends on the patient's smoking. A Bayesian network (BN) captures this insight graphically; it represents the distribution as a directed acyclic graph whose nodes represent the random variables and whose edges represent direct dependencies. The semantics of such a network is that each node is conditionally independent (in the probabilistic sense) of its non-descendants given values for its parents. This allows a very concise representation of the joint probability distribution over these random variables: we associate with each node a *conditional probability table*, which specifies for each node X the probability distribution over the values of X given each combination of values for its parents. The conditional independence assumptions associated with the BN imply that these numbers suffice to uniquely determine the probability distribution over these random variables.

Their probabilistic semantics and compact representation have also allowed statistical learning techniques to be used effectively in the task of learning Bayesian networks from data. Standard statistical parameter estimation techniques can be used for learning the parameters of a given network. Scoring functions such as *minimum description length (MDL)* and *Bayesian marginal likelihood* can be used to evaluate different candidate BN structures relative to a training set [5], allowing the construction of heuristic search algorithms for learning structure from data. These techniques allow a BN structure to be discovered from data. The learned structure can often give us insight about the nature of the connections between the variables in the domain. Furthermore, the graph structure can sometimes be interpreted causally [14], allowing us to reach conclusions about the consequences of intervening (acting) in the domain. Statistical learning techniques are also robust to the presence of missing data and hidden variables. Techniques such as *EM (expectation maximization)* can be used to deal with this issue in the context of parameter estimation [8] and have recently even be generalized to the harder problem of structure selection [3].

3   Probabilistic relational models

Over the last decade, BNs have been used with great success in a wide variety of real-world and research applications. However, despite their great success, BNs are often inadequate for as representation for large and complex domains. A BN for a given domain involves a prespecified set of random variables, whose relationship to each other is fixed in advance. Hence, a BN cannot be used to deal with domains where we might encounter several entities in a variety of configurations. This limitation of Bayesian networks is a direct consequence of the fact that they lack the concept of an "object" (or domain entity). Hence, they cannot represent general principles about multiple similar objects which can then be applied in multiple contexts.

Probabilistic relational models (PRMs) extend Bayesian networks with the concepts of individuals, their properties, and relations between them. In a way, they are to Bayesian networks as relational logic is to propositional logic. A PRM has a coherent formal semantics in terms of probability distributions over sets of relational logic interpretations. Given a set of ground objects, a PRM specifies a probability distribution over a set of interpretations involving these objects (and perhaps other objects).

3.1 Basic language

Our discussion of PRMs is based on the presentation in [4, 7]. It also accommodates and generalizes the probabilistic logic programming approach of [10, 13].

The basic entities in a PRM are *objects* or domain entities. Objects in the domain are partitioned into a set of disjoint *classes* $X_1, \ldots, X_n$. Each class is associated with a set of *attributes* $A(X_i)$. Each attribute $A_j \in A(X_i)$ takes on values in some fixed domain of values $V(A_j)$. We use $X.A$ to denote the attribute A of an object in class X. The other main component of the semantics is a set of typed *relations* $R_1, \ldots, R_m$. The classes and relations define the *schema* (or vocabulary) for our model.

It will be useful to define a directed notion of a relation, which we call a *slot*. If $R(X_1, \ldots, X_k)$ is any relation, we can project R onto its i-th and j-th arguments to obtain a binary relation $\rho(X_i, X_j)$, which we can then view as a *slot* of X_i. For any x in X_i, we let $x.\rho$ denote all the elements y in X_j such that $\rho(x, y)$ holds. Objects in this set are called ρ-*relatives* of x. We can concatenate slots to form longer *slot chains* $\tau = \rho_1. \cdots .\rho_m$, defined by composition of binary relations. (Each of the ρ_i's in the chain must be appropriately typed.) We use $X.\tau$ to denote the set of objects that are τ-relatives of an object in class X.

Consider, for example, a simple genetic model of the inheritance of a single gene that determines a person's blood type. Each person has two copies of the chromosome containing this gene, one inherited from her mother, and one inherited from her father. There is also a possibly contaminated test that attempts to recognize the person's blood type. Our schema contains two classes *Person* and *Blood-Test*, and three relations *Father*, *Mother*, and *Test-of*. Attributes of *Person* are *Gender*, *P-Chromosome* (the chromosome inherited from the father), *M-Chromosome* (inherited from the mother). The attributes of *Blood-Test* are *Contaminated* and *Result*.

An *instance* $\mathcal{I}$ of a schema is simply a standard relational logic interpretation of this vocabulary. For an object $\mathcal{I}$ and one of its attributes A, we use $\mathcal{I}_{x.a}$ to denote the value of $x.A$ in $\mathcal{I}$. A *probabilistic relational model (PRM)* defines a probability distribution over a set of instances of a schema. Most simply, we assume that the set of objects and the relations between them are fixed, i.e., external to the probabilistic model. Then, the PRM defines only a probability distribution over the attributes of the objects in the model. More precisely, a *skeleton structure* σ of a relational schema is a partial specification of an instance of the schema. It specifies the set of objects $\mathcal{O}^\sigma(X_i)$ for each class and the relations that hold between the objects. However, it leaves the values of the attributes unspecified. A PRM then specifies a probability distributions over *completions* $\mathcal{I}$ of the skeleton.

The PRM specifies the probability distribution using the same underlying principles used in specifying Bayesian networks. The assumption is that each of the random variables in the PRM — in this case the attributes $x.a$ of the individual objects x — is directly influenced by only a few others. The PRM therefore defines for each $x.a$ a set of *parents*, which are the direct influences on it, and a local probabilistic model that specifies the dependence on these parents. However, there are two primary differences between PRMs and BNs. First, a PRM defines the dependency model at the class level, allowing it to be used for any object in the class. In some sense, it is analogous to a universally quantified statement. Second, the PRM explicitly uses the relational structure of the model, in that it allows the probabilistic model of an attribute of an object to depend also on attributes of related objects. The specific set of related objects can vary with the skeleton σ; the PRM specifies the dependency in a generic enough way that it can apply to an arbitrary relational structure.

Formally, a PRM consists of two components: the qualitative dependency structure, $\mathcal{S}$, and the parameters associated with it, $\theta_{\mathcal{S}}$. The dependency structure is defined by associating with each attribute $X.A$ a set of *parents* $\mathrm{Pa}(X.A)$. These correspond to *formal* parents; they will be instantiated in different ways for different objects in X. Intuitively, the parents are attributes that are "direct influences" on $X.A$.

We distinguish between two types of formal parents. The attribute $X.A$ can depend on another probabilistic attribute B of X. This formal dependence induces a corresponding dependency for individual objects: for any object x in $\mathcal{O}^\sigma(X)$, $x.a$ will depend probabilistically on $x.b$. The attribute $X.A$ can also depend on attributes of related objects $X.\tau.B$, where τ is a slot chain. To understand the semantics of this formal dependence for an individual object x, recall that $x.\tau$ represents the *set* of objects that are τ-relatives of x. Except in cases where the slot chain is guaranteed to be single-valued, we must specify the probabilistic dependence of $x.a$ on the multiset $\{y.b \;:\; y \in x.\tau\}$.

The notion of *aggregation* from database theory gives us precisely the right tool to address this issue; i.e., $x.a$ will depend probabilistically on some aggregate property of this multiset. There are many natural and useful notions of aggregation: the mode of the set (most frequently occurring value); mean value of the set (if values are numerical); median, maximum, or minimum (if values are ordered); cardinality of the set; etc. More formally, our language allows a notion of an aggregate γ; γ takes a multiset of values of some ground type, and returns a summary of it. The type of the aggregate can be the same as that of its arguments. However, we allow other types as well, e.g., an aggregate that reports the size of the multiset. We allow $X.A$ to have as a parent $\gamma(X.\tau.B)$; the semantics is that for any $x \in X$, $x.a$ will depend on the value of $\gamma(x.\tau.b)$. We define $V(\gamma(X.\tau.b))$ in the obvious way.

Given a set of parents $\mathrm{Pa}(X.A)$ for $X.A$, we can define a local probability model for $X.A$. We associate $X.A$ with a *conditional probability distribution* that specifies $P(X.A \mid \mathrm{Pa}(X.A))$. Let U be the set of parents of $X.A$. Each of these parents U_i — whether a simple attribute in the same relation or an aggregate of a set of τ relatives — has a set of values $V(U_i)$ in some ground type. For each tuple of values $\mathbf{u} \in V(\mathbf{U})$, we specify a distribution $P(X.A \mid \mathbf{u})$ over $V(X.A)$. This entire set of parameters comprises θ_S.

3.2 PRM semantics

Given any skeleton, we have a set of random variables of interest: the attributes of the objects in the skeleton. We want the PRM to specify a probability distribution over the possible assignments of values to these random variables. In order to guarantee that the local probability models associated with these variables define a coherent distribution, we must ensure that our probabilistic dependencies are acyclic, so that a random variable does not depend, directly or indirectly, on its own value. Consider the parents of an attribute $X.A$. When $X.B$ is a parent of $X.A$, we define an edge $x.b \to_\sigma x.a$; when $\gamma(X.\tau.B)$ is a parent of $X.A$ and $y \in x.\tau$, we define an edge $y.b \to_\sigma x.a$. We say that a dependency structure S is *acyclic* relative to a skeleton σ if the directed graph defined by $\to_\sigma$ over the variables $x.a$ is acyclic. In this case, we are guaranteed that the PRM defines a coherent probabilistic model over complete instantiations $\mathcal{I}$ consistent with σ.

$$P(\mathcal{I} \mid \sigma, S, \theta_S) = \prod_{X_i} \prod_{A \in \mathcal{A}(X_i)} \prod_{x \in \mathcal{O}^\sigma(X_i)} P(\mathcal{I}_{x.a} \mid \mathcal{I}_{\mathrm{Pa}(x.a)}) \tag{1}$$

This construction allows us to check whether a dependency structure S is acyclic relative to a fixed skeleton σ. However, we often want stronger guarantees: we want to ensure that our dependency structure is acyclic for any skeleton that we are likely to encounter. How do we guarantee acyclicity for an arbitrary skeleton? A simple approach is to ensure that dependencies among attributes respect some order, i.e., they are stratified. More precisely, we say that $X.A$ *directly depends* on $Y.B$ if either $X = Y$ and $X.B$ is a parent of $X.A$, or $\gamma(X.\tau.B)$ is a parent of $X.A$ and the τ-relatives of X are of class Y. We require that $X.A$ directly depends only on attributes that precede it in the order.

While this simple approach clearly ensures acyclicity, it is too limited to cover many important cases. In our genetic model, for example, the genotype of a person depends on the genotype of her parents; thus, we have *Person.P-Chromosome* depending directly on *Person.P-Chromosome*, which clearly violates the requirements of our simple approach. In this model, the apparent cyclicity at the attribute level is resolved at the level of individual objects, as a person cannot be his/her own ancestor. That is, the resolution of acyclicity relies on some prior knowledge that we have about the domain. We want to allow the user to give us information such as this, so that we can make stronger guarantees about acyclicity.

We allow the user to assert that certain slots $\mathcal{R}_{ga} = \{\rho_1, \ldots, \rho_k\}$ are *guaranteed acyclic*; i.e., we are guaranteed that there is a partial ordering $\prec_{ga}$ such that if y is a ρ-relative for some $\rho \in \mathcal{R}_{ga}$ of x, then $y \prec_{ga} x$. We say that τ is guaranteed acyclic if each of its components ρ's is guaranteed acyclic. This prior knowledge allows us to guarantee the legality of certain dependency models [4]. We start by building a graph that describes the direct dependencies between the attributes. In this graph, we have a *yellow* edge $X.B \to X.A$ if $X.B$ is a parent of $X.A$. If $\gamma(X.\tau.B)$ is a parent of $X.A$, we have an edge $Y.B \to X.A$ which is *green* if τ is guaranteed acyclic and *red* otherwise. (Note that there might be several edges, of different colors, between two attributes). The intuition is that dependency along green edges relates objects that are ordered by an acyclic order. Thus these edges by themselves or combined with intra-object dependencies (yellow edges) cannot cause a cyclic dependency. We must take care with other dependencies, for which we do not have prior knowledge, as these might form a cycle. This intuition suggests the following definition: A (colored) dependency graph is *stratified* if every cycle in the graph contains at least one green edge and no red edges. It can be shown that if the colored dependency graph of S and $\mathcal{R}_{ga}$ is stratified, then for any skeleton σ for which the slots in $\mathcal{R}_{ga}$ are jointly acyclic, S defines a coherent probability distribution over assignments to σ.

This notion of stratification generalizes the two special cases we considered above. When we do not have any guaranteed acyclic relations, all the edges in the dependency graph are colored either yellow or red. Thus, the graph is stratified if and only if it is acyclic. In the genetics example, all the relations would be in $\mathcal{R}_{ga}$. Thus, it suffices to check that dependencies within objects (yellow edges) are acyclic. Checking for stratification of a colored graph can be done, using standard graph algorithms, in time linear in the number of edges in the graph.

4 Inference

PRMs are significantly more expressive than Bayesian networks. Performing inference on a BN — answering queries about one or more random variables given evidence about others — is already an expensive operation (the task is NP-hard [1]). It is natural to suspect that the additional expressive power of PRMs might make the inference problem significantly harder. Surprisingly, we have strong evidence that the additional expressive power helps, rather than hinders, to perform the inference task.

A PRM makes explicit two types of structure which are often present in a BN but only implicitly: encapsulation of influence, and model reuse. As we will see, making this structure explicit allows the inference algorithm to exploit it, and often to achieve better performance.

The random variables in a BN are typically induced by more than one "object" present in the model; but having no notion of an "object", the BN has no way of making that knowledge explicit. The PRM does make this knowledge explicit, and it turns out to be extremely useful. In practice, it is often the case that an attribute of an object is influenced mostly by other attributes of the same object; there are relatively few inter-object dependencies. In general, BN inference algorithms [9] use a "divide and conquer" approach, doing localized computation over the graphical structure of the BN and putting the results together. By making the locality structure explicit, we can give our BN algorithm guidance on how to perform this partitioning effectively.

The other useful structure is induced by the class structure. A PRM makes explicit the fact that several "chunks" of the model are derived from the same probabilistic model — the class model. If we have multiple objects of the same class, without any evidence telling us that they are necessarily different, we can often do a single inference subroutine for one and reuse it for the others. In large structured domains with multiple objects, the savings can be considerable.

In [12], we present experiments with this approach on the challenging real-world domain of military situation assessment. We show that by using the structure of the PRM, we can gain orders of magnitude savings over the straightforward BN inference algorithms. In particular, we constructed a PRM for this domain, and considered its behavior over a skeleton with a large number of objects. The BN over the attributes of these objects has over 5500 random variables. A standard BN inference algorithm, applied to this BN, took over twenty minutes to answer a query. The PRM inference algorithm that takes advantage of the additional structure took nine seconds.

5   Learning

One of the main advantages of probabilistic model is that the same representation language accommodates both reasoning and learning. As discussed in the introduction, the underlying probabilistic framework provides many advantages, including the availability of: good statistical parameter estimation techniques; techniques for dealing with missing data; and well-motivated scoring functions for structure selection.

PRMs are built on the same foundations as BNs. They share the same underlying probabilistic semantics and the use of local independence models to allow compact representation of complex distributions. This similarity allows many of the BN learning techniques developed over the last few years to be extended to PRMs. As a first step [6], we have shown how to apply EM (Expectation Maximization [2]) to the problem of learning parameters θ_S for a PRM whose dependence structure S is known. More recently [4], we have attacked the more challenging problem of learning the dependency structure S from data. Given a relational database as a training set, our algorithm discovers probabilistic dependencies between attributes of related entities. For example, in a database of movies and actors, it learned that the *Role-Type* played by an actor in a movie depends on the *Gender* of the actor and the *Genre* of the movie.

6 Structural uncertainty

So far, we have assumed that the skeleton is external to the probabilistic model. In fact, our framework can be extended to accommodate a generative model over skeletons as well as their properties. We now provide a brief sketch of this extension, which is fully described in [7, 12].

Restricting attention to binary relations, we define a probability distribution over the relational structure relating to slots of a given class. For example, let us assume that the class *Professor* has a slot *Student*. We can introduce an attribute into the class called *num(Student)*, which takes on integer values in some finite range $0, \ldots, k$. The value of this attribute represents the number of students that the professor has. Now, consider a particular professor in this class. Each choice of value for this attribute is associated with a different skeleton, where the professor has a different set of students. We can specify a probability distribution over the values of this attribute, which induces a probabilistic model over the skeletons of this schema.

Our framework allows this uncertainty over structure to interact with the model in interesting ways. In particular, we view the attribute *num(Student)* as a random variable, and it can be used in the same ways as any other random variable: it can depend probabilistically on the values of other attributes in the model (both of the associated object and of related ones) and can influence probabilistically the values of attributes in the model. For example, the attribute *num(Student)* can depend on the amount of funding — e.g., via an aggregate *Sum* over *Professor.Contract.Amount*, and can influence their stress level.

Note that the semantics of this extension are significantly more subtle. A set of objects and relations between them no longer specifies a complete schema. For example, assume we are given a single professor and one student for her. A priori, the PRM may give positive probability to instances $\mathcal{I}$ where the professor has zero students, one student, two students, or more. Instances where the professor has zero students are inconsistent with our evidence that the professor has at least one. We must therefore use Bayesian conditioning to update the distribution to accommodate this new fact. There are also instances where the professor has more than one student. In general, these are not inconsistent with our observations. They will merely contain new "generic" objects of the *Student* class, about which nothing is known except that they are students of this particular professor.

In [7, 12], we discuss some other forms of representing uncertainty over the relational structure of the model. We also show how some of the ideas for guaranteeing acyclic model structure can be extended to this richer setting.

7 Conclusions and further directions

PRMs provide a formal foundation for a rich class of models that integrates the expressive power of Bayesian networks and of relational models. On the one hand, they allow Bayesian networks to scale up to significantly more complex domains.

On the other, they provide a coherent and robust treatment of uncertainty, and can therefore deal with domains where deterministic first-order frameworks could not reasonably be applied. As we showed in [7], PRMs allow existing knowledge bases to be annotated with probabilistic models, greatly increasing their ability to express meaningful knowledge in real-world applications.

By carefully designing the language features of PRMs and their semantics, we have managed to achieve this increase in expressive power without losing the properties that made Bayesian networks so attractive: the sound probabilistic semantics, the ability to answer an entire range of queries, and the existence of effective inference and learning algorithms that exploit the structure. Indeed, we have shown that by making this higher level structure explicit, we allow inference algorithms to exploit it and achieve even better performance than on the equivalent BN.

PRMs provide a new coherent framework for combining logical and probabilistic approaches. They therefore raise many new challenges. Some of the the most important of these are in the area of discovering structure from complex data; some important tasks include: automated discovery of hidden variables, discovering causal structure, automatically learning a class hierarchy, and more. Solving these problems and others will almost certainly require an integration of techniques from probabilistic learning and from inductive logic programming.

Acknowledgements All of the work described in this paper was done jointly with Avi Pfeffer. Some is also joint work with Nir Friedman and Lise Getoor. This work was supported by the Office of Naval Research, by DARPA's HPKB program, by DARPA's DMIF program under subcontract to Information Extraction and Transport, by the Army Research Office under the MURI program "Integrated Approach to Intelligent Systems," and by the generosity of the Powell Foundation and the Sloan Foundation.

References

1. G.F. Cooper. The computational complexity of probabilistic inference using Bayesian belief networks. *Artificial Intelligence*, 42:393–405, 1990.
2. A. Dempster, N. Laird, and D. Rubin. Maximum likelihood from incomplete data via the EM algorithm. *Journal of the Royal Statistical Society*, 39 (Series B):1–38, 1977.
3. N. Friedman. Learning belief networks in the presence of missing values and hidden variables. In *Proc. ICML*, 1997.
4. N. Friedman, L. Getoor, D. Koller, and A. Pfeffer. Learning probabilistic relational models. In *Proc. IJCAI*, 1999.
5. D. Heckerman. A tutorial on learning with Bayesian networks. Technical Report MSR-TR-95-06, Microsoft Research, 1995.
6. D. Koller and A. Pfeffer. Learning probabilities for noisy first-order rules. In *Proc. IJCAI*, pages 1316–1321, 1997.
7. D. Koller and A. Pfeffer. Probabilistic frame-based systems. In *Proc. AAAI*, 1998.

8. S. L. Lauritzen. The EM algorithm for graphical association models with missing data. *Computational Statistics and Data Analysis*, 19:191–201, 1995.

9. Steffen L. Lauritzen and David J. Spiegelhalter. Local computations with probabilities on graphical structures and their application to expert systems. *Journal of the Royal Statistical Society*, B 50(2):157–224, 1988.

10. L. Ngo and P. Haddawy. Answering queries from context-sensitive probabilistic knowledge bases. *Theoretical Computer Science*, 1996.

11. J. Pearl. *Probabilistic Reasoning in Intelligent Systems: Networks of Plausible Inference*. Morgan Kaufmann, 1988.

12. A. Pfeffer, D. Koller, B. Milch, and K. Takusagawa. SPOOK: A system for probabilistic object-oriented knowledge representation. Submitted to UAI '99, 1999.

13. D. Poole. Probabilistic Horn abduction and Bayesian networks. *Artificial Intelligence*, 64:81–129, 1993.

14. P. Spirtes, C. Glymour, and R. Scheines. *Causation, prediction, and search*. Springer Verlag, 1993.

Inductive Databases
(Abstract)

Heikki Mannila

Microsoft Research, One Microsoft Way, Redmond, WA 98052-6399, USA
mannila@microsoft.com

Abstract. Data mining aims at trying to locate interesting patterns or regularities from large masses of data. Data mining can be viewed as part of a data analysis or knowledge management. In data analysis tasks one can see a continuous spectrum of information needs, starting from very simple database queries ("what is the address of customer NN"), moving to more complex aggregate information ("what are the sales by product groups and regions") to data mining type of queries ("give me interesting trends on sales"). This suggests that it is useful to view data mining as querying the theory of the database, i.e., the set of sentences that are true in the database. An *inductive database* is a database that conceptually contains in addition to normal data also all the generalizations of the data from a given language of descriptors. Inductive databases can be viewed as analogues to deductive databases: deductive databases conceptually contain all the facts derivable from the data and the rules. In this talk I describe a formal framework for inductive databases and discuss some theoretical and practical problems in the area.

Some Elements of Machine Learning[*]
(Extended Abstract)

J. R. Quinlan

School of Computer Science and Engineering
UNSW
Sydney Australia 2052
quinlan@cse.unsw.edu.au

1 Introduction

This talk will revisit some important elements of ML lore, focusing on the design of classifier-learning systems. Within ML, the key desiderata for such systems have been predictive accuracy and interpretability. Although Provost, Fawcett and Kohavi (1998) have shown that accuracy alone is a poor metric for comparing learning systems, it is still important in most real-world applications. The quest for intelligibility, stressed from earliest days by Michie, Michalski and others, is now crucial for those data-mining applications whose main objective is insight. Scalability is also vital if the learning system is to be capable of analyzing the burgeoning numbers of instances and attributes in commercial and scientific databases.

The design of classifier-learning systems is guided by several perceived truths, including:

- Learning involves generalization.
- Most ML models are structures (exceptions being Naive Bayes and some instance-based models).
- A model is an element in a lattice of possible models, so search is unavoidable.
- General-to-specific and specific-to-general search are both important – most systems will use both.
- Similar instances probably belong to the same class (the *similarity assumption*).
- Learned models should not blindly maximize accuracy on the training data, but should balance resubstitution accuracy against generality, simplicity, interpretability, and search parsimony.
- Error can be decomposed into components arising from bias and variance, thereby helping to understand the behavior of learning systems.

We might all accept these, but that does not mean that their consequences and possibilities have been thoroughly explored. I would like to illustrate this with four mini-topics relevant to the design of classifier-learning systems: creating structure, removing excessive structure, using search effectively, and finding an appropriate tradeoff between accuracy and complexity.

---

[*] This extended abstract also appears in the Proceedings of the Sixteenth International Conference on Machine Learning, published by Morgan Kaufmann.

2 Structured Models

Two commonly-used approaches used in ML are *divide-and-conquer*, which produces tree-structured models, and *cover*, which generally yields sequence models such as rulesets and Horn Clause programs. Both divide-and-conquer and cover can transform any parametric model class into a structured model class, reducing its bias but at the same time increasing its variance.

In propositional learning, model components such as leaves or rules are associated with contiguous regions in the instance space, and can thus be justified under the similarity assumption. But "closeness" in the instance space is not the only way to measure similarity; two instances can also be regarded as similar if they are mapped to the same output by some function. For example, consider the application of divide-and-conquer to Naive Bayes. Whereas Kohavi's (1996) NBTree generates a tree-structured model based on the familiar regional partition of the instance space, an alternative divides the instances on the basis of the class predicted by the current Naive Bayes model.

3 Right-Sizing Models

The downside of structured models is their potential to overfit the training data. In ML we generally accept that it is better to construct a model and then post-process the structure to remove unhelpful parts. The methods used to decide whether structure is warranted can be grouped into

- syntactic heuristics such as MML/MDL, cost-complexity pruning, and structural risk minimization, and
- non-syntactic heuristics such as cross-validation, reduced error pruning, and pessimistic pruning.

MML/MDL is appealing – it has a firm basis in theory, does not require construction of additional models, uses all the training data, and avoids strong assumptions. However its performance depends critically on the way in which the conceptual messages are encoded. For example, MDL fares poorly in evaluations conducted by Kearns, Mansour, Ng, and Ron (1997). Wallace, the founder of MML, has questioned the coding approach used by Kearns et al and shows that an alternative scheme produces much better results.

4 Computation-Intensive Learning

Structured models imply vast model spaces, so early ML algorithms used greedy heuristics in order to make the search tractable. As cycles have become exponentially cheaper, researchers have experimented with more thorough search. The results have been rather unexpected – theories have been found that are both simpler and fit the data better, but predictive accuracy has often suffered. Examples are provided by Webb's (1993) work with finding optimal rules, and

Cameron-Jones' and my (1995) experiments varying the amount of search. (In hindsight, we might have expected this, since the phenomenon of overtraining is well-known in Neural Networks.)

Domingos (1998) has recently developed a "process-oriented" approach that relates true error rate directly to search complexity, much as MML/MDL relates it to theory complexity. An ideal formalism would take into account resubstitution error, theory complexity, and search complexity.

5 Boosting

Freund and Schapire's (1996) *boosting* has been acclaimed by ML researchers and statisticians alike. All empirical studies have found that boosting usually increases predictive accuracy, often dramatically.

On the other hand, boosted classifiers can become totally opaque. For instance, it is possible to construct a single decision tree that is exactly equivalent to a boosted sequence of trees, but the single tree can become enormous even when the sequence is as short as three.

Is there a middle ground? I will discuss a fledgling technique for using boosting to improve the predictive accuracy of a rule-based classifier without increasing its complexity. A more ambitious goal would be to find a comprehensible approximation to a boosted classifier.

6 Looking Ahead

ML is a mature field with unique features that distinguish it from related disciplines such as Statistics. My list of its most valuable assets includes:

- A head start in relational learning (one decade at least).
- A substantial body of theory (eg, PAC-learnability, weak learnability, identification in the limit).
- Links between theory and system development (eg, boosting).
- An understanding of search and heuristics (a legacy of ML's roots in AI).
- A lack of hang-ups about optimality.

If I were given one wish regarding future directions in ML, it would be that we pay more attention to interpretability. For example, I would like to see:

- A model of interpretability (or, alternatively, of opacity).
- Approaches for constructing understandable approximations to complex models.
- Ways of reformulating models to improve their intelligibility.

Acknowledgements Thanks to Sašo Džeroski and Ivan Bratko for comments on a draft of this abstract.

References

1. Domingos, P. (1998) A process-oriented heuristic for model selection. *Proceedings ICML'98*, 127-135. San Francisco: Morgan Kaufmann.
2. Freund, Y., and Schapire, R.E. (1997) A decision-theoretic generalization of on-line learning and an application to boosting. *Journal of Computer and System Sciences, 55*, 119-139.
3. Kearns, M., Mansour, Y., Ng, A.Y., and Ron, D. (1997) An experimental and theoretical comparison of model selection methods. *Machine Learning, 27*, 1, 7-50.
4. Kohavi, R. (1996) Scaling up the accuracy of naive-Bayes classifiers: a decision-tree hybrid. *Proceedings KDD-96*.
5. Provost, F., Fawcett, T., and Kohavi, R. (1998) The case against accuracy estimation for comparing induction algorithms. *Proceedings ICML'98*, 445-453. San Francisco: Morgan Kaufmann.
6. Quinlan, J.R., and Cameron-Jones, R.M. (1995) Oversearchinhg and layered search in empirical learning. *Proceedings IJCAI'95*, 1019-1024. San Francisco: Morgan Kaufmann.
7. Webb, G. (1993) Systematic search for categorical attribute-value data-driven machine learning. *Proceedings 6th Australian Joint Conference on Artificial Intelligence*, 342-347. Singapore: World Scientific.

Part II

Contributed Papers

Refinement Operators Can Be (Weakly) Perfect

Liviu Badea and **Monica Stanciu**

AI Lab, Research Institute for Informatics
8-10 Averescu Blvd., Bucharest, Romania
e-mail: **badea@ici.ro**

Abstract. Our aim is to construct a *perfect* (i.e. minimal and optimal) ILP refinement operator for hypotheses spaces bounded below by a most specific clause and subject to syntactical restrictions in the form of input/output variable declarations (like in Progol). Since unfortunately no such optimal refinement operators exist, we settle for a weaker form of optimality and introduce an associated weaker form of subsumption which exactly captures a first incompleteness of Progol's refinement operator. We argue that this sort of incompleteness is not a drawback, as it is justified by the examples and the MDL heuristic.
A second type of incompleteness of Progol (due to subtle interactions between the requirements of non-redundancy, completeness and the variable dependencies) is more problematic, since it may sometimes lead to unpredictable results. We remove this incompleteness by constructing a sequence of increasingly more complex refinement operators which eventually produces the first (weakly) *perfect* refinement operator for a Progol-like ILP system.

1 Introduction

Learning logic programs from examples in Inductive Logic Programming (ILP) involves traversing large spaces of hypotheses. Various heuristics, such as information gain or example coverage, can be used to guide this search. A simple search algorithm (even a complete and non-redundant one) would not do, unless it allows for a flexible traversal of the search space, based on an external heuristic. Refinement operators allow us to decouple the heuristic from the search algorithm.

In order not to miss solutions, the refinement operator should be (weakly) complete. In order not to revisit already visited portions of the search space it should also be non-redundant. Such weakly complete non-redundant refinement operators are called *optimal*.

Various top-down ILP systems set a lower bound (usually called most specific clause (MSC) or saturant) on the hypotheses space in order to limit its size. Syntactical restrictions in the form of mode declarations on the predicate arguments are also used as a declarative bias.

Devising an optimal refinement operator for a hypotheses space bounded below by a MSC in the presence of input/output ($\pm$) variable dependencies is not only a challenging issue given the subtle interactions of the above- mentioned features, but also a practically important one since refinement operators represent the core of an ILP system.

The Progol refinement operator [4], for example, is incomplete in two ways. First, it is incomplete w.r.t. ordinary subsumption since each literal from the MSC has *at most one* corresponding literal in each hypothesis (only variabilized *subsets* of the MSC are considered as hypotheses). Rather than being a drawback, we argue that this incompleteness is exactly the sort of behavior we would expect. In order to make this observation precise, we introduce a weaker form of subsumption under which the refinement operator is complete.

The second type of incompleteness (see also example 30 of [4]) is more problematic since it cannot be characterized in a clean way and since it depends on the ordering of mode declarations and examples. In order to achieve non-redundancy and at the same time obey the ±variable dependencies imposed by the mode declarations, Progol scans the MSC left-to-right and non-deterministically decides for each literal whether to include it in (or exclude it from) the current hypothesis. A variabilized version of the corresponding MSC literal is included in the current hypothesis only if all its input (+) variables are preceded by suitable output (−) variables. This approach is incomplete since it would reject a literal l_i that obtains a +variable from a literal l_j that will be considered only later:

$$\ldots, l_i(\cdots, +\overrightarrow{X, \cdots}), \ldots, l_j(\cdots, -X, \cdots), \ldots$$

although l_j, l_i would constitute a valid hypothesis.

Note that a simple idea like reordering the literals in the MSC would not help in general, since the MSC may exhibit cyclic variable dependencies while still admitting acyclic subsets.

The following example illustrates the above-mentioned incompleteness:

```
:- modeh(1, p(+any, +t))?    :- modeb(1, f(-any, -t))?
:- modeb(1, g(+any, +t))?    :- modeb(1, h(-any, -t))?
p(1,a).  p(2,a).  p(3,a).    :-p(4,a).
f(1,b).  f(2,b).  f(3,b).    f(4,b).
g(1,a).  g(2,c).  g(3,c).
h(1,a).  h(2,c).  h(3,c).    h(4,a).
```

As long as the mode declaration for h precedes that of h, Progol will produce a MSC p(A,B) :- f(A,C), g(A,B), h(A,B) in which the g literal cannot obtain its +variables from h since the former precedes the latter in the MSC. Thus Progol will miss the solution p(A,B) :- h(A,C), g(A,C) which can be found only if we move the mode declaration for h before that of g. This type of incompleteness may sometimes lead to unpredictable results and a reordering of the mode declarations will not always be helpful in solving the problem.

Although Progol's algorithm for constructing the MSC makes sure that each +variable occurrence is preceded by a corresponding −variable, there may be several other −variable occurrences in literals ordered after the literal containing the +variable. These potential "future links" will be missed by Progol. In cases of many such "future links", the probability of the correct ordering being in the search space is exponentially low in the number of "future links".

For a *very small* number of literals in the body and/or a small variable depth, this incompleteness may not be too severe, especially if we order the mode declarations appropriately. The problem becomes important for hypotheses with a larger number of literals.

2 Refinement Operators

In order to be able to guide the search in the space of hypotheses by means of an external heuristic, we need to construct a refinement operator. For a top-down search, we shall deal with a *downward* refinement operator, i.e. one that constructs clause *specializations*. In the following we will consider refinement operators w.r.t. the subsumption ordering between clauses.

Definition 1. Clause C *subsumes* clause D, $C \succeq D$ iff there exists a substitution θ such that $C\theta \subseteq D$ (the clauses being viewed as sets of literals). C *properly subsumes* D, $C \succ D$ iff $C \succeq D$ and $D \not\succeq C$. C and D are *subsume-equivalent* $C \sim D$ iff $C \succeq D$ and $D \succeq C$.

Lemma 2. *[5] For a most general literal L w.r.t. clause C (one with new and distinct variables), C properly subsumes $C \cup \{L\}$ iff L is incompatible with all literals in C (i.e. it has a different predicate symbol).*

The somewhat subtle and counter-intuitive properties of subsumption are due to the incompatibility of the induced subsumption-equivalence relation $\sim$ with the elementary operations of a refinement operator, such as adding a literal or performing a substitution.

Remark. Note that not all reduced specializations D of a reduced clause C can be obtained just by adding one literal or by making a simple substitution $\{X/Y\}$. It may be necessary to add several literals and make several simple substitutions in one refinement step, since each of these elementary operations applied separately would just produce a clause that is subsume- equivalent with C.

Definition 3. ρ is a (downward) *refinement operator* iff for all clauses C, ρ produces only specializations of C: $\rho(C) \subseteq \{D \mid C \succeq D\}$.

Definition 4. A refinement operator ρ is called

- *(locally) finite* iff $\rho(C)$ is finite and computable for all C.
- *proper* iff for all C, $\rho(C)$ contains no $D \sim C$.
- *complete* iff for all C and D, $C \succ D \Rightarrow \exists E \in \rho^*(C)$ such that $E \sim D$.
- *weakly complete* iff $\rho^*(\square) =$ the entire set of clauses.
- *non-redundant* iff for all C_1, C_2 and D, $D \in \rho^*(C_1) \cap \rho^*(C_2) \Rightarrow C_1 \in \rho^*(C_2)$ or $C_2 \in \rho^*(C_1)$.
- *ideal* iff it is locally finite, proper and complete.

- *optimal* iff it is locally finite, non-redundant and weakly complete.
- *minimal* iff for all C, $\rho(C)$ contains only downward covers[1] and all its elements are incomparable ($D_1, D_2 \in \rho(C) \Rightarrow D_1 \not\succeq D_2$ and $D_2 \not\succeq D_1$).
- *(downward) cover set* iff $\rho(C)$ is a maximal set of non- equivalent downward covers of C.
- *perfect* iff it is minimal and optimal.

Theorem 5. *[6]. For a language containing at least one predicate symbol of arity ≥ 2, there exist no ideal (downward) refinement operators.*

The nonexistence of ideal refinement operators is due to the incompleteness of the (unique) cover set of a clause C, because of *uncovered infinite ascending chains* $C \succ \ldots \succ E_{i+1} \succ E_i \succ E_{i-1} \succ \ldots \succ E_1$ (for which there exists no maximal element $E \succeq E_i$ for all i, such that $C \succ E$). Indeed, since none of the E_i can be a downward cover of C, C cannot have a complete downward cover set.

Every ideal refinement operator ρ determines a finite and complete downward cover set $\rho^{dc}(C) \subseteq \rho(C)$, obtained from $\rho(C)$ by removing all E covered by some $D \in \rho(C): D \succeq E$.

3 Ideal versus optimal refinement operators

The subsumption lattice of hypotheses is far from being tree-like: a given clause D can be reachable from several incomparable hypotheses $C_1, C_2, \ldots$.

Theorem 6. *A refinement operator cannot be both* complete *(a feature of ideal operators) and* non-redundant *(a feature of optimal operators).*

Proposition 7. *For each ideal refinement operator ρ we can construct an optimal refinement operator $\rho^{(o)}$.*

$\rho^{(o)}$ is obtained from ρ such that for $D \in \rho(C_1) \cap \ldots \cap \rho(C_n)$ we have $\exists i.D \in \rho^{(o)}(C_i)$ and $\forall j \neq i.D \notin \rho^{(o)}(C_j)$.

The efficiency of ideal and respectively optimal refinement operators depends on the density of solutions in the search space. *Ideal* operators are preferable for search spaces with *dense solutions,* for which almost any refinement path leads to a solution. In such cases, an optimal (non-redundant) operator might get quite close to a solution C but could backtrack just before finding it for reasons of non-redundancy (for example because C is scheduled to be visited on a different path and thus it avoids revisiting it). Despite this problem, the solutions are dense, so an optimal operator would not behave too badly, after all.

On the other hand, *optimal* operators are preferable for search spaces with rare solutions, case in which a significant portion of the search space would be traversed and any redundancies in the search due to an ideal operator would be very time consuming.

---

[1] D is a downward cover of C iff $C \succ D$ and no E satisfies $C \succ E \succ D$.

Thus, unless we are dealing with a hypotheses space with a very high solution density, we shall prefer an optimal operator over an ideal one. However, in practice we shall proceed by first constructing an ideal refinement operator ρ and only subsequently modifying it, as in proposition 7, to produce an optimal operator $\rho^{(o)}$.

4   Refinement operators for hypotheses spaces bounded below by a MSC

Limiting the hypotheses space below by a most specific (bottom) clause $\perp$ leads to a more efficient search.[2] This strategy has proven successful in state-of-the-art systems like Progol, which search the space of hypotheses C between the most general clause (for example the empty clause $\square$) and the most specific clause $\perp$: $\square \succeq C \succeq \perp$ (for efficiency reasons, the generality ordering employed is subsumption rather than full logical implication).

Formalizing Progol's behavior amounts to considering hypotheses spaces consisting of clause-substitution pairs $C = (cl(C), \theta_\perp(C))$ such that $cl(C)\theta_\perp(C) \subseteq \perp$. (For simplicity, we shall identify in the following $cl(C)$ with C.[3])

The following refinement operator is a generalization of Laird's operator in the case of hypotheses spaces bounded below by a MSC $\perp$.

$D \in \rho_\perp^{(L)}(C)$ iff either

(1) $D = C \cup \{L'\}$ with $L \in \perp$ (L' denotes a literal with the same predicate symbol as L, but with new and distinct variables), or

(2) $D = C\{X_j/X_i\}$ with $\{X_i/A, X_j/A\} \subseteq \theta_\perp(C)$.

Note that in (2) we unify only variables X_i, X_j corresponding to the same variable A from $\perp$ (since otherwise we would obtain a clause more specific than $\perp$).

$\rho_\perp^{(L)}$ is finite, complete, but improper. The lack of properness is due to the possibility of selecting a given literal $L \in \perp$ several times in the current hypothesis (using (1)). It can be easily shown that the nonexistence result 5 for ideal refinement operators can be restated in the case of hypotheses spaces bounded below by a MSC. Therefore, we cannot hope to convert $\rho_\perp^{(L)}$ (which is improper) to an ideal operator.

On the other hand, the Progol implementation uses a slightly weaker refinement operator that considers each literal $L \in \perp$ for selection *only once*. This weaker operator is no longer complete, anyway not w.r.t. ordinary subsumption. For example, if $\perp = \ldots \leftarrow p(A, A)$, then the weaker refinement operator would construct only hypotheses with a single p-literal, such as $H_1 = \ldots \leftarrow$

---

[2] In the following, we restrict ourselves for simplicity to refinement operators for *flattened definite Horn clauses*.

[3] In general, for a given clause C there can be several distinct substitutions θ_i such that $C\theta_i \subseteq \perp$. Viewing the various clause-substitution pairs (C, θ_i) as distinct hypotheses amounts to distinguishing the $\perp$-literals associated to each of the literals of C.

$p(X, X)$, or $H_2 = \ldots \leftarrow p(X, Y)$, but it will never consider hypotheses with multiple p-literals, like $H_3 = \ldots \leftarrow p(X, Y), p(Y, X)$, or $H_4 = \ldots \leftarrow p(X, Y), p(Y, Z)$, $p(Z, W)$, etc. since such hypotheses could be constructed only if we would allow selecting (suitably variabilized versions of) the literal $p(A, A)$ *several times* (and not just once, as in Progol). Note that H_3 is strictly more general (w.r.t. subsumption) than H_1, but also strictly more specific than H_2: $H_2 \succ \boxed{H_3} \succ H_1$. Since H_3 is not even in the search space, Progol's refinement operator is, in a way, incomplete.[4] This incompleteness is due to the fact that $\bot$ is scanned only once for literal selection. It could be easily bridged by scanning $\bot$ repeatedly, so that a given literal can be selected several times. Unfortunately, in principle we cannot bound the number of traversals, although in practice we can set an upper bound.

On the other hand, looking at the above-mentioned incompleteness more carefully, we are led to the idea that it is somehow *justified by the examples* and the MDL principle.

In our previous example, if $p(A, A)$ is the only p-literal in $\bot$, then it may be that something like: p(a,a). p(b,b). p(c,c). [ex] are the only examples. In any case, we could not have had examples like p(a,b). p(b,a). which would have generated $\bot = \ldots \leftarrow p(A, B), p(B, A)$ instead of $\bot = \ldots \leftarrow p(A, A)$. Now, it seems reasonable to assume that a hypothesis like $H = \ldots \leftarrow p(X, Y), p(Y, X)$, although logically consistent with the examples [ex], is not "required" by them. So, although Progol generally returns the most general hypothesis consistent with the examples, in the case it has to choose between hypotheses with multiple occurrences of the same literal from $\bot$, it behaves as if it would always prefer the more specific one (the one with just one occurrence). A justification of this behavior could be that the more general hypotheses are not "required" by the examples. Also, the more general hypotheses (with several occurrences of some literal from $\bot$) are always longer (while covering the same number of examples) and thus will be discarded by the MDL principle anyway.

As we have already mentioned, the subtle properties of subsumption are due to the possibility of clauses with more literals being more general than clauses with fewer literals. This is only possible in the case of multiple occurrences of literals with the same predicate symbol (as for example in uncovered infinite ascending chains).

In the following, we introduce a weaker form of subsumption, which exactly captures Progol's behavior by disallowing substitutions that identify literals.

Definition 8. Clause C *weakly-subsumes* clause D *relative to* $\bot$, $C \succeq_w D$ iff $C\theta \subseteq D$ for some substitution θ that does not identify literals (i.e. for which there are no literals $L_1, L_2 \in C$ such that $L_1\theta = L_2\theta$) and such that $\theta_\bot(D) \circ \theta = \theta_\bot(C)$.

Note that although in the above example $H_3 \succ H_1$ w.r.t. (ordinary) subsumption, they become incomparable w.r.t. weak subsumption because the substitution $\theta = \{Y/X\}$ that ensures the subsumption relationship $H_3 \succ H_1$ identifies the literals $p(X, Y)$ and $p(Y, X)$.

---

[4] It's *search* however, is complete if we use the MDL heuristic. See below.

Although Progol's refinement operator is in a way incomplete w.r.t. ordinary subsumption, it is complete w.r.t. weak subsumption. Disallowing substitutions that identify literals entails the following properties of weak subsumption.

Proposition 9. *If $C \succeq_w D$ then $|C| \leq |D|$ (where $|C|$ is the length of the clause C, i.e. the number of its literals).*

Lemma 10. *(a) In the space of clauses ordered by weak subsumption there exist no infinite ascending chains (and therefore no uncovered infinite ascending chains).*
(b) there exist no uncovered infinite descending chains.

Lemma 10(a) implies the existence of *complete downward cover sets*, which can play the role of ideal operators for weak subsumption.

A form of subsumption even weaker than weak subsumption is *subsumption under object identity* [1]: $C \succeq_{OI} D$ iff $C\theta \subseteq D$ for some substitution θ that does not unify variables of C. For example, $p(X, Y) \nsucceq_{OI} p(X, X)$, showing that subsumption under object identity is too weak for our purposes.

A form of subsumption slightly stronger than weak subsumption (but still weaker than ordinary subsumption) is *"non-decreasing" subsumption*: $C \succeq_{ND} D$ iff $C\theta \subseteq D$ and $|C| \leq |D|$. (Such a substitution θ can identify literals of C, but other literals have to be left out when going from C to D to ensure $|C| \leq |D|$. This leads to somewhat cumbersome properties of "non-decreasing" subsumption.)

Concluding, we have the following chain of increasingly stronger forms of subsumption: $C \succeq_{OI} D \Rightarrow C \succeq_w D \Rightarrow C \succeq_{ND} D \Rightarrow C \succeq D$.

We have seen that Laird's operator $\rho_{\perp}^{(L)}$ is locally finite, complete, but improper and that it cannot be converted to an ideal operator w.r.t. subsumption. However, it can be converted to an *ideal operator w.r.t. weak subsumption* by selecting each literal $L \in \perp$ at most once:

$D \in \rho_{\perp}^{(1)}(C)$ iff either

(1) $D = C \cup \{L'\}$ with $L \in \perp \setminus C\theta_{\perp}(C)$ (L' being L with new and distinct variables), or
(2) $D = C\{X_j/X_i\}$ with $\{X_i/A, X_j/A\} \subseteq \theta_{\perp}(C)$.

Since literals from $\perp$ are selected only once, $\rho_{\perp}^{(1)}$ turns out proper, and although it looses completeness w.r.t. ordinary subsumption, it is still complete w.r.t. weak subsumption.

4.1 From ideal to optimal refinement operators

We have already seen (theorem 6) that, due to completeness, ideal refinement operators cannot be non-redundant and therefore optimal. As already argued in section 3, non-redundancy is extremely important for efficiency. We shall therefore transform the ideal refinement operator $\rho_{\perp}^{(1)}$ to an optimal operator $\rho_{\perp}^{(1o)}$ by replacing the stronger requirement of completeness with the weaker one of weak completeness. Non-redundancy is achieved (like in proposition 7) by assigning a successor $D \in \rho_\perp^{(1)}(C_i) \cap \ldots \cap \rho_\perp^{(1)}(C_n)$ to one and only one of its predecessors C_i: $D \in \rho_\perp^{(1o)}(C_i)$ and $\forall j \neq i.D \notin \rho_\perp^{(1o)}(C_j)$. The refinement graph of such a non-redundant operator becomes tree-like. If the operator is additionally weakly complete, then every element in the search space can be reached through exactly one refinement chain.

The essential cause for the redundancy of a refinement operator (like $\rho_\perp^{(1)}$) is the *commutativity* of the operations of the operator (such as literal addition (1) and elementary substitution (2) in the case of $\rho_\perp^{(1)}$). For example, $D' \cup \{L_1, L_2\}$ can be reached both from $D' \cup \{L_2\}$ by adding L_1 and from $D' \cup \{L_1\}$ by adding L_2. This redundancy is due to the commutativity of the operations of adding literal L_1 and literal L_2 respectively. A similar phenomenon turns up in the case of substitutions.

The assignment of D to one of its successors C_i is largely arbitrary, but has to be done for ensuring non-redundancy. This can be achieved by imposing an ordering on the literals in $\perp$ and making the selection decisions for the literals $L_i \in \perp$ in the given order. We also impose an ordering on the variable occurrences in $\perp$ and make the unification decisions for these variable occurrences in the given order. Finally, we have to make sure that literal additions (1) do not commute with elementary substitutions (2). This is achieved by allowing only substitutions involving newly introduced ("fresh") variables (the substitutions involving "old" variables having been performed already).

Optimal refinement operators have been introduced in [2] for the system CLAUDIEN. However, the refinement operator of CLAUDIEN is optimal only w.r.t. literal selection (which makes the problem a lot easier since variabilizations are not considered). One could simulate variabilizations by using explicit equality literals in the DLAB templates, but the resulting algorithm is no longer optimal since the transitivity of equality is not taken into account. For example, in case of a template containing $\ldots \leftarrow [X = Y, X = Z, Y = Z]$, the algorithm would generate the following equivalent clauses: $\ldots \leftarrow X = Y, X = Z$ and $\ldots \leftarrow X = Y, Y = Z$.

In the following, we construct an optimal operator $\rho_\perp^{(1o)}$ (w.r.t. weak subsumption) associated to the ideal operator $\rho_\perp^{(1)}$. We start by assuming an ordering of the literals $L_k \in \perp$: L_k precedes L_l in this ordering iff $k < l$. This ordering will be used to order the selection decisions for the literals of $\perp$: we will not consider selecting a literal L_k if a decision for L_l, $l > k$ has already been made (we shall call this rule the 'literal rule').

The ordering of the selection decisions for literals also induces an ordering on the variable occurrences[5] in $\perp$: X_i precedes X_j in this ordering ($i < j$) iff X_i is a variable occurrence in a literal selected before the literal containing X_j, or X_i precedes X_j in the same literal.

To achieve non-redundancy, we will impose an order in which the substi-

---

[5] To each argument of each literal of $\perp$ we assign a new and distinct variable X_i (denoting a variable occurrence).

tutions are to be performed. Namely, we shall disallow substitutions $\{X_j/X_i\}$, $i < j$ if some X_k with $k > j$ had already been involved in a previous substitution $\{X_k/X_l\}$ (we shall refer to this rule as the 'substitution rule'). Roughly speaking, we make substitutions in increasing order of the variables involved. This ensures the nonredundancy of the operation of making substitutions.

Having operators for selecting literals and making substitutions that are nonredundant if taken separately, does not ensure a non-redundant refinement operator when the two operators are combined: we also have to make sure that literal additions (1) and elementary substitutions (2) do not commute. For example, if $\perp = \ldots \leftarrow p(A, A), q(B)$, the clause $\ldots \leftarrow p(X, X), q(Z)$ could be obtained either by adding the literal $\overline{q(Z)}$ to $C_1 = \ldots \leftarrow p(X, X)$ or by making the substitution $\{Y/X\}$ in $C_2 = \ldots \leftarrow p(X, Y), q(Z)$. The latter operation should be disallowed since it involves no "fresh" variables (assuming that $\overline{q(Z)}$ was the last literal added, Z is the only "fresh" variable).

In general, we shall allow only substitutions involving at least a "fresh" variable (we shall call this rule the 'fresh variables rule'). The set of "fresh" variables is initialized when adding a new literal L with the variables of L. Variables involved in subsequent substitutions are removed from the list of "fresh" variables. Substitutions involving no fresh variables are assumed to have already been tried on the ancestors of the current clause and are therefore disallowed.

The three rules above (the literal, substitution and fresh variables rules) are sufficient to turn $\rho_\perp^{(1)}$ into an optimal operator w.r.t. weak subsumption. However, the substitution rule forces us to explicitly work with variable occurrences, instead of just working with the substitutions $\theta_\perp(C)$ (if X_l and X_k are variable occurrences, then the substitution $\{X_k/X_l\}$ would eliminate X_k when working just with substitutions, and later on we wouldn't be able to interdict a substitution $\{X_j/X_i\}$ for $j < k$ because we would no longer have X_k).

Fortunately, it is possible to find a more elegant formulation of the substitution and fresh variable rules combined. For each clause C, we shall keep a list of fresh substitutions $\mathcal{F}(C)$ that is initialized with $\theta_\perp(L)$ when adding a new literal L. As before, we shall allow only substitutions $\{X_j/X_i\}$ involving a fresh variable X_j. But we eliminate from $\mathcal{F}(C)$ not just X_j/A, but all X_k/B with $k \leq j$ ('prefix deletion rule'). This ensures that after performing a substitution of X_j, no substitution involving a "smaller" X_k will ever be attempted. This is essentially the substitution rule in disguise, only that now we can deal with substitutions instead of a more cumbersome representation that uses variable occurrences.

The optimal refinement operator can thus be defined as:

$D \in \rho_\perp^{(1o)}(C)$ iff either

(1) $D = C \cup \{L'\}$ with $L \in \perp \setminus \text{prefix}_\perp(C\theta_\perp(C))$, where $\text{prefix}_\perp(C) = \{L_i \in \perp \mid \exists L_j \in C$ such that $i \leq j\}$ and L' is L with new and distinct variables.
$\theta_\perp(D) = \theta_\perp(C) \cup \theta_\perp(L')$, $\mathcal{F}(D) = \theta_\perp(L')$, or

(2) $D = C\{X_j/X_i\}$ with $i < j$, $\{X_i/A, X_j/A\} \subseteq \theta_\perp(C)$ and $X_j/A \in \mathcal{F}(C)$.
$\theta_\perp(D) = \theta_\perp(C) \cup \{X_j/X_i\}$, $\mathcal{F}(D) = \mathcal{F}(C) \setminus \{X_k/B \in \mathcal{F}(C) \mid k \leq j\}$.

Example 1. Let $\bot = p(A, A, A, A)$ and $C_1 = p(X_1, X_2, X_3, X_4)$, $\theta_\bot(C_1) = \{X_1/A, X_2/A, X_3/A, X_4/A\}$, $\mathcal{F}(C_1) = \{\underbrace{X_1/A, X_2/A, X_3/A}, X_4/A\}$. The substitution $\{X_3/X_1\}$ eliminates the entire prefix $\{X_1/A, X_2/A, X_3/A\}$ from $\mathcal{F}(C_1)$: $C_2 = C_1\{X_3/X_1\} = p(X_1, X_2, X_1, X_4)$, $\theta_\bot(C_2) = \{X_1/A, X_2/A, X_4/A\}$, $\mathcal{F}(C_2) = \{X_4/A\}$. Now, only the substitutions involving X_4 are allowed for C_2.

5 Refinement operators for clauses with variable dependencies

Most implemented ILP systems restrict the search space by providing mode declarations that impose constraints on the types of the variables. Also, variables are declared as either input $(+)$ or output $(-)$. In this setting, *valid* clauses (clauses verifying the mode declarations) are *ordered* sets of literals such that every input variable $+X$ in some literal L_i is preceded by a literal L_j containing a corresponding output variable $-X$.[6] These variable dependencies induced by the $\pm$mode declarations affect a refinement operator for an unrestricted language (like $\rho_\bot^{(1o)}$), since now not all refinements according to the unrestricted $\rho_\bot^{(1o)}$ are valid clauses. Nevertheless, we can use $\rho_\bot^{(1o)}$ to construct an optimal refinement operator $\rho_\bot^{(1o)(\pm)}$ for clauses with $\pm$variable dependencies by repeatedly using the "unrestricted" $\rho_\bot^{(1o)}$ to generate refinements until a valid refinement is obtained. One-step refinements w.r.t. $\rho_\bot^{(1o)(\pm)}$ can thus be multi-step refinements w.r.t. $\rho_\bot^{(1o)}$ (all intermediate steps being necessarily invalid).

$$\rho_\bot^{(1o)(\pm)}(C) = \{D_n \mid D_1 \in \rho_\bot^{(1o)}(C), D_2 \in \rho_\bot^{(1o)}(D_1), \ldots, D_n \in \rho_\bot^{(1o)}(D_{n-1})$$
$$\text{such that } D_n \text{ is valid but } D_1, \ldots, D_{n-1} \text{ are invalid}\}.$$

(Here, a clause C is called valid iff it admits an ordering that satisfies the mode declarations. Such an ordering can easily be obtained with a kind of topological sort.)

Note that $\rho_\bot^{(1o)(\pm)}$ is optimal, but *non-minimal*, since it may add more than one literal in one refinement step. For example, if $\bot = \ldots \leftarrow p(+A), q(-A)$, it would generate both $C_1 = \ldots \leftarrow q(-X), p(+X)$ and $C_2 = \ldots \leftarrow q(-X)$ as one-step refinements of $\square$, whereas it may seem more natural to view C_1 as a one-step refinement of C_2 (rather than of $\square$).

To obtain a *minimal* optimal (i.e. a *perfect*) refinement operator, we need to postpone the choice of unselectable (variabilizations of) literals until they become selectable, instead of making a selection decision right away. We also have to make sure that selectable literals obtain all their $+$variables from previous $-$variables by making all the corresponding substitutions in one refinement step.

(1) add a new literal (to the right of all selected ones) and link all its $+$variables according to "old" substitutions

---

[6] This is true for literals in the body of the clause. Input variables in the head of the clause behave exactly like output variables of body literals. To simplify the presentation, we shall not explicitly refer to the head literal.

(2) make a substitution (involving at least a "fresh" variable)
(3) wake-up a previously unselectable literal (to the left of the rightmost selected literal).

If several literals can be added at a given time, we shall add them in the order induced by $\perp$. In other words, we shall disallow adding a literal $L_2 < L_1$ after adding L_1 if L_2 was selectable even before adding L_1 (since otherwise we would redundantly generate C, L_1, L_2 both from C, L_1 by adding L_2 and from C, L_2 by adding L_1).

On the other hand, the multiple +variables of several literals can be linked to the same −variable ("source"). For example, if $\perp = \ldots \leftarrow p_1(+A), p_2(+A), q(-A)$, then $\rho(\square) = \{C_1\}$, $\rho(C_1) = \{C_2, C_3\}$, $\rho(C_2) = \{C_4\}$ and $\rho(C_3) = \rho(C_4) = \emptyset$, where $C_1 = \ldots \leftarrow q(-X)$, $C_2 = \ldots \leftarrow q(-X), p_1(+X)$, $C_3 = \ldots \leftarrow q(-X), p_2(+X)$, $C_4 = \ldots \leftarrow q(-X), p_1(+X), p_2(+X)$. Note that both $p_1(+X)$ and $p_2(+X)$ use the same "source" $q(-X)$. Also note that adding $p_2(+X)$ to C_2 is allowed since $p_2 > p_1$, while adding $p_1(+X)$ to C_3 is disallowed because $p_1 < p_2$ was selectable even before adding p_2 (to C_1).

Using the notation $\theta_\perp^+(L')$ (and respectively $\theta_\perp^-(L')$) for the substitutions of +(−)variables of $\theta_\perp(L')$, we obtain the following *perfect* (*minimal*[7] and *optimal*) refinement operator $\rho_\perp^{(1 \circ \pm)}$ for clauses with variable dependencies.

$D \in \rho_\perp^{(1 \circ \pm)}(C)$ iff either

(1) $D = C \cup \{L'\}$ with $L \in \perp \setminus \text{prefix}_\perp(C\theta_\perp(C))$, where L' is L with new and distinct −variables[8], and +variables such that $\theta_\perp^+(L') \subseteq \theta_\perp(D) = \theta_\perp(C) \cup \theta_\perp^-(L')$.
$\mathcal{F}(D) = \theta_\perp^-(L') \setminus \{X_k/B \in \theta_\perp^-(L') \mid k \leq j$ for some $X_j/A \in \theta_\perp^+(L') \cup \theta_\perp^-(L')\}$,
or

(2) $D = C\{X_j/X_i\}$ with $i < j$, $\{X_i/A, X_j/A\} \subseteq \theta_\perp(C)$ and $X_j/A \in \mathcal{F}(C)$.
$\theta_\perp(D) = \theta_\perp(C) \cup \{X_j/X_i\}$, $\mathcal{F}(D) = \mathcal{F}(C) \setminus \{X_k/B \in \mathcal{F}(C) \mid k \leq j\}$, or

(3) $D = C \cup \{L'\}$ with $L \in \text{prefix}_\perp(C\theta_\perp(C)) \setminus C\theta_\perp(C)$, where L' is L with new and distinct −variables[7], and +variables such that $\theta_\perp^+(L') \subsetneq \theta_\perp(D) = \theta_\perp(C) \cup \theta_\perp^-(L')$, and for all $L_i \in C$ such that $L_i > L'$, $\text{first}_{L_i}(C) \cup \{L'\}$ is invalid, where $\text{first}_{L_i}(C)$ are the literals added to C before L_i.
$\mathcal{F}(D) = \theta_\perp^-(L') \setminus \{X_k/B \in \theta_\perp^-(L') \mid k \leq j$ for some $X_j/A \in \theta_\perp^+(L') \cup \theta_\perp^-(L')\}$.

Observe that substitutions (2) involving −variables (controlled by $\mathcal{F}$) are to be performed right away when $\mathcal{F}$ allows it, because later additions of woken-up literals will reset $\mathcal{F}$ and make those substitutions impossible. On the other hand, we can always wake-up literals (by solving their +variables) (3) *after*

---

[7] The refinement operator of *Markus* is not minimal (no description of this operator is available in [3], but see his footnote 4). As far as we know, our refinement operator is the first *minimal* and *optimal* one (w.r.t. weak subsumption).

[8] The −variables of L' are preceded by all −variables of C in our variable ordering. (This variable ordering is *dynamical* since it is induced by the selection decisions for literals.)

making those substitutions. In other words, we firmly establish our "sources" (i.e. −variables) before waking-up the "consumers" (i.e. +variables).

The following example illustrates the functioning of $\rho_{\perp}^{(1o\pm)}$.

Example 2. For $\perp = \ldots \leftarrow r(+B), q_1(+A, -B), q_2(+A, -B), p(-A)$, $\rho(\square) = \{C_1\}$, $\rho(C_1) = \{C_2, C_3\}$, $\rho(C_2) = \{C_4, C_5\}$, $\rho(C_3) = \{C_6\}$, $\rho(C_4) = \{C_7\}$, $\rho(C_5) = \{C_8, C_9\}$, $\rho(C_7) = \{C_{10}\}$, $\rho(C_6) = \rho(C_8) = \rho(C_9) = \rho(C_{10}) = \emptyset$, where

$C_1 = \ldots \leftarrow p(-X)$

$C_2 = \ldots \leftarrow p(-X), q_1(+X, -Y)$

$C_3 = \ldots \leftarrow p(-X), q_2(+X, -Y)$

$C_4 = \ldots \leftarrow p(-X), q_1(+X, -Y), r(+Y)$

$C_5 = \ldots \leftarrow p(-X), q_1(+X, -Y), q_2(+X, -Y')$

$C_6 = \ldots \leftarrow p(-X), q_2(+X, -Y), r(+Y)$

$$C_7 = \ldots \leftarrow p(-X), q_1(+X, -Y), r(+Y), q_2(+X, -Y')$$
$$C_8 = \ldots \leftarrow p(-X), q_1(+X, -Y), q_2(+X, -Y)$$
$$C_9 = \ldots \leftarrow p(-X), q_1(+X, -Y), q_2(+X, -Y'), r(+Y')$$
$$C_{10} = \ldots \leftarrow p(-X), q_1(+X, -Y), q_2(+X, -Y), r(+Y).$$

Note that $C_{10} \notin \rho(C_8)$ because $q_2 > r$ in $\perp$ and $first_{q_2}(C_8) \cup \{\overline{r(+Y)}\} = C_2 \cup \{\overline{r(+Y)}\} = C_4$ is valid, thereby violating the condition of step (3). In other words, we cannot wake up $r(+Y)$ in C_8 because it was already selectable in C_2 (otherwise we would obtain the redundancy $C_{10} \in \rho(C_7) \cap \rho(C_8)$). For similar reasons, we don't have $C_7 \in \rho(C_5), C_5 \in \rho(C_3)$ or $C_9 \in \rho(C_6)$.

On the other hand, $C_{10} \notin \rho(C_9)$ because the substitution $\{Y'/Y\}$ in C_9 is disallowed by $\mathcal{F}(C_9) = \emptyset$ (the last literal added, $r(+Y')$, having no −variables).

Note that the incompleteness of Progol's refinement operator (which applies only steps (1) and (2)) is due to obtaining the substitutions of +variables only from −variables of already selected literals, whereas they could be obtained from −variables of literals that will be selected in the future (as in step (3)). For example, if $\perp = \ldots \leftarrow p(-A), q(+A), r(-A)$, then Progol's refinement of $C = \ldots \leftarrow p(-X)$ will miss the clause $D = \ldots \leftarrow p(-X), r(-Y), q(+Y)$ in which q obtains its $+Y$ from r.

We have implemented the refinement operators described in this paper and plan to use them as a component in a full ILP system.

References

1. Esposito F., A. Laterza, D. Malerba, G. Semeraro. *Refinement of Datalog Programs.* Workshop on Data Mining and ILP, Bari 1996.
2. De Raedt L., M. Bruynooghe. *A theory of clausal discovery.* IJCAI-93, 1058-1063.
3. Grobelnik M. *Induction of Prolog programs with Markus.* LOPSTR'93, 57-63.
4. Muggleton S. *Inverse entailment and Progol.* New Generation Computing Journal, 13:245-286, 1995.
5. van der Laag P. *An Analysis of Refinement Operators in ILP.* PhD Thesis, Tinbergen Inst. Res. Series 102, 1995.
6. van der Laag P., S.H. Nienhuys-Cheng. *Existence and Nonexistence of Complete Refinement Operators.* ECML-94, 307-322.

Combining Divide-and-Conquer and Separate-and-Conquer for Efficient and Effective Rule Induction

Henrik Boström and Lars Asker

Dept. of Computer and Systems Sciences
Stockholm University and Royal Institute of Technology
Electrum 230, 164 40 Kista, Sweden
{henke,asker}@dsv.su.se

Abstract. Divide-and-Conquer (DAC) and Separate-and-Conquer (SAC) are two strategies for rule induction that have been used extensively. When searching for rules DAC is maximally conservative w.r.t. decisions made during search for previous rules. This results in a very efficient strategy, which however suffers from difficulties in effectively inducing disjunctive concepts due to *the replication problem*. SAC on the other hand is maximally liberal in the same respect. This allows for a larger hypothesis space to be searched, which in many cases avoids the replication problem but at the cost of lower efficiency. We present a hybrid strategy called Reconsider-and-Conquer (RAC), which handles the replication problem more effectively than DAC by reconsidering some of the earlier decisions and allows for more efficient induction than SAC by holding on to some of the decisions. We present experimental results from propositional, numerical and relational domains demonstrating that RAC significantly reduces the replication problem from which DAC suffers and is several times (up to an order of magnitude) faster than SAC.

1 Introduction

The two main strategies for rule induction are Separate-and-Conquer and Divide-and-Conquer. Separate-and-Conquer, often also referred to as Covering, produces a set of rules by repeatedly specialising an overly general rule. At each iteration a specialised rule is selected that covers a subset of the positive examples and excludes the negative examples. This is repeated until all positive examples are covered by the set of rules. The reader is referred to [7] for an excellent overview of Separate-and-Conquer rule learning algorithms. Divide-and-Conquer produces a hypothesis by splitting an overly general rule into a set of specialised rules that cover disjoint subsets of the examples. The rules that cover positive examples only are kept, while the rules that cover both positive and negative examples are handled recursively in the same manner as the first overly general rule.

For Separate-and-Conquer, the computational cost (measured as the number of checks to see whether or not a rule covers an example) grows quadratically in the size of the example set, while it grows linearly using Divide-and-Conquer.[1] This follows from the fact that Separate-and-Conquer searches a larger hypothesis space than Divide-and-Conquer [2]. For any hypothesis in this larger space there is a corresponding hypothesis with identical coverage in the narrower space. Hence none of the strategies is superior to the other in terms of expressiveness. However, for many of the hypotheses within the narrower space there is a hypothesis with identical coverage but fewer rules within the larger space. Since the number of rules in a hypothesis provides a bound on the minimal number of examples needed to find it, this means that Separate-and-Conquer often requires fewer examples than Divide-and-Conquer to find a correct hypothesis. In particular this is true in domains in which the *replication problem* [13] is frequent, i.e. when the most compact definition of the target concept consists of disjuncts whose truth values are (partially or totally) independent, e.g. $p(x_1, x_2, x_3, x_4) \leftarrow (x_1 = 1 \wedge x_2 = 2) \vee (x_3 = 0 \wedge x_4 = 1)$.

The two strategies can be viewed as extremes w.r.t. how conservative they are regarding earlier decisions when searching for additional rules. Divide-and-Conquer can be regarded as maximally conservative and Separate-and-Conquer as maximally liberal. We propose a hybrid strategy, called Reconsider-and-Conquer, which combines the advantages of Divide-and-Conquer and Separate-and-Conquer and reduces their weaknesses. The hybrid strategy allows for more effective handling of the replication problem than Divide-and-Conquer by reconsidering some decisions made in the search for previous rules. At the same time it allows for more efficient induction than Separate-and-Conquer by holding on to some of the earlier decisions.

In the next section we introduce some basic terminology. In section three, we formally describe Reconsider-and-Conquer, and in section four we present experimental results from propositional, numerical and relational domains demonstrating that the hybrid approach may significantly reduce the replication problem from which Divide-and-Conquer suffers while at the same time it is several times faster than Separate-and-Conquer. In section five, we discuss related work and in section six finally, we give some concluding remarks and point out directions for future research.

2   Preliminaries

The reader is assumed to be familiar with the logic programming terminology [11].

A *rule r* is a definite clause $r = h \leftarrow b_1 \wedge \ldots \wedge b_n$, where h is the head, and $b_1 \wedge \ldots \wedge b_n$ is a (possibly empty) body.

A *rule g* is *more general* than a rule s w.r.t. a set of rules B (background predicates), denoted $g \succeq_B s$, iff $M_{\{g\} \cup B} \supseteq M_{\{s\} \cup B}$, where M_P denotes the least Herbrand model of P (the set of all ground facts that follow from P).

The *coverage* of a set of rules H, w.r.t. background predicates B and a set of atoms A, is a set $A_{HB} = \{a : a \in A \cap M_{H \cup B}\}$. We leave out the subscript

---

[1] assuming that the maximum number of ways to specialise a rule is fixed.

B when it is clear from the context. Furthermore, if H is a singleton $H = \{r\}$, then $A_{\{r\}}$ is abbreviated to A_r.

Given a rule r and background predicates B, a *specialisation operator* σ computes a set of rules, denoted $\sigma_B(r)$, such that for all $r' \in \sigma_B(r)$, $r \succeq_B r'$. Again we leave out the subscript if B is clear from the context.

Given a rule r, background predicates B, and a specialisation operator σ, a *split* of r is a set of rules $s = \{r_1, \ldots, r_n\}$, such that $r_i \in \sigma(r)$, for all $1 \leq i \leq n$, and $M_{\{r_1, \ldots, r_n\} \cup B} = M_{\{r\} \cup B}$. Furthermore, s is said to be a *non-overlapping* split if $M_{\{r_i\} \cup B} \cap M_{\{r_j\} \cup B} = M_B$ for all $i, j = 1, \ldots, n$ such that $i \neq j$.

3 Reconsider-and-Conquer

Reconsider-and-Conquer works like Separate-and-Conquer in that rules are iteratively added to the hypothesis while removing covered examples from the set of positive examples. However, in contrast to Separate-and-Conquer, which adds a single rule on each iteration, Reconsider-and-Conquer adds a set of rules. The first rule that is included in this set is generated in exactly the same way as is done by Separate-and-Conquer, i.e. by following a branch of specialisation steps from an initial rule into a rule that covers positive examples only. However, instead of continuing the search for a subsequent rule from the initial rule, Reconsider-and-Conquer backs up one step to see whether some other specialisation step could be taken in order to cover some of the remaining positive examples (i.e. to complete another branch). This continues until eventually Reconsider-and-Conquer has backed up to the inital rule. The way in which this set of rules that is added to the hypothesis is generated is similar to how Divide-and-Conquer works, but with one important difference: Reconsider-and-Conquer is less restricted than Divide-and-Conquer regarding what possible specialisation steps can be taken when having backed up since the specialisation steps are not chosen independently by Divide-and-Conquer due to that the resulting rules should constitute a (possibly non-overlapping) split.

One condition used by Reconsider-and-Conquer to decide whether or not to continue from some rule on a completed branch is that the fraction of positive examples among the covered examples must never decrease anywhere along the branch (as this would indicate that the branch is focusing on covering negative rather than positive examples). However, in principle both weaker and stronger conditions could be employed. The weakest possible condition would be that each rule along the branch should cover at least one positive example. This would make Reconsider-and-Conquer behave in a way very similar to Divide-and-Conquer. A maximally strong condition would be to always require Reconsider-and-Conquer back up to the initial rule, making the behaviour identical to that of Separate-and-Conquer.

In Figure 1, we give a formal description of the algorithm. The branch of specialisation steps currently explored is represented by a stack of rules together with the positive and negative examples that they cover. Once a branch is completed, i.e a rule that covers only positive examples is added to the hypothesis, the stack is updated by removing all covered examples from the stack. Furthermore, the stack is truncated by keeping only the bottom part where the fraction of positive examples covered by each rule does not decrease compared to those covered by the preceding rule.

---

function Reconsider-and-Conquer(E^+, E^-)
  $H := \emptyset$
  while $E^+ \neq \emptyset$ **do**
    $r :=$ an initial rule such that $E_r^+ \neq \emptyset$
    $H' :=$ Find-Rules$(r, [], E_r^+, E_r^-)$
    $E^+ := E^+ \setminus E_{H'}^+$
    $H := H \cup H'$
  return H

function Find-Rules(r, S, E^+, E^-)
  if $E^- \neq \emptyset$ **then**
    $r' :=$ a rule $\in \sigma(r)$
    $H :=$ Find-Rules$(r', (r, E^+, E^-) \cdot S, E_{r'}^+, E_{r'}^-)$
  else $H := \{r\}$
  repeat
  Update S w.r.t. H
  if $S \neq []$ **then**
    Pop $(r, E^\oplus, E^\ominus)$ from S
    if there is a rule $r' \in \sigma(r)$ such that $\frac{|E_{r'}^\oplus|}{|E_{r'}^\oplus \cup E_{r'}^\ominus|} \geq \frac{|E^\oplus|}{|E^\oplus \cup E^\ominus|}$ **then**
      $H' :=$ Find-Rules$(r', (r, E^\oplus, E^\ominus) \cdot S, E_{r'}^\oplus, E_{r'}^\ominus)$
      $H := H \cup H'$
      $S := (r, E^\oplus, E^\ominus) \cdot S$
  until $S = []$
  return H

Fig. 1. The Reconsider-and-Conquer algorithm.

An Example Assume that the target predicate is $p(x_1, x_2, x_3, x_4) \leftarrow (x_1 = 1 \wedge x_2 = 1) \vee (x_3 = 1 \wedge x_4 = 1) \vee (x_3 = 1 \wedge x_4 = 2)$, and that we are given 100 positive and 100 negative instances of the target predicate, i.e. $|E^+| = 100$ and $|E^-| = 100$. Assume further that our specialisation operator is defined as $\sigma(h \leftarrow b_1 \wedge \ldots \wedge b_n) = \{h \leftarrow b_1 \wedge \ldots \wedge b_n \wedge x = c | x \text{ is a variable in } h \text{ and } c \in \{1, \ldots, 4\}\}$. Now assuming that Reconsider-and-Conquer starts with the initial rule $r_0 = p(x_1, x_2, x_3, x_4)$, Find-Rules recursively generates a sequence of more specialised rules, say:

$$r_1 = p(x_1, x_2, x_3, x_4) \leftarrow x_3 = 1 \qquad\qquad |E_{r_1}^+| = 50 \; |E_{r_1}^-| = 10$$
$$r_2 = p(x_1, x_2, x_3, x_4) \leftarrow x_3 = 1 \wedge x_4 = 1 \; |E_{r_2}^+| = 25 \; |E_{r_2}^-| = 0$$

where the last rule is included in the hypothesis.

Find-Rules then updates the stack by removing all covered (positive) examples and keeping only the bottom part of the stack that corresponds to a sequence of specialisation steps that fulfills the condition of a non-decreasing fraction of covered positive examples. In this case, the bottom element r_1 is kept as it covers 25 positive and 10 negative examples compared to 75 positive and 100 negative examples that are covered by the initial rule. So in contrast to Separate-and-Conquer, Reconsider-and-Conquer does not restart the search from the initial rule but continues from rule r_1 and finds a specialisation that does not decrease the fraction of positive examples, say:

$$r_3 = p(x_1, x_2, x_3, x_4) \leftarrow x_3 = 1 \wedge x_4 = 2 \; |E_{r_3}^+| = 25 \; |E_{r_3}^-| = 0$$

After the stack is updated, no rules remain and hence Reconsider-and-Conquer restarts the search from an initial rule, and may choose any specialisation without being restricted by the earlier choices. This contrasts to Divide-and-Conquer, which would have had to choose some of the other rules in the (non-overlapping) split from which r_1 was taken (e.g. $\{p(x_1, x_2, x_3, x_4) \leftarrow x_3 = 2, p(x_1, x_2, x_3, x_4) \leftarrow x_3 = 3, p(x_1, x_2, x_3, x_4) \leftarrow x_3 = 4\}$). Assuming the same initial rule (r_0) is chosen again, the sequence of rules produced by Find-Rules may look like:

$$r_4 = p(x_1, x_2, x_3, x_4) \leftarrow x_1 = 1 \qquad\qquad |E_{r_4}^+| = 50 \; |E_{r_4}^-| = 20$$
$$r_5 = p(x_1, x_2, x_3, x_4) \leftarrow x_1 = 1 \wedge x_2 = 1 \; |E_{r_5}^+| = 50 \; |E_{r_5}^-| = 0$$

The last rule is included in the hypothesis and now all positive examples are covered so Reconsider-and-Conquer terminates. Hence, the resulting hypothesis is:

$$r_2 = p(x_1, x_2, x_3, x_4) \leftarrow x_3 = 1 \wedge x_4 = 1$$
$$r_3 = p(x_1, x_2, x_3, x_4) \leftarrow x_3 = 1 \wedge x_4 = 2$$
$$r_5 = p(x_1, x_2, x_3, x_4) \leftarrow x_1 = 1 \wedge x_2 = 1$$

It should be noted that Divide-and-Conquer has to induce seven rules to obtain a hypothesis with identical coverage, as the disjunct that corresponds to r_5 above has to be replicated in five rules:

$$p(x_1, x_2, x_3, x_4) \leftarrow x_3 = 1 \wedge x_4 = 1$$
$$p(x_1, x_2, x_3, x_4) \leftarrow x_3 = 1 \wedge x_4 = 2$$
$$p(x_1, x_2, x_3, x_4) \leftarrow x_3 = 1 \wedge x_4 = 3 \wedge x_1 = 1 \wedge x_2 = 1$$
$$p(x_1, x_2, x_3, x_4) \leftarrow x_3 = 1 \wedge x_4 = 4 \wedge x_1 = 1 \wedge x_2 = 1$$
$$p(x_1, x_2, x_3, x_4) \leftarrow x_3 = 2 \wedge x_1 = 1 \wedge x_2 = 1$$
$$p(x_1, x_2, x_3, x_4) \leftarrow x_3 = 3 \wedge x_1 = 1 \wedge x_2 = 1$$
$$p(x_1, x_2, x_3, x_4) \leftarrow x_3 = 4 \wedge x_1 = 1 \wedge x_2 = 1$$

4 Empirical Evaluation

We first describe how the experiments were performed and then present the experimental results.

4.1 Experimental setting

Reconsider-and-Conquer (RAC) was compared to Divide-and-Conquer (DAC) and Separate-and-Conquer (SAC) in several propositional, numerical and relational domains. The domains were obtained from the UCI repository [1], except for two relational domains: one consists of four sets of examples regarding structure-activity comparisons of drugs for the treatment of Alzheimer's desease, and was obtained from Oxford University Computing Laboratory and the other domain is about learning the definite clause grammar (DCG) in [3, p 455].[2]

All three algorithms were tested both with information gain heuristics and probability metrics based on the hypergeometric distribution, which for DAC are those given in [14] and [12] respectively, while the information gain heuristic modified for SAC (and RAC) is taken from [10, p 165], and the modified version of the probability metric in [12] for SAC and RAC is:

$$P(|E_{r'}^+|, |E_{r'}^-|, |E_r^+|, |E_r^-|) = \frac{\binom{|E_r^+|}{|E_{r'}^+|} \binom{|E_r^-|}{|E_{r'}^-|}}{\binom{|E_r^+ \cup E_r^-|}{|E_{r'}^+ \cup E_{r'}^-|}}$$

where $r' \in \sigma(r)$. The specialisation r' of r with lowest probability is chosen from $\sigma(r)$ given that

$$\frac{|E_{r'}^+|}{|E_{r'}^+ \cup E_{r'}^-|} \geq \frac{|E_r^+|}{|E_r^+ \cup E_r^-|}$$

Following [5], cut-points for continuous-valued attributes were chosen dynamically from the boundary points between the positive and negative examples in the training sets for the numerical and relational domains.

An experiment was performed in each domain, in which the entire example set was randomly split into two partitions corresponding to 90% and 10% of the examples respectively. The larger set was used for training and the smaller for testing. The same training and test sets were used for all algorithms. Each experiment was iterated 30 times and the mean accuracy on the test examples as

---

[2] The set of positive examples consists of all sentences of up to 10 words that can be generated by the grammar (2869 sentences) and the equal sized set of negative examples was generated by applying the following procedure to each positive example: i) replace a randomly selected word in the sentence with a randomly selected word from the corpus, ii) go to step i with a probability of 0.5 and iii) restart the procedure if the resulting sentence is a positive example.

well as the amount of work performed measured as the cpu time[3] are presented below. In addition, we also present the mean number of rules in the produced hypotheses.

4.2 Experimental results

In Table 1, we present the accuracy, cpu time and number of rules in the hypothesis produced by each algorithm using both the probability metrics and the information gain heuristics for all domains. The domains within the first group in the table are propositional, the domains within the second group are numerical, and the domains in the last group are relational. For all accuracies, bold face indicates that there is a statistically significant difference between the method and some less accurate method and no significant difference between the method and some more accurate method (if any). Furthermore, underline indicates that there is a statistically significant difference between the method and some more accurate method and no significant difference between the method and some less accurate method (if any).

The accuracies of the three methods are shown in columns 2-4. To summarise these results, one can see that DAC has a best/worst score (as indicated by bold and underline in the table) of 3/10 (5/8) (the first score is for the probability metrics and the second is for the information gain heuristics). The corresponding score for SAC is 9/3 (8/3) and for RAC 8/3 (8/2). Looking more closely at the domains, one can see that there is a significant difference in accuracy between DAC and SAC in favour of the latter in those (artificial) domains in which the replication problem was expected to occur (Tic-Tac-Toe, KRKI) but also in several of the other (natural) domains (most notably Student loan and Alzh. chol.). One can see that RAC effectively avoids the replication problem in these domains and is almost as accurate as, or even more accurate than, SAC.

DCG is the only relational domain in which DAC is significantly more accurate than SAC and RAC (although the difference is small). In this domain the replication problem is known not to occur since the shortest correct grammar is within the hypothesis space of DAC. The difference in accuracy can here be explained by the different versions of the probability metrics and information gain heuristics that are used for DAC and SAC/RAC. For DAC these reward splits that discriminate positive from negative examples while for SAC/RAC they reward rules with a high coverage of positive examples.

In columns 5-7, the cputime of the three methods are shown. The median for the cpu time ratio SAC/DAC is 5.68 (5.77) and for the cpu time ratio RAC/DAC

---

[3] The amount of work was also measured by counting the number of times it was checked whether or not a rule covers an example, which has the advantage over the former measure that it is independent of the implementation but the disadvantage that it does not include the (small) overhead of RAC due to handling the stack. However, both measures gave consistent results and we have chosen to present only the former. All algorithms were implemented in SICStus Prolog 3 #6 and were executed on a SUN Ultra 60, except for the numerical domains which were executed on a SUN Ultra I.

Domain	Accuracy (percent)			Time (seconds)			No. of rules		
	DAC	SAC	RAC	DAC	SAC	RAC	DAC	SAC	RAC
Shuttle	97.98	99.17	99.17	0.13	0.34	0.17	9.9	5.8	5.8
	98.33	99.17	99.17	0.13	0.33	0.16	8.1	5.8	5.8
Housevotes	93.26	94.11	93.95	1.78	4.98	2.29	17.1	13.8	15.1
	93.64	93.95	93.64	1.73	5.00	2.20	16.7	13.9	15.4
Tic-Tac-Toe	85.59	99.58	99.03	2.04	7.10	4.13	108.3	13.0	21.2
	85.63	99.55	99.13	1.74	6.74	3.96	107.2	12.4	20.3
KRvsKP	99.58	99.20	99.30	96.90	379.77	119.93	18.5	17.4	16.2
	99.59	99.18	99.23	95.77	386.40	145.31	18.2	18.1	20.4
Splice (n)	92.97	91.67	92.41	284.76	3508.04	904.60	163.9	82.7	118.8
	92.88	90.07	91.88	278.53	3636.01	897.20	162.7	84.9	123.4
Splice (ei)	95.29	96.32	96.23	208.49	2310.56	318.57	79.6	30.6	42.9
	95.43	96.04	96.09	204.64	2344.55	311.55	77.4	31.7	42.9
Splice (ie)	93.77	93.29	93.55	243.76	4109.09	375.68	111.8	47.4	67.1
	94.10	93.01	93.51	235.31	3980.19	419.59	106.7	46.9	67.3
Monks-2	66.44	70.28	73.89	2.03	31.73	5.31	129.2	107.3	108.7
	72.44	68.78	73.11	0.88	31.52	5.00	121.0	107.9	109.1
Monks-3	96.79	96.42	96.42	0.69	3.98	1.15	27.1	23.7	23.7
	97.03	96.30	96.48	0.52	3.87	1.12	26.4	23.6	23.8
Bupa	62.25	65.59	65.00	39.62	192.75	75.88	37.4	25.1	29.4
	63.92	65.69	65.88	43.00	193.31	74.13	36.3	26.9	31.9
Ionosphere	88.10	86.86	88.29	1201.02	1965.23	1273.14	9.1	5.8	7.2
	88.19	86.57	87.05	1371.10	1916.97	1035.10	8.3	7.7	9.6
Pima Indians	72.73	71.26	71.95	323.73	3079.90	587.48	57.5	38.4	45.1
	72.60	71.99	70.39	329.26	2756.38	537.69	56.4	40.2	49.9
Sonar	71.27	71.90	73.49	2049.23	3484.61	2319.63	9.7	6.5	8.5
	72.70	74.13	74.60	2123.46	3247.45	2254.65	9.3	6.8	9.4
WDBC	91.40	94.09	91.99	4872.89	6343.40	4885.81	9.1	6.6	8.4
	91.99	93.63	92.63	4870.71	6656.17	4758.54	8.9	6.7	10.2
KRKI	98.03	98.90	99.17	50.37	101.90	55.46	26.8	9.2	13.0
	98.07	98.90	99.13	50.08	101.75	55.39	26.7	9.4	12.7
DCG	99.99	99.93	99.92	43.83	205.76	129.40	28.0	28.8	28.5
	99.99	99.97	99.95	44.17	204.05	130.55	28.0	28.1	28.1
Student loan	90.53	96.57	96.57	10.72	60.94	21.00	113.4	35.9	44.0
	92.03	96.83	96.40	10.13	58.50	21.48	96.7	36.7	44.7
Alzh. toxic	77.53	81.50	81.84	238.27	1581.34	406.28	198.4	83.5	92.7
	77.68	81.54	81.91	195.89	1593.38	417.64	190.9	84.8	95.4
Alzh. amine	86.14	85.60	85.56	208.13	2146.01	337.96	148.8	81.6	92.0
	85.89	85.85	84.15	162.83	1854.61	330.25	144.8	82.6	94.0
Alzh. scop.	56.15	59.84	60.21	215.50	2673.01	501.71	263.1	124.5	135.4
	55.47	60.99	60.36	195.14	2259.70	528.71	261.5	121.4	132.3
Alzh. chol.	64.76	75.06	74.99	452.24	10148.40	1063.30	450.4	228.2	240.8
	64.86	75.54	75.31	364.41	9980.11	1103.79	438.8	226.0	244.9

Table 1. Accuracy, cpu time, and number of rules using probability metrics (first line) and information gain (second line).

it is 1.71 (1.78). The domain in which the SAC/RAC ratio is highest is Splice(ie) where the ratio is 10.94 (9.5). Except for Monks-2, the domain for which the SAC/DAC ratio is highest is Alz. chol., where it is 27.31 (22.44). The RAC/DAC ratio in this domain is 3.03 (2.35). In Monks-2, the SAC/DAC ratio is even higher for the probability metrics (35.82) but lower for the information gain heuristics (15.63). The RAC/DAC ratio reaches its highest value in this domain (5.68 for the probability metric).

In columns 8-10, the average number of rules produced are shown. DAC produces more rules than SAC in all domains except one (DCG). The median for the number of rules produced by SAC is 28.8 (28.1), for RAC 29.4 (31.9) and for DAC 57.5 (56.4). These results are consistent with the fact that SAC and RAC search a larger hypothesis space than DAC in which more compact hypotheses may be found.

In summary, both RAC and SAC outperform DAC in most domains tested in the experiments, mainly due to the effective handling of the replication problem. But although RAC is about as accurate as SAC, it is up to an order of magnitude faster.

5 Related Work

Two previous systems, IREP [8] and RIPPER [4], are able to efficiently process large sets of noisy data despite the use of Separate-and-Conquer. The main reason for this efficiency is the use of a technique called *incremental reduced error pruning*, which prunes each rule immediately after it has been induced, rather than after all rules have been generated. This speeds up the induction process as the pruned rules allow larger subsets of the remaining positive examples to be removed at each iteration compared to the non-pruned rules. It should be noted that this technique could also be employed directly in Reconsider-and-Conquer, improving the efficiency (and accuracy) further, especially in noisy domains.

Like Reconsider-and-Conquer, a recently proposed method for rule induction, called PART, also employs a combination of Divide-and-Conquer and Separate-and-Conquer [6]. One major difference between PART and Reconsider-and-Conquer is that the former method uses Divide-and-Conquer to find *one* rule that is added to the resulting hypothesis, while the latter method uses (a generalised version of) Divide-and-Conquer for generating *a set of* rules that is added. The purpose of the former method to use Divide-and-Conquer is not to gain efficiency over Separate-and-Conquer, but to avoid a problem called *hasty generalisation* that may occur when employing incremental reduced error pruning, like IREP and RIPPER do. Again, the former method may in fact be used as a pruning technique in conjunction with Reconsider-and-Conquer rather than Separate-and-Conquer.

In C4.5rules [16], a set of rules is first generated using Divide-and-Conquer, and then simplified by a post-pruning process. However, the cost of this process is cubic in the number of examples [4], which means that it could be even more expensive than using Separate-and-Conquer in the first place to overcome the replication problem. Still, the post-pruning techniques employed by C4.5rules (and other systems e.g. RIPPER) could be useful for both Separate-and-Conquer as well as Reconsider-and-Conquer. The main advantage of using Reconsider-and-Conquer for generating the initial set of rules compared to Divide-and-Conquer as used in C4.5rules is that significantly fewer rules need to be considered by the post-pruning process when having employed the former.

There have been other approaches to the replication problem within the framework of decision tree learning. One approach is to restrict the form of the trees when growing them, which then allows for merging of isomorphic subtrees [9]. It should be noted that these techniques are, in contrast to Reconsider-and-Conquer, yet restricted to propositional and numerical domains.

6   Concluding Remarks

A hybrid strategy of Divide-and-Conquer and Separate-and-Conquer has been presented, called Reconsider-and-Conquer. Experimental results from propositional, numerical and relational domains have been presented demonstrating that Reconsider-and-Conquer significantly reduces the replication problem from which Divide-and-Conquer suffers and that it is several times (up to an order of magnitude) faster than Separate-and-Conquer. In the trade-off between accuracy and amount of cpu time needed, we find Reconsider-and-Conquer in many cases to be a very good alternative to both Divide-and-Conquer and Separate-and-Conquer.

There are a number of directions for future research. One is to explore both pre- and post-pruning techniques in conjunction with Reconsider-and-Conquer. The techniques that have been developed for Separate-and-Conquer can in fact be employed directly as mentioned in the previous section. Another direction is to investigate alternative conditions for the decision made by Reconsider-and-Conquer regarding whether or not the search should continue from some rule on a completed branch. The currently employed condition that the fraction of covered positive examples should never decrease worked surprisingly well, but other conditions, e.g. based on some significance test, may be even more effective.

Acknowledgements This work has been supported by the European Community ESPRIT Long Term Research Project no. 20237 *Inductive Logic Programming II* and the Swedish Research Council for Engineering Sciences (TFR).

References

1. Blake C., Keogh E. and Merz C.J., *UCI Repository of machine learning databases*, Irvine, CA: University of California, Department of Information and Computer Science (1998)
2. Boström H., "Covering vs. Divide-and-Conquer for Top-Down Induction of Logic Programs", *Proc. of the Fourteenth International Joint Conference on Artificial Intelligence*, Morgan Kaufmann (1995) 1194–1200
3. Bratko I., *Prolog Programming for Artificial Intelligence* , (2nd edition), Addison-Wesley (1990)
4. Cohen W. W., "Fast Effective Rule Induction", *Machine Learning: Proc. of the 12th International Conference*, Morgan Kaufmann (1995) 115–123
5. Fayyad U. and Irani K., "On the Handling of Continuos-Valued Attributes in Decision Tree Generation", *Machine Learning* 8 (1992) 87–102
6. Frank E. and Witten I. H., "Generating Accurate Rule Sets Without Global Optimization", *Machine Learning: Proc. of the Fifteenth International Conference*, Morgan Kaufmann (1998) 144–151
7. Fürnkranz J., "Separate-and-Conquer Rule Learning", *Articial Intelligence Review* **13(1)** (1999)
8. Fürnkranz J. and Widmer G., "Incremental Reduced Error Pruning", *Machine Learning: Proc. of the Eleventh International Conference*, Morgan Kaufmann (1994)
9. Kohavi R. and Li C-H., "Oblivious Decision Trees, Graphs and Top-Down Pruning", *Proc. of the Fourteenth International Joint Conference on Artificial Intelligence*, Morgan Kaufmann (1995) 1071–1077
10. Lavrač N. and Džeroski S., *Inductive Logic Programming: Techniques and Applications*, Ellis Horwood (1994)
11. Lloyd J. W., *Foundations of Logic Programming*, (2nd edition), Springer-Verlag (1987)
12. Martin J. K., "An Exact Probability Metric for Decision Tree Splitting and Stopping", *Machine Learning* **28** (1997) 257–291
13. Pagallo G. and Haussler D., "Boolean Feature Discovery in Empirical Learning", *Machine Learning* **5** (1990) 71–99
14. Quinlan J. R., "Induction of Decision Trees", *Machine Learning* **1** (1986) 81–106
15. Quinlan J. R., "Learning Logical Definitions from Relations", *Machine Learning* **5** (1990) 239–266
16. Quinlan J. R., *C4.5: Programs for Machine Learning*, Morgan Kaufmann (1993)

Refining Complete Hypotheses in ILP

Ivan Bratko

University of Ljubljana, Faculty of Computer and Information Sc.
Trzaska 25, 1000 Ljubljana, Slovenia
bratko@fri.uni-lj.si

Abstract. Most ILP systems employ the covering algorithm whereby hypotheses are constructed iteratively clause by clause. Typically the covering algorithm is greedy in the sense that each iteration adds the best clause according to some local evaluation criterion. Some typical problems of the covering algorithm are: unnecessarily long hypotheses, difficulties in handling recursion, difficulties in learning multiple predicates. This paper investigates a non-covering approach to ILP, implemented as a Prolog program called HYPER, whose goals were: use intensional background knowledge, handle recursion well, and enable multi-predicate learning. Experimental results in this paper may appear surprising in the view of the very high combinatorial complexity of the search space associated with the non-covering approach.

1 Introduction

Most ILP systems employ the covering algorithm whereby hypotheses are induced iteratively clause by clause. Examples of such systems are Quinlan's FOIL [5], Grobelnik's Markus [2], Muggleton's PROGOL [3] and Pompe's CLIP [4]. The covering algorithm builds hypotheses gradually, starting with the empty hypothesis and adding new clauses one by one. Positive examples covered by each new clause are removed, until the remaining positive examples are reduced to the empty set, that is, the clauses in the hypothesis cover all the positive examples.

Typically the covering algorithm is greedy in the sense that on each iteration it chooses to add the clause that optimises some evaluation criterion. Such a clause tends to be optimal locally, with respect to the current set of clauses in the hypothesis. However there is no guarantee that the covering process will result in a globally optimal hypothesis. A good hypothesis is not necessarily assembled from locally optimal clauses. On the other hand, locally inferior clauses may cooperate well as a whole, giving rise to an overall good hypothesis.

Some typical problems due to the greedy nature of the covering algorithm are:

- Unnecessarily long hypotheses with too may clauses
- Difficulties in handling recursion
- Difficulties in learning multiple predicates simultaneously

In view of these difficulties a non-covering approach where a hypothesis (with all its clauses) would be constructed as a whole, would seem to be a better idea. Of course a strong practical reason against this, and in favour of the covering approach, is the combinatorial complexity involved. The local optimisation of individual clauses is complex enough, so the global optimisation of whole hypotheses would seem to be out of question. Experimental results in this paper are possibly surprising in this respect.

In this paper we investigate a non-covering approach and study its performance on typical small ILP learning problems that require recursion. We develop such a non-covering algorithm, implemented as a Prolog program called HYPER (Hypothesis Refiner, as opposed to the majority of ILP programs that are "clause refiners"). The design goals of the HYPER program were:

- simple, transparent and short
- handle intensional background knowledge
- handle recursion well
- enable multipredicate learning
- handle reasonably well typical basic ILP benchmark problems (member/2, append/3, path/3, sort/2, arches/3, etc.) without having to resort to special tricks, e.g. unnatural declaration of argument modes

HYPER does not address the problem of noisy data. So it aims at inducing short hypotheses that are consistent with the examples, that is: cover all the positive examples and no negative one.

2 Mechanisms of HYPER

According to the design goal of simplicity, the program was developed in the following fashion. First, an initial version was written which is just a simple generator of possible hypotheses for the given learning problem (i.e. bakground predicates and examples). The search strategy in this initial version was simple iterative deepening. Due to its complexity, this straightforward approach, as expected, fails even for simplest learning problems like member/2 or append/3. Then additional mechanisms were added to the program, such as better search and mode declarations, to improve its efficiency. Thirteen versions were written in this way with increasingly better performance. Once a reasonable performance on the basic benchmark problems was obtained, the added mechanisms were selectively switched off to see which of them were essential. Eventually, the final version was obtained with the smallest set of added mechanisms which still performs reasonably well. The mechanisms that were experimentally found to be essential are described in detail below. Later we also discuss mechanisms that somewhat surprizingly proved not to be particularly useful.

2.1 Search

HYPER constructs hypotheses in the top-down fashion by searching a refinement tree in which the nodes correspond to hypotheses. A hypothesis H_0 in this tree has successors H_i, where hypotheses H_i are the least specific (in some sense) refinements of of H_0. Refinements are defined by HYPER's refinement operator described in the next section. Each newly generated hypothesis is more specific than or equal to its predecessor in the sense of theta-subsumption. So a hypothesis can only cover a subset of the examples covered by the hypothesis' predecessor. The learning examples are always assumed noise-free, and the goal of search is to find a hypothesis that is consistent with the examples. That is, it covers all the positive examples and no negative example. If a hypothesis is generated that does not cover all the positive examples, it is immediately discarded because it can never be refined into a consistent hypothesis. Excluding such hypotheses from the search tree reduces the tree considerably. During search, new hypotheses are not checked whether they are duplicates or in any sense equivalent to already generated hypotheses.

Search starts with a set of initial hypotheses. This set is the set of all possible bags of user-defined start clauses of up to the user-defined maximal number of clauses in a hypothesis. Multiple copies of a start clause typically appear in a start hypothesis. A typical start clause is something rather general and neutral, such as: append(L1, L2, L3).

HYPER performs a best-first search using an evaluation function that takes into account the size of a hypothesis and its accuracy in a simple way by defining the cost of a hypothesis H as:

$$Cost(H) = w_1 * Size(H) + w_2 * NegCover(H)$$

where NegCover(H) is the number of negative examples covered by H. The definition of 'H covers example E' in HYPER roughly corresponds to 'E can be logically derived from H'. There are however some essential procedural details described later. w_1 and w_2 are weights. The size of a hypothesis is defined simply as a weighted sum of the number of literals and number of variables in the hypothesis:

$$Size(H) = k_1 * \#literals(H) + k_2 * \#variables(H)$$

All the experiments with HYPER described later were done with the following settings of the weights: $w_1=1$, $w_2=10$, $k_1=10$, $k_2=1$, which corresponds to:

$$Cost(H) = \#variables(H) + 10 * \#literals(H) + 10 * NegCover(H)$$

These settings are ad hoc, but their relative magnitudes are intuitively justified as follows. Variables in a hypothesis increase its complexity, so they should be taken into account. However, the literals increase the complexity more, hence they contribute to the cost with a greater weight. A covered negative example contributes to a hypothesis' cost as much as a literal. This corresponds to the intuition that an extra literal should at least prevent one negative example from being covered. It should be noted that these weights can be varied considerably withought affecting the search performance. For example, changing k_1 from 1 to 5 had no effect on search in the experiments.

2.2 Hypothesis refinement

To refine a clause, perform one of the following:

1. Unify two variables in the clause, e.g. X1 = X2.
2. Refine a variable in the clause into a background term, e.g. replace variable L0 with term [X|L].
3. Add a background literal to the clause.

Some pragmatic details of these operations are as follows:

(a) The arguments of literals are typed. Only variables of the same type can be unified. The user defines background knowledge, including "back-literals" and "back-terms". Only these can be used in refining a variable (of the approapriate type) into a term, and in adding a literal to a clause.
(b) Arguments in back-literals can be defined as input or output. When a new literal is added to a clause, all of its input arguments have to be unified (non-deterministically) with the existing non-output variables in the clause (that is those variables that are assumed to have their values instantiated at this point of executing the clause).

To refine a hypothesis H_0, choose one of the clauses C_0 in H_0, refine clause C_0 into C, and obtain a new hypothesis H by replacing C_0 in H_0 with C. This says that the refinements of a hypothesis are obtained by refining *any* of its clauses. There is a useful heuristic that often saves complexity. Namely, if a clause is found in H_0 that alone covers a negative example, then only refinements arising from this clause are generated. The reason is that such a clause necessarily has to be refined before a consistent hypothesis is obtained. This will be referred to as "covers-alone heuristic".
This refinement operator aims at producing least specific specialisations (LSS). However, it really only approximates LSS. This refinement operator does LSS under the constraint that the number of clauses in a hypothesis after refinement stays the same. Without this restriction, an LSS operator should be more appropriately defined as:

$$\text{refs\_hyp}(H_0) = \{ H_0 - \{C_0\} \cup \text{refs\_clause}(C_0) \mid C_0 \in H_0\}$$

where refs_hyp(H_0) is the set of all LSS of hypothesis H_0, and refs_clause(C_0) is the set of all LSS of clause C_0. This unrestricted definition of LSS was not implemented in HYPER for the obvious reason of complexity.

2.3 Interpreter for hypotheses

To prove an example, HYPER uses intensional background knowledge together with the current hypothesis. To this end HYPER includes a Prolog meta-interpreter which does approximately the same as the Prolog interpreter, but takes care of the possibility of falling into infinite loops. Therefore the length of proofs is limited to a specified maximal number of proof steps (resolution steps). This was set to 6 in all the experiments mentioned in this paper. It is important to appropriately handle the cases where this bound is exceeded. It would be a mistake to interpret such cases simply as 'fail'. Instead, the following interpretation was designed and proved to be essential for the effectiveness of HYPER. The interpreter is implemented as the predicate:

prove(Goal, Hypo, Answer)

Goal is the goal to be proved using the current hypothesis Hypo and background knowledge. The predicate prove/3 always succeeds and Answer can be one of the following three cases:

Answer = yes   if Goal is derivable from Hypo in no more than D steps (max. proof length)
Answer = no   if Goal is not derivable even with unlimited proof length
Answer = maybe   if proof search was terminated after D steps

The interpretation of these answers, relative to the standard Prolog interpreter, is as follows. 'yes' means that Goal under the standard interpreter would definitely succeed. 'no' means that Goal under the standard interpreter would definitely fail. 'maybe' means any one of the following three possibilities:

1. The standard Prolog interpreter (no limit on proof length) would get into infinite loop.
2. The standard Prolog interpreter would eventually find a proof of length greater than D.
3. The standard Prolog interpreter would find, at some length greater than D, that this derivation alternative fails. Therefore it would backtrack to another alternative and there possibly find a proof (of length possibly no greater than D), or fail, or get into an infinite loop.

The question now is how to react to answer 'maybe' when processing the learning examples. HYPER reacts as follows:

- When testing whether a positive example is covered, 'maybe' is interpreted as 'not covered'.
- When testing whether a negative example is not covered, 'maybe' is interpreted as not 'not covered', i.e. as 'covered'.

A clarification is in order regarding what counts as a step in a proof. Only resolution steps involving clauses in the current hypothesis count. If backtracking occurs before proof length is exceeded, the backtracked steps are discounted. When proving the conjunction of two goals, the sum of their proof lengths must not exceed max. proof length. Calls of background predicates, defined in Prolog, are delegated to the standard Prolog interpreter and do not incur any increase in proof length. It is up to the user to ensure that the standard Prolog interpreter does not get into an infinite loop when processing such "background" goals.

2.4 Example

HYPER is implemented in Prolog. In this implementation, a hypothesis is represented as a list of clauses. A clause is a list of literals accompanied by a list of variables and their types. For example:

```
[member( X0, [X1 | L1]), member( X0, L2)] /
[X0:item, X1:item, L1:list, L2:list]
```

corresponds to the Prolog clause:

```
member( X0, [X1 | L1])   :- member( X0, L2).
```

where the variables X0 and X1 are of type item, and L1 and L2 are of type list. The types are user-defined.

Figure 1 shows the specification accepted by HYPER of the problem of learning two predicates simultaneously: even(L) and odd(L), where even(L) is true if L is a list with an even number of elements, and odd(L) is true if L is a list with an odd number of elements. In this specification,

```
backliteral( even( L), [L:list], []).
```

means: even(L) can be used as a background literal when refining a clause. The argument L is of type list. L is an input argument; there are no oputput arguments. prolog_predicate(fail) means that there are no background predicates defined in Prolog. The predicate term/3 specifies how variables of given types (in this case 'list') can be refined into terms, comprising variables of specified types. Start hypotheses are all possible bags of up to max_clauses = 4 start clauses of the two forms given in Fig. 1. For this learning problem HYPER finds the following hypothesis consistent with the data:

```
even( [ ] ).
even([ A, B | C ] )     :-     even( C).
odd( [ A | B ] )     :-     even( B).
```

Before this hypothesis is found, HYPER has generated altogether 66 hypotheses, refined 16 of them, kept 29 as further candidates for refinement, and discarded the remaining 21 as incomplete (i.e. not covering all the positive examples). To reach the final hypothesis above from the corresponding start hypothesis, 6 refinement steps are required. The size of the complete refinement forest of up to 6 refinement steps from the start hypotheses in this case, respecting the type constraints as specified in Fig. 1, is 22565. The actual number of hypotheses generated during search was thus less than 0.3% of the total refinement forest to depth 6.

This learning problem can also be defined more restrictively by only allowing term refinements on lists to depth 1 only, thus suppressing terms like [X1,X2 | L]. This can be done by using type "list(Depth)" in the definition of refine_term/3 and start_clause/1 as follows:

```
term( list( D), [ X | L ], [ X:item, L:list(1) ] ) :-
    var( D).      % list(1) cannot be refined further!
term( list( D), [ ], [ ]).
start_clause( [ odd( L) ] / [ L:list( D) ] ).
start_clause( [ even( L) ] / [ L:list( D) ] ).
```

Using this problem definition, HYPER finds the mutually recursive definition of even/2 and odd/2:

```
even( [ ] ).
odd( [A | B ] )    :-   even( B ).
even( [ A | B ] )   :-   odd( B ).
```

2.5 Mechanisms that did not help

Several mechanisms were parts of intermediate versions of HYPER, but were eventually left out because they were found not to be clearly useful. They did not significantly improve search complexity and at the same time incurred some complexity overheads of their own. Some of these mechanisms are mentioned below as possibly useful "negative lessons":

- Immediately discard clause refinements that render the corresponding hypothesis unsatisfiable (i.e. cannot succeed even on the most general query).
- Checking for redundant or duplicate hypotheses where "duplicate" may mean either literally the same under the renaming of the variables, or some kind of equivalence between sets of clauses and literals in the clauses, or redundancy based on theta-subsumption between hypotheses. One such idea is to discard those newly generated and complete hypotheses that subsume any other existing candidate hypothesis. This requires special care because the subsuming hypothesis may later be refined into a hypothesis that cannot be reached from other hypotheses. Perhaps surprizingly no version of such redundancy or duplicate test

was found that was clearly useful. Also it is hard to find a useful subsumption-based test that would correspond well to the procedurally oriented interpretation of hypotheses.

```
% Inducing odd and even length property for lists

% Background literals

backliteral( even( L), [ L:list], [ ]).
backliteral( odd( L), [ L:list], [ ]).

% Term refinements

term( list, [ X | L ], [ X:item, L:list]).
term( list, [ ], [ ]).

% Background predicates defined in Prolog

prolog_predicate( none).      % No background predicate in Prolog

% Start clauses

start_clause( [ odd( L) ] / [ L:list]).
start_clause( [ even( L) ] / [ L:list]).

% Positive examples

ex( even( [ ] ) ).
ex( even( [a,b] ) ).
ex( odd( [a] ) ).
ex( odd( [b,c,d] ) ).
ex( odd( [a,b,c,d,e] ) ).
ex( even( [a,b,c,d] ) ).

% Negative examples

nex( even( [a] ) ).
nex( even( [a,b,c] ) ).
nex( odd( [ ] ) ).
nex( odd( [a,b] ) ).
nex( odd( [a,b,c,d] ) ).
```

Fig. 1: Definition of the problem of learning even/1 and odd/1 simultaneously.

- "Closing" induced clauses as in Markus [2] to avoid the problem with uninstanted outputs of a target predicate. Closing a hypothesis means to "connect" all the output arguments to instantiated variables (i.e. unifying all the output arguments with other arguments). There are typically many ways of closing a hypothesis. So in evaluating a hypothesis, a "best" closing would be sought (one that retains the completeness and covers the least negative examples). This is, however, not only combinatorially inefficient, but requires considerable elaboration because often the closing is not possible without making the hypothesis incomplete (closing is sometimes too coarse a specialisation step).

3 Experiments

Here we describe experiments with HYPER on a set of typical ILP test problems. All of them, except arches/3, concern relations on lists and require recursive definitions. The problems are:

```
member(X,List)
append(List1,List2,List3)
even(List) + odd(List)  ( learning simultaneously even and odd length list)
path(StartNode,GoalNode,Path)
insort(List,SortedList)    (insertion sort)
arch(Block1,Block2,Block3)    (Winston's arches with objects taxonomy)
invariant(A,B,Q,R)  (Bratko and Grobelnik's program loop invariant [1])
```

For all of these problems, correct definitions were induced from no more than 6 positive and 9 negative examples in execution times typically in the order of a second or a few seconds with Sicstus Prolog on a 160 MHz PC. No special attention was paid to constructing particularly friendly example sets. Smaller example sets would possibly suffice for inducing correct definitions. Particular system settings or mode declarations to help in particular problems were avoided throughout. Details of these experiments are given in Table 1. The definitions induced were as expected, with the exception of a small surprise for path/3. The expected definition was:

```
path( A, A, [A]).
path( A, B, [A | C])   :-
  link( A, D), path( D, B, C).
```

The induced definition was slightly different:

```
path( A, A, [A]).
path( C, D, [C, B | A]):-
  link( C, B), path( B, D, [E | A]).
```

This might appear incorrect because the last literal would normally be programmed as path(B, D, [B | A]), stating that the path starts with node B and not with the undefined E. However, the heads of both induced clauses take care of eventually instantiating E to B.

The main point of interest in Table 1 are the search statistics. The last five columns give: the refinement depth RefDepth (the number of refinement steps needed to construct the final hypothesis from a start hypothesis), the number of all generated hypotheses, the number of refined hypotheses and the number of candidate hypotheses waiting to be refined, and the total size of the refinement forest up to depth RefDepth. This size corresponds to the number of hypotheses that would have to be generated if the search was conducted in the breadth-first fashion. The number of all generated hypotheses is greater than the sum of refined and to-be-refined hypotheses. The reason is that those generated hypotheses that are not complete (do not cover all the positive examples) are immediately discarded. Note that all these counts include duplicate hypotheses because when searching the refinement forest the newly generated hypotheses are not checked for duplicates. The total size of the refinement forest is determined by taking into account the covers-alone heuristic. The sizes would have been considerably higher without this heuristic, as illustrated in Table 2. This table tabulates the size of the search forest and the size of the refinement forest by refinement depth, and compares these sizes with or without covers-alone heuristic and duplicate checking. The total sizes of the refinement forests in Table 1 were determined by generating these trees, except for append/3 and path/3. These trees were too large to be generated, so their sizes in Table 1 are estimates, obtained by extrapolating the exponential growth to the required depth. These estimates are considerable underestimates.

Tables 1 and 2 indicate the following observations:

- In most of these cases HYPER only generates a small fraction of the total refinement forest up to solution depth.
- The losses due to no duplicate checking are not dramatic, at least for the tabulated case of member/2. Also, as Table 2 shows, these losses are largely alleviated by the covers-alone heuristic.

Search in HYPER is guided by two factors: first, by the constraint that only complete hypotheses are retained in the search; second, by the evaluation function. In the cases of Table 1, the evaluation function guides the search rather well except for invariant/3.

One learning problem, not included in Fig. 1, where it seems HYPER did not perform satisfactorily, is the learning of quick-sort. In this problem, the evaluation function does not guide the search well because it does not discriminate between the hypotheses on the path to the target hypothesis from other hypotheses. The target hypothesis emerges suddenly "from nothing". HYPER did induce a correct hypothesis for quick-sort with difference lists, but the definition of the learning problem (input-output modes) had to be defined in a way that was judged to be too unnatural assuming the user does not guess the target hypothesis sufficiently closely. Natural handling of such learning problems belongs to future work.

Table 1. Complexity of some learning problems and corresponding search statistics. "Total size" is the number of nodes up to Refine depth in the refinement forest defined by HYPER's refinement operator, taking into account the "covers-alone" heuristic.

Learning problem	Backgr. pred.	Pos. exam.	Neg. exam.	Refine depth	Hypos. refined	To be refined	All ge- nerated	Total size
member	0	3	3	5	20	16	85	1575
append	0	5	5	7	14	32	199	$> 10^9$
even + odd	0	6	5	6	23	32	107	22506
path	1	6	9	12	32	112	658	$> 10^{17}$
insort	2	5	4	6	142	301	1499	540021
arches	4	2	5	4	52	942	2208	3426108
invariant	2	6	5	3	123	2186	3612	18426

Table 2. Complexity of the search problem for inducing member/2. D is refinement depth, N is the number of nodes in refinement forest up to depth D with covers-alone heuristic, N(uniq) is the number of unique such hypotheses (i.e. after eliminating duplicates); N(all) is the number of all the nodes in refinement forest (no covers-alone heuristic), N(all,uniq) is the number of unique such hypotheses.

D	N	N(uniq)	N(all)	N(all,uniq)
1	3	3	6	6
2	13	13	40	31
3	50	50	248	131
4	274	207	1696	527
5	1575	895	12880	2151

4 Conclusions

The paper investigates the refinement of complete hypotheses. This was experimentally investigated by designing the ILP program HYPER which refines complete hypotheses, not just clauses. It does not employ a covering algorithm, but constructs a complete hypothesis "simultaneously". This alleviates problems with recursive definitions, specially with mutual recursion (when *both* mutually recursive clauses are needed for each of them to be found useful). The obvious worry with this approach is its increased combinatorial complexity in comparison with covering. The experimental results are possibly surprising in this respect as shown inTable 1. In most of the experiments in typical simple learning problems that involve recursion, HYPER's search heuristics cope well with the complexity of the hypothesis space.

The heuristics seem to be particularly effective in learning predicates with structured arguments (lists). On the other hand, the heuristics were not effective for invariant/4 whose arguments are not structured, and background predicates are arithmetic.

Some other useful properties of the HYPER approach are:

1. The program can start with an arbitrary initial hypothesis that can be refined to the target hypothesis. This is helpful in cases when the user's intuition allows start the search with an initial hypothesis closer to the target hypothesis.

2. The target predicate is not necessarily the one for which the examples are given. E.g., there may be examples for predicate p/1, while an initial hypothesis contains the clauses: q(X) and p(X) :- r(X,Y), q(Y).

3. The program always does a general to specific search. This monotonicity property allows to determine bounds on some properties of the reachable hypotheses. E.g. if H covers P positive examples and N negative examples, then all the hypotheses reachable through refinements will cover at most P and N examples respectively.

Acknowledgements

This work was partly supported by the Slovenian Ministry of Science and Technology, and the Commission of the European Union within the project ILP2. Part of this work was done during the author's visit at the AI Laboratory, School of Computer Sc. and Eng., University of New South Wales, Sydney, Australia, that also provided support for the visit. I would like to thank Marko Grobelnik, Uros Pompe and Claude Sammut for discussion.

References

1. Bratko, I., Grobelnik, M. (1993) Inductive learning applied to program construction and verification. *Proc. ILP Workshop 93*, Bled, Slovenia.
2. Grobelnik, M. (1992) Markus – an optimised model inference system. *Proc. ECAI Workshop on Logical Approaches to Machine Learning*, Vienna.
3. Muggleton, S. (1995) Inverse entailment and Progol. *New Generation Computing*, **13** (1995), 245-286.
4. Pompe, U. (1998) *Constraint Inductive Logic Programming*. Ph.D. Thesis, University of Ljubljana, Faculty of Computer and Info. Sc. (In Slovenian).
5. Quinlan, J.R. (1990) Learning logical definitions from relations. *Machine Learning*, **5** (1990), 239-266.

Acquiring Graphic Design Knowledge with Nonmonotonic Inductive Learning

Kazuya CHIBA[1], Hayato OHWADA[2] and Fumio MIZOGUCHI[2]

[1] Corporate Research Laboratories, Fuji Xerox Co., Ltd.
Email: chiba.kazuya@fujixerox.co.jp
[2] Faculty of Science and Engineering, Science University of Tokyo
Email: {ohwada, mizo}@ia.noda.sut.ac.jp

Abstract. In this paper, we present a new method based on nonmonotonic learning where the Inductive Logic Programming (ILP) algorithm is used twice and apply our method to acquire graphic design knowledge. Acquiring design knowledge is a challenging task because such knowledge is complex and vast. We thus focus on principles of layout and constraints that layouts must satisfy to realize automatic layout generation. Although we do not have negative examples in this case, we can generate them randomly by considering that a page with just one element moved is always wrong. Our nonmonotonic learning method introduces a new predicate for exceptions. In our method, the ILP algorithm is executed twice, exchanging positive and negative examples. From our experiments using magazine advertisements, we obtained rules characterizing good layouts and containing relationships between elements. Moreover, the experiments show that our method can learn more accurate rules than normal ILP can.

1 Introduction

As the World Wide Web (or simply "Web") has spread recently, more amateurs (not professional graphic designers) have begun to design web documents. This indicates the need to support them and is our motivation for studying how to acquire graphic design knowledge, or more generally, visual design knowledge. Our ultimate target is automated graphic design; to automatically generate a high-quality design conforming to the given intention from materials and intention of document. To realize this, we believe that knowledge-based approaches should be taken. There are two approaches for acquiring design knowledge. The first one is acquisition from experts, i.e., graphic designers. However, it is not easy to extract their expertise and to make it machine-processable. The other is to acquire design knowledge from examples. We think this is suitable for this domain. Lieberman pointed out that graphic designers communicate expert knowledge through specific example designs [Lieberman 95].

There has been some previous work on acquiring design knowledge from examples. The first kind of such work uses a statistical approach. For example, Ishiba et al. [Ishiba 97] analyzed the relationships between human feelings and design attributes of simple business documents, using linear regression. Typical human feelings are "warm," "simple," "powerful," and "unique." The design attributes include "the font used in the title" and "space between lines." In work of this kind, impressions are represented by a linear function of a fixed number of parameters.

However, this approach can be applied only to designs of similar forms. In simple business documents, a page can be described by parameters as Ishiba did. However, in posters or advertisements, elements on the page differ for differing samples. For example, parameters for title could not be set because some sample would have no specific title or would have two titles. Thus, we need to model a page at the element level, not at the page level. In this case, a set of parameters is needed for each element, not only for a whole page. Thus a page requires a set of parameter sets. Since the number of parameters differs for samples, regression cannot be applied to this case.

Another kind of work on acquiring design knowledge is based on command sequences. *Mondrian* [Lieberman 93, 96] is an example of this kind of system. Mondrian is a graphical editor that can learn new graphical procedures by example (through *programming by demonstration*). Mondrian records and generalizes procedures presented as sequences of graphical editing commands. However, the acquired knowledge is in procedural form, not in declarative form. The procedures learned are not sufficiently general; they can be used only on "analogous" examples. Moreover, existing documents cannot be used as examples for learning.

In contrast to the two approaches above, we adopt *Inductive Logic Programming* (ILP) [Muggleton 91]. ILP can handle element-level page models. For example, the rule

```
property1(Page) :- has(Page,Element),
    attribute1(Element).
```

states that a page is `property1` if the page has (at least) one element which is `attribute1`. In this example, `attribute1` is a parameter for each element, and a page can be described as a set of an arbitrary number of parameters such as `attribute1(element1), attribute1(element2),...`

Moreover, since ILP uses logic programs as knowledge representation, complex and declarative design knowledge can be acquired. Since ILP can also learn relations, it can acquire design knowledge represented as relationships between elements on pages. In addition, we introduce our new methods where the ILP algorithm is used twice. Details are described later.

The paper is organized as follows. Section 2 clarifies the precise scope of this study. The dataset used is described in Section 3; the positive and negative examples, in Section 4; and the background knowledge, in Sections 5. Section 6 presents our learning methods and the results of the experiments using three different algorithms. Finally, Section 7 concludes with a discussion and an outline of directions for further work.

2 Target

Acquiring graphic design knowledge is a challenging task because the whole knowledge is complex and vast, so we limit the scope of our study. We think the knowledge can be divided roughly into two kinds, knowledge about layout and knowledge about other things (color, pattern, texture, etc.). Here we exclude typesetting knowledge since it has already been investigated a lot. The latter can be represented mainly using attributes and is considered to be covered mostly by statistical approaches. Therefore, we deal with the layout part.

The layout knowledge can be divided into two kinds.

(1) Principles of layout - Basic rules about goodness of layout, i.e. rules by which to judge that a particular layout is good or bad (or medium). For example, layouts generated by designers are good ones, and layouts consisting of randomly placed elements are bad ones.

(2) Relationships between layout and feelings - Knowledge about design alternatives conforming to the layout principles. Different layouts convey different human feelings, such as dynamic, stable, powerful, rhythmical, motive, orderly, or adventurous.

Knowledge type (1) can realize automated layout generation, whereas knowledge type (2) can realize evaluation only. Therefore, we focus on the principles of layout.

3 Page model and its representation

To show that ILP is effective for acquiring design knowledge, we deal with advertisements which the statistical approaches cannot handle. More precisely, we deal with one-page advertisements in technology magazines, using such advertisements found in *BYTE* [BYTE 97] as our data. Since electronic data are not available, we have to make our dataset by hand.

First, we model pages for our purpose. In our model, each element on a page, such as a block of text, a picture, or an illustration, is called an object. Note that an object is not uniquely identified while making a dataset. A page is considered a set of objects. For the sake of simplicity, we model an object as a circumscribing rectangle. Ruled lines and frames are ignored, as are background images. Figure 1 illustrates an example of our page model. The figure is derived from an actual advertisement page in *BYTE*. The large object (a) is actually two columns of text which flows around the overlapping illustration (b).

The following features are extracted from objects (the last three ones are only for text):

- *type*: text, image, or illustration. Illustrations include charts, graphs, or logos. Decorated or deformed text (usually a title) is considered an image.

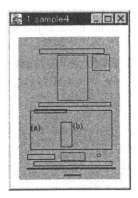

Fig. 1. Example of our model

- *location*: represented as *p(L,U,R,D)*, where *L, U* are the *X, Y* coordinates of the upper left of the rectangle and *R, D* are the *X, Y* coordinates of the lower right of the rectangle. Coordinates are measured in millimeters.
- *number of columns*.
- *alignment between text lines*: left, right, center, or justify (just). Alignment for a single line is just.
- *font size*: The size of font used most frequently, in points (= 1/4 mm).

These features are represented as Prolog facts like `smpl(PageID,ObjectID,Object)`. We give an example of the real representation of a page below:

```
smpl(4,1,obj(text(1,just,36),p(40,22,164,31))).
smpl(4,2,obj(illustration,p(74,34,132,119))).
smpl(4,3,obj(illustration,p(141,33,174,63))).
                         :
smpl(4,13,obj(text(1,just,8),p(86,259,117,261))).
```

4   Positive and negative examples

In this task, we do not have the negative examples needed for ILP. Thus our case can be regarded as nonmonotonic inductive logic programming setting [De Raedt 93].

To generate negative examples, we now consider applying the *Closed World Assumption* (CWA). In other words, any layout different from the original one is considered a negative example. However, CWA does not always hold in the design domain. Thus, in our study we assume the situation that the last element is to be located to a page on which all other elements already have been located. In this situation, we think it is always wrong to place the last element in any location except the right location. In this way, we apply CWA and generate many negative examples. For instance, in Figure 2, (a) shows a positive example, and (b), (c), and (d) show negative examples when the black object is to be located.

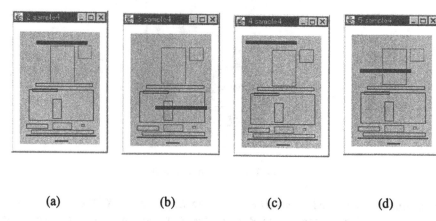

(a)   (b)   (c)   (d)

Fig. 2. Positive and negative examples

The target predicate for our learning experiments is `good_locate1(Case,Location)`, where `Case` is a term `case(PageID,ObjectID)` and `Location` is a term `loc(X,Y)`. This says that on the page `PageID`, it is good to place the object `ObjectID` at location (X,Y). For instance, a positive example is represented as `good_locate1(case(4,1),loc(40,22))`.

5 Background Knowledge

To determine the background knowledge for our experiments, we investigated actual advertisement pages. First, we tried to detect and describe basic rules about goodness of layout from the pages as well as we could, consulting design textbooks. Next, we determined the predicates needed to describe such rules and defined the predicates, partly referring to [Honda 94]. Our background knowledge consisting of 15 predicates and their definitions is shown below.

For an object:
- `form_obj(Case,Location,Obj)`: From Case and Location, an object Obj is formed, referring to smp1. For example, `form_obj(case(4,1),loc(40,22),obj(text(1,just,36), p(40,22,124,144)))` holds when smp1 is defined as shown in Section 3.
- `obj_type(Obj,Type)`: The type of Obj is Type.
- `obj_width(Obj,Length)`: The width of Obj is Length, in millimeters.
- `obj_height(Obj,Length)`: The height of Obj is Length, in millimeters.
- `h_position(Obj,Pos)`: The approximate horizontal position of Obj is Pos. Pos is left, middle, or right.

- v_position(Obj, Pos): The approximate vertical position of Obj is Pos. Pos is top, middle, or bottom.
- h_centered(Obj): Obj is horizontally centered. 4 mm or less error is allowed.

For text:
- text_align(Obj, AlignType): Alignment type between lines in Obj is AlignType.
- font_size(Obj, F): The size of font used in Obj is F, in millimeters.
- column(Obj, N): the number of columns in Obj is N.

For relationships between objects:
- h_align(Case, Obj1, Obj2, AlignType): On page PageID (in Case), Obj1 and Obj2 are horizontally aligned. AlignType is left, right, center, or just.
- v_align(Case, Obj1, Obj2, AlignType): Obj1 and Obj2 are vertically aligned. AlignType is top, bottom, center, or just. Note that for these two predicates, 1 mm error is allowed in alignment.
- above(Case, Obj1, Obj2, Distance): Obj1 is located above Obj2 and the distance between the two is Distance, in millimeters.
- direct_above(Case, Obj1, Obj2, Distance): Obj1 is located directly (no object exists between the two) above Obj2.
- overlapping(Case, Obj1, Obj2): Obj1 and Obj2 overlap each other.

Our page model and our background knowledge used here are unintentionally similar to the ones used in document layout recognition problems [Esposito 94]. However, there are differences, such as permission of overlapping and features for text, because different problems are treated.

6 Learning methods and experimental results

In our experiments, we use three different learning methods.

6.1 Normal ILP

We sampled 20 advertisement pages from the magazine *BYTE* and constructed a positive example set from all objects on the pages. Among randomly generated examples, only ones whose corresponding object falls within the page area form the negative example set. In all experiments, we used this dataset comprising 228 positive examples and 1039 negative examples. We use an ILP system *Progol* (CProgol ver4.4) [Muggleton 95].

Below, we show the 11 rules generated by Progol when the noise parameter was 60%. The noise parameter indicates the percentage of the negative examples that learned rules are allowed to predict. The running time (on a Sun Enterprise5000) was approximately 29 minutes.

```
(1)  good_locate1(A,B)  :- form_obj(A,B,C),
         h_align(A,C,D,left).
(2)  good_locate1(A,B)  :- form_obj(A,B,C),
         h_align(A,C,D,right).
(3)  good_locate1(A,B)  :- form_obj(A,B,C),
         h_align(A,C,D,center).
(4)  good_locate1(A,B)  :- form_obj(A,B,C),
         obj_type(C,image).
(5)  good_locate1(A,B)  :- form_obj(A,B,C),
         v_align(A,C,D,center), v_position(C,bottom).
(6)  good_locate1(A,B)  :- form_obj(A,B,C),
         h_position(C,right), v_position(C,bottom).
(7)  good_locate1(A,B)  :- form_obj(A,B,C),
         v_align(A,C,D,center), v_align(A,C,D,top),
         v_position(C,top).
(8)  good_locate1(A,B)  :- form_obj(A,B,C),
         v_align(A,C,D,top), obj_type(C,illustration),
         h_position(C,right), obj_type(D,illustration).
(9)  good_locate1(A,B)  :- form_obj(A,B,C),
         v_position(C,bottom), obj_height(C,D), 16=<D,
         D=<16.
(10) good_locate1(A,B)  :- form_obj(A,B,C),
         v_position(C,bottom), obj_height(C,D), 28=<D,
         D=<28.
(11) good_locate1(A,B)  :- form_obj(A,B,C), obj_width(C,D),
         obj_height(C,E), 14=<E, 168=<D.
```

The first rule learned states that B is a good location in case A if the object C located at B is left aligned with another object D. Six learned rules out of 11 contain predicates representing relationships between objects. It shows that ILP is suitable for acquiring layout knowledge because only ILP can generate such rules. While most rules are general and characterize good layouts, rules (4) and (11) are not useful, since they do not say anything about locations. We think rules (6), (9), and (10) characterize this particular dataset, and rules (7) and (8) seem to be overly specific.

We measured predictive accuracy on unseen cases using five-fold cross validations. Twenty sample pages were split into five folds, each of which contains four pages. Figure 3 shows the performance results as the noise parameter was varied. We do not use conventional accuracy because the number of negative examples is arbitrary. Instead, we measured accuracy independently for positive and negative examples. In Figure 3, Predictive value(+) = TP/R^+, where TP is the number of correctly predicted positive examples, and R^+ is the number of positive examples. Similarly, Predictive value(-) = TN/R^-, where TN is the number of correctly predicted negative examples, and R^- is the number of negative examples.

To average, we adopted the F_1 score [Slattery 98, Rijsbergen 79]. This is defined as: $F_1 = 2P^+P^-/(P^++P^-)$, where P^+ and P^- are predictive values(+) and (-), respectively. In our experiment, the F_1 score peaked at 77.7% when the noise was 30%.

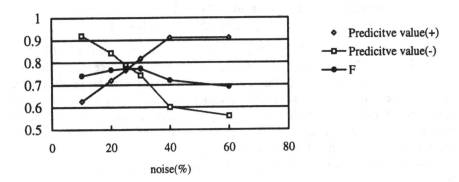

Fig. 3. Performance of normal learning procedure. F stands for F_1 score.

6.2 Nonmonotonic learning

Here we present a repeat learning method based on nonmonotonic learning. This method can treat layout exceptions, prohibiting rules in design knowledge which are naturally described using negation. In our method, the ILP algorithm is executed twice, and positive and negative examples are exchanged in the second learning session.

This method introduces a new predicate for exceptions in a way similar to the nonmonotonic learning of *Closed World Specialization* (CWS) [Bain 91, Srinivasan 92]. Whereas CWS first selects an over-general clause then specializes it with a new predicate, our method specializes a whole logic program (a set of clauses). In our approach, the ILP algorithm is not modified but is treated as a component.

The following is our nonmonotonic learning algorithm. In the algorithm, *ILP(BK,Pos,Neg)* outputs a (possibly over-general) logic program by an ILP algorithm.

Input: background knowledge *BK*, a set of positive examples *Pos*, and a set of
   negative examples *Neg*
   $H_1 = ILP(BK,Pos,Neg)$
   $Neg2$ = subset of *Neg* covered by H_1
   $H_2 = ILP(BK,Neg2,Pos)$
Output: $H = H_1 \wedge \sim H_2$

In Prolog, we have to rename the predicates in the head of H_1 and H_2 individually and add a rule using negation as failure like:

```
target(V1,...,Vn) :- target1(V1,...,Vn),
    not(target2(V1,...,Vn)).
```

In our experiment, we add the following rule:

```
good_locate1(Case,Loc) :-
        good_locate1_learned1(Case,Loc),
        not(good_locate1_learned2(Case,Loc)).
```

We use Progol as the ILP algorithm. The noise parameter for the first learning session is set to 60% so that rules generated include numerous exceptions, since our preliminary experiments showed that a higher initial noise parameter yields a higher final F_1 score. In our experiment, 464 examples remained as negative examples for the second learning. Note that method requires many negative examples in the beginning, so that enough examples remain. In our case, fortunately, this requirement is met by the Closed World Assumption.

This algorithm generated the following 11 rules when the noise in the second learning was 5%.

```
(1) good_locate1(A,B) :- form_obj(A,B,C), obj_height(C,D),
        font_size(C,D).
(2) good_locate1(A,B) :- form_obj(A,B,C),
        obj_type(C,image), overlapping(A,C,D),
        obj_type(D,illustration).
(3) good_locate1(A,B) :- form_obj(A,B,C),
        h_position(C,right), overlapping(A,C,D),
        h_position(D,right).
(4) good_locate1(A,B) :- form_obj(A,B,C),
        v_position(C,top), obj_height(C,D), D=<2.000.
(5) good_locate1(A,B) :- form_obj(A,B,C),
        v_position(C,top), overlapping(A,C,D),
        text_align(D,just).
(6) good_locate1(A,B) :- form_obj(A,B,C),
        overlapping(A,C,D), v_align(A,D,E,center),
        obj_type(D,image).
(7) good_locate1(A,B) :- form_obj(A,B,C),
        overlapping(A,C,D), overlapping(A,C,E),
        overlapping(A,D,E).
(8) good_locate1(A,B) :- form_obj(A,B,C),
        v_align(A,C,D,center), obj_type(C,text),
        overlapping(A,C,E), h_centered(E).
(9) good_locate1(A,B) :- form_obj(A,B,C),
        v_position(C,top), overlapping(A,C,D),
        h_align(A,D,E,left), above(A,D,E,F).
(10) good_locate1(A,B) :- form_obj(A,B,C),
        overlapping(A,C,D), overlapping(A,C,E),
        overlapping(A,D,F), above(A,F,E,G).
```

```
(11) good_locate1(A,B) :- form_obj(A,B,C),
     overlapping(A,C,D), overlapping(A,C,E),
     overlapping(A,E,F), above(A,D,E,G).
```

We think all rules except rule (1) correctly state prohibited positions in layouts. For example, rule (4) says that an object whose height is 2 mm or less should not be placed on the top area of a page. Rule (7) says that no three different objects should overlap.

Figure 4 shows the accuracy (of H) using similar five-fold cross validations, with varying noise in the second learning session. The F_1 score peaked at 84.8% when the noise was 5%, demonstrating that our nonmonotonic algorithm outperforms the normal learning.

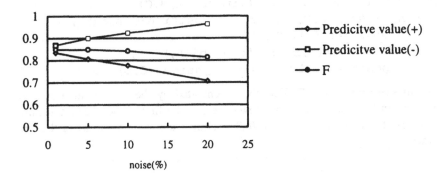

Fig. 4. Performance of nonmonotonic learning. F stands for F_1 score.

6.3 Another repeat learning

The location of an element satisfies many rules, not one. Here we introduce another repeat learning method mainly to learn many such rules. This method is similar to the one given in the previous section, except that positive and negative examples for the second learning session are reversed. This method also introduces a new predicate in a way similar to that in the concept learning tool *CLT* [Wrobel 94] of *MOBAL*. Both introduce a new predicate for positive examples of the target concept. As in CWS, CLT specializes an over-general clause. That is the difference between our method and CLT.

The following is our repeat learning algorithm.

Input: background knowledge *BK*, a set of positive examples *Pos*, and a set of negative examples *Neg*
  $H_1 = ILP(BK,Pos,Neg)$
  $Neg2$ = subset of *Neg* covered by H_1
  $H_2 = ILP(BK, Pos, Neg2)$
Output: $H = H_1 \wedge H_2$

In Prolog, as in the previous method, we have to rename the predicates in the head of H_1 and H_2 individually and add a rule like:

```
target(V1,...,Vn) :- target1(V1,...,Vn),
  @ @arget2(V1,...,Vn).
```

Similarly, we used Progol as the ILP algorithm. The noise parameter for the first session is set to 60%. We show a subset of 11 generated rules when the noise in the second learning session was 40%.

```
(2) good_locate1(A,B) :- form_obj(A,B,C), h_centered(C).
(6) good_locate1(A,B) :- form_obj(A,B,C),
      h_align(A,C,D,center), text_align(C,center),
      h_align(A,D,E,center).
(8) good_locate1(A,B) :- form_obj(A,B,C),
      h_align(A,C,D,center), h_position(C,right),
      v_position(C,bottom).
(9) good_locate1(A,B) :- form_obj(A,B,C),
      v_position(C,bottom), obj_height(C,D), D=<2.
```

Most rules are more specific than those generated by the first learning session. These rules can be regarded as new knowledge that the first session cannot acquire. For accuracy, the F_1 score peaked at 76.9%, almost the same value as in the first experiment.

7 Conclusions

We applied Inductive Logic Programming to the graphic design domain, which is novel for ILP. As a result of our experiments using real-world data, we obtained rules characterizing good layouts and including relationships between elements. Moreover, we presented a new method based on nonmonotonic learning where the ILP algorithm is used twice. Our experiments showed that the method can learn more accurate rules than normal ILP can. This proves the power of the method.

The rules obtained here can be directly used for automated layout of "the last element." Since rules can be regarded as constraints, a locating problem can be regarded as a constraint-satisfying problem. Although a constraint satisfying problem can be over-constrained or under-constrained, it is handled well by introducing *constraint hierarchy* [Borning 87], which we think is suitable for this layout problem. In our approach, constraint hierarchies can be easily constructed by specifying the rules generated by the first and second learning sessions with different strengths.

Realizing an automated element locating system is a topic for further study. Another topic for future work is improving predictive accuracy. We plan to improve or increase the background knowledge, guided by analysis of examples predicted incorrectly. Other topics are increasing samples by automated data transformation from electronic documents and experimenting with other kind of advertisements than

BYTE or other kinds of documents. We believe our proposed nonmonotonic learning approach is applicable to domains other than graphic design, especially to domains in which the Closed World Assumption can be used to give many negative examples initially.

References

[Bain 91] M. Bain and S. Muggleton. Non-monotonic learning. In D. Michie, editor, *Machine Intelligence* 12:105-120. Oxford University Press, 1991.

[Borning 87] A. Borning, R. Duisberg, B. Freeman-Benson, A. Kramer, and M. Woolf. Constraint Hierarchies. *ACM OOPSLA*, Oct. 1987, pp. 48-60.

[BYTE 97] *BYTE*, 22(12), McGraw-Hill, 1997.

[De Raedt 93] L. De Raedt and M. Bruynooghe, A theory of clausal discovery. in *Proceedings of the 13th International Joint Conference on Artificial Intelligence*, pp. 1058-1063, Morgan Kaufmann, 1993.

[Esposito 94] F. Esposito, D. Malerba and G. Semeraro. Multistrategy Learning for Document recognition. *Applied Artificial Intelligence: An International Journal*, 8(1):33-84, 1994.

[Honda 94] K. Honda, C. Kato, H. Ohwada, N. Ichihara and F. Mizoguchi. A Floor Planning System Using Constraint Logic Programming. In *Proc. of The 2nd International Conference on the Practical Applications of Prolog*,1994.

[Ishiba 97] M. Ishiba et al. A Document Generation System using the Kansei Model. *IPSJ SIG Report*, 97-HI-70, pp. 71-78, 1997. (In Japanese)

[Lieberman 93] H. Lieberman. Mondrian: A Teachable Graphical Editor. in *Watch What I Do: Programming by Demonstration*, Allen Cypher, ed., MIT Press, 1993.

[Lieberman 95] H. Lieberman. The Visual Language of Experts in Graphic Design. *IEEE Symposium on Visual Languages*, Darmstadt, Germany, September 1995.

[Lieberman 96] H. Lieberman. Intelligent Graphics. *Communications of the ACM*, 39(8):38-48, 1996.

[Muggleton 91] S. Muggleton. Inductive logic programming. *New Generation Computing*, 8(4):295-318, 1991.

[Muggleton 95] S. Muggleton. Inverse entailment and Progol. *New Generation Computing*, 13:245-286, 1995.

[Rijsbergen 79] C. J. van Rijsbergen. *Information Retrieval*. chapter 7. Butterworths, 1979.

[Slattery 98] S. Slattery and M. Craven. Combining Statistical and Relational Methods for Learning in Hypertext Domains. *Proceedings of the 8th International Conference on Inductive Logic Programming*, Springer-Verlag, 1998.

[Srinivasan 92] A. Srinivasan, S. Muggleton, and M. Bain. Distinguishing exceptions from noise in non-monotonic learning. In *Proceedings of the Second Inductive Logic Programming Workshop*, pp. 97-107, Tokyo, 1992.

[Wrobel 94] S. Wrobel. Concept Formation During Interactive Theory Revision. *Machine Learning*, 14:169-191, 1994.

Morphosyntactic Tagging of Slovene Using Progol

James Cussens,[1] Sašo Džeroski,[2] Tomaž Erjavec[2]

[1] University of York,
Heslington, York YO10 5DD, UK
jc@cs.york.ac.uk
[2] Department for Intelligent Systems, Jožef Stefan Institute,
Jamova 39, SI-1000 Ljubljana, Slovenia
saso.dzeroski@ijs.si, tomaz.erjavec@ijs.si

Abstract. We consider the task of tagging Slovene words with morphosyntactic descriptions (MSDs). MSDs contain not only part-of-speech information but also attributes such as gender and case. In the case of Slovene there are 2,083 possible MSDs. P-Progol was used to learn morphosyntactic disambiguation rules from annotated data (consisting of 161,314 examples) produced by the MULTEXT-East project. P-Progol produced 1,148 rules taking 36 hours. Using simple grammatical background knowledge, e.g. looking for case disagreement, P-Progol induced 4,094 clauses in eight parallel runs. These rules have proved effective at detecting and explaining incorrect MSD annotations in an independent test set, but have not so far produced a tagger comparable to other existing taggers in terms of accuracy.

1 Introduction

While tagging has been extensively studied for English and some other Western European languages, much less work has been done on Slavic languages. The results for English do not necessarily carry over to these languages. The tagsets for Slavic languages are typically much larger (over 1000), due to their many inflectional features; on the other hand, training corpora tend to be smaller.

In work related to this [9] a number of taggers were applied to the problem of tagging Slovene. Four different taggers were trained and tested on a hand annotated corpus of Slovene, the translation of the novel '1984' by G. Orwell. The taggers tested were the HMM tagger [6, 15], Brill's Rule based tagger [3], the Maximum Entropy Tagger [14], and the Memory-based Tagger [7]. Accuracies on 'known' words were mostly a little over 90%, with the Memory-Based Tagger achieving 93.58%. Known words are those found in a lexicon that accompanies the corpus. Our goal here was to see whether ILP (specifically P-Progol) could be used to learn rules for tagging, to analyse the rules and to compare empirically with these other approaches to tagging.

2 Morphosyntactic Descriptions

The EU-funded MULTEXT-East project [8] developed corpora, lexica and tools for six Central and East-European languages. The centrepiece of the corpus is the novel "1984" by George Orwell, in the English original and translations [11]. The novel has been hand-tagged with disambiguated morphosyntactic descriptions (MSDs) and lemmas. The novel is marked up for sentences and tokens; these can be either punctuation or words. Each punctuation symbol has its own corpus tag (e.g. XMDASH), while the words are marked by their morphosyntactic descriptions.

The syntax and semantics of the MULTEXT-East MSDs are given in the *morphosyntactic specifications* of the project [10]. These specifications have been developed in the formalism and on the basis of specifications for six Western European languages of the EU MULTEXT project [1]; the MULTEXT project produced its specifications in cooperation with EAGLES (Expert Advisory Group on Language Engineering Standards) [4].

The MULTEXT-East morphosyntactic specifications contain, along with introductory matter, also:

1. the list of defined categories (parts-of-speech)
2. common tables of attribute-values
3. language particular tables

Of the MULTEXT-East *categories*, Slovene uses Noun (N), Verb (V), Adjective (A), Pronoun (P), Adverb (R), Adposition (S),[1] Conjunction (C), Numeral (M), Interjection (I), Residual (X),[2] Abbreviation (Y), and Particle (Q).

The morphosyntactic specifications provide the grammars for the MSDs of the MULTEXT-East languages. The greatest worth of these specifications is that they provide an attempt at a morphosyntactic encoding standardised across languages. In addition to already encompassing seven typologically very different languages, the structure of the specifications and of the MSDs is readily extensible to new languages.

To give an impression of the information content of the Slovene MSDs and their distribution, Table 1 gives, for each category, the number of *attributes* in the category, the total number of *values* for all attributes in the category; the number of different MSDs in the *lexicon*, and, finally, in the annotated MULTEXT-East Slovene '1984' *corpus*.

To exemplify the annotation use, Fig 1 gives the MSD-annotated first sentence of the Slovene translation of the novel: *It was a bright cold day in April, and the clocks were striking thirteen.* The Bil/Vcps-sma annotation shows that "Bil" is a singular masculine past participle in the active voice, and the jasen/Afpmsnn annotation shows that "jasen" is an adjective which is indefinite, nominative, singular, masculine, positive and qualificative.

---

[1] Adpositions include prepositions and postpositions; Slovene uses only prepositions.

[2] Residual is a category encompassing unknown (unanalysable) lexical items. It appears only once in the Slovene lexicon, for 2+2=5; in our experiment we also used it to mark punctuation.

Table 1. Slovene morphosyntactic distribution

PoS	Att	Val	Lex	Cor
Noun	5	16	99	74
Verb	8	26	128	93
Adjective	7	22	279	169
Pronoun	11	36	1,335	594
Adverb	2	4	3	3
Adposition	3	8	6	6
Conjunction	2	4	3	2
Numeral	7	23	226	80
Interjection	0	0	1	1
Residual	0	0	1	1
Abbreviation	0	0	1	1
Particle	0	0	1	1
All	45	139	2,083	1,025

```
Bil/Vcps-sma je/Vcip3s--n jasen/Afpmsnn &comma;/XCOMMA
mrzel/Afpmsnn aprilski/Aopmsn dan/Ncmsn in/Ccs
ure/Ncfpn so/Vcip3p--n bile/Vmps-pfa trinajst/Mcnpnl &period;/XPERIOD
```

Fig. 1. First MSD-annotated sentence of Slovene translation of Orwell's "1984"

3 Method

Following the basic approach taken in [5, 12], we used ILP to learn MSD elimination rules each of which identify a set of MSDs that cannot be correct for a word in a particular context. The context for a word is given as the MSDs of all words to the left and to the right of the word. Not using the actual words in the context simplified the learning, and is justified on the grounds that MSDs (unlike, say, Penn Treebank PoS tags) provide very specific information about the words.

The MULTEXT-East lexicon provides an *ambiguity class* for the Slovene words appearing in the corpus. For a given word, this is the set of possible MSDs for that word. Elimination rules can then be applied to reduce this ambiguity class in a particular context, ideally reducing it to a single MSDs. Note that each rule requires a word's context to be sufficiently disambiguated so that it can fire. This motivates using elimination rules in tandem with another tagger.

3.1 Examples

Each ambiguous word generated a single negative example and one or more positive examples. Each negative example is represented as a triple of left context, correct MSD and right context. The correct MSD generates a negative example for the induction of elimination rules since it identifies an MSD which it would be incorrect to eliminate. Positive examples contain MSDs which are incorrect (positive examples of MSDs to eliminate) but which are in the focus word's ambiguity class.

The left context is reversed so that the MSD immediately to the left of the focus is at the head of the list. Figure 2 show two positive and one negative example generated from a single occurrence of a word with ambiguity class {pp3fsg__y_n,vmip3s__n,vcip3s__n}. In this context, vcip3s__n is the correct MSD and hence appears in a negative example of elimination. MSDs are represented as constants for efficiency. We used exactly the same training data that had been used for training the other taggers in [9]. This data, together with other resources to reproduce our experiments, can be found at: http://alibaba.ijs.si/et/project/LLL/tag/. We produced 99,261 positive and 81,805 negative examples giving a total of 181,066 examples.

```
%rmv(LeftReversed,Focus,Right)
%2 POSITIVE EXAMPLES
rmv([vcps_sma],[pp3fsg__y_n],[afpmsnn,xcomma,afpmsnn,aopmsn,ncmsn,ccs,
ncfpn,vcip3p__n,vmps_pfa,mcnpnl,xperiod]).
rmv([vcps_sma],[vmip3s__n],[afpmsnn,xcomma,afpmsnn,aopmsn,ncmsn,ccs,
ncfpn,vcip3p__n,vmps_pfa,mcnpnl,xperiod]).

%1 NEGATIVE EXAMPLE
rmv([vcps_sma],[vcip3s__n],[afpmsnn,xcomma,afpmsnn,aopmsn,ncmsn,ccs,
ncfpn,vcip3p__n,vmps_pfa,mcnpnl,xperiod]).
```

Fig. 2. Examples created from a single occurrence of an ambiguous word

3.2 Background Knowledge

The use of ILP for tagging is particularly well motivated when the tags (here MSDs) have considerable structure. The background knowledge was designed to take advantage of that structure. Figure 3 shows some of the background predicates used.

Working through Figure 3, we have firstly, msd/2 which explodes MSDs from constants into lists so that other predicates can extract the relevant structure from the MSDs; there were 1703 such msd/2 facts in our background knowledge. Many of the background predicates consume an initial portion of a word's context (left or right) and return the remainder of the context as an output in the second argument. For example, noun(A,B) is true if A begins with a noun and is followed by B. We have the predicates gender/3, case/3 and number/3, which identify gender, case and number or fail for MSDs where these are not defined. Figure 3 shows two of the gender/2 clauses which show that the gender identifier is the 3rd attribute for noun MSDs and the 4th for pronoun. The most important predicates are `disoncase/2 disongender/2` and `disonnumb/2` which indicate when two MSDs disagree in case, gender or number.

We also have simple phrasal definitions. Noun phrases `np/1` are defined as zero or more adjectives followed by one or more nouns. This is clearly not a full definition of noun phrase, but is included on the grounds that the simple noun phrases so defined will be useful features for the elimination rules. Finally, we have `isa/2` which identifies particular MSDs and `skip_over/2` which is used to skip over apparently unimportant tokens which do not have case, number or gender defined.

```
%EXPLODING MSD CONSTANTS
msd(afcfda, [a,f,c,f,d,a]).
msd(afcfdg, [a,f,c,f,d,g]).
msd(afcfdl, [a,f,c,f,d,l]).

%Parts of speech, always first letter
noun([M|T],T) :- msd(M,[n|_]).
verb([M|T],T) :- msd(M,[v|_]).

%GENDER
gender([M|T],Gender,T) :- msd(M,[n,_,Gender|_]).
gender([M|T],Gender,T) :- msd(M,[p,_,_,Gender|_]).

%DISAGREEMENT ON CASE, GENDER OR NUMBER
disoncase(M1,M2) :- case(M1,C1,_), case(M2,C2,_), \+ C1 = C2.
disongender(M1,M2) :- gender(M1,C1,_), gender(M2,C2,_), \+ C1 = C2.
disonnumb(M1,M2) :- numb(M1,C1,_), numb(M2,C2,_), \+ C1 = C2.

%NOUN PHRASE
np(A,B) :- adjective_star(A,C), noun_plus(C,B).
%and backwards ..
np1(A,B) :- noun_plus(A,C), adjective_star(C,B).

noun_plus(A,B) :- noun(A,B).
noun_plus(A,B) :- noun(A,C), noun_plus(C,B).

%IDENTIFYING PARTICUAR MSDS
isa([H|T],H,T).

%FOR SKIPPING TO IMPORTANT WORDS
skip_over(A,B) :-
        all_undefined_plus(A,B),
        some_defined(B).
```

Fig. 3. Excerpt of background knowledge

3.3 Splitting the Data

P-Progol is currently unable to accept 181,065 (fairly complex) examples directly. The data was therefore split according to the part-of-speech of the focus MSD (the 3rd argument of the examples). This formed the 8 data sets for Noun (n), Verb (v), Adjective (a), Pronoun (p), Adverb (r), Adposition (s), Numeral (m) and Other (o) described in Table 2. The "Other" dataset covered conjunctions (c) and particles (q) together. Although large by ILP standards, each of these datasets was sufficiently small for P-Progol 2.4.7 running on Yap Prolog 4.1.15.

Although motivated by pragmatics, this splitting had a number of beneficial effects. The split meant that all eight datasets could have been processed in parallel as eight separate Yap processes. In fact, due to a lack of suitable machines the work was spread between the first author's Viglen laptop (233 MHz Pentium, 80 MBytes RAM) and Steve Moyle's PC (266 MHz, 128 MBytes RAM). These machines are denoted Y and O respectively in Table 2. Since we had 8 rule sets induced for specific parts-of-speech we were able to index on the part-of-speech by altering the induced rules to have the relevant part-of-speech as a first argument.

In effect, we performed a single initial greedy split of the data as would be done as the first step in a decision tree inducer such as TILDE[2]. Since many of the clauses induced in earlier work on random samples of the complete data set were specific to a particular part-of-speech (e.g. rmv(L,F,R) :- noun(L,L2) ...), we will not have missed many good clauses as a result of our greediness.

3.4 P-Progol Parameters and Constraints

As well as limiting the amount of data input to a particular P-Progol run, we also constrained the Progol search in two major ways. The basic Progol algorithm consists of taking a 'seed' uncovered positive example, producing a most specific 'bottom clause' which covers it and then using the bottom clause to guide the search for the 'best' clause that covers the seed.

P-Progol has a number of built-in cost functions: the 'best' clause is that which minimises this cost. In this work, we choose m-estimation [13, p.179–180] to estimate the accuracy of clauses, and searched for the clause that maximised estimated accuracy. An m value of 1 was chosen. Such a low value of m might allow overfitting, so as a guard against this, only clauses which covered at least 10 positives were allowed. Such a stopping rule has the advantage of allowing the search to be pruned. If a clause dips below 10 positives then there is no point considering any specialisations of that clause, since they will also cover fewer than 10 positives. Also, only clauses with at least 97% training accuracy were allowed.

Two more constraints were required for learning to be feasible. Firstly, we restricted each Progol search to a maximum of 5000 clauses—many searches hit this threshold. Secondly, we limited clauses to a maximum of four literals, the only exception being the Numeral (m) run because of its small example set. Caching ([5]) was only used on two small runs to avoid any risk of running out of RAM.

4 Results

4.1 The Induction Process

Considerable effort was expended in tracking down bugs in earlier versions of Yap Prolog which involved indexing problems for large data sets. Ashwin Srinivasan and the first author also implemented improvements to P-Progol which considerably improved its efficiency. Despite these (productive) efforts, the large number of examples and the nature of the Progol search meant long P-Progol runs sometimes lasting a few days (see Table 2).

Table 2. Data set and induction statistics

PoS	Pos	Neg	Tot	Rules	Time (hrs)	Searches	Machine	Caching	$|C|$
a	29099	5709	34808	1148	36.1	1513	Y	on	4
m	1972	843	2815	223	2.6	305	Y	off	5
n	20125	14569	34694	809	54.0	2767	O	off	4
o	2279	21946	24225	36	15.8	1960	Y	on	4
p	26585	8480	35065	1291	54.5	2750	O	off	4
r	2500	4980	7480	42	5.3	1941	O	off	4
s	4865	6025	10890	90	2.3	293	Y	off	4
v	11836	19253	31089	455	25.6	1599	O	off	4
All	99261	81805	181066	4094	196.2	13128			

4.2 Structure of Induced Theories

P-Progol associates a clause label with each induced clause which gives the positive and negative cover, and the clause's 'score'. In our case the score was clause accuracy as estimated by the m-estimate. This allowed us to parameterise the induced theory, converting a clause such as

```
rmv(L,F,R) :- case(R,n,R2), disonnumb(F,R2), disonnumb(F,R).
```

from the adjective theory, to:

```
rmv(a,L,F,R,score(1283,1,0.999094)) :-
  case(R,n,R2), disonnumb(F,R2), disonnumb(F,R).
```

This allowed us to produce subsets of the complete theory by thresholding on the m-estimated accuracy (*EstAcc*). For example, filtering out all rules with $EstAcc < 0.999$ results in an under-general theory but with only ultra-reliable rules remaining. Note also the added "a" index which indicates that the rule only applies when F (the focus word) is an adjective.

The isa/3 predicate appears very often in the induced theory, indicating the importance of MSD-specific rules. Also, as expected many of the rules look for disagreement between neighbouring words. In the *EstAcc* ≥ 0.999 exactly half of the 240 rules used the disagreement predicates. Many of those that did not, used two literals to specify particular disagreements.

In the complete theory, 2069 of the 4094 rules used only features of chunks (words or simple phrases) right next to the focus word. In the *EstAcc* ≥ 0.999 subtheory, 173 out of the 240 rules used only such features, showing that most highly reliable rules are quite simple, identifying anomalies between neighbouring words. Of the remaining 67 rules with *EstAcc* ≥ 0.999, all of them only looked one chunk beyond neighbouring chunks.

```
rmv(a,L,F,R,score(1130,0,0.999855)) :-
 case(F,n,D), numb(F,d,D), disonnumb(F,R).
rmv(a,L,F,R,score(748,0,0.999781)) :-
 case(R,1,R2), gender(R,f,R2), gender(F,m,_).
rmv(v,L,F,R,score(619,0,0.999001)) :-
 numb(F,p,D), gender(F,n,D), isa(L,vcip3s__n,L2).
rmv(n,L,F,R,score(600,0,0.999301)) :-
 numb(F,d,_), isa(L,sps1,L2).
rmv(n,L,F,R,score(433,0,0.999032)) :-
 case(F,a,_), isa(L,spsg,L2).
rmv(m,L,F,R,score(14,0,0.980036)) :-
 gender(F,f,_), isa(L,spsi,L2),
 numb(L2,_,L3), case(L3,_,L4).
```

Fig. 4. A subset of the induced disambiguation theory

4.3 Consistency Checking and Ambiguity Reduction

Here we tested the consistency of each test sentence with the rules. As Table 3 shows, a good half of the correct readings are deemed inadmissible by the complete theory. This is because it only takes one disambiguation rule to incorrectly fire for a whole sentence to be rejected.

Table 3. Proportion of test sentence annotations rejected

EstAcc >	0	96.0	97.0	98.0	98.5	99.0	99.5	99.7	99.9
	49.5	48.6	46.4	36.9	32.4	24.7	15.8	10.9	3.5

To measure ambiguity reduction, we selected those 263 sentences from the test set, which had fewer than 2000 possible annotations according to the ambiguity classes of the words in the sentences. Many sentences have millions of possible annotations, most of them plainly absurd, so we do not wish to receive credit for eliminating these. Table 4 shows the ambiguity reduction factor (ARF) for each subtheory: we summed the number of possible annotations for each sentences in the test set giving a total of 81634 annotations. To get the ARF we divided this number by the number of annotations consistent with the rules. We also give the rejection error rate (RER), the percentage of times that the annotation given in the test set was inconsistent with the rules.

Table 4. Per sentence ambiguity reduction factor and rejection rate, for sentences with fewer than 2000 possible annotations

$EstAcc >$	0	96.0	97.0	98.0	98.5	99.0	99.5	99.7	99.9
ARF	67.3	65.1	56.6	38.0	29.4	21.1	10.6	6.9	2.7
RER	25.5	24.7	22.1	17.5	13.3	8.7	3.0	2.3	0.4

The ambiguity reduction factor is good, even the $EstAcc > 0.999$ theory reduces sentence ambiguity by nearly a third. However, to use the rules to reduce ambiguity, we should be almost guaranteed not to reject the correct annotation; this means only the small theories composed only of highly reliable rules should be used.

4.4 Error Detection

The 0.4% RE for the $EstAcc > 0.999$ was due to a single test set annotation being rejected. The annotated test sentence was: "[Winston/npmsn] [in/ccs] [Julia/npfsn] [sta/vcip3d__n] [se/px_____y] [očarana/afpmdn] [objela/vmps_sfa] [./xperiod]" ("Delighted, Winston and Julia embraced.") This annotation was rejected by this rule:

```
rmv(a,L,F,R,score(1130,0,0.999855)) :-
    case(F,n,D), numb(F,d,D), disonnumb(F,R).
```

on the grounds that dual nominative adjectives can not be followed by any word that does not have the same number. This rules out the "očarana/afpmdn, objela/vmps_sfa" annotation

Upon inspection we found that the rule was correct to reject this annotation: "objela" (embraced) should have been tagged as dual not singular. This lead us to use the $EstAcc > 0.999$ theory to look for other possible errors in the complete test set. To help us do this we wrote a simple Prolog interface which flagged possible errors and *explained why* they were suspected errors. Figure 5 shows how the interface flagged the "objela" error.

This demonstrates two points. Firstly our disambiguation rules can be used to detect incorrect annotations, *and provide an explanation of* why *the annotation is incorrect.* Secondly, our rules are constraints that apply not only to

```
**ERROR DETECTED**
[(Winston_BOS,npmsn),(in,ccs),(Julija,npfsn),(sta,vcip3d__n),(se,px_____y)]
ocxarana,afpmdn <= HERE
[(objela,vmps_sfa),(.,xperiod)]

Constraint number 1 confidence score(1130,0,0.999855)

because:
ocxarana,afpmdn is ambiguous, and is (apparently) an adjective

and we can not also have:
ocxarana,afpmdn with case: n
ocxarana,afpmdn with numb: d
objela,vmps_sfa and ocxarana,afpmdn disagreeing on number
**********
Enter y if this is a real error
|: |:
```

Fig. 5. Interface for annotation error flagging

the focus word. Here, "očarana", the focus word, was annotated correctly—the inconsistency was detected in its context.

However, of the 24 alleged test set errors flagged by our constraints, only 9 turned out to be actual errors. The other 15 were examples of rare atypical constructions. All the constraints which incorrectly flagged errors had $EstAcc >$ 0.999. For example, one had covered 761 positives and 0 negatives in the training data. So the large number of errors is perhaps surprising and points to possible over-fitting with an inadequately large training dataset. On the other hand, as an annotation validation tool, performance is reasonable, and it would be easy to expand the explanations and allow the user to correct (real) errors as they are presented.

4.5 Tagging Accuracy

Our MSD elimination rules can not be used as a standalone tagger: they rely too heavily on disambiguated context and there is no guarantee that a single MSD will be returned for each word after incorrect MSDs have been eliminated. We propose that they can be used as a filter to reject inconsistent annotations produced by another tagger, such as those mentioned in Section 1.

Here we combine our rules with the simplest tagger—one that returns the most likely tag based on lexical statistics, without taking context into account. Our goal is to measure the degree to which accuracy increases once the rules are used to filter out incorrect annotations.

Due to problems with Sicstus Prolog, experiments were conducted on a subset of 526 of the original 650 test sentences. These were sentences with fewer than 2000 possible annotations. Choosing the most likely tag according to lexical statistics produces an accuracy of 83.3% on this test set. We combined this tagger with our rules by doing a uniform cost search i.e. (A^* with $h = 0$) for the most probable sentence annotation according to the lexical statistics, which was consistent with our rules.

Using the complete theory we achieved 86.6%. Some subtheories did a little better, for example the $EstAcc \geq 0.985$ accuracy was 87.5% So we have an improvement, albeit a modest one. Our experiments with error flagging reported in Section 4.4 indicate that a major barrier to improved performance is that our constraints frequently reject correct annotations.

It remains to be seen what improvement, if any, can be achieved when marrying our rules to more sophisticated taggers such as those mentioned in Section 1. Clearly the combination examined here has far lower performance than the taggers mentioned in Section 1.

5 Conclusions and Future Work

In this work, we have established the following positive results:

1. P-Progol can be applied directly to datasets of at least 30,000 examples. With appropriate use of sampling, it is likely that this could upper limit could be increased considerably.
2. We have induced MSD elimination rules which can be used to filter out incorrect annotations. The symbolic nature of the rules means that an *explanation* is also supplied. This makes using these rules particularly appropriate for an interactive system—we intend to use the rules induced here to check the existing MULTEXT-East corpus

We have also established the following negative result:

1. The performance of the MSD elimination rules as a standalone system or in tandem with a crude tagger based on lexical statistics is considerably worse than that of competing taggers.

Apart from checking the MULTEXT-East corpus with the rules, we also intend to use the rules to check the annotations proposed by the taggers mentioned in Section 1. By filtering out at least some incorrect annotations, the tagging accuracy should increase.

Acknowledgements

Special thanks are due to Steve Moyle for allowing us to run Yap/P-Progol on his machine—this was essential to get the work finished in time. Thanks to Ashwin Srinivasan for enhancements and bug fixes to P-Progol and to Vitor Santos Costa for allowing us to "go places no one has been before" with Yap4.1.15. Finally, thanks and apologies to Gill, Jane and Robert for putting up with the first author during the writing of this paper. The work presented here was supported by the ESPRIT IV Project 20237 ILP2.

References

1. N. Bel, Nicoletta Calzolari, and Monica Monachini (eds.). Common specifications and notation for lexicon encoding and preliminary proposal for the tagsets. MULTEXT Deliverable D1.6.1B, ILC, Pisa, 1995.
2. H. Blockeel and L. De Raedt. Top-down induction of first-order logical decision trees. *Artificial Intelligence*, 101(1-2):285–297, 1999.
3. Eric Brill. Transformation-based error-driven learning and natural language processing: A case study in part-of-speech tagging. *Computational Linguistics*, 21(4):543–565, 1995.
4. Nicoleta Calzolari and John McNaught (eds.). Synopsis and Comparison of Morphosyntactic Phenomena Encoded in Lexicons and Corpora: A Common Proposal and Applications to European Languages. EAGLES Document EAG—CLWG— MORPHSYN/R, ILC, Pisa, 1996.
5. James Cussens. Part-of-speech tagging using Progol. In *Inductive Logic Programming: Proceedings of the 7th International Workshop (ILP-97). LNAI 1297*, pages 93–108. Springer, 1997.
6. D. Cutting, J. Kupiec, J. Pedersen, and P. Sibun. A practical part-of-speech tagger. In *Proceedings of the Third Conference on Applied Natural Language Processing*, pages 133–140, Trento, Italy, 1992.
7. Walter Daelemans, Jakub Zavrel, Peter Berck, and Steven Gillis. Mbt: A memory-based part of speech tagger-generator. In Eva Ejerhed and Ido Dagan, editors, *Proceedings of the Fourth Workshop on Very Large Corpora*, pages 14–27, Copenhagen, 1996.
8. Ludmila Dimitrova, Tomaž Erjavec, Nancy Ide, Heiki-Jan Kaalep, Vladimír Petkevič, and Dan Tufiş. Multext-East: Parallel and Comparable Corpora and Lexicons for Six Central and Eastern European Languages. In *COLING-ACL '98*, pages 315–319, Montréal, Québec, Canada, 1998.
9. Sašo Džeroski, Tomaž Erjavec, and Jakub Zavrel. Morphosyntactic tagging of slovene: Evaluating pos taggers and tagsets. Technical Report IJS TechReport DP-8018, Jozef Stefan Institute, 1999.
10. Tomaž Erjavec and Monica Monachini (eds.). Specifications and notation for lexicon encoding. MULTEXT-East Final Report D1.1F, Jožef Stefan Institute, Ljubljana, December 1997. http://nl.ijs.si/ME/CD/docs/mte-d11f/.
11. Tomaž Erjavec and Nancy Ide. The MULTEXT-East corpus. In Antonio Rubio, Natividad Gallardo, Rosa Castro, and Antonio Tejada, editors, *First International Conference on Language Resources and Evaluation, LREC'98*, pages 971–974, Granada, 1998. ELRA. URL: http://ceres.ugr.es/ rubio/elra.html.
12. Nikolaj Lindberg and Martin Eineborg. Learning constraint grammar-style disambiguation rules using inductive logic programming. In *Proc. COLING/ACL98*, 1998.
13. Tom Mitchell. *Machine Learning*. McGraw-Hill, 1997.
14. Adwait Ratnaparkhi. A maximum entropy part of speech tagger. In *Proc. ACL-SIGDAT Conference on Empirical Methods in Natural Language Processing*, pages 491–497, Philadelphia, 1996.
15. Rene Steetskamp. An implementation of a probabilistic tagger. Master's thesis, TOSCA Research Group, University of Nijmegen, Nijmegen, 1995. 48 p.

Experiments in Predicting Biodegradability

Sašo Džeroski (1), Hendrik Blockeel (2), Boris Kompare (3),
Stefan Kramer (4), Bernhard Pfahringer (4), Wim Van Laer (2)

(1) Department of Intelligent Systems, Jozef Stefan Institute
Jamova 39, SI-1000 Ljubljana, Slovenia
(2) Department of Computer Science, Katholieke Universiteit Leuven
Celestijnenlaan 200A, B-3001 Heverlee, Belgium
(3) Faculty of Civil Engineering and Geodesy, University of Ljubljana
Hajdrihova 28, SI-1000, Ljubljana, Slovenia
(4) Austrian Research Institute for Artificial Intelligence
Schottengasse 3, A-1010 Vienna, Austria

Abstract. We present a novel application of inductive logic programming (ILP) in the area of quantitative structure-activity relationships (QSARs). The activity we want to predict is the biodegradability of chemical compounds in water. In particular, the target variable is the half-life in water for aerobic aqueous biodegradation. Structural descriptions of chemicals in terms of atoms and bonds are derived from the chemicals' SMILES encodings. Definition of substructures are used as background knowledge. Predicting biodegradability is essentially a regression problem, but we also consider a discretized version of the target variable. We thus employ a number of relational classification and regression methods on the relational representation and compare these to propositional methods applied to different propositionalisations of the problem. Some expert comments on the induced theories are also given.

1 Introduction

The persistence of chemicals in the environment (or to environmental influences) is welcome only until the time the chemicals fulfill their role. After that time or if they happen to be at the wrong place, the chemicals are considered pollutants. In this phase of chemicals' life-span we wish that the chemicals disappear as soon as possible. The most ecologically acceptable (and a very cost-effective) way of 'disappearing' is degradation to components which are not considered pollutants (e.g. mineralization of organic compounds). Degradation in the environment can take several forms, from physical pathways (erosion, photolysis, etc.), through chemical pathways (hydrolysis, oxydation, diverse chemolises, etc.) to biological pathways (biolysis). Usually the pathways are combined and interrelated, thus making degradation even more complex. In our study we focus on biodegradation in an aqueous environment under aerobic conditions, which affects the quality of surface- and groundwater.

The problem of properly assessing the time needed for ultimate biodegradation can be simplified to the problem of determining the half-life time of that process. However, very few measured data exist and even these data are not taken under controlled conditions. It follows that an objective and comprehensive database on biolysis half-life times can not be found easily. The best we were able to find was in a handbook of degradation rates [10]. The chemicals described in this handbook were used as the basis of our study.

Usually, authors try to construct a QSAR model/formula for only one class of chemicals, or congeners of one chemical, e.g. phenols. This approach to QSAR model construction has an implicit advantage that only the variation with respect to the class mainstream should be identified and properly modelled. Contrary to the described situation, our database comprises several families of chemicals, e.g. alcohols, phenols, pesticides, chlorinated aliphatic and aromatic hydrocarbons, acids, diverse other aromatic compounds, etc. From this point of view, the construction of adequate QSAR models/formulae is a much more difficult task.

We apply several machine learning methods, including several inductive logic programming methods, to the above database in order to construct SAR/QSAR models for biodegradability. The remainder of the paper is organized as follows. Section 2 describes the dataset and how the representations used by the different machine learning systems were generated. Section 3 lists the representation and the machine learning systems employed, and describes the experimental setup. Section 4 presents the experimental results, including expert comments on some of the induced rules. Section 5 gives further discussion, Section 6 comments on related work, and Section 7 concludes and gives some directions for further work.

2 The dataset

The database used was derived from the data in the handbook of degradation rates [10]. The authors have compiled from available literature the degradation rates for 342 widely used (commercial) chemicals. Where no measured data on degradation rates were available, expert estimation was performed. The main source of data employed was the Syracuse Research Corporation's (SRC) Environmental Fate Data Bases (EFDB), which in turn used as primary sources of information DATALOG, CHEMFATE, BIOLOG, and BIODEG files to search for pertinent data.

For each considered chemical the book contains degradation rates in the form of a range of half-life times (low and high estimate) for overall, biotic and abiotic degradation in four environmental compartments, i.e., soil, air, surface water and ground water. We focus on surface water here. The overall degradation half-life is a combination of several (potentially) present pathways, e.g., surface water photolysis, photooxydation, hydrolysis and biolysis (biodegradation). These can occur simultaneously and have even synergistic effects, resulting in a half-life time (HLT) smaller than the HLT for each of the basic pathways. We focus on biodegradation here, which was considered to run in unacclimated aqueous conditions, where biota (living organisms) are not adapted to the specific pollutant considered. For biodegradation, three environmental conditions were considered:

aerobic, anaerobic, and removal in waste water treatment plants (WWTP). In our study we focus on aqueous biodegradation HLT's in aerobic conditions.

The target variable for machine learning systems that perform regression was the natural logarithm of the arithmetic mean of the low and high estimate of the HLT for aqueous biodegradation in aerobic conditions, measured in hours.

A discretized version of the arithmetic mean was also considered in order to enable us to apply classification systems to the problem. Four classes were defined : chemicals degrade *fast* (mean estimate HLT is up to 7 days), *moderately fast* (one to four weeks), *slowly* (one to six months), or are *resistant* (otherwise).

From this point on, we proceeded as follows. The CAS (Chemical Abstracts Service) Registry Number of each chemical was used to obtain the SMILES [22] notation for the chemical. In this fashion, the SMILES notations for 328 of the 342 chemicals were obtained.

The SMILES notation contains information on the two-dimensional structure of a chemical. So, an atom-bond representation, similar to the representation used in experiments to predict mutagenicity, can be generated from a SMILES encoding of a chemical. A DCG-based translator that does this has been written by Michael de Groeve and is maintained by Bernhard Pfahringer. We used this translator to generate atom-bond relational representations for each of the 328 chemicals. Note that the atom-bond representation here is less powerful than the QUANTA-derived representation, which includes atom charges, atom types and a richer selection of bond types. Especially the types carry a lot of information on the substructures that the respective atoms/bonds are part of.

A global feature of each chemical is its molecular weight. This was included in the data. Another global feature is logP, the logarithm of the compound's octanol/water partition coefficient, used also in the mutagenicity application. This feature is a measure of hydrophobicity, and can be expected to be important since we are considering biodegradation in water.

The basic atom and bond relations were then used to define a number of background predicates defining substructures / functional groups that are possibly relevant to the problem of predicting biodegradability. These predicates are: nitro $(-NO_2)$, sulfo $(-SO_2$ or $-O-S-O_2)$, methyl $(-CH_3)$, methoxy $(-O-CH_3)$, amine, aldehyde, ketone, ether, sulfide, alcohol, phenol, carboxylic acid, ester, amide, imine, alkyl_halide (R-Halogen where R is not part of a resonant ring), ar_halide (R-Halogen where R is part of a resonant ring), epoxy, n2n $(-N=N-)$, c2n $(-C=N-)$, benzene (resonant C_6 ring), hetero_ar_6_ring (resonant 6 ring containing at least 1 non-C atom), non_ar_6c_ring (non-resonant C_6 ring), non_ar_hetero_6_ring (non-resonant 6 ring containing at least 1 non-C atom), six_ring (any type of 6 ring), carbon_5_ar_ring (resonant C_5 ring) non_ar_5c_ring (non-resonant C_5 ring), non_ar_hetero_5_ring (non-resonant 5 ring containing at least 1 non-C atom), and five_ring (any type of 5 ring). Each of these predicates has three arguments: MoleculeID, MemberList (list of atoms that are part of the functional group) and ConnectedList (list of atoms connected to atoms in MemberList, but not in MemberList themselves).

3 Experiments

3.1 Representations

Molecular weight, logP and the abovementioned predicates form the basic relational representation (denoted by R1) considered in our experiments. Two propositional representations were derived from this. The first one (denoted P1) has an attribute $fgCount$ for each three-argument predicate fg of the background knowledge, which is the number of distinct functional groups of type fg in a molecule. Including logP and molecular weight, this representation has 31 attributes.

The second propositional representation (denoted P2) has been derived by counting all substructures of two and three atoms plus all four-atom substructures of a star-topology (no chains). Substructures that appear in at least three compounds (59 of them) are taken into account. For each such substructure we have a feature counting the number of distinct substructures of that kind in a molecule. The second propositional representation also includes logP and molecular weight.

Many of the functional groups have been selected from the PTE (predictive toxicology evaluation) domain theory [20], where the task is to predict carcinogenicity of chemicals. In this domain, the approach of Dehaspe and Toivonen [7] to discover (count) most frequent substructures that occur in the dataset and use these in conjunction with propositional learners has been among the most successful. Our small substructure representation has been derived along these lines.

3.2 Systems

A variety of classification and regression systems were applied to the classification, respectively regression version of the biodegradability problem. Propositional systems were applied to representations P1 and P2. For classification, these were the decision-tree inducer C4.5 [16] and the rule induction program RIPPER [6]. For regression, the regression-tree induction program M5' [21], a re-implementation of M5 [17] was used. It can construct linear models in the leaves of the tree.

Relational learning systems applied include ICL [8], which induces classification rules, SRT [15] and TILDE [1]. The latter are capable of inducing both classification and regression trees. ICL is an upgrade of CN2 [5] to first-order logic, TILDE is an upgrade of C4.5, and SRT is an upgrade of CART [3]. TILDE cannot construct linear models in the leaves of its trees; SRT can.

Finally, FFOIL [18] was also applied to the classification version of the problem. It used a representation (denoted R2) based on the atom and bond relations, designed to avoid problems with indeterminate literals. New predicates are introduced for conjunctions of the form $atom(M, X, Element1, \_, \_)$, $bond(M, X, Y, BondType), atom(M, Y, Element2, \_, \_)$.   E.g., $o2s(M, X, Y)$ stands for $atom(M, X, o, \_, \_), bond(M, X, Y, 2), atom(M, Y, s, \_, \_)$.

Table 1. Performance of machine learning systems predicting biodegradability.

System	Representation	Accuracy	Accuracy (+/-1)	Correlation (r)
C4.5	P1	55.2	86.2	-
C4.5	P2	56.9	82.4	-
RIPPER	P1 (-S0)	52.6	89.8	-
RIPPER	P2	57.6	93.9	-
M5'	P1	53.8	94.5	0.666
M5'	P2	59.8	94.7	0.693
FFOIL	R2	53.0	88.7	-
ICL	R1	55.7	92.6	-
SRT-C	P1	51.3	88.2	-
SRT-C	P1+R1	55.0	90.0	-
SRT-R	P1	49.8	93.8	0.580
SRT-R	P1+R1	52.6	93.0	0.632
TILDE-C	R1	51.0	88.6	-
TILDE-C	P1+R1	52.0	89.0	-
TILDE-R	R1	52.6	94.0	0.622
TILDE-R	P1+R1	52.4	93.9	0.623
BIODEG				0.607

Regarding parameter settings, default settings were employed for all systems wherever possible. Deviations from default parameter settings will be mentioned where appropriate in the results section.

3.3 Evaluation

Performance on unseen cases was estimated by performing five 10-fold cross-validations. The same folds were used by all systems. Performances reported are averages over the 5 cross-validations. Some of the induced models were inspected by B. Kompare, acting here as a domain expert, who provided some comments on their meaning and agreement with existing knowledge in the domain.

For the regression systems, correlation between the actual and predicted values of the log mean half-time of aerobic aqueous biodegradation is reported. We also measure classification accuracy (as described below) achieved by discretizing the real-valued predictions.

For the classification systems, classification accuracy is reported. We are dealing with ordered class values and misclassification of, e.g., fast as slow is a bigger mistake than misclassification of fast as moderate. We thus also record accuracy where only misclassification by more than one class up or down counts as an error (e.g., fast as slow, or resistant as moderate). This is denoted as Accuracy (+/-1) in Table 1.

4 Results

Table 1 gives an overview of the performance of the different classification and regression systems as applied to the problem of predicting biodegradability. SRT-C denotes SRT used to learn classification trees, while SRT-R denotes SRT used

```
resistant :- logP>=4.91, 'C[H]'<=15 (27/4).
  % Nonpolar (hydrophobic) compounds degrade less readily
resistant :- 'C[Cl]'>=3, mweight<=165.834 (7/1).
  % Halogenated compounds are resistant
fast :- mweight<=110.111, 'O[H]'>=1 (18/4).
  % Alcohols (alkyl -OH) are fast to degrade
fast :- mweight<=108.096, 'C=O'>=1 (15/7).
  % C=O readily degrades
slow :- 'N=O'>=1, mweight<=130.19 (10/0).
  % Compounds with N(-)O degrade slowly
slow :- logP>=1.52, 'C[H]'<=5 (31/16).
slow :- 'CN'>=1, logP>=1.7, mweight>=249.096 (11/3).
  % Very heavy and possibly toxic
slow :- 'C=O'<=0, mweight>=121.182, 'CN'>=1 (23/15).
default moderate (85/51).
```

Fig. 1. Rules for predicting biodegradability induced by RIPPER.

to learn regression trees. TILDE-C and TILDE-R have similar meaning. The first column lists the system applied, the second the representation used. The second column also lists some parameters changed from their default values. The representations are described in Section 3.1 (P1,P2, R1) and 3.2 (R2). The next three columns list performance measures as described in Section 3.3.

C4.5 was used on the two different propositional representations. Better performance was achieved using P2. Default parameters were used. The trees generated were too bushy for expert inspection. C4.5 performs worst in terms of large misclassification (e.g. fast as slow) errors, i.e. in terms of the measure Accuracy (+/-1).

RIPPER achieves highest accuracy of the classification systems applied. With its default parameters RIPPER prunes drastically, producing small rule sets. The rule set derived from the entire dataset for representation P2 is given in Figure 1, together with some comments provided by our domain expert.

The expert liked the rule-based representation and the concise rules very much (best of the representations shown to him, which included classification and regression trees induced by M5', SRT and TILDE, as well as clausal theories induced by ICL). The rules make sense, but are possibly pruned too much and cover substantial numbers of negative examples.

Pruning was then turned down in RIPPER (option -S0), producing larger sets of longer rules, at a moderate loss of accuracy. The accuracy for representation P2 is in this case 54.8 % (again estimated by doing five 10-fold cross-validations).

M5' achieves best results among the systems applied in terms of both regression accuracy (almost 0.7) and classification accuracy (almost 60 %, respectively 95 %). M5' was used with pruning turned down (-f0.0), as this seemed to perform best in terms of accuracy. Linear models are by default allowed in the leaves of the trees. Trees generated with these settings were too large to interpret.

Trees were generated from the entire dataset with more intensive pruning to ensure they were of reasonable size for interpretation by the domain expert. The tree generated from representation P2 is shown in Figure 2. The setting -f1.2

```
logP <= 4.005
|    mweight <= 111.77
|    |    'O[H]' <= 0.5 LM1 (80/49.7%)
|    |    'O[H]' > 0.5 LM2 (22/50.7%)
|    mweight > 111.77
|    |    'C=O' <= 0.5 LM3 (112/65.4%)
|    |    'C=O' > 0.5
|    |    |    'CO' <= 1.5
|    |    |    |    'CN[H]' <= 1.5
|    |    |    |    |    'C[Cl]' <= 1.5 LM4 (7/0%)
|    |    |    |    |    'C[Cl]' > 1.5 LM5 (2/6.68%)
|    |    |    |    'CN[H]' > 1.5 LM6 (9/33.8%)
|    |    |    'CO' > 1.5
|    |    |    |    'C[H]' <= 12.5
|    |    |    |    |    'N[H]' <= 0.5
|    |    |    |    |    |    'CO' <= 2.5 LM7 (5/0%)
|    |    |    |    |    |    'CO' > 2.5 LM8 (10/46.1%)
|    |    |    |    |    'N[H]' > 0.5 LM9 (5/16.3%)
|    |    |    |    'C[H]' > 12.5
|    |    |    .   |    logP <= 2.26 LM10 (5/0%)
|    |    |    |    |    logP > 2.26 LM11 (4/2.42%)
logP > 4.005
|    logP <= 4.895 LM12 (27/53.9%)
|    logP > 4.895
|    |    'C[H]' <= 15.5 LM13 (31/55%)
|    |    'C[H]' > 15.5 LM14 (9/45.9%)

Linear models at the leaves:
  Unsmoothed (simple):
    LM1: class = 6.1 + 0.525'C[Cl]' + 0.618'CN' - 1.09'C=O' - 0.559'CN[H]'
    LM2: class = 4.71
    LM3: class = 7.38 - 0.00897mweight + 0.889'C[Br]' + 0.576'C[Cl]' + 0.522'CN' + 0.113'N=O'
    LM4: class = 6.04
    LM5: class = 6.7
    LM6: class = 9.83 - 1.8'N[H]'
    LM7: class = 4.56
    LM8: class = 5.6
    LM9: class = 6.15
    LM10: class = 6.04
    LM11: class = 6.52 - 0.252'O[H]'
    LM12: class = 6.77 + 0.182'C[Cl]' - 0.357'CO'
    LM13: class = 9.43 - 1.52'CN'
    LM14: class = 12.2 - 0.0157mweight
```

Fig. 2. Regression tree for predicting biodegradability induced by M5'.

was used for pruning. The numbers in brackets denote the number of examples in a leaf and the relative error of the model in that leaf on the training data: LM1 was constructed from 80 examples and has 49.7 % relative error on them.

Unsurprisingly, the most important feature turns out to be logP, the hydrophobicity measure. For compounds to biodegrade fast in water, it helps if they are less hydrophobic. When a compound is not very hydrophobic (logP < 4.005), molecular weight is an important feature. With relatively low molecular weight (< 111.77), the presence of an $-OH$ group indicates smaller half-life times. With no $-OH$ groups (LM1), halogenated compounds degrade more slowly and so do compounds with CN substructures (positive coefficients in LM1). This is also consistent with the expert comments on the RIPPER rules.

FFOIL uses the R2 representation (Section 3.2). The settings -d10 and -a65 were used; -d10 allows the introduction of "deeper variables" (this does not seem to have any impact), and -a65 means that a clause must be 65% correct or better (FFOIL's default is 80 %, which seems too demanding in this domain).

```
activ(A,B)
carbon_5_ar_ring(A,C,D) ?
+--yes: [9.10211]  % Aromatic compounds are relatively slow to degrade
+--no:  aldehyde(A,E,F) ?
        +--yes: [4.93332] % Aldehydes are fast
        +--no: atm(A,G,h,H,I) ? % If H not present should degrade slowly
               +--yes: mweight(A,J) , J =< 80 ?
               |       +--yes: [5.52184] % Low weight ones degrade faster
               |       +--no: ester(A,K,L) ? % Esters degrade fast
               |              +--yes:mweight(A,M) , M =< 140 ?
               |              |      +--yes: [4.93332]
               |              |      +--no:  [5.88207]
               |              +--no: mweight(A,N) , N =< 340 ?
               |                     +--yes:carboxylic_acid(A,O,P) ? % Acids degrade fast
               |                     |      +--yes:[5.52288]
               |                     |      +--no: ar_halide(A,Q,R) ? % Halogenated - slow
               |                     |             +--yes: alkyl_halide(A,S,T) ?
               |                     |             |       +--yes: [11.2742]
               |                     |             |       +--no:  [7.81235]
               |                     |             +--no:  phenol(A,U,V) ?
               |                     |                     +--yes:mweight(A,W) , W =< 180 ?
               |                     |                     |      +--yes:[4.66378]
               |                     |                     |      +--no: [7.29547]
               |                     |                     +--no: [6.86852]
               |                     +--no: [8.28685]
               +--no:  mweight(A,X) , X =< 100 ?
                       +--yes: [6.04025]
                       +--no:  [8.55286]
```

Fig. 3. A regression tree for predicting biodegradability induced by TILDE.

FFOIL only uses the atom and bond relations, molecular weight and logP, but not the functional group relations/predicates. On the entire dataset, FFOIL induces 54 rules. It is interesting that some of these rules use negation. The rule activity(A,fast):-mw(A,C), logp(A,D), not(c1cl(A,_1,_2)), C>104.151, D>1.52, C <=129.161, D<=3.45,!. states that a compound A degrades fast if it is not halogenated, is relatively light, and relatively nonhydrophobic.

ICL was applied to representation R1. In terms of accuracy, it achieves better results than all other systems not using P2, and in terms of Accuracy (+/-1) it performs better than all classification systems except RIPPER on P2. The theory induced from the entire dataset contains 87 rules.

An example rule is: moderate(M) :- atom(M,A1,Elem1,_,_), Elem1 = s, mweight(M,MW),lt(MW,190),gt(MW,90). It states that a compound with a sulphur atom and molecular weight between 90 and 190 degrades moderately fast. The expert comments that sulphur slows down biodegradation.

Another rule states that a compound is fast to degrade if it contains a benzene and a phenol group and is lighter that 170. The expert comments that in this case degradability is probably due to hydrolisis and photolysis.

SRT upgrades CART to a relational representation, as mentioned above. From CART it inherits error-complexity pruning. It can construct linear models in the leaves and extends CART methodology by cross-validating these models. No linear models in the leaves were allowed in the experiments reported here.

The SRT results were not obtained by using default settings. Results for unmodified error-complexity pruning were not competitive. We thus forced SRT to overfit: from the sequence of pruned trees ordered by increasing complexity we took the first tree after the most accurate tree that was within one standard error of the former. The resulting trees were too large for inspection.

Both a propositional (P1) and a relational representation (P1+R1) were used. Adding the relational information improves accuracy, the greatest jump being observed for classification accuracy of SRT-C. Using P2 in addition (P1+P2+R1) only improves the regression results marginally. SRT-C is better than SRC-R on accuracy, but worse on Accuracy (+/-1).

TILDE was used for both classification and regression, once using R1 and once using P1+R1. TILDE-C was used with default settings. TILDE-R was used with its ftest parameter set to 0.01, which causes maximal pre-pruning.

The use of P1 in addition to R1 does not change the performance of TILDE. Better performance is achieved with regression, not in terms of Accuracy but in terms of Accuracy (+/-1). Using P2 in addition (P1+P2+R1) yields worse regression results ($r=0.58$).

An example regression tree induced by TILDE-R from the entire dataset is given in Figure 3. This tree has actually been generated without using logP information. It was analysed and commented upon by the domain expert. The fact that it does not use logP actually makes it easier for the influence of the functional groups on biodegradability to be identified. Namely, when logP is used, a large part of the tree uses logP only. Some of the expert comments are given in the tree itself.

5 Discussion

Overall, propositional systems applied to representation P2 yield best performance. M5' on this representation yields the highest overall accuracy, Accuracy (+/-1) and correlation. RIPPER follows with the second best classification accuracy and Accuracy (+/-1) matched only by TILDE-R. Of the relational learning systems, ICL performs best with highest classification accuracy and Accuracy (+/-1) comparable to that of SRT-R and TILDE-R.

Regression systems perform better than classification ones. This does not clearly show when one looks at accuracy alone, but it becomes clearer when one looks at Accuracy (+/-1). It thus seems that regression problems can best be handled by regression systems.

Using relational information in addition to the propositional formulation P1 does not bring drastic improvements. SRT and TILDE perform slightly better or the same on P1 + R1 as compared to P1. SRT and TILDE used for regression on P1 + R1 still perform (slightly) worse than M5' on P1. The reason for this might be the fact that M5' was using linear regression in the leaves, while SRT and TILDE were not.

Note that the propositional representations P1 and P2 contain structural features derived 1) directly from the functional group relations and 2) from the atom and bond relations. These features count occurrences of substructures within compounds. P1 contains definitions of both small and larger groups (such as rings), while P2 mainly contains small structures (up to 4 atoms).

The biodegradation rates used in this study were expert estimates rather than measurements for the most part. We have thus been modeling expert opinions on biodegradation rates, and not biodegradation rates themselves. This means that we have also modeled expert estimation errors. To the authors' knowledge, only small datasets containing measured biodegradation rates for structurally related chemicals are publicly available at present.

6   Related work

Related work includes QSAR applications of machine learning and ILP, on one hand, and constructing QSAR models for biodegradability, on the other hand. On the ILP side, QSAR applications include drug design (e.g. [13]), mutagenicity prediction (e.g. [19]), and toxicity prediction [20]. The latter two are closely related to our application. In fact, we have used a similar representation and reused parts of the background knowledge developed for them.

On the biodegradability side, [11] is closest to our work. The last row of Table 1, marked BIODEG, gives the correlation between the actual values of the continuous class and predictions made by the BIODEG program [12]. The correlation is calculated for all 328 chemicals in our database, since the BIODEG program has been derived independently. This program estimates the probability of rapid aerobic biodegradation in the presence of mixed populations of environmental organisms. It uses a model derived by linear regression [11].

The best results of our experiments (correlation of 0.7) are considerably better than the BIODEG program predictions (correlation 0.6). Furthermore, while the reported performance results for the machine learning systems are for unseen cases, some of the 200 chemicals used in developing BIODEG also appear in our database. In [11], CAS numbers for 144 of the 200 chemicals used to derive BIODEG are provided; of these, 21 also appear in our database. The correlation of BIODEG predictions is thus probably even lower than 0.6 for unseen cases.

Work on applying machine learning to predict biodegradability includes [14], who compared several AI tools on the same domain and data and found these to yield better results than the classical statistical and probabilistic approaches, [23, 4] who applied neural nets, and [9] who applied several different approaches.

7   Conclusions and further work

Predicting biodegradability is a QSAR problem, similar to predicting mutagenicity or toxicity. Based on a handbook of biodegradation rates, we have developed a relational dataset including a structural representation of compounds and background knowledge on potentially relevant substructures. This dataset is suitable for both propositional and relational learning. Particular attention was paid to data quality issues: many datasets of this kind have surprisingly many errors, such as incorrect SMILES codes, which essentially result in incorrect descriptions of the compounds and affect the resulting QSAR theories accordingly. The dataset itself is thus a contribution on its own.

We have applied a range of machine learning systems, including ILP systems, to several representations derived from the relational description of the compounds. Best performance was achieved on good propositionalisations derived by counting substructures. This is in agreement with, e.g., the predictive toxicology evaluation results (cf. this volume) where best results were achieved by propositional systems using relational features representing the presence/count of frequent substructures.

M5', which achieves the best results, outperforms an approach derived by biodegradability experts, implemented in the program BIODEG. The theories induced by the machine learning systems were easy to interpret (size permitting) and made sense to the domain expert. Given that the biodegradation rates that we used as values of the target variable are mostly estimates and not measured values, overall performance is satisfactory.

There is a variety of directions for further work. One possibility is to study overall degradation and biodegradation comparatively. Identifying chemicals for which degradation and biodegradation time differ is an important topic. Characterising such chemicals would be an interesting learning problem.

Another important issue is how performance is evaluated when only estimates of the target variable are provided. One could argue that if the learned theory predicts a value which is between the low and high estimate provided by an expert, its prediction is correct. In a sense, we may have applied a too strict evaluation criterion here, trying to fit the log mean half-life time, while providing a value in the provided interval may have been sufficient.

Predicting the logarithm of the mean of the low and high estimates of the degradation rate is close to predicting the logarithm of the high estimate. Predicting the (logarithm of the) low estimate and combining the two predictions might yield better results. This should also be investigated in further work.

Acknowledgements: This work was supported in part by the ESPRIT IV Project 20237 ILP2. It is also part of the project *Carcinogenicity Detection by Machine Learning*, funded by the Austrian Federal Ministry of Science and Transport, which also provides general financial support for the Austrian Research Institute for AI. Thanks are due to: Irena Cvitanič for help with preparing the dataset in computer-readable form; Christoph Helma for help in preparing the background knowledge and calculating logP; Ross King and Ashwin Srinivasan for providing some definitions of the functional group predicates.

References

1. Blockeel, H. and De Raedt, L. 1998. Top-down induction of first order logical decision trees. *Artificial Intelligence*, 101(1-2): 285–297.
2. Boethling, R.S., and Sabljic, A. 1989. Screening-level model for aerobic biodegradability based on a survey of expert knowledge. *Environ. Sci. Technol.* 23: 672–679.
3. Breiman, L., Friedman, J.H., Olshen, R.A., and Stone, C.J. 1984. *Classification and Regression Trees*. Wadsworth, Belmont.

4. Cambon, B., and Devillers, J. 1993. New trends in structure-biodegradability relationships. *Quant. Struct. Act. Relat.* 12(1): 49–58.
5. Clark, P., and Boswell, R. 1991. Rule induction with CN2: some recent improvements. In *Proc. 5th European Working Session on Learning*, pages 151–163. Springer, Berlin.
6. Cohen W. 1995. Fast effective rule induction. In *Proc. 12th Intl. Conf. on Machine Learning*, pages 115–123. Morgan Kaufmann, San Mateo, CA.
7. Dehaspe, L., and Toivonen, H. 1999. Frequent query discovery: a unifying ILP approach to association rule mining. *Data Mining and Knowledge Discovery*.
8. De Raedt, L., and Van Laer, W. 1995. Inductive constraint logic. In *Proc. 6th Intl. Workshop on Algorithmic Learning Theory*, pages 80–94. Springer, Berlin.
9. Gamberger, D., Sekuak, S., and Sabljič, A. 1993. Modelling biodegradation by an example-based learning system. *Informatica* 17: 157–166.
10. Howard, P.H., Boethling, R.S., Jarvis, W.F., Meylan, W.M., and Michalenko, E.M. 1991. *Handbook of Environmental Degradation Rates*. Lewis Publishers.
11. Howard, P.H., Boethling, R.S., Stiteler, W.M., Meylan, W.M., Hueber, A.E., Beauman, J.A., and Larosche, M.E. 1992. Predictive model for aerobic biodegradability developed from a file of evaluated biodegradation data. *Environ. Toxicol. Chem.* 11: 593–603.
12. Howard, P. and Meylan, W. 1992. User's Guide for the Biodegradation Probability Program, Ver. 3. Syracuse Res. Corp., Chemical Hazard Assessment Division, Environmental Chemistry Center, Syracuse, NY 13210, USA.
13. King, R.D., Muggleton, S.H., Lewis, R.A., and Sternberg, M.J.E. 1992. Drug design by machine learning : the use of inductive logic programming to model the structure-activity relationship of trimethoprim analogues binding to dihydrofolate reductase. *Proc. National Academy of Sciences USA*, 89: 11322–11326.
14. Kompare, B. 1995. *The use of artificial intelligence in ecological modelling.* Ph.D. Thesis, Royal Danish School of Pharmacy, Copenhagen, Denmark.
15. Kramer, S. 1996. Structural regression trees. In *Proc. 13th Natl. Conf. on Artificial Intelligence*, pages 812–819. AAAI Press/The MIT Press.
16. Quinlan, J.R. 1993a. *C4.5: Programs for Machine Learning*. Morgan Kaufmann, San Mateo, CA.
17. Quinlan, J.R. 1993b. Combining instance-based and model-based learning. In *Proc. 10th Intl. Conf. on Machine Learning*, pages 236–243. Morgan Kaufmann, San Mateo, CA.
18. Quinlan, J.R. 1996. Learning first-order definitions of functions. *Journal of Artificial Intelligence Research*, 5:139–161.
19. Srinivasan, A., Muggleton, S.H., Sternberg, M.J.E., and King, R.D. 1996. Theories for mutagenicity: A study in first-order and feature-based induction. *Artificial Intelligence* 85(1-2): 277–299.
20. Srinivasan, A., King, R.D., Muggleton, S.H., and Sternberg, M.J.E. 1997. The predictive toxicology evaluation challenge. In *Proc. 15th Intl. Joint Conf. on Artificial Intelligence*, pages 4–9. Morgan Kaufmann, San Mateo, CA.
21. Wang, Y., and Witten, I.H. 1997. Inducing model trees for continuous classes. In *Poster Papers - 9th European Conf. on Machine Learning*, pages 128–137. Prague, Czech Republic. URL: http://www.cs.waikato.ac.nz/~ ml/publications.html.
22. Weininger D. 1988. SMILES, a Chemical and Information System. 1. Introduction to Methodology and Encoding Rules. *J. Chem. Inf. Comput. Sci.* 28(1): 31-6.
23. Zitko, V. 1991. Prediction of biodegradability of organic chemicals by an artificial neural network. *Chemosphere*, Vol. 23, No. 3: 305-312.

1BC: A First-Order Bayesian Classifier

Peter Flach and Nicolas Lachiche

University of Bristol, United Kingdom
{flach,lachiche}@cs.bris.ac.uk

Abstract. In this paper we present 1BC, a first-order Bayesian Classifier. Our approach is to view individuals as structured terms, and to distinguish between structural predicates referring to subterms (e.g. atoms from molecules), and properties applying to one or several of these subterms (e.g. a bond between two atoms). We describe an individual in terms of elementary features consisting of zero or more structural predicates and one property; these features are considered conditionally independent following the usual naive Bayes assumption. 1BC has been implemented in the context of the first-order descriptive learner Tertius, and we describe several experiments demonstrating the viability of our approach.

1 Introduction

In this paper we present 1BC, a first-order Bayesian Classifier. While the propositional Bayesian Classifier makes the naive Bayes assumption of statistical independence of elementary features (one attribute taking on a particular value) given the class value, it is not immediate which elementary features to use in the first-order case, where features may be constructed from arbitrary numbers of literals. A classification task consists in classifying new individuals given some examples. It requires therefore a clear notion of individuals. Our approach is to view individuals as structured terms, and to distinguish between structural predicates referring to subterms (e.g. atoms from molecules), and properties applying to one or several of these subterms (e.g. a bond between two atoms). An elementary first-order feature then consists of zero or more structural predicates and one property.

In section 2, we briefly recall the main ideas behind the propositional naive Bayesian classifier, and discuss possible ways to upgrade it to a first-order language. In section 3, we describe the first-order language used in 1BC. Section 4 gives some implementation details, and section 5 describes our experiments on 3 well-known datasets from Inductive Logic Programming (ILP). Section 6 discusses the main implications of our approach.

2 The Naive Bayesian Classifier

Like any learner, the naive Bayesian classifier manipulates descriptions of individuals. The classical naive Bayesian classifier uses an attribute-value language, a representation formalism that is commonly used in machine learning. Logically speaking an attribute-value language can be mapped to unary predicate logic, where hypotheses use a single universally quantified variable to express generalisation over all individuals, and examples are variable-free conjunctions concerning single individuals. Whereas this representation is, strictly speaking, not propositional, a learning system keeping track of the distinction between examples and hypotheses can actually drop the syntactic distinction and express both in a variable-free, essentially propositional formalism (the single representation trick). In Section 2.1 we recall the propositional naive Bayesian classifier. In Section 2.2 we discuss the general problem of upgrading it to deal with non-propositional representations.

2.1 The Propositional Case

Let $A_i, 1 \leq i \leq n$, be a set of attributes, and let Cl be the class attribute. Given that an individual takes on the values $a_1 \dots a_n$ for attributes $A_i \dots A_n$, in a Bayesian approach the most likely class value c is the one that maximises

$$P(c|a_1 \dots a_n) = \frac{P(a_1 \dots a_n|c)P(c)}{P(a_1 \dots a_n)} \tag{1}$$

Here we write $P(a_i)$ as an abbreviation for $P(A_i = a_i)$.

In order to decrease the number of probabilities involved in this calculation, and to increase the reliability of their estimates, usually the simplifying *naive Bayes assumption* is made that $P(a_1 \dots a_n|c) = P(a_1|c) \dots P(a_n|c)$, i.e. the values taken on by the different attributes are conditionally independent given the class value. The predicted class value c is the one that maximises $P(c)P(a_1|c) \dots P(a_n|c)$:

$$argmax_c P(c) \prod P(a_i|c) \tag{2}$$

(For a given individual the term $P(a_1 \dots a_n)$ is a constant normalising term that can be ignored if we're only interested in determining the most likely class value.)

The classifier which predicts by maximising the above expression is called the naive Bayesian classifier, or *Bayesian classifier* for short. Essentially, it reads the description of an individual to be classified, and then tries to estimate how likely it is to observe such an individual among each of the possible classes. Thus, the fundamental problem of a Bayesian classifier (naive or otherwise) is to estimate how likely it is to observe an individual satisfying a particular description among given sub-populations. In our case these estimates are obtained from the training set, under the naive Bayes assumption of conditional independence. Even in cases where this assumption is clearly invalid, the Bayesian classifier has been shown to give good results [5].

2.2 The First-Order Case

Upgrading the Bayesian classifier to first-order representations requires a perspective on how exactly learning in first-order logic generalises attribute-value learning. Recently, a number of such perspectives have been proposed [1, 17, 10]. Each of these approaches make certain assumptions on what an individual is, and how it is represented. Our approach is best understood by thinking of individuals as structured objects represented by first order terms in a strongly typed language [6]. Our actual implementation makes use of a flattened, function-free Prolog representation, as explained in Section 3.

As in the propositional case, we will assume that the domain provides a well-defined notion of an individual, e.g. a patient in a medical domain, a molecule in mutagenicity prediction, or a board position in chess. To each individual is associated its description (everything that is known about it except its classification) and its classification. In a first-order representation the description of an individual can be expressed by a single structured term. In the attribute-value case this term is a tuple (element of a cartesian product) of attribute values (constants). For instance, in a medical domain each patient could be represented by a five-tuple specifying name, age, sex, weight, and blood pressure of the patient. The first-order case generalises this by allowing other complex types at the top-level (e.g. sets, lists), and by allowing intermediate levels of complex subtypes before the atomic enumerated types are reached.

Example 1. Consider Michalski's east- and westbound trains learning problem. We start with a number of propositional attributes:
$Shape = \{\texttt{rectangle}, \texttt{u\_shaped}, \texttt{bucket}, \texttt{hexa}, \ldots\}$
$Length = \{\texttt{double}, \texttt{short}\}$
$Roof = \{\texttt{flat}, \texttt{jagged}, \texttt{peaked}, \texttt{arc}, \texttt{open}\}$
$Load = \{\texttt{circle}, \texttt{hexagon}, \texttt{triangle}, \ldots\}$
A car is a 5-tuple describing its shape, length, number of wheels, type of roof, and its load:
$Car = Shape \times Length \times Integer \times Roof \times Load$
And finally we define a train as a set of cars:
$Train = 2^{Car}$
Here is a term representing a train with 2 cars:
$\{(\texttt{u\_shaped}, \texttt{short}, 2, \texttt{open}, \texttt{triangle}), (\texttt{rectangle}, \texttt{short}, 2, \texttt{flat}, \texttt{circle})\}$.

In this example an individual is represented by a *set* of tuples of constants, rather than by a tuple of constants as in the propositional case.Notice that the complex type *set of tuples* leads to what has been called the *multiple-instance problem* [3]. It has been argued that the multiple instance problem represents most of the complexity of upgrading to a first-order representation [1]. However, we would like to stress that the above representation does not prevent a deeper nesting of types.

If we want to apply a Bayesian classifier to Example 1, we need a general mechanism to estimate the probability of observing an arbitrary set of tuples. Following a naive Bayesian approach we want to *decompose* the probability of a set, for instance into the probability of each of its members occurring separately. In our example, we would consider the event of one tuple occurring in the set independent of the events of other tuples occurring in it (given the class value).

For example, the probability of the above train occurring among eastbound trains could be assessed by estimating the probability of a u_shaped short open car with 2 wheels whose load is a triangle occurring in eastbound trains and the probability of a rectangle short car with a flat roof whose load is a circle occurring in eastbound trains. Notice however that this is not the only way to decompose a probability distribution over sets. For instance, the number of elements of the set may be governed by a separate distribution.

Now, how are the probabilities of particular cars estimated? Again, there are several possibilities. One possibility is to decompose again, using the propositional naive Bayesian decomposition over tuples. Another possibility is not to decompose cars, treating them as atomic terms instead whose probability should be estimated directly from the training set. Our approach is flexible, allowing the user a maximum depth until which the term can be decomposed. However, in this paper we will focus on a recursive decomposition until the deepest level. That is, the probability of the above train occurring among eastbound trains is assessed by estimating the probabilities $P(u\_shaped|eastbound)$, $P(rectangle|eastbound)$, $P(short|eastbound)$, $P(2|eastbound)$, $P(open|eastbound)$, $P(flat|eastbound)$, $P(triangle|eastbound)$, and $P(circle|eastbound)$.

In addition, we consider the negation of properties not satisfied by any car in the train. Indeed, the probability of the set $\{b,c\}$ as a subset of $\{a,b,c\}$ can be assumed inversely proportional to the probability of a. Therefore the probability of features not occurring in the previous train are considered, such as $P(\neg diamond|eastbound)$, $P(\neg long|eastbound)$, and $P(\neg 3|eastbound)$, provided some trains in the training set contain diamond-shaped cars, long cars, or cars with 3 wheels. The probability of the observed train is then approximated by the product of the aforementioned probabilities.

To summarise the discussion so far, the fundamental problem of a first-order Bayesian classifier is *how to decompose a probability distribution over a complex type possibly involving several levels of nesting*. The main difference with the propositional case is that there are a number of ways of approaching this problem, none of which seem *a priori* preferable. In the next section we describe our approach, which is a transformation approach in the sense that we use a flattened, function-free representation instead of the above term-based representation. The reason for this representation change is that 1BC is implemented on top of an existing system, implemented in C, which uses a flattened representation. Using a flattened representation means that we have to 'emulate' complex types such as tuples, lists, and sets. In fact, we will only be concerned with tuples, emulated by so-called structural functions, and sets, emulated by non-determinate structural predicates, as explained in the next section. Handling other non-determinate types such as lists is left for future work.

It is important not to confuse the flattening transformation with propositionalisation as e.g. done by LINUS [9]. Since individual-based representations can always – conceptually – be propositionalised, the distinguishing characteristic of propositionalisation approaches is that they transform the first-order data into propositional form. In contrast, 1BC operates directly on the first-order data.

3 A First-Order Language for Bayesian Classifiers

In this section we extend the representation formalism employed by the Bayesian classifier. We employ Prolog notation, with variables starting with capitals and constants starting with lowercase letters, and commas indicating conjunction between literals.

3.1 Structural Predicates and Properties

As explained above, a domain is thought of as a hierarchy of complex types. Instead of specifying this type hierarchy directly, the teacher associates with each complex type a structural predicate that can be used to refer to some of its subterms.

Definition 1. *A structural predicate is a binary predicate associated with a complex type representing the relation between that type with one of its parts.*

For instance, for an n-dimensional cartesian product, each of the n projection functions can be represented by a structural predicate (since it is a 1-to-1 relation, it is usually omitted). For a list type and a set type, list membership and set membership are structural predicates (notice that these are not functions, but 1-to-n relations). For example, the following conjunction of literals refers to the load L of some car C of a train T: train2car(T,C),car2load(C,L).

Definition 2. *A functional structural predicate, or structural function, refers to a unique subterm, while a non-determinate structural predicate is non-functional.*

In the above example car2load is functional and train2car is non-determinate. Our non-determinate structural predicates are similar to the structural literals of [17], however they are not required to be transitive.

Definition 3. *A property is a predicate characterising a subset of a type.*

A property is for instance the length of a car short(C), or the shape of a load load(L,triangle).

Definition 4. *A parameter is an argument of a property which is always instantiated. If a property has no parameter (or only one instantiation of its parameters), it is boolean, otherwise it is multivalued.*

Our parameters correspond to valued arguments of [15]. We also assume that the value of parameters depends functionally on the instantiation of the remaining (relational [15]) arguments.

Definition 5. *A property is propositional if it has only one argument which is not a parameter, and relational if it has more than one.*

The property shape(C,rectangle) is propositional, while bond(Atom1,Atom2,1) is relational.

3.2 Features

Definition 6. *An* individual variable *is a variable of the complex type describing the domain of interest. A* first-order feature *of an individual is a conjunction of structural predicates and of properties where:*

- *each structural predicate uses one of the variables already introduced, and introduces a new variable,*
- *properties only use the variables introduced by structural predicates or the individual variable,*
- *all variables are used either by a structural predicate or a property.*

For instance, the following is a first-order feature: `train2car(T,C),car2load(C,L), load(L,triangle)`. Note that all variables are existentially quantified except the individual variable, which is free.[1] This feature is true of any train which has a car which has a triangular load. The condition `train2car(T,C)` is not a first-order feature, and neither is `train2car(T,C1),train2car(T,C2),short(C1)` nor `load(L,triangle)`.

Definition 7. *A feature is* functional *if all structural predicates are functional, otherwise it is* non-determinate.

Definition 8. *A functional feature is* boolean *if it contains a single property and this property is boolean, otherwise it is* multivalued. *A non-determinate feature is always boolean.*

For instance, the feature `train2firstcar(T,C)`, `shape(C,Shape)`, where Shape indicates a parameter, is multivalued. The first car of a given train has only one shape. On the other hand, the feature `train2car(T,C)`, `shape(C,Shape)` is boolean rather than multivalued. The same train can have a car with a rectangular shape, and another car with a non-rectangular shape.

The distinction between structural predicates and properties is best understood in the context of a representation of individuals by terms: structural predicates refer to subterms (and introduce new variables), properties treat subterms as atomic (and consume variables). However, the same distinction can be made when using a flattened representation, which is in fact what we use in the 1BC system. Flattening requires introducing a name for all relevant subterms. For instance, the train of Example 1 could have the following flattened representation:

```
train(t1).
train2car(t1,c1).        train2car(t1,c2).
shape(c1,u_shaped).      shape(c2,rectangle).
length(c1,short).        length(c2,short).
wheels(c1,2).            wheels(c2,2).
roof(c1,open).           roof(c2,flat).
car2load(c1,l1).         car2load(c2,l2).
load(l1,triangle).       load(l2,circle).
```

---

[1] In a proper first-order language this feature would be written as
∃ C,L: `train2car(T,C)` ∧ `car2load(C,L)` ∧ `load(L,triangle)`.

Which predicates are structural and which are properties is part of the definition of the hypothesis language, as it cannot always be detected automatically, especially when the representation is flattened and no types are defined. Let's consider an example of the declarations required by 1BC.

```
--INDIVIDUAL
train 1 train cwa
--STRUCTURAL
train2car 2 1:train *:car * cwa
car2load 2 1:car 1:load * cwa
--PROPERTIES
eastbound 1 train * cwa
shape 2 car #shape * cwa
short 1 car * cwa
roof 2 car #kind * cwa
wheels 2 car #nb_wheels * cwa
load 2 load #l_shape * cwa
```

The first two lines define a single individual variable of type train. The next three lines define the structural predicates. train2car is a many-to-one relation, indicating that one train may contain many cars, but each car belongs to exactly one train. This functions is a language bias, since rules like eastbound(T1) :- train2car(T1,C), train2car(T2,C),eastbound(T2) will not be considered. Similarly, car2load(C,L) indicates that each car contains exactly one load. Finally, the following lines indicate the properties. The second argument's type of the second property #shape is preceded by #, indicating that it is a parameter which must always be instantiated in rules. The label cwa means that the Closed-World Assumption is used for these predicates.

These declarations are similar to mode declarations, albeit on the predicate level rather than the argument level. ILP systems such as Progol [11] and Warmr [2] use mode declarations such as train2car(+Train,-Car) indicating that the first argument is an input argument and should use a variable already occurring previously in the current hypothesis. They however do not distinguish between structural predicates and properties.

3.3 Elementary Features

From the naive Bayesian perspective, non-elementary features are those whose joint probability distribution is approximated from the distributions of the elementary features. Distinguishing between elementary and non-elementary features is crucial to the naive Bayesian approach.

To understand the distinction between elementary and non-elementary first-order features, consider the following features:

```
train2car(T,C),length(C,short)
train2car(T,C),roof(C,open)
train2car(T,C),length(C,short),roof(C,open)
```

The first feature is true of trains having a short car. The second feature is true of trains having an open car. The third feature is true of trains having a short, open car. From the naive Bayes perspective this third feature is non-elementary, as we assume (justifiably or otherwise) that the probability of a car being short is independent of the probability of a car being open, given the class value. Therefore our first-order Bayesian classifier needs to have access to the first and second feature, but not the third.

Definition 9. *A feature is* elementary *if it contains a single property.*

Notice that properties may express relations between subterms, e.g. mol2atom(M,A1), mol2atom(M,A2), bond(A1,A2) would be an elementary first-order feature which describes the case of a molecule containing two atoms with a bond between them.

4 Implementation

1BC has been implemented in C in the context of the first-order descriptive learner Tertius [7]. Let us first describe briefly Tertius' abilities which are used in 1BC.

Tertius is able to deal with extensional explicit knowledge (i.e. the truth value of all ground facts is given), with extensional knowledge under the Closed World Assumption (i.e. all true ground facts are given), or with intensional knowledge (i.e. truth values are derived using either prolog inference mechanism or a theorem prover). Tertius can also deal with (weakly) typed predicates, that is each argument of a predicate belongs to a named type and the set of constants belonging to one type defines its domain. Moreover, if a domain is continuous, Tertius allows one to discretise it into several intervals of one standard deviation and centered on the mean.

Given some knowledge concerning the domain, Tertius returns a list of interesting sets of literals. It performs a top-down search, starting with the empty set and iteratively refines it. In order to avoid to consider the same clauses several times (and their refinements!), the refinement steps (i.e. adding a literal, unifying two variables, and instantiating a variable) are ordered. Once a particular refinement step is applied, none of its predecessors are applicable anymore. The search space can be seen as a generalisation of set-enumeration trees [14] to first-order logic.

Since there might be an infinite number of refinements, the search is restricted to a maximum number of literals and of variables. Other language biases are the declaration of structural predicates and properties, the distinction between functional and non-determinate structural predicates, and the use of parameters, as explained in the previous section.

Elementary first-order features are generated by constraining Tertius to generate only hypotheses containing exactly one property and no unnecessary structural predicates. The features can optionally be read from a file. In Equation 2, the features $A_i = a_i$ are replaced by elementary first-order features f. Each conditional probability $P(f|c)$ of the feature value f given the value c of the class is then estimated from the training data. Writing $n(f \wedge c)$ for the number of individuals satisfying f and $Cl = c$, $n(c)$ for the number of individuals satisfying $Cl = c$, and F for the number of values of the feature (the number of possible values for a multivalued feature, 2 for a boolean or a non-determinate feature), the Laplace estimate $P(f|c) = \frac{n(f \wedge c)+1}{n(c)+F}$ is used in order to avoid null probabilities in the product in Equation 2.

5 Experiments

In this section we describe experimental results on mutagenesis, finite-element mesh design, and KRK-illegal.

5.1 Mutagenesis

This problem concerns identifying mutagenic compounds. We considered the "regression friendly" dataset and we used only the atom and bond structure of the molecule represented by a structural predicate atm(M,A) linking an atom A to its molecule M and four properties atomel(A,El), atomty(A,AType), atomch(A,Charge) and bond(A1,A2,BondType).

1BC gets an accuracy of 80.9% on the training set, which is comparable to Progol's accuracy of 79.8% but lower than regression's accuracy of 89.9% [16]. 1BC was also evaluated using a 3-fold cross-validation to be compared to the accuracy estimated on a randomly chosen test set of one third in [16]. The accuracy resulting from the 3-fold cross-validation is 74.5%. Progol and regression gave respectively 71.4% and 85.7%.

5.2 Finite Element Mesh Design

This domain is about finite element methods in engineering. The task is to predict how many elements should be used to model each edge of a structure [4]. The target predicate is mesh(Edge,Number) where the Number of elements in the Mesh model can vary between 1 and 17. Each edge is described by three multivalued properties type(Edge,Type), support(Edge,Support) and load(Edge,Load). Three structural predicates neighbour_xy_r(E1,E2), neighbour_yz_r(E1,E2) and neighbour_zx_r(E1,E2) provide the functional representation of neighbour(E1,E2) which is necessary to define multivalued features. Structural predicates opposite_r(E1,E2) and equal_r(E1,E2) are also a functional representation of other topological relations.

The accuracy achieved by 1BC is 61.9% considering properties of the edge only, and 66.2% when considering features of the surrounding edges. This is lower than Golem's accuracy of 84.9% [4] but it shows an improvement of the accuracy when topological properties are used. This is confirmed on the next domain.

5.3 Illegal Chess Endgame Positions

The final experiment concerns the chess endgame domain White King and Rook vs. Black King (KRK) [12]. The classification task is to distinguish between illegal and legal board positions. The 1BC representation employs a structural function board2whiteking to refer to the position of the White King (similarly for the other two pieces), and two structural functions pos2rank and pos2file to translate a position into rank and file. We have two propositional properties rankeq and fileeq equating rank/file with a number, and three relational properties adj, eq and lt to compare rank/files. The propositional elementary features in this domain are exemplified by board2whiteking(A,B),rankeq(B,1) and board2blackking(A,B),fileeq(B,8). The relational elementary features are of the form board2whiteking(A,B),board2whiterook(A,C),pos2rank(B,D), pos2rank(C,E),eq(E,D).

Following the results reported in [9], we used 5 training sets of 100 board positions each, and a test set of 5000 positions. Table 1 gives the accuracy over the training set, and the accuracy over the test set, averaged over the 5 training sets. 1BC 2/2 refers to features with no more than 2 literals and 2 variables, i.e. the propositional features referred to above (in this case pos2file and pos2rank are used as properties with a parameter as second argument). Similarly, 1BC 5/5 refers to features with up to 5 literals and 5 variables, which includes both the propositional and the relational features. 1BC FO refers to relational features only (the two propositional properties rankeq and fileeq were removed from the representation).

Table 1. Results in the KRK-illegal domain.

System	Training accuracy	Test accuracy
Majority class	64.0% sd. 3.0%	66.3%
MLC++	79.0% sd. 3.1%	57.0% sd. 2.6%
1BC 2/2	79.0% sd. 3.5%	56.2% sd. 1.4%
1BC 5/5	91.2% sd. 2.5%	84.3% sd. 5.2%
1BC FO	93.8% sd. 3.6%	88.3% sd. 2.8%

The results show that KRK-illegal is a difficult domain for a Bayesian classifier, since the best result reported in [9] was 98.1% on the test set, achieved by LINUS. Nevertheless, the experiment clearly demonstrates that the use of first-order features considerably improves the performance of the Bayesian classifier. With only propositional features, the result on the test set drops well below the majority class. This means that propositional features have actually negative information content [8]. To verify that this was not due to a bug in 1BC, we also ran the Bayesian Classifier in MLC++ on the same data, and got virtually the same results for the propositional features only.

6 Discussion

In this paper we presented a first-order Bayesian classifier. While many propositional learners have been upgraded to first-order logic in ILP, the case of the Bayesian classifier poses a problem that has not been satisfyingly solved before, namely how to distinguish between elementary and non-elementary first-order features. Treating each Prolog literal as a feature, as is done in LINUS [9] is not a solution, because many literals do not contain a reference to an individual, and thus the relative frequency associated with that literal cannot be attributed to an individual. Our approach gives a clear picture of how an individual-based first-order representation upgrades attribute-value learning, namely by allowing relational and non-determinate features. In this respect, the work extends previous work on the relationship between propositional and first-order learning [1, 6, 10, 15, 17].

One can argue that any individual-based first-order learning problem, as defined in this paper, can be transformed to attribute-value learning, by introducing an attribute for any first-order feature in the hypothesis language. However, one should distinguish between transformation of the hypothesis language and transformation of the data (propositionalisation). 1BC does the first but not the second. Furthermore, the transformation of the hypothesis language is mostly conceptual: it is perfectly possible to explain how 1BC operates on a multiple-instance problem by decomposing a probability distribution on sets. Thus, 1BC clearly extends the propositional naive Bayesian engine. That being said, notice that 1BC is able to consider the same features and is guaranteed to perform at least as well as a purely propositional Bayesian classifier, as was demonstrated in the KRK-illegal domain. This is a desirable property that is currently shared by only a few ILP systems.

Pompe and Kononenko also describe an application of naive Bayesian classifiers in a first-order context [13]. However, in their approach the naive Bayesian formula is used in a post-processing step to combine the predictions of several, independently learned first-order rules. As far as we are aware, the present paper is the first to describe a first-order naive Bayesian *learner*.

Future work includes refining the declarative bias specification of Tertius and 1BC. We would also like to handle other non-determinate types such as lists. Finally, we would like to extend 1BC to an interactive truth-value predictor, which could answer ground Prolog queries from an extensional database.

Acknowledgements

We acknowledge the useful comments of three anonymous reviewers. Part of this work was supported by the Esprit IV Long Term Research Project 20237 *Inductive Logic Programming 2*.

References

1. L. De Raedt. Attribute value learning versus inductive logic programming: The missing links (extended abstract). In D. Page, editor, *Proc. of the 8th Int. Conference on Inductive Logic Programming*, LNAI 1446, pages 1–8. Springer-Verlag, 1998.

2. L. Dehaspe and L. De Raedt. Mining association rules in multiple relations. In S. Džeroski and N. Lavrač, editors, *Proc. of the 7th Int. Workshop on Inductive Logic Programming*, LNAI 1297, pages 125–132. Springer-Verlag, 1997.

3. T. G Dietterich, R. H. Lathrop, and T. Lozano-Perez. Solving the multiple instance problem with axis-parallel rectangles. *Artificial Intelligence*, 89:31–71, 1997.

4. B. Dolšak, I. Bratko, and A. Jezernik. Finite element mesh design: An engineering domain for ILP application. In S. Wrobel, editor, *Proc. of the 4th Int. Workshop on Inductive Logic Programming*, GMD-Studien 237, pages 305–320, 1994.

5. P. Domingos and M. Pazzani. On the optimality of the simple Bayesian classifier under zero-one loss. *Machine Learning*, 29:103–130, 1997.

6. P.A. Flach, C. Giraud-Carrier, and J.W. Lloyd. Strongly typed inductive concept learning. In D. Page, editor, *Proc. of the 8th Int. Conference on Inductive Logic Programming*, LNAI 1446, pages 185–194. Springer-Verlag, 1998.

7. P.A. Flach and N. Lachiche. A first-order approach to unsupervised learning. Submitted, 1999.

8. I. Kononenko and I. Bratko. Information-based evaluation criterion for classifier's performance. *Machine Learning*, 6:67–80, 1991.

9. N. Lavrač and S. Džeroski. *Inductive Logic Programming: Techniques and Applications*. Ellis Horwood, 1994.

10. R. Piola M. Botta, A. Giordana. FONN: Combining first order logic with connectionist learning. In *Proc. of the 14th Int. Conference on Machine Learning*, pages 46–56, 1997.

11. S. Muggleton. Inverse entailment and Progol. *New Generation Computing*, 13(3-4):245–286, 1995.

12. S. Muggleton, M. Bain, J. Hayes-Michie, and D. Michie. An experimental comparison of human and machine learning formalisms. In *Proc. Sixth Int. Workshop on Machine Learning*, pages 113–118. Morgan Kaufmann, 1989.

13. U. Pompe and I. Kononenko. Naive Bayesian classifier within ILP-R. In L. De Raedt, editor, *Proc. of the 5th Int. Workshop on Inductive Logic Programming*, pages 417–436. Dept. of Computer Science, Katholieke Universiteit Leuven, 1995.

14. R. Rymon. Search through systematic set enumeration. In *Proc. Third Int. Conf. on Knowledge Representation and Reasoning*, pages 539–550. Morgan Kaufmann, 1992.

15. M. Sebag. A stochastic simple similarity. In D. Page, editor, *Proc. of the 8th Int. Conference on Inductive Logic Programming*, LNAI 1446, pages 95–105. Springer-Verlag, 1998.

16. A. Srinivasan, S. H. Muggleton, R. D. King, and M. J. E. Sternberg. Mutagenesis: ILP experiments in a non-determinate biological domain. In S. Wrobel, editor, *Proc. of the 4th Int. Workshop on Inductive Logic Programming*, GMD-Studien 237, pages 217–232, 1994.

17. J.-D. Zucker and J.-G. Ganascia. Learning structurally indeterminate clauses. In D. Page, editor, *Proc. of the 8th Int. Conference on Inductive Logic Programming*, LNAI 1446, pages 235–244. Springer-Verlag, 1998.

Sorted Downward Refinement: Building Background Knowledge into a Refinement Operator for Inductive Logic Programming

Alan M. Frisch

Intelligent Systems Group, Department of Computer Science,
University of York, York YO10 5DD, United Kingdom
frisch@cs.york.ac.uk
http://www.cs.york.ac.uk/~frisch

Abstract. Since its inception, the field of inductive logic programming has been centrally concerned with the use of background knowledge in induction. Yet, surprisingly, no serious attempts have been made to account for background knowledge in refinement operators for clauses, even though such operators are one of the most important, prominent and widely-used devices in the field. This paper shows how a sort theory, which encodes taxonomic knowledge, can be built into a downward, subsumption-based refinement operator for clauses.

1 Introduction

Since its inception, the field of inductive logic programming (ILP) has been centrally concerned with the use of background knowledge in induction. Yet, surprisingly, no serious attempts have been made to account for background knowledge in refinement operators for clauses, even though such operators are one of the most important, prominent and widely-used devices in the field.

As a first step to developing methods for incorporating background knowledge into refinement, this paper develops a downward refinement operator for clauses into which is built a simple form of background knowledge—a sort theory, which encodes taxonomic knowledge. The approach to achieving this is straightforward. The clauses in the space of refinements are sorted in that each variable is associated with a sort and the variable ranges over only elements in that sort. The background knowledge that is built into refinement is a theory stating how sorts are related and what objects belong to what sorts. The background knowledge is incorporated into subsumption, which underlies the downward refinement operator, in one simple way: by restricting attention to those substitutions that are well-sorted in that the term substituted for a variable denotes an object that belongs to the sort associated with the variable. The development of a sorted downward refinement operator based on this new subsumption relation follows the same lines used by Nienhuys-Cheng and De Wolf [6] to develop an unsorted refinement operator based on unsorted subsumption.

The idea of building a theory into a system through its mechanisms for instantiation has been well explored and exploited in automated deduction. And a very general definition of instantiation with built-in theories has been presented by Frisch and Page [4]. I conjecture that it is possible for ILP systems to also benefit greatly from using instantiation with built-in theories. Frisch and Page [3, 8, 7] have already explored this idea in the context of generalisation. This paper takes a first step towards exploring this idea in the context of refinement.

2 Sorted Logic

The logical language used in this paper is a very simple sorted logic. It is almost identical to ordinary first-order predicate calculus; syntactically it provides some simple extensions and semantically it uses the same kind of models.

In addition to the usual function and predicate symbols, the lexicon of the sorted language contains a disjoint set of sort symbols. Typographically, sort symbols are written entirely in small capitals as such: MAMMAL. Semantically, a sort symbol, like a monadic predicate symbol, denotes a subset of the domain, called a sort.

The sorted clauses with which refinement works are constructed in the same way as ordinary clauses except that sorted variables are used instead of ordinary variables. A sorted variable is a pair, $x{:}\tau$, where x is a variable name and τ is a sort symbol. For example, $x{:}\text{DOG}$ is a sorted variable. To avoid confusion I never write a formula containing two distinct variables that have the same variable name. That is, no formula contains both $x{:}\tau$ and $x{:}\tau'$ where τ and τ' are distinct. τ and ω are used as meta-linguistic symbols that always stand for sort symbols.

Semantically, a sorted variable ranges over only the subset of the domain denoted by its sort symbol. The simplest way to define the semantics of universally-quantified sorted sentences is in terms of their equivalence to ordinary sentences: $\forall x{:}\tau\ \phi$ is logically equivalent to $\forall x\ \neg\tau(x) \vee \phi'$, where ϕ' is the result of substituting x for all free occurrences of $x{:}\tau$ in ϕ. The formula that results from removing all sorted variables from a formula ϕ by rewriting with this equivalence is called the *normalisation* of ϕ and is denoted by ϕ^N. So, for example, the normalisation of $\forall x{:}\text{MAN}\ \forall y{:}\text{BLONDE}\ Loves(x,y) \vee Loves(y,x)$ is $\forall x,y\ \neg Man(x) \vee \neg Blonde(y) \vee Loves(x,y)) \vee Loves(y,x)$, and the two sentences are, by definition, logically equivalent. Notice that the normalisation of a sorted clause is itself a clause; such a clause is referred to as a *normalised clause*.

The background knowledge that is to be built into the instantiation, subsumption and refinement of sorted clauses is known as a sort theory. A sort theory is a *finite* set of sentences that express relationships among the sorts and the sortal behaviour of the functions. Sentences of the sort theory are constructed like ordinary sentences of first-order predicate calculus except that they contain no ordinary predicate symbols; in their place are sort symbols acting as monadic predicate symbols. Hence, every atomic formula of the sort theory is of the form $\tau(t)$, where τ is a sort symbol and t is an ordinary term. Formulas of the sort theory are assigned truth values in the usual Tarskian manner.

To keep matters simple, we restrict the form of the sort theory. In particular each sentence of the sort theory will have one of only two forms: function sentences and subsort sentences. Each *function sentence* is of the form

$$\forall x_1, \ldots, x_n \ \tau_1(x_1) \wedge \cdots \wedge \tau_n(x_n) \to \tau(f(x_1, \ldots, x_n)) \ ,$$

where each x_i is a distinct variable and f is an n-ary function symbol. If $n = 0$, then f is a constant symbol and the form of the function sentence is simply $\tau(f)$. Each *subsort sentence* is of the form $\forall x \ \tau_1(x) \to \tau_2(x)$. We can think of the subsort sentences of the sort theory as forming a graph where each sort symbol that occurs in some subsort sentence is a node and there is an arc directed from τ_2 to τ_1 if and only if the sort theory contains the formula $\forall x \ \tau_1(x) \to \tau_2(x)$. We require that the sort theory is such that its graph is acyclic and singly rooted. We shall assume that the root is the sort symbol UNIV.

Notice that every sentence of a sort theory is a notational variant of a definite clause. We will sometimes treat these sentences as clauses, such as when we apply the resolution rule of inference to them.

Where ϕ is any formula (ordinary or sorted), we say that the *universal closure* of ϕ is the result of universally quantifying all free variables in ϕ, and we denote the universal closure of ϕ by $\overline{\forall}\phi$.

Let Σ be a sort theory. We say that sentence ϕ_1 Σ-*entails* sentence ϕ_2 if and only if $\Sigma \cup \{\phi_1\} \models \phi_2$, and we write $\phi_1 \models_\Sigma \phi_2$. Two clauses—sorted or unsorted—are said to be Σ-*equivalent* if their universal closures Σ-entail each other. A *quasi-ordering*, or *preorder*, is a relation that is reflexive and transitive. It is straightforward to verify that $\models_\Sigma$ is a quasi-ordering on sentences.

Notationally, throughout the paper θ and σ always denote substitutions, ϕ always denotes a formula and Σ always denotes a sort theory. C and D always denote sorted clauses unless otherwise stated. To denote a normalised clause, C^N and D^N are usually used. Sorted and unsorted clauses are treated as sets, though they are sometimes written as disjunctions. If C is a sorted or unsorted clause—that is, a set of literals—and L is a literal, then $C \vee L$ is a clause with literals $C \cup \{L\}$.

3 Sorted Substitution and Sorted Subsumption

Intuitively, a substitution is a sorted substitution if the term substituted for each variable respects the sort associated with the variable. More precisely, a substitution θ is said to be a *sorted substitution* or Σ-*substitution* if for every variable $x{:}\tau$, it is the case that $\Sigma \models \overline{\forall} \ \tau(t)$ where t is $(x{:}\tau)\theta$. A sorted clause C is Σ-*more general* than another D if there is Σ-substitution θ such that $C\theta = D$. In this case we write $C \geq_\Sigma D$ and say that D is a Σ-*instance* of C.

Frisch [2] shows that the identity substitution is a Σ-substitution and that the composition of two Σ-substitutions is also a Σ-substitution. It follows from this that $\geq_\Sigma$ is a quasi-ordering.

If σ is a renaming substitution then θ and $\theta \cdot \sigma$ are said to be *variants*. Also, C and $C\sigma$ are said to be variants.

The following theorems provide justification for the given definition of Σ-substitution by telling us that they have the significant properties that ordinary substitutions have, hence we hope that this will lead sorted subsumption to have many of the important properties of ordinary subsumption.

Theorem 1 (Sorted Herbrand Theorem [2]). *Let C be a set of sorted clauses and let $C_{\Sigma gr}$ be a set containing every ground clause that is a Σ-instance of some clause in C. Then $\Sigma \cup \overline{\forall} C$ is satisfiable if and only if $C_{\Sigma gr}$ is.*

This Herbrand Theorem, like the ordinary Herbrand Theorem, relates the satisfiability of non-ground clauses to the satisfiability of ground clauses. Notice that this Herbrand theorem relates $\Sigma \cup C$, which contains a sort theory and sorted variables, to $C_{\Sigma gr}$, which contains no sort theory and no sorted variables (hence no sort symbols). Thus, for purposes of satisfiability, *all* that is relevant about sorts has been built into the process of taking Σ-instances.

For ordinary clauses we know that instantiation is a stronger relation than entailment, but that over the set of ordinary atoms, the two relations are the same. The corresponding result holds for sorted clauses and sorted atoms.

Theorem 2 ([4]). *If $C \geq_\Sigma D$ then $\overline{\forall} C \models_\Sigma \overline{\forall} D$. Furthermore, if C and D are sorted atoms, then the converse holds.*

Let us now turn our attention to sorted subsumption and begin by recalling the definition of ordinary (unsorted) subsumption: unsorted clause E *subsumes* unsorted clause F, written $E \succeq F$, if and only if $E\theta \subseteq F$ for some substitution θ. The definition of sorted subsumption is identical, except that only sorted substitutions are considered: sorted clause C Σ-*subsumes* sorted clause D, written $C \succeq_\Sigma D$, if and only if $C\theta \subseteq D$ for some Σ-substitution θ.

Since both the $\subseteq$ and $\geq_\Sigma$ relations are quasi-orders, it follows that the $\succeq_\Sigma$ relation is also a quasi-order. Corresponding to the well-known result that subsumption implies entailment, Σ-subsumption implies Σ-entailment:

Theorem 3. *If $C \succeq_\Sigma D$ then $\overline{\forall} C \models_\Sigma \overline{\forall} D$.*

Proof. If $C \succeq_\Sigma D$ then, by definition $C\theta \subseteq D$ for some Σ-substitution θ. From Theorem 2, we have $\overline{\forall} C \models_\Sigma \overline{\forall}(C\theta)$. Since $C\theta \subseteq D$, the semantic definition of disjunction tells us that $\overline{\forall}(C\theta) \models_\Sigma \overline{\forall} D$. From the previous two statements and the transitivity of $\models_\Sigma$, we have that $\overline{\forall} C \models_\Sigma \overline{\forall} D$. $\qquad\square$

4 The Building Blocks of Sorted Substitution

The definition of sorted substitution has a semantic component. This section presents two purely-syntactic characterisations. The first characterisation shows how sorted substitutions can be made up by composing elementary sorted substitutions, which themselves are syntactically defined. The second characterisation is based on inference rules that operate on normalised clauses. Because these inference rules have a correspondence to elementary sorted instantiation we call them *ESI inference rules*. After defining elementary substitutions and the ESI inference rules, this section proves their correspondence and then proves that they provide a sound and complete basis for sorted substitution. Though the ESI inference rules are not used in subsequent sections, they are central to this section's proof of the completeness of elementary sorted substitutions and they provide insight into the close relationship between elementary sorted substitutions and well-known inference rules.

Definition 1 (Elementary Σ-Substitution). *An elementary Σ-substitution for C is*

1. $\{x{:}\tau \mapsto y{:}\tau\}$, *where $x{:}\tau$ and $y{:}\tau$ are distinct variables that occur in C.*
2. $\{z{:}\tau \mapsto f(x_1{:}\tau_1, \ldots, x_n{:}\tau_n)\}$ *where $z{:}\tau$ occurs in C and $\bar{\forall}\,\tau_1(x_1) \wedge \cdots \wedge \tau_n(x_n) \rightarrow \tau(f(x_1, \ldots, x_n))$ is a variant of a function sentence in Σ such that $x_1{:}\tau_1, \ldots, x_n{:}\tau_n$ do not occur in C.*
3. $\{x{:}\tau_1 \mapsto y{:}\tau_2\}$, *where $x{:}\tau_1$ occurs in C and $\forall x\, \tau_2(x) \rightarrow \tau_1(x)$ is a variant of a subsort sentence in Σ such that $y{:}\tau_2$ does not occur in C.*

Definition 2 (ESI Inference Rules and Derivations). *The ESI inference rules are:*

1. Binary sort factorisation: *Let C^N be a normalised clause whose form is $\neg\tau_1(x_1) \vee \cdots \vee \neg\tau_n(x_n) \vee C'$, where C' is a clause containing only ordinary predicates symbols. For all $1 \leq i, j \leq n$, such that $\tau_i = \tau_j$ we say that $C^N\{x_i \mapsto x_j\}$ is a binary sort factor of C^N.*
2. Binary f-resolution: *If C^N is a normalised clause and ϕ is a function sentence, then any binary resolvent of C^N and ϕ is a binary f-resolvent of C^N and ϕ.*
3. Binary ss-resolution: *If C^N is a normalised clause and ϕ is a subsort sentence, then any binary resolvent of C^N and ϕ is a binary ss-resolvent of C^N and ϕ.*

A finite sequence of unsorted clauses, $C_0, \ldots, C_n$, is an ESI-derivation of C_n from $\{C_0\} \cup \Sigma$ if for all $1 \leq i \leq n$, C_i can be obtained by applying an ESI inference rule to C_{i-1} and a sentence in Σ.

Proposition 1. *The resolvent of a normalised clause with a clause from a sort theory is always a normalised clause. Furthermore, an ESI-inference rule applied to a normalised clause always produces a normalised clause.*

The operation of the three types of elementary substitutions in the domain of sorted clauses corresponds directly to the operation of the three inference rules in the domain of normalised clauses.

Theorem 4 (Correspondence Theorem). *Let C and D be sorted clauses. Then:*

1. $D = C\theta$ for some θ, a type 1 elementary Σ-substitution for C, if and only if D^N is a binary sorted factor of C^N.
2. D is a variant of $C\theta$ for some θ, a type 2 elementary Σ-substitution for C, if and only if D^N is a variant of a binary f-resolvent of C^N and some function sentence of Σ.
3. D is a variant of $C\theta$ for some θ, a type 3 elementary Σ-substitution for C, if and only if D^N is a variant of a binary ss-resolvent of C^N and some subsort sentence of Σ.

Proof. Let $y_1{:}\tau_1, \ldots, y_n{:}\tau_n$ be the variables of C and let C^N be $\neg\tau_1(y_1) \vee \cdots \vee \neg\tau_n(y_n) \vee C'$.

1. Distinct variables $x{:}\tau$ and $y{:}\tau$ occur in C if and only if $\tau(x)$ and $\tau(y)$ are distinct atoms that appear in C^N. Thus $\theta = \{x{:}\tau \mapsto y{:}\tau\}$ is a type 1 elementary Σ-substitution for C if and only if C^N has a binary sort factor using substitution $\theta' = \{x \mapsto y\}$. The reader can verify that this sort factor is $(C\theta)^N$.
2. For each function sentence $\phi \in \Sigma$ we show the correspondence holds between the type 2 elementary Σ-substitutions using ϕ and the binary f-resolutions using ϕ. Let $\phi' = \overline{\forall}\, \tau_1(x_1) \wedge \cdots \wedge \tau_n(x_n) \rightarrow \tau(f(x_1, \ldots, x_n))$ be a variant of ϕ such that $x_1{:}\tau_1, \ldots, x_n{:}\tau_n$ do not occur in C. Then $z{:}\tau$ occurs in C if and only if $\tau(z)$ occurs in C^N. Thus $\theta = \{z{:}\tau \mapsto f(x_1{:}\tau_1, \ldots, x_n{:}\tau_n)\}$ is a type 2 elementary Σ-substitution for C if and only if there is a binary f-resolution of ϕ' and C^N upon the atom $\tau(z)$. The reader can verify that the resolvent is $(C\theta)^N$.
3. For each subsort sentence $\phi \in \Sigma$ we show the correspondence holds between the type 3 elementary Σ-substitutions using ϕ and the binary ss-resolutions using ϕ. Let $\phi' = \forall x\, \tau_2(x) \rightarrow \tau_1(x)$ be a variant of ϕ such that $x{:}\tau_2$ does not occur in C. Then $x{:}\tau_1$ occurs in C if and only if $\neg\tau_1(x)$ occurs in C^N. Thus $\theta = \{x{:}\tau_1 \mapsto y{:}\tau_2\}$ is a type 3 elementary Σ-substitution for C if and only if there is a binary ss-resolution of ϕ' and C^N upon the atom $\tau_1(x)$ The reader can verify that the resolvent is $(C\theta)^N$. $\quad\Box$

The soundness of elementary Σ-substitutions follows directly from the definitions of Σ-substitution and elementary Σ-substitution. Then, the soundness of ESI-derivations follows immediately from the soundness of elementary substitutions and the Correspondence Theorem (Theorem 4).

Theorem 5 (Soundness of Elementary Σ-Substitutions). *Every elementary Σ-substitution is a Σ-substitution.*

Corollary 1 (Soundness of ESI-Derivations). *D is a Σ-instance of C if there is an ESI inference rule that in one step derives D^N from $\{C^N\} \cup \Sigma$.*

We now turn our attention to the task of proving the completeness of ESI-derivations and, hence, also elementary substitutions. We first introduce some useful notation and concepts and prove two lemmas before turning to the main proof.

Let ϕ be any formula with n *top-level term occurrences*, that is, n occurrences of terms as arguments to predicates. Number the occurrences from 1 to n in left-to-right order, as they appear in ϕ. We use $\phi[t_1, \ldots, t_n]$ to denote a formula whose ith top-level term occurrence is t_i, for all $1 \leq i \leq n$. Subsequently we use $\phi[t_1', \ldots, t_n']$ to denote the formula that results from replacing the ith top-level term occurrence in $\phi[t_1, \ldots, t_n]$ with t_i', for all $1 \leq i \leq n$.

We establish the completeness of ESI-derivations by showing their correspondence to SLD-style derivations. The SLD derivations we use are of the more general form presented by Nienhuys-Cheng and De Wolf [6]. In this form the top clause and all derived clauses may be any Horn clause, though the side clauses must still be definite and resolution must still be upon the positive literal of the side clause. In this general setting, the subsumption theorem does not hold if a fixed selection function is used;[1] so we shall ignore selection functions and, to avoid confusion, call such derivations *LD-derivations*. Thus, in an LD derivation any negative literal of a center clause may be resolved upon.

Lemma 1. *If C and D are sorted atoms such that $C^N \succeq D^N$ then some variant of D^N can be derived from C^N using (zero or more applications of) only sorted binary factoring.*

Proof. Let C^N be $\neg\tau(x_1) \vee \cdots \vee \neg\tau_n(x_n) \vee Head$. Then, since D is atomic, D^N can be written as

$$T \vee \neg\tau_1(x_1\theta) \vee \cdots \vee \neg\tau_n(x_n\theta) \vee Head\theta \,, \tag{1}$$

where θ is a substitution and T is a possibly empty disjunction of negative sort literals, none of which are $\tau_i(x_i\theta)$ $(1 \leq i \leq n)$. Then θ must map every x_i $(1 \leq i \leq n)$ to a variable, otherwise (1) would not be a normalised clause. Thus, either θ is a renaming substitution, or it "collapses" two or more variables in the sense that it maps them to the same variable. Whatever collapses it does can be considered as a sequence of collapses each of which collapses exactly two distinct variables. Consider a collapse of two distinct variables, x_i and x_j. Then τ_i and τ_j must be the same, otherwise (1) would not be a normalised clause. Now observe that this collapse of x_i and x_j is a variant of the collapse produced by applying binary sorted factorisation to the literals $\neg\tau_i(x_i)$ and $\neg\tau_j(x_j)$. Hence the sequence of collapses can be produced by a sequence of applications of binary sorted factorisations, and the effect of applying θ to C^N can be achieved by a series of zero or more binary sorted factorings followed by the application of a renaming substitution. By Proposition 1 $C^N\theta$ must be a normalised clause; therefore T must be empty, otherwise (1) would not be a normalised clause. Thus (1) can be produced from C^N by application of a series of zero or more binary sorted factorings followed by the application of a renaming substitution. $\quad\square$

Lemma 2. *Let C and D be sorted atoms. Then every LD derivation of D^N from $\{C^N\} \cup \Sigma$ is an ESI derivation of D^N from $\{C^N\} \cup \Sigma$.*

---

[1] This point is not stated explicitly by Nienhuys-Cheng and De Wolf.

Proof. Note that D^N, C^N and all members of Σ are definite clauses. Let P be the predicate symbol in the positive literal of D^N. Also note that in an LD derivation the positive literals of all derived clauses and of the top clause are all the same. Thus the top clause must be C^N as no clause in Σ contains P. And all of the other input clauses to the derivation must be members of Σ. Hence every resolution in the LD derivation is a binary ss-resolution or a binary f-resolution. □

Theorem 6 (Completeness of ESI-Derivations). *If $C \geq_\Sigma D$ then there is an ESI derivation of a variant of D^N from $\{C^N\} \cup \Sigma$.*

Proof. Let us write C as a disjunction of distinct sorted literals, $C_1 \vee \cdots \vee C_n$— which we shall call $C^\vee[t_1, ..., t_k]$. Then $C \geq_\Sigma D$ if and only there exists a disjunction, $D_1 \vee \cdots \vee D_n$—which we shall call $D^\vee[t'_1, ..., t'_k]$—and a Σ-substitution, θ, such that $D = \{D_i \mid 1 \leq i \leq n\}$ and $C_i\theta = D_i$ for all $1 \leq i \leq n$. Let P be a predicate symbol of arity k that does not appear in C, D or Σ. Observe that $D^\vee[t'_1, ..., t'_k] = C^\vee[t_1\theta, ..., t_k\theta]$. Thus $P(t_1, ..., t_k)\theta = P(t'_1, ..., t'_k)$, which, from the work of Frisch and Page [4], implies that $\bar{\forall} P(t_1, ..., t_k) \models_\Sigma \bar{\forall} P(t'_1, ..., t'_k)$. This, in turn, implies that $\bar{\forall} P(t_1, ..., t_k)^N \models_\Sigma \bar{\forall} P(t'_1, ..., t'_k)^N$. Since Σ, $P(t_1, ..., t_k)^N$, and $P(t'_1, ..., t'_k)^N$ are all Horn clauses, the subsumption theorem for LD-derivations [6] tells us that there is a definite clause A that is LD-derivable from $\{P(t_1, ..., t_k)^N\} \cup \Sigma$ such that A subsumes $P(t'_1, ..., t'_k)^N$. From Lemmas 1 and 2 we know that this implies that there is a definite clause A that is ESI-derivable from $\{P(t_1, ..., t_k)^N\} \cup \Sigma$ and a variant of $P(t'_1, ..., t'_k)^N$ that is ESI-derivable from $\{A\} \cup \Sigma$. Hence, there is an ESI derivation of a variant of $P(t'_1, ..., t'_k)^N$ from $\{P(t_1, ..., t_k)^N\} \cup \Sigma$. Now let us replace each clause in this derivation, which is of the form $P(s_1, ..., s_k)^N$, with $C^\vee[s_1, ..., s_k]^N$. The resulting derivation is the desired ESI derivation—from $\{C^N\} \cup \Sigma$ to a variant of D^N. □

The completeness of elementary substitutions follows immediately from the completeness of ESI-derivations and the Correspondence Theorem (Theorem 4).

Corollary 2 (Completeness of Elementary Substitutions). *If $C \geq_\Sigma D$ then there exists a finite sequence of clauses, $C_0, ..., C_n$ such that $C_0 = C$, clause C_n is a variant of D, and for every $1 \leq i \leq n$ there is some σ, an elementary Σ-substitution for C_{i-1}, such that $C_{i-1}\sigma = C_i$.*

5 Sorted Downward Refinement

A downward refinement operator in general is used to generate specialisations of a formula; the particular downward operator introduced by this paper operates on sorted clauses and it produces sorted clauses that are specialisations in the sense that they are Σ-subsumed by the clause operated on.

Starting with a set of one or more initial clauses, a refinement operator can be used repeatedly to generate more clauses to add to the set. This defines a set of clauses, called a refinement space, that a learning algorithm can search in an attempt to find a suitable hypothesis.

An important question that needs to be addressed is what formulas would we like to be in the refinement space. That is, what formulas make reasonable hypotheses? In the unsorted setting, a common and simple answer to this question is that the space should include every clause subsumed by an initial clause. But in the case of sorted clauses the question is trickier because not every clause is, in a certain sense, sensible. The answer we shall adopt here is that clauses in the refinement space should contain only terms that conform to the sort theory in the the sense that they are *well sorted*, as we now define.

Definition 3 (Well Sorted Terms and Clauses). *Term t has sort τ with respect to Σ if $\Sigma \models \bar{\forall}\tau(t)$. In addition, t is well sorted with respect to Σ if for some sort symbol τ term t has sort τ with respect to Σ. By extension, we say that a clause is* well sorted *with respect to Σ if every term that occurs in it is well sorted with respect to Σ. Where Σ is obvious, we shall simply say "well sorted."*

A number of simple consequences of this definition are worth noting, and we do so without proof:

Proposition 2. *If Σ is an arbitrary sort theory then:*

1. *The empty clause is well sorted with respect to Σ.*
2. *With respect to Σ, a variable, $x{:}\tau$, has sort τ and is therefore well sorted.*
3. *$f(t_1, \ldots, t_n)$ has sort τ with respect to Σ if and only if Σ entails some function sentence of the form $\forall x_1, \ldots, x_n\ \tau_1(x_1) \wedge \cdots \wedge \tau_n(x_n) \rightarrow \tau(f(x_1, \ldots, x_n))$ such that each t_i has sort τ_i, for $1 \leq i \leq n$.*
4. *If $f(t_1, \ldots, t_n)$ is well sorted with respect to Σ, then so are $t_1, \ldots, t_n$.*

Point 4, which is an immediate consequence of point 3, is useful for simplifying the test for well sortedness.

More importantly, the set of well-sorted formulas has the property that it is closed under the application of sorted substitutions.

Theorem 7. *If t is a term that has sort τ with respect to Σ and θ is a Σ-substitution then $t\theta$ has sort τ with respect to Σ. Thus if e is a term or clause that is well sorted with respect to Σ, then so is $e\theta$.*

Proof. This is proved by induction on the structure of t. In the base case, t is a constant or a variable. In the case in which t is a constant, the theorem holds trivially since $t = t\theta$. In the case in which t is a variable, let $x{:}\omega$ be t and let s be $(x{:}\omega)\theta$. Since θ is a Σ-substitution, by definition $\Sigma \models \bar{\forall}\omega(s)$. Thus, by Definition 3, s, which is equal to $t\theta$, has sort τ with respect to Σ.

For the inductive case, let t be $f(t_1, \ldots, t_n)$ and assume (inductive hypothesis) that the theorem holds for for $t_1, \ldots, t_n$. By point 3 of Proposition 2 Σ entails some function sentence ϕ of the form $\forall x_1, \ldots, x_n\ \tau_1(x_1) \wedge \cdots \wedge \tau_n(x_n) \rightarrow \tau(f(x_1, \ldots, x_n))$ such that each t_i has sort τ_i, for $1 \leq i \leq n$. Then by the inductive hypothesis each $t_i\theta$ has sort τ_i, for $1 \leq i \leq n$. This means that Σ entails $\forall \tau_1(t_1\theta) \wedge \cdots \wedge \tau_n(t_n\theta)$. And since Σ entails ϕ, it must also entail $\bar\forall\, \tau(f(t_1\theta,\ldots,t_n\theta))$. Thus, by the Definition 3, $t\theta$, which is $f(t_1\theta,\ldots,t_n\theta)$, has sort τ. $\qquad\square$

Consequently, when a refinement operator generates a new term by applying a Σ-substitution to a well sorted term, there is no need to test that the resulting term is well sorted.

Definition 4 (Sorted Downward Refinement). *If C is a sorted clause, its downward Σ-refinement, written $\rho_\Sigma(C)$, is the smallest set such that:*

1. *For each θ that is an elementary Σ-substitution for C, $\rho_\Sigma(C)$ contains $C\theta$.*
2. *For each n-ary predicate symbol P, let x_1:UNIV, $\ldots$, x_n:UNIV be distinct variables not appearing in C. Then $\rho_\Sigma(C)$ contains $C \vee P(x_1:\text{UNIV},\ldots,x_n:\text{UNIV})$ and $C \vee \neg P(x_1:\text{UNIV},\ldots,x_n:\text{UNIV})$.*

$\rho_\Sigma^*(C)$ is the smallest set such that $C \in \rho_\Sigma^*(C)$ and if $D \in \rho_\Sigma^*(C)$ then $\rho_\Sigma(D) \subseteq \rho_\Sigma^*(C)$.

We now present a simple lemma and then use it to show that this downward refinement operator has the desired properties.

Lemma 3. *If $C \geq_\Sigma D$ then $\rho_\Sigma^*(C)$ contains a variant of D.*

Proof. Since ρ_Σ can apply any elementary Σ-substitution, this lemma is an immediate consequence of Theorem 2. $\qquad\square$

Theorem 8 (Sorted Downward Refinement Theorem). *ρ_Σ is*

- *Correct: If $D \in \rho_\Sigma(C)$ then $C \succeq_\Sigma D$ and if C is well sorted with respect to Σ then so is D;*
- *Finite: If the set of predicate symbols in the language is finite then $\rho_\Sigma(C)$ is finite; and*
- *Complete: If C and D are well sorted clauses with respect to Σ and $C \succeq_\Sigma D$ then some variant of D is a member of $\rho_\Sigma^*(C)$.*

Proof. Correct: Consider as two cases the two forms of downward refinement given in the definition of downward refinement (Definition 4). If D is generated in case 1 then $D = C\theta$ for some elementary Σ-substitution θ. Hence, by the soundness of elementary sorted substitutions (Theorem 5), $C \succeq_\Sigma D$ and, by Theorem 7, if C is well sorted with respect to Σ then so is D.

If D is generated in case 2, then $C \subseteq D$ so, by definition, $C \succeq_\Sigma D$. If C is well sorted with respect to Σ then so is D since every term in D is either in C or is of the form x:UNIV—which is well sorted by point 2 of Proposition 2.

Finite: Let v be the number of variables occurring in C; s be the number of subsort sentences in Σ; f be the number of function sentences in Σ; and p be the number of predicate symbols in the language. Case 1 of the definition of downward refinement produces a refinement by applying an elementary Σ-substitution to C. The number of elementary Σ-substitutions for C of type 1, 2 and 3 is bounded by $v(v-1)/2$, $f \cdot v$ and $s \cdot v$ respectively. The number of refinements produced by case 2 of the definition of downward refinement is $2p$.

Complete: Let θ be a Σ-substitution such that $C\theta \subseteq D$. From Lemma 3 we know that $C\theta$ is a variant of a member of $\rho_\Sigma^*(C)$. Below we shall show that D is a variant of a member of $\rho_\Sigma^*(C\theta)$. From these two facts we can conclude that D is a variant of a member of $\rho_\Sigma^*(C)$.

To show that D is a variant of a member of $\rho_\Sigma^*(C\theta)$ we show that ρ_Σ^* can extend a clause by adding any one well sorted literal; hence it can extend a clause by adding any finite number of well sorted literals. More precisely we show that if A is a well sorted clause and L is a well sorted literal then $A \vee L$ is a variant of a member of $\rho_\Sigma^*(A)$. Let L be of the form $P(t_1, \ldots, t_n)$ (or $\neg P(t_1, \ldots, t_n)$) and let L' be $P(x_1:\text{UNIV}, \ldots, x_n:\text{UNIV})$ (or $\neg P(x_1:\text{UNIV}, \ldots, x_n:\text{UNIV})$), where $x_1, \ldots, x_n$ are variable names that do not occur in A. Observe that L'—and, hence, $A \vee L'$—is well sorted with respect to Σ and that $A \vee L$ is a Σ-instance of $A \vee L'$. Hence, from Lemma 3, $A \vee L$ is a variant of a member of $\rho_\Sigma(A \vee L')$. From case 2 of the definition of downward refinement (Definition 4) $A \vee L' \in \rho_\Sigma(A)$. From these last two sentences we reach our desired conclusion: $A \vee L$ is a variant of a member of $\rho_\Sigma^*(A)$. $\qquad\square$

6   A Comparison of Sorted and Unsorted Refinement

This section compares the sorted downward refinement operator ρ_Σ defined in this paper with the unsorted downward refinement operator ρ_L presented by Nienhuys-Cheng and De Wolf [6] and credited to Laird [5]. This comparison is conducted by considering ρ_Σ as operating on the set of normalised clauses (to be precise, $\rho_\Sigma(C^N) = \{D^N \mid D \in \rho_\Sigma(C)\}$) and ρ_L as operating on unsorted clauses whose predicate symbols are either ordinary predicates symbols or sort symbols.

In a couple of ways ρ_Σ generates a smaller space than does ρ_L. If C is a well sorted clause, then every member of $\rho_\Sigma(C^N)$ is the normalisation of a well sorted clause. However this is not the case for ρ_L: $\rho_L(C^N)$ may contain clauses that are the normalisation of no sorted clause or of a sorted clause that is not well sorted. Furthermore, it can be shown that every member of $\rho_\Sigma(C^N)$ is Σ-equivalent to some member of $\rho_L(C^N)$. However the containment doesn't hold the other way.

Another difference between the two refinement operators is that ρ_Σ takes account of Σ in the order that it generates clauses, whereas ρ_L does not. To illustrate this let Σ be $\{\forall x \; \text{ODD}(x) \to \text{INTEGER}(x)\}$, let C^N be $P(x) \vee \neg \text{INTEGER}(x)$, let D^N be $P(x) \vee \neg \text{ODD}(x)$, and let D' be $P(x) \vee \neg \text{INTEGER}(x) \vee \neg \text{ODD}(x)$. Observe that $\rho_L^*(C^N)$ contains D^N but $\rho_\Sigma^*(C^N)$ does not contain D^N—though it does contain the Σ-equivalent clause D'. Thus the ρ_L space fails to recognise the equivalence of D^N and D' and locates them in different places in the refinement space.

7 Further Work and Conclusions

Of the numerous issues that require and deserve further study, two seem more immediate than the others. First, the relationship between the sorted subsumption relation $\succeq_\Sigma$ and Buntine's [1] generalised subsumption relation is a very close one and deserves explication. Second, in certain cases some of the immediate sorted refinements of a sorted clause may be Σ-instances of others. This redundancy is undesirable and methods for eliminating it need to be investigated.

To conclude the reader is asked to observe the degree to which this paper's development of sorted subsumption and sorted refinement parallels that of the unsorted case except with sorted substitution replacing unsorted substitution. Though proving the completeness of elementary sorted substitutions requires a fair amount of new mechanism, this paper's approach to sorted refinement presents no surprises. And *that* is the point. One can build background knowledge into subsumption and refinement by building it into substitution—and nowhere else. And, unlike other routes, the approach to doing so is straightforward.

Acknowledgements

Most of this paper was written while I was a visiting researcher in the Meme Media Laboratory of Hokkaido University, Japan. I thank Akihiro Yamamoto for helpful discussions and for hosting my visit, and the anonymous referees for their comments.

References

1. Wray Buntine. Generalized subsumption and its applications to induction and redundancy. *Artificial Intelligence*, 36(2):149–176, 1988.
2. Alan M. Frisch. The substitutional framework for sorted deduction: Fundamental results on hybrid reasoning. *Artificial Intelligence*, 49:161–198, 1991.
3. Alan M. Frisch and C. David Page Jr. Generalization with taxonomic information. In *Proc. of the Eighth National Conf. on Artificial Intelligence*, pages 755–761, Boston, MA, July 1990.
4. Alan M. Frisch and C. David Page Jr. Building theories into instantiation. In *Proc. of the Fourteenth Int. Joint Conf. on Artificial Intelligence*, pages 1210–1216, Montreal, Canada, August 1995.
5. Philip D. Laird. *Learning from Good and Bad Data*. Kluwer Academic Publishers, Boston, MA, 1988.
6. Shan-Hwei Nienhuys-Cheng and Ronald de Wolf. *Foundations of Inductive Logic Programming*. Springer-Verlag, 1997.
7. C. David Page Jr. *Anti-Unification in Constraint Logics: Foundations and Applications to Learnability in First-Order Logic, to Speed-up Learning, and to Deduction*. PhD thesis, Department of Computer Science, University of Illinois at Urbana-Champaign, 1993.
8. C. David Page Jr. and Alan M. Frisch. Generalization and learnability: A study of constrained atoms. In Stephen H. Muggleton, editor, *Inductive Logic Programming*, chapter 2, pages 29–61. Academic Press, London, 1992.

A Strong Complete Schema for Inductive Functional Logic Programming*

J. Hernández-Orallo   M.J. Ramírez-Quintana

DSIC, UPV, Camino de Vera s/n, 46020 Valencia, Spain.
{jorallo,mramirez}@dsic.upv.es

Abstract. A new IFLP schema is presented as a general framework for the induction of functional logic programs (FLP). Since narrowing (which is the most usual operational semantics of FLP) performs a unification (mgu) followed by a replacement, we introduce two main operators in our IFLP schema: a generalisation and an inverse replacement or intra-replacement, which results in a generic inversion of the transitive property of equality. We prove that this schema is *strong* complete in the way that, given some evidence, it is possible to induce any program which could have generated that evidence. We outline some possible restrictions in order to improve the tractability of the schema. We also show that inverse narrowing is just a special case of our IFLP schema. Finally, a straightforward extension of the IFLP schema to function invention is illustrated.

Keywords: Functional Logic Programming, Inductive Logic Programming, Function Invention, Induction of Auxiliary Functions, Narrowing, Inverse Narrowing.

1 Introduction

Inductive logic programming (ILP) [9] is the branch of machine learning that studies concept learning in a logical framework. Namely, ILP deals with the induction of logic programs (i.e. finite sets of Horn clauses) from examples and background knowledge.

The use of logic programming for learning is mainly based on the idea that logic programs are a single representation for examples, background knowledge and hypotheses. However, logic languages like Prolog (the most representative language of this paradigm) lack some programming facilities such as evaluable and nested functions, types, higher order programming and lazy evaluation. Although these features are well supported by functional languages, they lack the computing power provided by logical variables and unification. Hence, the interest in the integration of both families of languages has grown over the last few years.

Integrated languages fully exploit the facilities of logic programming in a general sense: functions, predicates and equality. One relevant approach [4, 6]

---

* This work has been partially supported by CICYT under grant TIC 98-0445-C03-C1.

to integration is functional logic programming where the programs are logic programs which are augmented with Horn equational theories. A lot of work has been invested in the development of the semantics of integrated languages. Therefore, it has been shown that the main semantic properties of logic programs also hold for functional logic programs (least model, fixpoint semantics) [1][1]. Operational semantics is defined in terms of semantic unification or $\mathcal{E}$-unification [15] (i.e., general unification wrt an equational theory $\mathcal{E}$). Narrowing [5, 14] is a sound and complete $\mathcal{E}$-unification method for theories which satisfy some requirements (such as confluence and termination properties or the absence of extra variables in the condition of the equations). Narrowing can be seen as a combination of resolution from logic programming and term reduction from functional programming. Hence, it is widely accepted that narrowing is the key to describing operational semantics of functional logic languages.

In [3] we have presented a framework for the induction of functional logic programs (IFLP) from (positive and negative) examples. The evidence is composed of equations, and their rhs's are normalised wrt the background knowledge and the theory to be induced. In logic programming, the induction can be made top-down (starting from the most general program and refining it by specialisation) or bottom-up (starting from positive data as a program and generalising it). In the case of functional logic programs, we cannot follow a top-down direction because the examples are equations, and the most general program $X = Y$ would not make the program terminating nor confluent. As a consequence, the kernel of our method was an inverse narrowing mechanism (similar to the inverse resolution operator of ILP) which selects pairs of equations to obtain an equation which is usually more general than the original ones. The starting set of equations is a generalisation of the positive examples which is made by replacing terms by variables at some occurrences. In fact, the algorithm combines inverse narrowing and generalisation in each step. The method is effective, but it is too specific for those cases where auxiliary terms are involved.

Let us show this with an example.

Example 1. Consider the following evidence

$$E^+ = \left\{ \begin{array}{l} e_1^+ : f(a) = r(g(b,b)) \\ e_2^+ : h(a,b) = r(a) \end{array} \right\}$$

and suppose that sufficient negative examples are provided to justify the program

$$P = \left\{ \begin{array}{l} r_1 : h(Y,a) = g(Y,b) \\ r_2 : f(X) = r(h(b,X)) \\ r_3 : h(a,b) = r(a) \end{array} \right\}$$

However, P could never be induced by inverse narrowing. This is because the example e_1^+ directly relates the function symbols f, r and g (we are not considering other constant symbols in the equations), whereas the equations r_1 and r_2 from P define the function f in terms of r and g but through the function h. This last function can be thought of as an auxiliary function in the definition

---

[1] In this paper we do not address any questions related to declarative semantics.

of f. The generalisation step in the inverse narrowing approach does not take this possibility into account since there is no positive evidence that links the symbols f and h nor the symbols h and g.

In this paper, we define a new framework, the IFLP schema, as a general and strong complete framework for solving the IFLP problem. By strong completeness we refer to the capability of inducing *all* possible programs such that the positive examples hold wrt them but the negative examples do not. The term 'strong' is due to the fact that, in this context, weak completeness makes no sense since it is always possible to find a program that covers all the positive examples and none of the negative ones: the positive examples themselves. Other completeness results could be stated in terms of some extra conditions that the program should follow (e.g. Progol). The idea is to generalise the way in which the narrowing relation is inverted to induce theories which use auxiliary functions. The inductive method proposed is closely related to the transitive property of equality. More exactly, we define a new operator that reverses the direction in which transitivity is applied. Then, we prove that the schema is complete in the sense mentioned above. We also show that the IFLP schema is rather general to have inverse narrowing as one of its instances. Finally, we deal with the function invention problem which can be easily formalised in our schema. In this context, we can consider an invented function as an auxiliary function of a new signature that extends the hypothesis language with new functions.

The work is organised as follows. In Section 2, we recall the main concepts of functional logic programming and we formalise the narrowing semantics we focus on. Section 3 reviews the inverse narrowing approach and analyses the way in that theories are induced. This motivates the introduction of new operators to overcome the limitations of inverse narrowing. The IFLP schema is defined in Section 4. The strong completeness of the schema is discussed in Section 5. Section 6 shows that inverse narrowing is an instance of our schema. In Section 7, the setting is easily changed to include function invention. Finally, Section 8 concludes the paper and discusses future work.

2 Preliminaries

We briefly review some basic concepts about equations, Term Rewriting Systems and $\mathcal{E}$-unification. For any concept which is not explicitly defined, the reader may refer to [2, 8, 15].

Let Σ be a set of *function symbols* (or functors) together with their arity[2] and let $\mathcal{X}$ be a countably infinite set of *variables*. Then $\mathcal{T}(\Sigma, \mathcal{X})$ denotes the set of *terms* built from Σ and $\mathcal{X}$. The set of variables occurring in a term t is denoted $Var(t)$. This notation naturally extends to other syntactic objects (like clause, literal, ...). A term t is a *ground term* if $Var(t) = \emptyset$. A *substitution* is defined as a mapping from the set of variables $\mathcal{X}$ into the set of terms $\mathcal{T}(\Sigma, \mathcal{X})$. An *occurrence* u in a term t is represented by a sequence of natural numbers. $O(t)$ and $\bar{O}(t)$

---

[2] We assume that Σ contains at least one constant.

denote the *set of occurrences* and *non-variable occurrences* of t respectively. $t_{|u}$ denotes the *subterm* of t at the occurrence u and $t[t']_u$ denotes the *replacement* of the subterm of t at the occurrence u by the term t'. An equation is an expression of the form $l = r$ where l and r are terms. l is called the left hand side (lhs) of the equation and r is the right hand side (rhs). An equational theory $\mathcal{E}$ (which we call *program*) is a finite set of equational clauses of the form $l = r \Leftarrow e_1, \ldots, e_n$. with $n \geq 0$ where e_i is an equation, $1 \leq i \leq n$. The theory (and the clauses) are called *conditional* if $n > 0$ and *unconditional* if $n = 0$. An equational theory can also be viewed as a (Conditional) Term Rewriting System (CTRS) since the equation in the head is implicitly oriented from left to right and the literals e_i in the body are ordinary non-oriented equations. Given a (C)TRS $\mathcal{R}$, $t \rightarrow_{\mathcal{R}} s$ is a rewrite step if there exists an ocurrence u of t, a rule $l = r \in \mathcal{R}$ and a substitution θ with $t_{|u} = \theta(l)$ and $s = t[\theta(r)]_u$. A term t is said to be in *normal form* wrt $\mathcal{R}$ if there is no term t' with $t \rightarrow_{\mathcal{R}} t'$. We say that an equation $t = s$ is normalized wrt $\mathcal{R}$ if t and s are in normal form. $\mathcal{R}$ is said to be *canonical* if the binary one-step rewriting relation $\rightarrow_{\mathcal{R}}$ is terminating (there is no infinite chain $s_1 \rightarrow_{\mathcal{R}} s_2 \rightarrow_{\mathcal{R}} s_3 \rightarrow_{\mathcal{R}} \ldots$) and confluent ($\forall s_1, s_2, s_3 \in \mathcal{T}(\Sigma, \mathcal{X})$ such that $s_1 \rightarrow_{\mathcal{R}}^* s_2$ and $s_1 \rightarrow_{\mathcal{R}}^* s_3, \exists s \in \mathcal{T}(\Sigma, \mathcal{X})$ such that $s_2 \rightarrow_{\mathcal{R}}^* s$ and $s_3 \rightarrow_{\mathcal{R}}^* s$). An $\mathcal{E}$-unification algorithm defines a procedure for solving an equation $t = s$ within the theory $\mathcal{E}$. Narrowing is a sound and complete method for solving equations wrt canonical programs. Given a program P, a term t *narrows* into a term t' (in symbols $t \stackrel{u, l=r, \theta}{\leadsto}_P t'$ [3]) iff $u \in \bar{O}(t)$, $l = r$ is a new variant of a rule from P, $\theta = mgu(t_{|u}, l)$ and $t' = \theta(t[r]_u)$. We write $t \leadsto_P^n t'$ if t narrows into t' in n narrowing steps.

3 The Inverse Narrowing Approach

In this section, we briefly outline the inverse narrowing approach we have presented in [3]. The algorithm was composed of two operators: Consistent Restricted Generalisation and Inverse Narrowing.

Since we had to ensure posterior satisfiability, the inverse narrowing method began generating all possible restricted generalisations from each positive example which was consistent with both positive and negative examples. It was computed by the Consistent Restricted Generalisation operator.

Definition 1. Consistent Restricted Generalisation CRG
An equation $e = \{l_1 = r_1\}$ is a consistent restricted generalisation (CRG) wrt E^+ and E^- and an existing theory $T = B \cup P$ if and only if e is a restricted generalisation for some equation of E^+ [4] (always oriented left to right) and there does not exist: (1) a narrowing chain using e and T that yields some equation

---

[3] Or simply $t \stackrel{l=r, \theta}{\leadsto}_P t'$ or $t \stackrel{\theta}{\leadsto}_P t'$ if the occurrence or the rule is clear from the context. Also, the subscript P will usually be dropped when clear from the context.

[4] An equation $t = s$ is a restricted generalisation of an equation $r = m$ if $\exists \sigma : \sigma(t) = r \wedge \sigma(s) = m$ and $\forall x (x \in Var(s) \Rightarrow x \in Var(t))$.

of E^-, and (2) a narrowing chain using e and T that yields a different normal form for some lhs different from the rhs which appeared in the equations of E^+.

Secondly, the inverse narrowing operator was defined as an operator that generates an equation from two equations.

Definition 2. Inverse Narrowing

Given a functional logic program P, we say that a term t conversely narrows into a term t', and we write $t \stackrel{u,l=r,\theta}{\leftrightarrow}_P t'$, iff $u \in O(t)$, $l = r$ is a new variant of a rule from P, $\theta = mgu(t_{|u}, r)$ and $t' = \theta(t[l]_u)$. The relation $\leftrightarrow_P$ is called the inverse narrowing relation.

Now, we will concentrate our attention on how the inverse narrowing approach induces equations. Suppose that $s = t$ and $l = r$ are the equations selected by the algorithm, such that $t_{|u}$ unifies with r with $\theta = mgu(t_{|u}, r)$. Then, $s = \theta(t[l]_u)$ and $l = r$ are the two equations induced in an inverse narrowing approach step. It is easy to see the relationship between this algorithm and the transitive property of equality. In what follows, for the sake of legibility, we consider x, y and z to be subterms at the occurrence ϵ. The next rationale is still valid for any other occurrence in a term.

The transitive property is expressed as:

$$x \rightarrow y \wedge y \rightarrow z \Rightarrow x \rightarrow z \ (1)$$

whereas an inverse narrowing approach step can be also represented as:

$$x \rightarrow z \wedge y \rightarrow z \Rightarrow x \rightarrow y \wedge y \rightarrow z \ (2)$$

where $x \rightarrow y$ in (2) is the equation computed by inverse narrowing from $x \rightarrow z$ and $y \rightarrow z$. However, (2) is not a real inversion of transitivity because it begins from two equations (one of the premises and the result) of the formula (1) and it generates its other premise. To have a constructive inversion of the transitivity of equality, the behaviour of the algorithm should be as follows:

$$x \rightarrow z \Rightarrow x \rightarrow y \wedge y \rightarrow z \ (3)$$

where $x \rightarrow y$ and $y \rightarrow z$ are the result of this constructive inverse narrowing. Notice that the term y in the above formula (3) is new. The following schema not only extends the setting to cope with this inverse transitive, but also to cope with inverse replacement. This is the mechanism which will allow us to introduce auxiliary functions in the inductive process.

4 IFLP Schema

Let us denote the set of function symbols of arity ≥ 0 which appear in a program P as Σ_P. In the same way, Σ_{E^+}, or simply Σ^+, denotes the set of function symbols of arity ≥ 0 which appear in the positive evidence E^+.

As we have stated, narrowing is based on a mgu, which is a specialisation, followed by a replacement. It is logical then to base the induction of functional logic programs on an inversion of these deductive operators. Consequently, we introduce two operators: an inverse specialisation, namely a generalisation, and an inverse replacement.

Definition 3. Unrestricted Generalisation (UG)
An equation $e' = \{l' = r'\}$ is an unrestricted generalisation (UG) of an equation $e = \{l = r\}$ if and only if there exists a substitution θ such that $\theta(l') = l$ and $\theta(r') = r$.

Definition 4. Single Intra-Replacement (SIR)
Given an equation $s = t$, choose any occurrence ω of t and any function symbol $F \in \Sigma^+$ to construct a new term q in the following way:
$$q = t[\phi]_\omega$$
where $\phi = F(X_{k,1}, X_{k,2}, \ldots, X_{k,n})$, $n \geq 0$ is the arity of F and $X_{k,i}$ are different fresh variables. The subscript k is used to distinguish these variables from other variables in previous or subsequent uses of this operator.

As output, the SIR operator produces a first equation D_k as: $\quad s = q$, *and a second equation E_k as:* $\quad q_{|\omega} = t_{|\omega}$

The first result from this definition is that D_k and E_k make true that $s \hookrightarrow^2 t$, i.e. s can be narrowed into t in two narrowing steps, because $s \overset{\epsilon, s=q, \emptyset}{\hookrightarrow} q$ and $q \overset{\omega, q_{|\omega}=t_{|\omega}, \emptyset}{\hookrightarrow} t$. Following the definition, and taking into account both D_k and E_k, the operator SIR can only generalise. However, if the occurrence ω is a variable X, the second equation is of the form $t = X$. If we remove this equation, it can be said that SIR specialises. Despite this seemingly contradictory behaviour, the operator must be used interactively in order to specialise a variable into a term which has more than one function symbol.

Example 2. Suppose an original equation $f(g(a)) = b$ and $\Sigma^+ = \{f, g, h, a, b\}$ with their corresponding arities. By choosing the occurence $\omega = \epsilon$ and $F = h$, we generate the following two equations:
a first equation D_k as: $\quad f(g(a)) = h(X_{k,1}, X_{k,2})$
and a second equation E_k as: $\quad h(X_{k,1}, X_{k,2}) = b$
We can apply the same operator to D_k at occurrence $\omega' = 2$ and $F = a$. This gives
a third equation D_{k+1} as: $\quad f(g(a)) = h(X_{k,1}, a)$
and a fourth equation E_{k+1} as: $\quad a = X_{k,2}$
It is easy to show that the original equation is covered by the program which can be constructed from $D_k, E_k, D_{k+1}, E_{k+1}$. However, it would be interesting to be able to specialise the lhs of E_k's and to allow more then one new symbol on the lhs.

Both things can be obtained by using the following simple operator:

Definition 5. Syntactic Folding (SF)
Given two equations $E_1 = \{l_1 = r_1\}$ and $E_2 = \{l_2 = r_2\}$ with r_1 being a variable such that there exists an occurrence ω such that $r_1 \equiv (l_2)_{|\omega}$, a new folded equation

can be constructed as $l_2[l_1]_\omega = r_2$. The same applies if such an occurrence is in r_2.

In the previous example E_{k+1} and E_k could be folded into $h(X_{k,1}, a) = b$ by using the occurrence $\omega=2$.

Example 3. Consider Example 1 again. If the first equation from the evidence is selected, i.e. $f(a) = r(g(b, b))$, and the SIR operator is applied at occurrence $\omega = 1$ and with function symbol h, the following two equations are generated:

a first equation D_k is: $\qquad f(a) = r(h(X_{k,1}, X_{k,2}))$

and a second equation E_k as: $\qquad h(X_{k,1}, X_{k,2}) = g(b, b)$

We can apply the same operator to D_k at occurrence $\omega' = 1.1$ and $F = b$. This produces:

a third equation D_{k+1} as: $\qquad f(a) = r(h(b, X_{k,2}))$

and a fourth equation E_{k+1} as: $\qquad b = X_{k,1}$

If SIR is applied again to D_{k+1} but now at occurrence $\omega' = 1.2$ and $F = a$, this gives:

a fifth equation D_{k+2} as: $\qquad f(a) = r(h(b, a))$

and a sixth equation E_{k+2} as: $\qquad a = X_{k,2}$

Equation D_{k+2} can be generalised into $f(X_{k,2}) = r(h(b, X_{k,2})$ which is one rule of program P. By using the SF operator, E_k and E_{k+2} can be folded into $h(X_{k,1}, a) = g(b, b)$ and then folded again by using E_{k+1} into $h(b, a) = g(b, b)$ which can then be generalised into $h(X_{k,1}, a) = g(X_{k,1}, b)$, which is another rule of the program.

These three operators are able to construct virtually any term as the following lemma and theorem show:

Lemma 1. *Select any term r constructable from $T(\Sigma)$. Given any equation $s = t$ and any occurrence ω of t there exists a finite combination of the SIR and SF operators that generates these two equations:*

a first equation D as: $\qquad s = q$

and a second equation E as: $\qquad q_{|\omega} = t_{|\omega}$

where $q = t[r]_\omega$.

Proof. Let us prove this lemma by mathematical induction. Consider d equal to the depth of the tree which can be drawn from r, e.g. $f(g(a, h(a, a)))$ has depth 4.

For $d = 1$, the lemma is obvious because it is only necessary to apply the SIR operator at occurrence ω with the term $\phi = r$.

Let us suppose the hypothesis that the lemma is true for k. Then, we have to show that it is true for $k+1$. Consider that $r_{|u} = g(a_1, a_2, \ldots, a_n)$ where a_i are function symbols of arity 0, i.e. constants, and $u = x_1.x_2.\ldots.x_k$ and there is no other occurrence at level $k+1$ but the a_i. By hypothesis we have been able to construct two equations for depth k:

a first equation D_k as: $\qquad s = q$

and a second equation E_k as: $\qquad q_{|\omega} = t_{|\omega}$

where $q = t[r']_\omega$, with r' being $r[a]_{x_1.x_2.\ldots.x_k}$ where this a does not appear again in r'. Since this a appears once, it is obvious that this step could have been avoided and we could have a variable X instead of a term a as well.

Let us apply the SIR operator to the first equation at occurrence $\omega' = x_1.x_2.\ldots.x_k$ with $\phi = g(X_{k,1}, X_{k,2}, \ldots, X_{k,n})$, $n \geq 0$ is the arity of F and $X_{k,i}$ are different fresh variables. This generates two equations:

a first equation D_{k+1} as: $\qquad s = q'$

and a second equation E_{k+1} as: $\qquad q'_{|\omega'} = q_{|\omega'}$

where $q' = q[\phi]_{\omega'}$. We can apply the SIR operator n times with function symbol a to D_{k+1} at all its n positions giving respectively:

a first equation D_i as: $\qquad s = q'[a_i]_i$

and a second equation E_i as: $\qquad a = X_{k,i}$

These E_i can be used jointly with D_{k+1} by operator SF to construct a new equation A, $s = q[g(a_1, a_2, \ldots, a_n)]_{\omega'}$, which is equal to $s = t[r]_\omega$, and D_i can be used jointly with D_{k+1} by operator SF for a second equation, $q[g(a_1, a_2, \ldots, a_n)]_{\omega'} = q_{|\omega'}$. Finally, since the rhs of this last equation is X, we can apply a SF operator to this last equation and E_k giving an equation B, $r = t_{|\omega}$. Both A and B are precisely the equations D and E of the lemma.

Since this holds for $k+1$ if it holds for k, we can affirm that it holds for all k. $\square$

Theorem 1. *Select any term r' which is constructable from $T(\Sigma, \mathcal{X})$. Given any equation $s = t$ and any occurrence ω of t, there exists a finite combination of the SIR, the SF and the UG operators that generates these two equations:*

a first equation D'_k as: $\quad s = q'$, *and a second equation E'_k as:* $\quad q'_{|\omega} = t_{|\omega}$,

where $q' = t[r']_\omega$.

Proof. Given the equation $s = t$ and any term r', consider a new term r such that any variable in r' is substituted by a function symbol of arity 0. Obviously, this r is ground, and, by lemma 1 it can be constructed by a finite combination of the operators SIR and SF, resulting in a first equation D_k as $s = q$, and a second equation E_k as $q_{|\omega} = t_{|\omega}$, where $q = t[r]_\omega$.

Take D_k and use a UG to obtain a new equation $s = t[r']_\omega$ which is equal to $s = q'$. In the same way all the E_k can be generalised to obtain a new equation $r' = t_{|\omega}$. $\square$

5 Strong Completeness of the IFLP Schema

Theorem 1 is essential to be able to show that any possible intermediate term that may be used in a derivation can be induced by using the operators of the IFLP Schema. This leads to the following strong completeness result:

Theorem 2. Strong Completeness

Given a finite program P, and a finite evidence E generated from P, such that every rule of P is necessary for at least one equation of the positive evidence (i.e. if removed some positive example is not covered), and $\Sigma_P = \Sigma^+$, i.e., all function symbols of the program appear in the positive evidence, then the program can be induced by a finite combination of the operators presented in the IFLP schema, that is to say, Unrestricted Generalitation (UG), Single Intra-Replacement (SIR) and Syntactic Folding (SF).

Proof. Select any rule $r \equiv \{s = t\}$ from P. Since it is necessary, it is used in at least one derivation of one example, say $a_0 = a_n$. We express this derivation as:

$$a_0 \overset{u_1, l_1 = r_1, \theta_1}{\hookrightarrow} a_1 \overset{u_2, l_2 = r_2, \theta_2}{\hookrightarrow} a_2 \hookrightarrow \ldots \overset{u_n, l_n = r_n, \theta_n}{\hookrightarrow} a_n$$

If $n = 1$, i.e. the derivation $a_0 \overset{u_1, l_1 = r_1, \theta_1}{\hookrightarrow} a_1$ then we have that under the IFLP schema we can generate a first equation D_k as: $a_0 = a_0$, and a second equation E_k as: $(a_0)_{|\omega} = (a_1)_{|\omega}$, such that $\omega = u_1$, and what has to be introduced is $q = (a_0)_{|\omega}$. This can be done as was shown in Theorem 1. The last equation E_k can be generalised in order to match $l_1 = r_1$.

Let us assume the hypothesis that we have been able to generate all the $l_i = r_i$ upto $n - 1$. Then, for n we have :

$$a_0 \overset{u_1, l_1 = r_1, \theta_1}{\hookrightarrow} a_1 \overset{u_2, l_2 = r_2, \theta_2}{\hookrightarrow} a_2 \hookrightarrow \ldots \overset{u_n, l_n = r_n, \theta_n}{\hookrightarrow} a_n$$

Since it has been generated to a_{n-1} we only have to show that it is possible to generate the equation that allows for narrowing from a_{n-1} to a_n, i.e. $a_{n-1} \overset{u_n, l_n = r_n, \theta_n}{\hookrightarrow} a_n$. However, this step is no different from the step we proved for $n = 1$, so we can find this $l_n = r_n$ and the hypothesis is true for all n. Thus, the theorem is proven. $\square$

Strong Completeness is not usual in the inductive literature (except [12]), because, without additional information (e.g. modes) it entails intractability. However, the previous theorem discovers a set of operators which are sufficient to induce *any possible* program. Further work is centred on finding restrictions which preserve completeness or bring the schema to tractability. Among the latter there are at least two ways possible. A first option is to fix a selection criterion (e.g. compression) ensuring completeness wrt this criterion by using an ordered search space and mode declarations (e.g. [11]). A second one is to study uncomplete but still powerful instances of the schema and provide efficient algorithms for them. The first option is in progress by the authors through the use of genetic programming as in [17]. The second option was precisely undertaken in [3] and the next section discusses its relation to the preceding schema.

6   Inverse Narrowing as an Instance of the IFLP Schema

In this section, we show that Inverse Narrowing is just an instance of our generic IFLP Schema. This relationship allows a more detailed study of our previous algorithm, its limitations and its extensions to cover more difficult cases without falling into intractability.

First of all, it is evident that, according to the definition given in Section 3, CRG is just a restriction of the UG. Secondly, Inverse narrowing was defined as an operator that generates an equation from two equations. On the contrary, SIR generates two equations from one equation. This operator, iterated and combined with the other operators of the IFLP Schema is a generalisation of inverse narrowing as the following corollary shows:

Corollary 1. *For any equation $s = t$ such that we can make an inverse narrowing step: $t \overset{u, l = r, \theta}{\hookleftarrow}_p t'$ to obtain a pair of equations $s = t'$ and $l = r$, then these two equations can be obtained in the IFLP schema.*

Proof. Just apply the operators of the IFLP schema to obtain a first equation D_k as: $s = q$, and a second equation E_k as: $q_{|\omega} = t_{|\omega}$, such that $\omega = u$, where $q = t[l]_\omega$ and $t_{|\omega} = r$.

The only difference is that $t' = \theta(q)$, i.e., a substitution is applied, but this difference vanishes if we select $q = \theta(t[l]_\omega)$ and then we generalise the second equation E_k to make it match $l = r$. $\square$

7 Extending Inverse Narrowing

As we have stated before, the IFLP Schema should suggest different ways to generalise inverse narrowing to cope with more complex cases. In this work, it has been shown that if a function symbol did not appear in some convenient conditions, it could not be induced by inverse narrowing. In this way, we can extend inverse narrowing to allow fresh variables on the rhs's and where the secondary equation can be obtained either from a set of generalised equations from the evidence or by the introduction of a new term function symbol $F(X_1', X_2', \ldots, X_m')$ into an equation of the form $F(X_1', X_2', \ldots, X_m') = Y$, which obviously can be used in any occurrence of the other equation since Y unifies with anything.

7.1 Function Invention

The invention of predicates is an open area of research in ILP [13, 16, 10, 7]. In the case of unconditional functional logic programs it is expected that function invention would be even more necessary than First Order Horn Logic [16].

In our strong completeness theorem, we assumed that $\Sigma_P = \Sigma^+$, i.e., all function symbols of the program appear in the positive evidence.

One of the reasons for the introduction of this general schema is that in the case where the relation $\Sigma_P \supset \Sigma^+$ is strict, we can extend Σ^+ with new and fresh function symbols of different arities, thus making the invention of new functions possible. The set of *inventable* functions is denoted by Σ^i, and the SIR operator can then construct terms by using function symbols from $\Sigma^+ \cup \Sigma^i$.

Under the extension of the signature, it is clear that the IFLP Schema is able to invent functions. The procedure resembles the approach presented in [10], where maximal utilisation predicates are introduced and then refined. In our case, they are refined by the possible introduction of function symbols in different occurrences at different stages.

On the contrary, in order to extend our previous inverse narrowing approach [3] with function invention, we are forced to act in the reverse way due to the nature of this procedure. Our extended inverse narrowing is able to do inventions of this kind but adding equations of the form $F(a, a, \ldots, a) = Y$ where F is a new function symbol from Σ^i and a is a constant which appears in Σ^+. These equations can be used as secondary equations in an inverse narrowing step. The use of inverse narrowing on the lhs is also required (this was already done when learning from background knowledge in [3]). Therefore, the approach becomes too general for practical purposes, as the following example illustrates.

Example 4. Let us consider the example of inducing the product function from scratch, which requires the invention of a function for addition. To do this, make $\Sigma^i = \{+\}$ where $+$ has arity 2. Given the following evidence:

(E_1^+) $ss0 \times ss0 = ssss0$
(E_2^+) $sss0 \times ss0 = ssssss0$
(E_3^+) $sss0 \times s0 = sss0$
(E_4^+) $0 \times sss0 = 0$
(E_5^+) $ss0 \times 0 = 0$
(E_6^+) $ssss0 \times 0 = 0$
(E_7^+) $s0 \times ss0 = ss0$

(E_1^-) $ss0 \times sss0 = sssssssss0$
(E_2^-) $sss0 \times sss0 = ssssssss0$
(E_3^-) $ss0 \times sss0 = ssss0$
(E_4^-) $sss0 \uparrow ss0 = ssss0$
(E_5^-) $0 \times s0 = s0$
(E_6^-) $s0 \times 0 = ss0$

We can proceed as follows. The equation $\{0 \times X = 0\}$ is just a generalisation of E_4^+. From $\Sigma^i = \{+\}$, we introduce the equation $+(0,0) = Y$, which can be expressed in infix notation as $E_1 \equiv 0+0 = Y$. From Σ^+ we introduce the equations $E_2 \equiv s(0) = Y'$ and $E_3 \equiv 0 = Y''$. We make inverse narrowing at occurrence ϵ of the rhs of E_1 with E_3 and we have $E_4 \equiv 0+0 = 0$ that can be generalised into $X+0 = X$. By repeatedly using inverse narrowing on different occurrences we can obtain the following equation $X + s(Y) = s(X+Y)$. Although, in this case, this involves only three steps, in general it would be necessary to use heuristics or mode declarations. Even with all this, some systems (e.g. [11]) are helped by some examples of the addition in the evidence. The equation $sX + Y = X \times Y$ can be obtained as was shown in [3] since the equations of addition are already generated.

At the end of the process, the following program can be constructed: $P = \{0 \times X = 0, sX \times Y = X \times Y + Y, X + 0 = X, X + s(Y) = s(X+Y)\}$.

8   Conclusions and Future Work

The IFLP Schema is shown to be a general and strong complete framework for the induction of functional logic programs. Theoretically, this allows the induction of functional logic programs with auxiliary functions and, if the signature is conveniently extended, it can be used to invent functions. Moreover, although intricate combinations of the operators which have been presented may be needed in order to obtain the rules of the intended program, function symbols are introduced one by one. This makes extending our previous algorithm with the new operators possible, since it is based on genetic programming techniques.

This theoretical work is a necessary stage in a more long-term project to explore the advantages of extending the representational language of ILP to functional logic programs. This is also subject to a convenient extension of our schema to conditional theories, which will make it possible to use and compare the same examples and background knowledge as in ILP problems. A less theoretical ongoing work is centred on the development and implementation of a more powerful but still tractable algorithm than the one presented in [3].

References

1. P.G. Bosco, E. Giovannetti, G. Levi, C. Moiso, and C. Palamidessi. A complete semantic characterization of K-leaf, a logic language with partial functions. In *Proceedings of the IEEE Symposium on Logic Programming*, pages 318–327. IEEE Computer Society Press, N.W., Washington, 1987.

2. M. Hanus. The Integration of Functions into Logic Programming: From Theory to Practice. *Journal of Logic Programming*, 19-20:583–628, 1994.

3. J. Hernández and M.J. Ramírez. Inverse Narrowing for the Induction of Functional Logic Programs. In *Proc. Joint Conference on Declarative Programming, APPIA-GULP-PRODE'98*, pages 379–393, 1998.

4. S. Hölldobler. Equational Logic Programming. In *Proc. Second IEEE Symp. on Logic In Computer Science*, pages 335–346. IEEE Computer Society Press, 1987.

5. H. Hussmann. Unification in conditional-equational theories. Technical report, Fakultät für Mathematik und Informatik, Universität Passau, 1986.

6. J. Jaffar, J.-L. Lassez, and M.J. Maher. A logic programming language scheme. In D. de Groot and G. Lindstrom, editors, *Logic Programming, Functions, Relations and Equations*, pages 441–468. Prentice Hall, Englewood Cliffs, NJ, 1986.

7. K. Khan, S. Muggleton, and R. Parson. Repeat learning using predicate invention. In C.D. Page, editor, *Proc. of the 8th International Workshop on Inductive Logic Programming, ILP'98*, volume 1446 of *Lecture Notes in Artificial Intelligence*, pages 165–174. Springer-Verlag, Berlin, 1998.

8. J.W. Klop. Term Rewriting Systems. *Handbook of Logic in Computer Science*, I:1–112, 1992.

9. S. Muggleton. Inductive Logic Programming. *New Generation Computing*, 8(4):295–318, 1991.

10. S. Muggleton. Predicate invention and utilisation. *Journal of Experimental and Theoretical Artificial Intelligence*, 6(1):127–130, 1994.

11. S. Muggleton. Inverse entailment and progol. *New Generation Computing Journal*, 13:245–286, 1995.

12. S. Muggleton. Comnpleting inverse entailment. In C.D. Page, editor, *Proc. of the 8th International Workshop on Inductive Logic Programming, ILP'98*, volume 1446 of *Lecture Notes in Artificial Intelligence*, pages 245–249. Springer-Verlag, Berlin, 1998.

13. S. Muggleton and W. Buntine. Machine invention of first-order predicates by inverting resolution. In S. Muggleton, editor, *Inductive Logic Programming*, pages 261–280. Academic Press, 1992.

14. U.S. Reddy. Narrowing as the Operational Semantics of Functional Languages. In *Proc. Second IEEE Int'l Symp. on Logic Programming*, pages 138–151. IEEE, 1985.

15. J.H. Siekmann. Universal unification. In *7th Int'l Conf. on Automated Deduction*, volume 170 of *Lecture Notes in Computer Science*, pages 1–42. Springer-Verlag, Berlin, 1984.

16. I. Stahl. The Appropriateness of Predicate Invention as Bias Shift Operation in ILP. *Machine Learning*, 20:95–117, 1995.

17. A. Varsek. *Genetic Inductive Logic Programming*. PhD thesis, University of Ljubljana, Slovenia, 1993.

Application of Different Learning Methods to Hungarian Part-of-Speech Tagging

Tamás Horváth[1], Zoltán Alexin[2], Tibor Gyimóthy[3], and Stefan Wrobel[4,1]

[1] German National Research Center for Information Technology, GMD - AiS.KD,
Schloß Birlinghoven, D-53754 Sankt Augustin, `tamas.horvath@gmd.de`
[2] Dept. of Applied Informatics, József Attila University,
P.O.Box 652, H-6701 Szeged, `alexin@inf.u-szeged.hu`
[3] Research Group on Artificial Intelligence, Hungarian Academy of Sciences,
Aradi vértanuk tere 1, H-6720 Szeged, `gyimi@inf.u-szeged.hu`
[4] Otto-von-Guericke-Universität Magdeburg, IWS,
P.O.Box 4120, D-39106 Magdeburg, `wrobel@iws.cs.uni-magdeburg.de`

Abstract. From the point of view of computational linguistics, Hungarian is a difficult language due to its complex grammar and rich morphology. This means that even a common task such as part-of-speech tagging presents a new challenge for learning when looked at for the Hungarian language, especially given the fact that this language has fairly free word order. In this paper we therefore present a case study designed to illustrate the potential and limits of current ILP and non-ILP algorithms on the Hungarian POS-tagging task. We have selected the popular C4.5 and Progol systems as propositional and ILP representatives, adding experiments with our own methods AGLEARN, a C4.5 preprocessor based on attribute grammars, and the ILP approaches PHM and RIBL. The systems were compared on the Hungarian version of the multilingual morphosyntactically annotated MULTEXT-East TELRI corpus which consists of about 100.000 tokens. Experimental results indicate that Hungarian POS-tagging is indeed a challenging task for learning algorithms, that even simple background knowledge leads to large differences in accuracy, and that instance-based methods are promising approaches to POS tagging also for Hungarian. The paper also includes experiments with some different cascade connections of the taggers.

1   Introduction

Part-of-speech (POS) *tagging* is one of the first stages in natural language related processing (e.g., parsing, information extraction). The task of a POS tagger is, for a given text, to provide for each word in the text its contextually disambiguated part of speech *tag* representing the word's morphosyntactic category. Depending on source language grammar and application needs, a suitable tag set is chosen by linguists as basis for further analysis. Tagging is a difficult task in general because of the large number of ambiguities in natural language texts. For Finno-Ugric languages, like Hungarian in particular, this task is even more complex because they have rich morphology and fairly *free word-order*. While a reduced tag set containing 125 different tags overcomes the difficulty of the huge set of morphosyntactic categories in practice, the free-word order makes the POS tagging task for the Hungarian language a new challenging problem for learning algorithms.

In this paper, we therefore present a case study designed to illustrate the potential and limits of current ILP and non-ILP algorithms on the Hungarian POS-tagging task. We have selected the popular C4.5 and Progol systems as propositional and ILP representatives, adding experiments with our own methods AGLEARN, a C4.5 preprocessor based on attribute grammars, and the ILP approaches PHM and RIBL. For the experiments, we have used the annotated Hungarian TELRI corpus from the MULTEXT-East project which is currently the only available annotated corpus for Hungarian. The corpus contains about 100.000 tokens (which is relatively small compared to e.g. the Wall Street Journal corpus for English with its 3 million words). In the past, the MULTEXT-East corpus was already used to test Brill's tagger generator [4, 17] but there, only relatively poor per-word overall accuracy was reached, adding additional motivation to the experiments with a reduced tag set as described in the present paper.

The paper is organized as follows. In Section 2 we give a brief introduction to the POS tagging problem, describe previous work on generating taggers through learning, and then focus on issues related to the Hungarian language and the dataset that was used. In Section 3 we give our motivation for the design of our empirical case study, in particular the choice of learning algorithms. We also describe, for each chosen algorithm, how the POS tagging problem is mapped to the algorithm's internal representation. Section 4 contains the results of our experiments along with a discussion. The paper ends with a discussion and conclusions from our studies along with suggestions for further research.

2 POS Tagging and the Data Set

During language processing when a sentence is read each word is labelled by the set of its possible morphosyntactic descriptions, called *tags*. For example, the Hungarian word *'hét'* can be either a *number* ('seven') or a *noun* ('week'). In most of the cases a word's true tag is uniquely defined by its context in the sentence. Since each language has ambiguous words (i.e. that have several different taggings), a working tagger must contain a disambiguation module choosing the true tag from the assigned tag set for each word. Ideally, the task of such a module is defined as follows. *Given*

– a set S of correctly disambiguated tagged sentences,
– another correctly tagged set S_{query} of sentences containing ambiguous words,

find the prediction of the true tag for each ambiguous word from S_{query}.

2.1 Previous Work on Generating Taggers through Learning

Several methods have been developed for the automatic generation of POS taggers from annotated corpora. In [5] Cussens described a tagging system for English that has been generated by Progol (combined with a selection of the most frequent class in those cases where Progol's rules did not make a decision). Progol was trained on a corpus containing 3 million words and it generated *"removable"* rules for ambiguous tags: whenever such a rule applies to a word, the rule's tag is removed from the set of candidates. Using a simple linguistic background knowledge the generated tagger achieved 96.4% per word accuracy on the test data[1].

Daelemans & al. in [7] presented the MBT memory-based tagger generator system for different languages. They trained their system on a subset of the Wall Street Journal corpus (2 million words) for English and achieved 96.4% accuracy. For other languages they reached the following results: Dutch (95.7%), Spanish(97.8%) and Czech(93.6%).

Eineborg & Lindberg presented a tagging system for Swedish language [9]. They applied Progol and in a similar way to Cussens' approach they learned *removable* rules for ambiguous tags. The Swedish UMEÅ Corpus (1 million words) was used, and a 97% accuracy was achieved.

The learned taggers can be combined in order to get more accurate results. Halteren & al. in [13] discussed several possible combinations of four well-known tagger generator methods (HMM, Memory Based, Brill, Maximum Entropy). They showed that all combination taggers outperform their best component. Their best combined tagger named *pairwise-voting* obtained 97.92% accuracy for the LOB corpus (1 million words).

An application of the Brill's tagger generator to Hungarian is presented in [17]. The TELRI [11] corpus (100.000 words) was used but only 87.5% per word accuracy was reached. This empirical result showed that Brill's method has some difficulty with languages which are dissimilar in their characteristics from English.

2.2 The Data Set

Our experiments were based on an improved version of the TELRI corpus [11] in which several incorrect annotations had been corrected. This corpus was produced within the framework of "MULTEXT-East" project whose main goal was to prove the suitability of the tag coding convention MorphoSyntactic Description (MSD) to East-European languages. Orwell's famous novel, the "1984" was translated into six Eastern-European languages including Hungarian and annotated by MSD codes.

Words in the Hungarian language may have several thousand MSD codes. In order to reduce this huge set, linguists also propose the CTAG code convention

---

[1] Per word accuracy is computed on all words of the test text, i.e., including both unambiguous words (already tagged correctly by the lexicon) and ambiguous words (requiring the learned tagger module).

which leads to a smaller set containing only 125 different tags [19]. Since each CTAG code represents a set of MSD codes, the CTAG annotated version of a text contains at most as many ambiguities as its MSD annotation. Clearly, by using CTAGs we lose some linguistic information, however, as it is reported in [19], the CTAG annotation still usefully applies to a number of cases of processing Hungarian texts.

In our experiments we used the CTAG annotated Hungarian version of the TELRI corpus. From the corpus, we first created a tag lexicon by collecting for each word the list of tags that actually occurred in the corpus. This lexicon was then used to convert the sentences of the corpus into training data. For example the first sentence of the novel

"Derült, hideg áprilisi nap volt, az órák éppen tizenhármat ütöttek." [2]

was converted into the list

(asn, {asn, vmis3s}), wpunct, asn, asn, nsn, vmis3s,
wpunct, (t, {psn, t}), npn, rg, ms, vmis3p, spunct

If the tagging of a particular word is ambiguous (according to the lexicon) then the corresponding item is a pair the first element of which is the true tag (according to the annotation) and the second is the set of possible tags (according to the lexicon). Chapter 1 and 2 in the novel having been used as training data while chapter 3 and 4 served as test data. In Table 1 the number of tokens in the corpus is presented.

	Number of tokens		
Category	Training	Test	Altogether
word	59035	21673	80708
punctuation	12484	5235	17719
	71519	26908	98427

Table 1. The number of tokens in the Hungarian corpus

3 Empirical Evaluation Design

The goal of our case study was not to compare particular learning systems, but to examine the influence of the unusual and difficult properties of the Hungarian language (complex grammar, free word order) on the learning problem. We therefore selected a set of learning systems representative of different system classes that have been tried before on POS tagging tasks to see how their performance would be affected and whether phenomena observed in other experiments would carry over to Hungarian.

---

[2] It was a bright cold day in April, and the clocks were striking thirteen.

To this end, as reference standards we selected two learning systems representative of popular propositional and ILP learners used for tagging problems, C4.5 [20] and the C version of Progol 4.4 [18]. Since it appears that for other languages, memory-based methods are promising, we further included the instance-based ILP system RIBL [10, 3] in the comparison. To examine the strong influence of background knowledge (reported e.g. in [5]), we used AGLEARN, a learning system that adds additional attributes to the input of C4.5. These attributes are specified with the help of an attribute grammar and actually computed by a parser that is invoked on the context of the focus word. Finally, as we wanted to examine the influence of depth bounds (window sizes) on the learning problem, we included experiments with PHM [16, 14], a method that is capable of efficiently learning logic programs with colored path graph background knowledge without depth bound.

Below we sketch the particular representations used for each of these learning systems. However, let us first describe some general properties of our experimental setup. First, in contrast to experiments such as [5], where "*removable*" rules were learned, we learned "*choose*" rules, i.e., whenever such a rule applies, the rule's tag is made the chosen (i.e., predicted) tag. Second, in order to increase the specificity of the learned rules and also to reduce the high runtime complexity of the learning systems, we decided to split the learning problem by learning rules for each ambiguity class separately, and limited ourselves to those classes which occurred at least 50 times in the training set. These ambiguity classes represent 92.23% (6667 of 7229) of all ambiguity occurrences in the training set and 91.26% (2443 of 2677) of all ambiguous tokens in the test data set. In cases of C4.5, AGLEARN, and RIBL we considered a separate learning problem for each ambiguity class. For Progol and PHM a separate learning problem for $choose\_t_i\_from\_t_1\_\ldots\_t_k$ was created for each of the possible true tags for each ambiguity class $c = \{t_1, \ldots, t_k\}$.

In all *training* examples, the unique correct tags for surrounding words were used. In cases of C4.5, AGLEARN, Progol, and PHM, the learned set of rules was used for testing as follows: whenever exactly one rule applied, this was used as the learner's prediction; if none or more than one applied, the test example was taken as uncovered and was assigned, as in [5] to the most frequent candidate category. Note that a rule cannot be applied if it does not cover the focus word or it refers to at least one ambiguous token in the context of the focus word. Since the IBL paradigm is able to handle missing attribute values as well, in the case of RIBL such ambiguous tokens were considered as objects without class information.

In the rest of this section we describe briefly the different representations we employed. The results are discussed in Section 4 in details.

3.1 C4.5 and AGLEARN

In our experiments with C4.5 we represented the context of the focus words by fixed length lists of the tokens, the chosen window size being 7. Below we give an item from the C4.5 training data file:

empty, empty, ms, asn, nso, nsnx, wpunct, nsn, vmis3s, asn, npox, aso, t, asn, t

The first 7-7 columns describe the left, and right context respectively, and the last one is the true tag of the current token. If a context was shorter than 7 then it was padded with the special value empty. In order to extend the above description with some basic linguistic knowledge, we used the system AGLEARN [12]. AGLEARN is a learning method which extends a propositional learning table with extra columns containing "relational" information. The basic idea of AGLEARN is very similar to the ILP system LINUS [8], i.e. a relational learning problem is transformed into propositional form and the rules inferred by a propositional learner are transformed back into relational form. The difference is that AGLEARN uses *attribute grammar* formalism for the relational representation. Since AGLEARN applies C4.5, its application can be considered as an extension of the propositional language used by C4.5.

When setting up a learning task for AGLEARN a simple linguistic background knowledge was developed. The aim of this linguistic background knowledge was to recognize token groups and characteristic phrase structures called *syntagmas* in the context of the focus word. An attribute grammar was used for the computation of two new attribute values (group and syntagma). Group values were computed for the left and right contexts. The syntagma value was computed only for the right context. This value is based on the syntax of the context so it cannot be computed for the left context when the beginning of the syntactic structure is not known. AGLEARN generated training examples for C4.5 in which in addition to the CTAGs these new attribute values were appeared as new columns. Our findings showed that these new columns in several cases appeared in the learned rules [2].

3.2 Progol

As mentioned earlier, for each ambiguity class $c = \{t_1, \ldots, t_k\}$, and for each $t \in c$ a separate learning problem was considered over the target predicate choose_t_from_c/2. For each training token with ambiguity class c we added the positive (resp. negative) example choose_t_from_c(L, R) if its true tag is t (resp. is not t). Arguments L and R are the token's whole left (in reverse order) and right contexts, respectively (i.e., there are lists containing the true tags). In each Progol learning task we used the following "technical" background knowledge:

$$\bigcup_{s \in C} \{s(s)\} \cup \{\text{empty}([]), \text{first}(T, [T|\_]), \text{second}(T, [\_, T|\_]), \text{third}(T, [\_, \_, T|\_])\} ,$$

where C denotes the set of CTAGs. Atoms first, second, and third were used to select the ith token from their second list arguments for $i = 1, 2, 3$, respectively. Note that the above background knowledge defines a window size of 3. Progol then learned rules e.g. of the form

choose_cp_from_cp_rp(L, R) : $-$first$(L1, L)$, rg$(L1)$, second$(R2, R)$, nsn$(R2)$,

meaning that a token's true tag is predicted by *cp* if its ambiguity class is $\{cp, rp\}$, its left neighbor is a token of true tag *rg*, and its second right neighbor has true tag *nsn*.

3.3 PHM

The Product Homomorphism Method (PHM) introduced in [16] is a combinatorial approach for learning simple logic programs. By using PHM, positive PAC learning results can be proved to different classes of *structured* background knowledges including the class of *colored path graphs* [16, 15, 14]. The POS problem is basically a *sequential* problem, that can be represented by *colored path graphs*. As PHM does not require any bound on the depth, in contrast to the other methods investigated, we do not need any window technique.

A colored directed graph is given by a tuple $G = (V, E, Q_1, \ldots, Q_l)$, where V denotes the set of vertices, $E \subseteq V \times V$ the set of edges, and $Q_i \subseteq V$ for $i = 1, \ldots, l$ the colors of the vertices. Thus, a vertex may have more than one or possible no color. G is a colored path graph if the directed graph (V, E) is a set of disjoint directed paths. Given a colored path graph background knowledge $\mathcal{B}$ and a set of facts $E = \{P(b_1), \ldots, P(b_t)\}$, $b_i \in V$ for $i = 1, \ldots, t$, the reduced RLGG of E with respect to $\mathcal{B}$ can be computed in time $O(l \cdot t \cdot L_{\max})$ and space $O(l \cdot L_{\max})$, where $L_{\max}$ is the length of the longest path in $\mathcal{B}$ [14].

In order to apply PHM, the POS problem must be represented by using colored path graph background knowledges. In our experiment with the PHM we used the next background knowledge $\mathcal{B}$ defined by the training set as follows:

- a constant identifying the jth word in sentence i was introduced for every possible i, j,
- for every consecutive words identified by a and b, respectively, a fact $R(a, b)$ was added to $\mathcal{B}$ (hence, the ground R-atoms in $\mathcal{B}$ form a set of disjoint directed paths), and
- for each constant a, a fact $t(a)$ was added to $\mathcal{B}$ where t is the true tag of the word identified by a (hence, t can be considered as a color).

For each ambiguity class $c = \{t_1, \ldots, t_k\}$ and for each possible tag $t \in c$ we considered a *separate* learning problem with background knowledge $\mathcal{B}$ and training examples $E^+(c, t) \cup E^-(c, t)$ with respect to a target predicate choose_t_from_c/1, i.e.,

- $E^+(c, t)$ is the set of the atoms choose_t_from_c(a) for every training instance (token) a with ambiguity class c, and true tag t, and
- $E^-(c, t)$ is the set of the atoms choose_t_from_c(a) for every training instance a with ambiguity class c, and true tag different from t.

As the problem of finding a consistent hypothesis consisting of k clauses with the smallest k is NP-complete [14], we used a simple variant of *tabu search* [1] with tabu size 5 maximizing the *relative frequency* function $n_{correct}/n$, where $n_{correct}$ is the number of training examples correctly classified, and n is the number of the covered training examples. A clause discovered was accepted if its accuracy on the covered training examples was at least 90%, and it covered at least 10% of the positive examples.

3.4 RIBL

RIBL is an instance-based ILP algorithm first introduced in [10] and further developed in [3]. Although there are a number of user-defined parameters controlling the automatic similarity measure used by RIBL, one of the basic practical problems is the choice of an adequate representation of the learning problem. In the case of the POS problem, we considered two different representations.

Representation with Lists In this *non-flattened* representation we used a ternary predicate for describing the background knowledge. Its first *input* argument was used to identify instances (i.e., tag occurrences), and its second, and third *output* arguments, both of type *list*, were used to describe the left and right neighbors (i.e., the true tags) of the instance identified by the first argument. In both directions we considered only *two* words at most (i.e., their true tags). For each ambiguity class $c = \{t_1, \ldots, t_k\}$ investigated we took the set X_c of training instances with ambiguity class c and for each $x \in X_c$ we added a target atom $t(x)$ to the set of training instances, where t is the true tag of the instance identified by x. In order to compare arguments of type list, we used list edit distance supported directly by RIBL [3]. We used trivial cost [3] on the list alphabet (i.e., the set of possible tags).

Representation with Relations In this representation we used a binary background relation R describing the chain of the words, i.e., the background knowledge contains a fact $R(a, b)$ if and only if the two instances identified by a and b, respectively, are consecutive in this order. For each training instance a with true tag t we also added the fact true_tag(a, t) to the background knowledge.

As in the previous representation, for each ambiguity class c we considered a separate learning problem with the same training instances as in the previous non-flattened representation.

4 Experimental Results and Discussion

In this section we discuss the experimental results of the five learning systems on the domain described in Subsection 2.2. Since AGLEARN used extra linguistic background knowledge and is based on C4.5, the results with C4.5 and AGLEARN are discussed in the same item.

C4.5 and AGLEARN C4.5 could not disambiguate only 15 test queries, in other words, it made a decision in 99.4% of the 2443 ambiguous test queries. It predicted 1973 instances correctly, which is a 80.8% test accuracy for the whole test set containing 2443 instances. We also note that this corresponds to a relative accuracy of 81.3% for the set of 2428 disambiguated test examples.

In the extended representation used by AGLEARN, the number of undecided cases was 72, i.e., it disambiguated 97.1% of the test instances. On the other hand, even for this smaller set, the number of correctly classified queries was 2045, i.e., 83.7% of the test examples. This is a 86.3% relative accuracy with respect to the decided cases.

Progol We got slightly different results with Progol. Progol could decide only in 1606 cases, that is, only in 65.7% of the test domain. A similar experimental result with Progol is also reported in [5]. On the other hand, Progol classified 1482 examples correctly, i.e., 60.7% of the 2443 test instances. This is an excellent 92.3% relative accuracy with respect to the decided 1606 cases.

PHM The rules discovered by PHM disambiguated 1965 cases from the 2443 ambiguous test queries, i.e., 80.4% of the 2443 test instances. 1776 cases, namely 72.7% of the 2443 examples, were correctly classified, which corresponds to a relative accuracy of 90.4% for the disambiguated 1965 cases.

RIBL In the non-flattened representation the optimal number of neighbors $k = 11$ was estimated by the *leave-one-out* evaluation method on the training set. Since the true tags in the window of a test instance may be unknown, we introduced a special symbol. The cost of inserting, deleting or replacing this symbol with any symbol was set to 1. In contrast to the other four systems, RIBL did not leave undecided cases, and correctly classified 84.8% (i.e., 2072 out of 2443) of the test set.

The best training (as well as test) accuracy was achieved by depth bound 3 in the second representation. In this case, RIBL correctly classified 1794 test instances from the 2443, which is a 73.4% test set accuracy. This result show that a significant improvement on the accuracy can be gained by using lists with edit distance on this domain (see also [3]).

In the remaining part of this section we summarize the above mentioned experimental results. For RIBL we take the result with the list representation. C4.5, AGLEARN, and RIBL have very good disambiguation capabilities, that is, the number of undecided test queries was small for these systems. In contrast to RIBL, C4.5, and AGLEARN, the systems Progol and PHM could not disambiguate a significant part of the test queries. There was also a difference between Progol and PHM in this sense. On the other hand, Progol and PHM had the best relative accuracy for the decided cases, and Progol was better than PHM. We also note, that although the extra linguistic background knowledge used by AGLEARN increased the number of undecided cases, it improved the results with C4.5.

In order to compare the previous results, we disambiguated the undecided test queries by applying the simple tagger based on lexicon frequencies. The accuracy of this tagger was 76.1% on the set containing the 2443 ambiguous test instances. The final results are listed in Table 2. The table also contains the per-word overall accuracies without punctuation symbols. In order to compute them, we used the lexicon frequencies for the uncovered 234 cases. The line 'ambiguous' in Table 2 illustrates the accuracies for the 2443 ambiguous test instances covered by the 27 classes investigated.

	C4.5	AGLEARN	Progol	PHM	RIBL (lists)
ambiguous (%)	81.0	84.8	82.8	84.6	84.8
overall per-word (%)	97.60	98.03	97.80	98.00	98.03

Table 2. Final test set accuracy results expressed in percentage terms.

4.1 Cascade Connection of the Taggers

As mentioned earlier, our goal was not to compare the different learning systems, but to select the candidate components of a working combined tagger. As a first step into this direction, we investigated some cascade connections of the previous taggers. These combinations first employ systems which are very accurate but have low coverage (e.g. Progol and/or PHM) and fall back to RIBL (which leaves no uncovered instances) only for the undecided tokens. The results of some combinations investigated are given in Table 3 (the accuracy is computed with respect to the 2443 ambiguous test instances considered).

	Progol → RIBL	PHM → RIBL	Progol → PHM → RIBL
accuracy (%)	85.7	86.5	86.0

Table 3. Results with different cascade connections of Progol, PHM, and RIBL.

Although the cascade connection is a simple combination in contrast e.g. [13], the results show the potential of this approach. An interesting observation is that the cascade connection of Progol with PHM did not improve the accuracy which means that PHM has weaker decision capability on the undecided tokens left by the Progol tagger.

5 Conclusion

In this paper, we have presented an initial case study with five selected ILP and non-ILP algorithms on the problem of POS tagging for the Hungarian language.

The purpose of the experiments was not to compare the learning systems, but rather to examine how the unusual and difficult properties of Hungarian (complex grammar, large tag set, free word order) affect the properties of the problem. Our experiments indicate that Hungarian is indeed a particular challenge to the learning of POS tagging rules, whether using propositional or ILP methods.

More specifically, however, some generally observed properties of the problem seem to carry over from simpler languages to Hungarian. First, in [13], it was reported that memory-based methods (MBL) are particularly suited for learning POS taggers. Given the accuracy figures reported above, our experiments indicate that this might also be the case for the POS tagging problem in Hungarian: the instance-based ILP system RIBL shows good results on this domain both in coverage and accuracy aspects. Secondly, as already emphasized e.g. by Cussens [5], the use of linguistic background knowledge is of great importance and cannot be offset by the use of more powerful learners. In our experiments, even a very simple set of linguistic background knowledge, provided by AGLEARN to C4.5, has notably improved the learning results. Thirdly, as in the experiments by Cussens for English [5], we found that also for the Hungarian POS tagging problem, both rule-inducing ILP learners have very good accuracy in those cases when they could decide, however the number of uncovered cases is relatively high for these learners, indicating some need for further generalization ability e.g. by giving additional background knowledge.

In future work on continuing this case study, we are therefore going to use additional linguistic background knowledge provided by an expert in order to improve accuracies of the three ILP systems Progol, PHM, and RIBL. For RIBL in particular, this may also mean using an expert-provided editing cost matrix instead of the trivial one used in the present experiments. In the cases of Progol and PHM, a test query remained undecided if it was covered by no clause or by two or more clauses predicting different tags. In order to reduce the number of undecided instances, we are going to apply Bayesian method for these cases. Bayesian methods for POS tagging have also been investigated in [6]. For the PHM approach, we plan improvements using *local search*. Finally, given the encouraging results of [13] on taggers that combine different learning systems, we are going to investigate other more sophisticated combinations as well.

Acknowledgements

This work was supported partly by the project ESPRIT IV 20237 ILP2. The second and third authors were also supported by the Hungarian OTKA grant T25721.

References

[1] E. H. L. Aarts and J. K. Lenstra, editors. *Local Search in Combinatorial Optimization*. Discrete Mathematics and Optimization. Wiley-Interscience, 1997.

[2] Z. Alexin, S. Zvada, and T. Gyimóthy. Application of AGLEARN on Hungarian Part-of-speech Tagging. In D. Parigot and M. Mernik, editors, *Second Workshop on Attribute Grammars and their Applications, WAGA'99*, pages 133–152, Amsterdam, The Netherlands, 1999. INRIA Rocquencourt.

[3] U. Bohnebeck, T. Horváth, and S. Wrobel. Term comparisons in first-order similarity measures. In D. Page, editor, *Proc. 8th Int. Conference on Inductive Logic Programming (ILP98)*, pages 65–79. Springer Verlag, 1998.

[4] E. Brill. Some advances in transformation-based part of speech tagging. In *Proceedings of the 12th National Conference on Artificial Intelligence. Volume 1*, pages 722–727. AAAI Press, July 31–Aug. 4 1994.

[5] J. Cussens. Part-of-speech tagging using Progol. In N. Lavrač and S. Džeroski, editors, *Proceedings of the 7th International Workshop on Inductive Logic Programming*, volume 1297 of *LNAI*, pages 93–108. Springer, Sept. 17–20 1997.

[6] J. Cussens. Using prior probabilities and density estimation for relational classification. *Lecture Notes in Computer Science*, 1446:106–115, 1998.

[7] W. Daelemans, A. v. d. Bosch, and J. Zavrel. Rapid development of NLP modules with memory-based learning. In *Proc. of ELSNET in Wonderland, Utrecht*, pages 105–113, 1998.

[8] S. Dzeroski and N. Lavrac. Inductive learning in deductive databases. *IEEE Transactions on Knowledge and Data Engineering: Special Issue on Learning and Discovery in Knowledge-Based Databases*, 5(6):939–949, Dec. 1993.

[9] M. Eineborg and N. Lindberg. Induction of constraint grammar-rules using Progol. *Lecture Notes in Computer Science*, 1446:116–124, 1998.

[10] W. Emde and D. Wettschereck. Relational instance based learning. In L. Saitta, editor, *Machine Learning - Proceedings 13th International Conference on Machine Learning*, pages 122–130. Morgan Kaufmann Publishers, 1996.

[11] T. Erjavec, A. Lawson, and L. R. (eds.). East meets west: A compendium of multilingual resources, 1998. CD-ROM, produced and distributed by TELRI Association e.V., ISBN:3-922641-46-6.

[12] T. Gyimóthy and T. Horváth. Learning semantic functions of attribute grammars. *Nordic Journal of Computing*, 4(3):287–302, Fall 1997.

[13] H. v. Halteren, J. Zavrel, and W. Daelemans. Improving data driven wordclass tagging by system combination. In *Proc. of COLING-ACL'98, Montreal, Canada*, pages 491–497, 1998.

[14] T. Horváth. *Learning logic programs with structured background knowledge*. PhD thesis, German National Research Center for Information Technology, 1999.

[15] T. Horváth, R. H. Sloan, and G. Turán. Learning logic programs by using the product homomorphism method. In *Proceedings of the 10th Annual Conference on Computational Learning Theory*, pages 10–20. ACM Press, July 6–9 1997.

[16] T. Horváth and G. Turán. Learning logic programs with structured background knowledge. In L. D. Raedt, editor, *Advances in Inductive Logic Programming*, pages 172–191. IOS Press, 1996.

[17] B. Megyesi. Brill's rule based part-of-speech tagger for Hungarian. Master's thesis, University of Stockholm, 1998.

[18] S. Muggleton. Inverse entailment and Progol. *New Generation Computing, Special issue on Inductive Logic Programming*, 13(3-4):245–286, 1995.

[19] C. Oravecz. Morfoszintaktikai annotáció a magyar nemzeti szövegtárban. Technical report, Research Institute for Linguistics, Hungarian Academy of Sciences, 1998. (in Hungarian).

[20] J. R. Quinlan. *C4.5: Programs for Machine Learning*. Morgan Kaufmann, 1993.

Combining LAPIS and WordNet for the Learning of LR Parsers with Optimal Semantic Constraints

Dimitar Kazakov

University of York, Heslington, York YO10 5DD, UK
kazakov@cs.york.ac.uk,
WWW home page: http://www.cs.york.ac.uk/~kazakov/

Abstract. There is a history of research focussed on learning of shift-reduce parsers from syntactically annotated corpora by the means of machine learning techniques based on logic. The presence of lexical semantic tags in the treebank has proved useful for learning semantic constraints which limit the amount of nondeterminism in the parsers. The level of generality of the semantic tags used is of direct importance to that task. We combine the ILP system LAPIS with the lexical resource WordNet to learn parsers with semantic constraints. The generality of these constraints is automatically selected by LAPIS from a number of options provided by the corpus annotator. The performance of the parsers learned is evaluated on an original corpus also described in the article.

1 Introduction

In all but the simplest natural language corpora, the grammars used for syntactic annotation are ambiguous, i.e. for some sentences they generate more than one parse. When learning parsers from treebanks, that is, text corpora in which sentences are annotated with their parses, two of the central issues in the parser design are the reduction of the number of parses, and the choice of the best parse out of the remaining ones. The former issue can be addressed by adding new constraints to and modification of the grammar used by the parser. If the result is a deterministic grammar, then the latter issue mentioned is automatically settled. Otherwise, probabilistic techniques can be applied to assign a probability to each parse, and choose the most probable one.

There is a history of research focussed on limiting or removing the nondeterminism from shift-reduce parsers using machine learning techniques based on logic [9], [7], [3]. The latter work introduces the system LAPIS in which lexical semantic tags present in the treebank are used to learn semantic constraints limiting the amount of nondeterminism in the LR parsers produced by the system. The grain of the semantic tags used is of direct importance to that task. Too general semantic tags would result in rules with poor discriminating ability, whereas too specific ones would not permit sufficient coverage of unseen examples. It is possible to use the lexical database WordNet [2] for semantic tagging, as it provides several concepts of various generality for each sense of a given word. The choice of a single concept out of those to be used as a semantic tag should not be made by the corpus annotator, because, as Zelle remarks ([8], p.32), *"it is unlikely [that] a hand-crafted feature set will be complete enough... to make the distinctions that are necessary for accurate parsing in realistic domains"*.

The present work implements a technique previously outlined by the author [3] allowing the use of WordNet in a flexible framework, where nouns and verbs in the corpus are tagged with a list of all relevant tags, and for each word the tag which is optimal, i.e. best suited for disambiguation, is automatically selected by the learning system. The method is tested on an original corpus with suitable annotation.

2 LR Parsers

LR parsers belong to the family of shift-reduce parsers. The latter are bottom-up directional parsers which use a stack to keep the intermediary results. Two of the basic actions carried out by all shift-reduce parsers are to shift a symbol from the input stream onto the stack, and to reduce a number of symbols on top of the stack, i.e., replace them with another one. Characteristic for the LR parsers is that they cannot handle ambiguous grammars, on the other hand, they can detect a syntactic error as soon as it is possible to do so on a left-to-right scan of the input [1].

The LR parser stack always contains an odd number of elements. Starting from the bottom with the initial state of the parser, all odd slots contain indices of parser states. The even slots of the stack contain grammar symbols, either terminals or nonterminals (see Figures 1–2a). The current state of the parser is the one on top of the stack. Each internal state corresponds to a set of partially processed grammar rules which share the RHS symbols seen so far. Each subsequent action of the parser is selected from a *parsing table* according to the current state of the stack and a number of lookahead input symbols (a single one for the parsers studied here). LR parsing tables are always created with the help of a software tool, such as the well-known Yacc [1]. The attempt to construct a parsing table for an ambiguous grammar results in a table containing *conflicts*, i.e. for certain pairs of states and lookahead symbols there are several possible actions in the table. Starting from the initial state 0, four actions are possible for a given State and input Symbol.

Accept If State=EndState and Symbol=end_of_string, then halt. The input has been successfully parsed (see Figure 1).

Shift/NewState Push the current input symbol onto the stack and transit to NewState, i.e. put NewState on top of the stack (see Figure 1). NewState is chosen from a parsing table, where it is selected by State and Symbol.

Reduce/RuleNo Remove from the top of the stack the number of couples (state,symbol) corresponding to the number of symbols in the RHS of the grammar rule Rule, check out the state OldState now on top of the stack, push the LHS of Rule onto the stack, and transit to state NewState, i.e.

push it onto the stack (see Figure 2a). NewState is selected by OldState and LHS in the part **Goto** of the LR parsing table.

Error Fail. The current state and lookahead symbol indicate that an ungrammatical sentence is being processed.

For a given parsing table, the corresponding LR parser is easily represented as a logic program. The representation described here is similar to the one used by Zelle and Mooney [9]. The stack and input are represented as lists, and the tagged words have the format Word:PoS^SemTag. Then the actions accept and error can be represented as predicates of two arguments (Stack,Input) (see Figure 3). The examples shown read as follows: *"If in State 1 the lookahead input symbol is tagged as end-of-sentence, accept the sentence and print the parse"* (cf. Figure 1a), *"Announce an unsuccessful parse if in the initial state 0 the lookahead symbol is not a verb, noun, or determiner"*. The actions shift and reduce are similarly represented as predicates with two pairs of arguments describing the stack and input before and after the action. Figure 3 also shows a simplified version of the parser as defined by the predicates parse/1 and do_parse/2.

3 Related Work

In his PhD thesis [7], Samuelsson describes a technique for the development of an efficient LR parser based on Explanation-Based Learning (EBL) [5] and entropy-related information measures. The method uses a treebank to modify the provided set of grammar rules and replace some of them with partially unfolded ones. The new rules do not cover part of the syntactic readings, if those are only marginally represented in the treebank. As a result, the grammar is less ambiguous at the price of a certain loss of coverage. Using that grammar also results in considerably faster parsing, due to the pruned search space and the larger number of symbols in the right-hand side of the unfolded grammar rules, which are reduced by the LR parser in a single step.

Zelle and Mooney [9], [8] have developed a method for learning case-rôle grammars from a treebank in which the nonterminal nodes correspond to deep cases, such as Agent, Patient, Instrument, etc. The treebank is used to construct an overgeneral shift-reduce parser covering the sentences in the treebank. The parser is then specialised and made deterministic by using ILP. Whenever necessary, lexical semantic classes are automatically defined in order to achieve deterministic parsing. In the experiments with case-rôle grammars, the learning algorithm CHILL *"consistently invented interpretable word classes"* [8], such as animate, human, or food.

4 LAPIS

LAPIS is a system which builds on Zelle and Mooney's research on the induction of shift-reduce parsers and extends it to learning of LR parsers, while changing at the same time the focus of the learning task. LAPIS, similarly to CHILL,

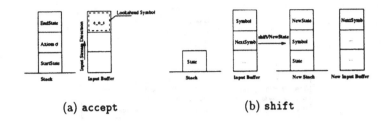

(a) accept   (b) shift

Fig. 1. LR parser accept and shift actions

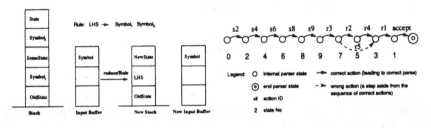

(a) LR parser reduce action   (b) Generation of positive and negative examples of actions

Fig. 2.

```
parse(ListOfTokens):-   do_parse([0],ListOfTokens).
%%%
do_parse(Stack,Input):- accept(Stack,Input).
do_parse(Stack,Input):- tagLookAheadSymbol(Input,TaggedI),
  (action_s(Stack,TaggedI,NewSt,NewI);action_r(Stack,TaggedI,NewSt,NewI)),
  do_parse(NewSt,NewI).

%%% accept(Stack,Input). Stack=[Top,...,Bottom].          Example:
accept([1,Parse|_],[_:e_o_s^_|_]):- write(Parse).

%%% error(Stack,Input).  Input=[LookaheadSymbol|More].  Example:
error([0|_],[_:AnyOf^_|_]):-  \+ member(AnyOf,[v,det,n]).

%%% action_s(Stack,Input,NewStack,NewInput). Example of shift action:
action_s([0|Stack],[n:Word^STag|Input],[2,n:Word^STag,0|Stack],Input).

%%% action_r(Stack,Input,NewStack,NewInput).  Example ( S --> n VP ):
action_r([3,vp(VP),State1,n:Word^STag,State2|RestOfStack],InputBuffer,
    [NewState,s([n:Word^STag,vp(VP)]),State2|RestOfStack],InputBuffer):-
    goto(State2,s,NewState).
%%%
goto(0,s,1).
```

Fig. 3. Logic representation of LR parsers

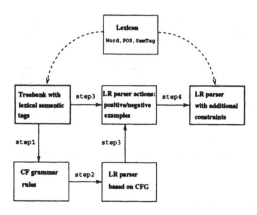

Fig. 4. LAPIS

uses lexical semantic classes as constraints for parse disambiguation. However, the assumption made in LAPIS is that semantic classes which are useful in disambiguation are present in language as words and idioms. The existence of a comprehensive source of such classes (WordNet), and even treebanks annotated with those classes (parts of the Brown Corpus [4]), poses the question whether WordNet semantic classes should not be used rather than learned from scratch.

The system LAPIS constructs LR parsers from treebanks of parse trees annotated with lexical semantic tags. LAPIS aims at the reduction of nondeterminism in the parsers it creates. This is achieved, as it will be shown further, by the means of lexicalisation and partial unfolding of the underlying grammar rules, in combination with the use of lexical semantic constraints.

The number of recursive grammar rules that are to be learned, and the lack of explicit negative examples make the learning of tools for syntactic analysis a particularly difficult task. In LAPIS, parser actions are learned rather than grammar rules. Although grammar rules and parser actions are closely related, the former are recursive concepts, whereas the latter are not.

For all trees in the treebank, each node and its immediate descendants represent the RHS and LHS of a CFG rule. The CFG derived from the treebank is used in LAPIS to define the for each sentence the set of all syntactically correct parses, then some of the parses, which are not present in the treebank, are used as negative examples. Again, learning parser actions instead of grammar rules allows to reduce the number of examples, only considering partial parses (subtrees) which differ from the correct parse in one, the topmost so far, node.

LAPIS (Learning Algorithm for Parser Induction Systems) consists of the following procedures (see Figure 4).

Step 1 For all trees in the treebank, the context-free grammar rules corresponding to all pairs <ParentNode,Daughters> are found. The result is a CFG which can produce all syntactic trees in the treebank. That CFG is usually ambiguous and produces a great number of spurious parses.

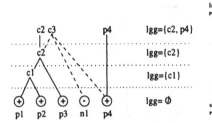

(a) Least general generalisations
of parser actions

(b) Inductive learning of parser actions

Fig. 5. Step 4

Step 2 Using the CFG rules obtained, the parsing table of a possibly nondeterministic LR parser is generated with Yacc. Each possible parser action (transition of that parser from one state to another) is represented as a Prolog clause. The logic program obtained can use the Prolog built-in backtracking mechanism to deal with any nondeterminism in the parser, and thus produce for a given sentence all possible parses.

Step 3 For each sentence in the treebank, the nondeterministic LR parser from Step 2 is used to generate the sequence of parser actions leading to the correct parse as shown in the treebank (Figure 2b). Each of these actions is an instantiation of one of the clauses generated in Step 2.

For each parser state in which nondeterminism occurs, e.g. State 7 in Figure 2b, the instantiation of the correct parser action (r2 in the example) is stored as a positive instance of that action. All other possible instantiations of parser actions for the given state and input symbol (here r5 for any input) are also generated and stored as negative instances of those actions (a detailed explanation with examples can be found in [3]).

Step 4 In the last step, the positive and negative instances of each parser action are used as input of a greedy ILP learning algorithm (shown in Figure 5b) based on syntactic least general generalisation [6] to learn a new definition of that action. The new definition is a set of clauses subsuming all positive examples, but none of the negative (see Figure 5a), and is usually more specific than the CFG-based definition of action generated in Step 2. If the former definition is substituted for the latter, the new parser obtained usually contains less nondeterministic states and hence does not produces some of the spurious parses generated by the CFG-based parser from Step 2.

The new parser can be viewed as using a unification grammar based on the backbone CFG of the parser from Step 2, but with rules additionally specialised (their coverage decreased). The difference between the CFG rules and those learned is threefold.

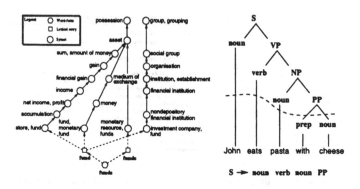

(a) Mapping from word-forms and lexical entries to synsets and their hypernyms in WordNet

(b) Grammar rule partial unfolding

Fig. 6.

1. Where the CFG rule is only looking for a terminal with a particular part of speech (e.g. noun), the new rule additionally requires that the terminal should belong to some semantic class.
2. In the new rules, a PoS can be narrowed down to a single word. In other words, the rules learned are partially *lexicalised*.
3. Some of the nonterminals in the RHS of the new rules are *unfolded*, i.e. replaced by some of their descendants in the parse tree, as shown in Figure 6b.

It can be seen from the rules learned that LAPIS combines rule unfolding with the use of lexical semantic tags to disambiguate the grammar. That, along with the partial lexicalisation makes the new grammar rules more specific than the original CFG ones, so that they produce a lower number of spurious parses.

5 WordNet as a Source of Semantic Tags

WordNet is an on-line lexical database which contains syntactic and semantic information for a large number of words and idioms. Originally developed for English [2], WordNet is also being implemented for other languages. The central building element of WordNet is called *synset*, or *lexicographer's entry*. A synset is a set of words or idioms which share a common meaning. For instance: {*(to) shut, (to) close*}. To simplify the internal representation, each synset is assigned a large integer used as a unique identifier. For instance, {*monetary resources, funds*} is Synset 109616555 in WordNet1.6. WordNet uses a set of rules and lists of exceptions to map word-forms to all relevant lexical entries. Figure 6a shows the word-form 'funds' which is recognised by WordNet as corresponding to two lexical entries, 'fund' and 'funds'. The lexical entry 'fund' appears in three synsets: {*store, fund*}, {*fund, monetary fund*}, and {*investment company, fund*}, respectively. The lexical entry 'funds' only appears in the synset {*monetary resource, funds*}. WordNet describes several semantic relations between synsets, such as meronymy (PART-OF), hypernymy or hyponymy. The latter two are identical up to the order of their arguments, and represent the two directions of the IS-A relationship, i.e. they bind a synset to a more general one: 'medium of exchange' is the hypernym of 'money', resp. 'money' is a hyponym of 'medium of exchange'. Once the mappings *Word-form → Lexical entry* and *Lexical entry → Synset* are carried out, WordNet semantic relations can be queried. Figure 6a displays all hypernyms possibly related to the word-form 'funds'. WordNet also contains a similar hierarchy of hypernyms for the verbs. In terms of graph theory, each of these two hierarchies can be described as a directed acyclic graph.

In the context of corpus-based parser learning, where the correct grain of semantic classes is difficult to be forseen, such a hierarchy of semantic tags can provide the necessary material for a flexible choice of the most appropriate semantic tags to be embedded in the parser. The idea is to allow the learning algorithm automatically to choose the appropriate level of generality.

That goal can be achieved by using lists as lexical semantic tags of the nouns and verbs in the treebank. Each noun or verb is tagged with a single list of hypernyms, from the most general to the most specific, ending with the WordNet synset representing the meaning of that word in the given context. Most of the synsets (word sense) have one immediate hypernym; in the opposite case usually one of the hypernyms is more relevant to the context, e.g. *person→life form, person→causal agent*, and it is selected by the annotator. Typical examples of words so tagged follow; to improve readability, synset indices have been replaced with one of the synonyms to which they correspond.

```
%Word:PoS^SemanticTag  pos/neg example
chauffeur:n^[entity,causal_agent,operator,driver,chauffeur] (+)
driver:n^[entity,causal_agent,operator,driver]              (+)
friend:n^[entity,causal_agent,person,friend]                (-)
```

Imagine the words so tagged appearing in otherwise identical instantiations of the same parser action, with the first two examples being positive and the last one negative. The generalisation step of the ILP algorithm will result in the following constraint for that terminal: Word:n^[entity,causal_agent,operator,driver|_]. Note that the internal representation of lists as binary trees makes possible the least general generalisation of lists of different length. In the current implementation of LAPIS, the most specific semantic tag which covers a number of positive examples, and is consistent with the negative, is learned. In general, there is a number of semantic tags covering the same positive and none of the negative examples, e.g. operator and driver in our example. It is possible to modify the algorithm according to the NLP application, so that the most general of those semantic tags is kept instead of the most specific one.

6   Dataset

The lexicon Lex5000, used in the experiments with structured semantic tags, consists of the following files and predicates:[1]

1. The files `noun.lex` and `verb.lex` contain the predicates `nlx/2`, and `vlx/2` respectively, which map noun and verb word-forms into lexical entries. For instance: `vlx(beginning,begin)`.

2. The files `noun_path_i.pl` and `verb_path_i.pl` contain the predicates `npath/2` and `vpath/2` respectively, which map a lexical entry into one of the possible semantic tags. For the sake of brevity, the original synset indices used in WordNet have been replaced by shorter, yet unique identifiers, `vpath(begin, [i948,i949,i950])`.

3. The file `i_map.pl` contains a single predicate, `imap/2` which maps the identifiers used in the predicates `npath/2` and `vpath/2` to the corresponding synset indices in WordNet1.6, e.g. `imap(i10,'100011937')`.

4. The file `ambig_lex.pl` contains a mapping from word-forms to lexical entries for the words other than nouns and verbs, along with a single top-level predicate `dict(WordForm,PoS,TopDownPath)` serving as a uniform interface to the whole lexicon.

The ratio between word-forms, lexical entries and semantic tags (paths of hypernyms) is 73 : 74 : 265 for the nouns, and 26 : 27 : 183 for the verbs. There are 84 different word-forms in the whole lexicon, and 468 combinations of a word-form, PoS and semantic tag, which corresponds to an average of 5.57 tags per word-form.

The treebank T5000 is an artificial resource, generated from 12 sentence templates, and the lexicon Lex5000. The treebank contains 5046 sentences and their parse trees. All words are tagged with their PoS, and nouns and verbs are also semantically tagged. Although the words in Lex5000 can have more than one semantic tag assigned, the treebank is generated with the help of an additional lexicon (`disamb_lex_i.pl`), from which only the correct semantic tag is taken for each lexical slot in the templates. The treebank consists of clauses of the predicate `parse(Sentence,Tree)`. Each of the templates has a unique parse tree assigned to the sentences it generates, except for one, which is treated as ambiguous. For each of the sentences corresponding to that template, there is a *pair* of `parse/2` clauses sharing the same first argument, i.e. referring to the same sentence, but assigning a different parse tree to it.

7   Results and Evaluation

In the experiments, the treebank T5000 has been split into a training set containing 4036 pairs <sentence,parse tree>, and a test set containing 1010 such pairs. Samples of different size have been subsequently taken from the training

---

[1] The structure of the lexicon benefitted from the joint work with James Cussens on a related task.

set, and LAPIS applied on them. For each training set sample, 2 different parsers were produced: (1) the CFG-based parser produced in Step 2 of the LAPIS algorithm; (2) the specialised parser learned in Step 4. Two modifications of the latter were considered: (2a) the parser as is, and (2b) the parser in which the lexical semantic tags were not used as semantic constraints, i.e. it only differed from the CFG-based parser in its use of partially unfolded and lexicalised rules.

The performance of these three parsers was compared on the test data set for two outputs: the first parse, resp. all parses produced for each sentence. The two main criteria used for evaluation were accuracy and precision. If c is the number of correct parses, w the number of the wrong ones, and u the number of examples for which no parse is generated, then accuracy is defined as $acc = \frac{c}{c+w+u}$, and precision as $prec = \frac{c}{c+w}$. Additionally, we measured the percentage of sentences for which a parse was generated, $cov = \frac{c+w}{c+w+u}$.

In the experiments where all possible parses were produced, the number of parses produced for each sentence $\#p$, and the number of correct parses per sentence $corr$ were also considered. The results averaged over 5 trials are displayed in Table 1, and Figure 7. Table 2 shows the average times (over 4 trials) for the most time consuming LAPIS Steps 3–4, and for parsing itself. Time complexity of Steps 3–4 is almost linear w.r.t. the treebank size. Parsing without semantic constraints takes about 15–25 ms to find the first parse, and 31–56 ms to find all of them. Parsing with semantic constraints is slower for two reasons, because of the additional lexicon lookup, and also because of the amount of backtracking that semantic ambiguity causes. The parser was specially designed to postpone semantic tagging until all semantic constraints have been applied to avoid backtracking. However, search for *all* parses using semantic constraints may become very time consuming because of the high level of lexical semantic ambiguity present in the corpus. For that reason no results have been reported on the average performance of parsing with semantic constraints for all parses.

Comparison between the performance of the CFG-based parser and the one learned with LAPIS is strongly in favour of the latter. Using lexical semantic constraints in the specialised parser descreases accuracy (by an average of 0.57% in the first-parse-only case), as the number of covered sentences goes down. At the same time, precision is increased (by 1.14% in average). The limited lexical repertoire of the treebank makes possible to resolve many syntactic ambiguities by lexicalisation of the grammar. With more realistic data, the rôle of semantic classes is expected to increase.

Even when the semantic constraints are not applied, the average number of parses produced for each sentence $1.12 < \#p < 1.42$, in comparison to the average of 15.12 parses per sentence produced by the CFG-based parser, shows reduction of the number of parses by order of magnitude 1. For the two extreme cases when $\#p = 1.42$, an average number of 1.22 (1.23) correct parses per sentence are actually produced, due to the presence in the corpus of some semantically ambiguous sentences, and also probably because some of the specialised clauses representing parser actions partially overlap, so producing the same parse tree more than once.

Tr.trees		CFG-based		Specialised parser										
				Without semantic constraints								With sem. c.		
				First parse only[1]			Average of all parses					First parse only[2]		
		1st	aver.											
no	[%]	acc	acc	acc	prec	cov	acc	prec	cov	#p	corr	acc	prec	cov
40	1	5.05	11.30	85.00	94.60	89.93	94.61	94.61	100.00	1.13	1.08	84.74	94.79	89.46
80	2	5.05	11.30	86.37	93.26	92.57	92.70	92.70	100.00	1.12	1.02	84.33	96.84	87.14
121	3	5.05	11.30	89.38	95.38	93.74	94.79	94.79	100.00	1.14	1.07	87.26	96.90	90.09
202	5	5.05	11.30	91.72	94.25	97.33	92.29	92.29	100.00	1.33	1.19	91.36	96.03	95.17
404	10	5.05	11.30	92.61	94.17	98.34	92.55	92.55	100.00	1.31	1.13	91.72	95.13	96.41
807	20	5.05	11.30	93.34	93.71	99.60	92.20	92.20	100.00	1.42	1.22	92.73	94.66	97.96
1211	30	5.05	11.30	93.66	93.86	99.78	92.39	92.39	100.00	1.32	1.13	93.05	94.79	98.16
1615	40	5.05	11.30	93.94	94.07	99.86	92.34	92.34	100.00	1.39	1.19	93.74	94.94	98.73
2018	50	5.05	11.30	94.04	94.09	99.94	92.46	92.46	100.00	1.35	1.15	93.70	94.94	98.69
2421	60	5.05	11.30	93.98	93.98	100.00	92.31	92.31	100.00	1.35	1.15	93.78	94.91	98.81
2825	70	5.05	11.30	94.12	94.23	99.88	92.55	92.55	100.00	1.37	1.18	93.78	95.00	98.71
3228	80	5.05	11.30	94.35	94.35	100.00	92.69	92.69	100.00	1.37	1.17	94.15	95.23	98.87
3632	90	5.05	11.30	94.39	94.39	100.00	92.69	92.69	100.00	1.42	1.23	94.15	95.23	98.87
3834	95	5.05	11.30	94.41	94.41	100.00	92.69	92.69	100.00	1.31	1.12	94.31	95.39	98.87
4036	100	5.05	11.30	94.45	94.45	100.00	92.69	92.69	100.00	1.36	1.16	94.33	95.41	98.87

Table 1. Results

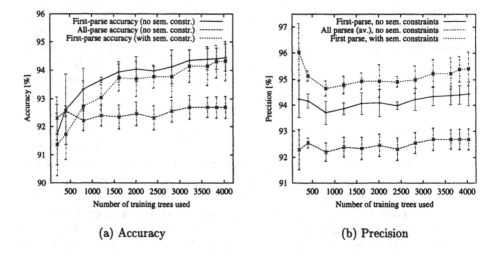

(a) Accuracy   (b) Precision

Fig. 7. Comparison of the three parsers

Tr. trees	40	80	121	202	404	807	1211	1615	2018	2421	2825	3228	3632	3834	4036
Step 3	13.8	48.5	64.8	115.8	222.0	461.2	758.2	1036.5	1357.2	1727.0	2097.0	2458.0	2860.2	3094.5	3310.2
Step 4	2.0	4.8	7.8	15.2	43.0	135.5	288.5	472.0	705.0	1015.2	1339.2	1789.0	2122.5	2442.5	2600.2
FPO[1] -sem.	0.015	0.016	0.017	0.018	0.020	0.022	0.023	0.025	0.024	0.025	0.025	0.023	0.022	0.022	0.021
AllP (total)	0.031	0.034	0.036	0.040	0.043	0.048	0.050	0.056	0.053	0.055	0.055	0.051	0.051	0.051	0.049
FPO[2] +sem.	4.548	7.262	3.010	0.684	0.542	0.387	0.380	0.298	0.283	0.292	0.338	0.281	0.284	0.266	0.250

Table 2. Time (in sec.) required for Steps 3–4 of Lapis, and for parsing.

8 Conclusions

The combination of LAPIS and WordNet proves its efficiency for the learning of specialised parsers, containing a very limited amount of nondeterminism. The dataset used, a treebank of semantically annotated parse trees, along with the semantic lexicon WordNet leads to the construction of parsers based on grammars with partially lexicalised and/or unfolded rules, with the additional help of lexical semantic constraints. The use of an artificial treebank was justified for two reasons. Firstly, the annotation of that part of the Brown Corpus which is tagged with WordNet synsets, comes in pairs of files, one for the syntactic trees and one for the semantic tags. Discrepancies between the two files make of their merging a nontrivial task. Also, we wanted to test the impact of semantic constraints on a noise-free data. Handling of noise is an issue on its own, which is still to be addressed in LAPIS. A promising future line of research is to use treebanks with all nodes annotated with their semantics in logic form, with the possible result being a parser which only produces parse trees corresponding to valid semantic interpretations of the whole sentence.

9 Acknowledgements

The author wish to thank James Cussens and the three anonymous referees for their thoughtful remarks. Part of the work on LAPIS and the treebank T5000 was done at CTU Prague. The author has been supported for this research by ESPRIT Projects 20237 ILP2, and 28623 ALADIN.

References

1. Alfred Aho, Ravi Sethi, and Jeffrey Ullman. *Compilateurs - Principles, techniques et outils*. InterEditions, Paris, 1989.
2. George A. Miller *et al.* Introduction to WordNet: An on-line lexical database. Technical report, University of Princeton, 1993.
3. Dimitar Kazakov. An inductive approach to natural language parser design. In Kemal Oflazer and Harold Somers, editors, *Proceedings of NeMLaP-2*, pages 209–217, Ankara, 1996. Bilkent University.
4. Mitchell P. Marcus, Beatrice Santorini, and Mary Ann Marcinkiewicz. Building a large annotated corpus of English: the Penn treebank. *Computational Linguistics*, 19, 1993.
5. Tom M. Mitchell. *Machine Learning*. McGraw-Hill, 1997.
6. G. Plotkin. A note of inductive generalization. In B. Meltzer and D. Mitchie, editors, *Machine Intelligence 5*, pages 153–163. Edinburgh University Press, 1970.
7. Ch. Samuelsson. *Fast Natural-Language Parsing Using Explanation-Based Learning*. PhD thesis, The Royal Institute of Technology and Stockholm University, 1994.
8. John M. Zelle. *Using Inductive Logic Programming to Automate the Construction of Natural Language Parsers*. PhD thesis, The University of Texas at Austin, 1995.
9. John M. Zelle and Raymond J. Mooney. Inducing deterministic Prolog parsers from treebanks: A machine learning approach. In *Proceedings of AAAI-94*, pages 748–753. AAI Press/MIT Press, 1994.

Learning Word Segmentation Rules for Tag Prediction

Dimitar Kazakov[1], Suresh Manandhar[2], and Tomaž Erjavec[3]

University of York, Heslington, York YO10 5DD, UK,
{kazakov,suresh}@cs.york.ac.uk,
WWW home page: [1] http://www.cs.york.ac.uk/~kazakov/ and
[2] http://www.cs.york.ac.uk/~suresh/

[3] Department for Intelligent Systems,
Jožef Stefan Institute, Ljubljana, Slovenia,
Tomaz.Erjavec@ijs.si,
WWW home page: http://nl.ijs.si/tomaz/

Abstract. In our previous work we introduced a hybrid, GA&ILP-based approach for learning of stem-suffix segmentation rules from an unmarked list of words. Evaluation of the method was made difficult by the lack of word corpora annotated with their morphological segmentation. Here the hybrid approach is evaluated indirectly, on the task of tag prediction. A pair of stem-tag and suffix-tag lexicons is obtained by the application of that approach to an annotated lexicon of word-tag pairs. The two lexicons are then used to predict the tags of unseen words in two ways, (1) by using only the stem and suffix generated by the segmentation rules, and (2) for all matching combinations of stem and suffix present in the lexicons. The results show high correlation between the constituents generated by the segmentation rules, and the tags of the words in which they appear, thereby demonstrating the linguistic relevance of the segmentations produced by the hybrid approach.

1 Introduction

Word segmentation is an important subtask of natural language processing with a range of applications from hyphenation to more detailed morphological analysis and text-to-speech conversion. In our previous work [5] we introduced a hybrid, GA&ILP-based approach for learning of stem-suffix segmentation rules from an unmarked list of words. Evaluation of the method was made difficult by the lack of word corpora annotated with their morphological segmentation. Here the quality of the segmentation rules learned with the hybrid approach is assessed, indirectly, through the task of morphosyntactic tag prediction.

Tag prediction of unknown words is an important preprocessing step performed by taggers. However, currently taggers either employ some simple heuristics for tag prediction based on the majority class tag, or word affixes [1]. In this paper we show that word segmentation information can be exploited to predict the possible tags of unknown words with high accuracy. There are several methods which would not require the segmentation of training words to learn tag prediction rules from *tagged* lexicons. The tag predicion task is employed here to prove the close correlation between morphosyntactic tags and word segments produced by our rules. Success in this task would also imply the possibility of using those segments as a substitute for morphosyntactic tags when learning NLP tools from *unnanotated* corpora.

An advantage of our approach is that it does not require a presegmented corpus for training. Instead, the system can be trained by supplying it with the same kind of lexicon of word-tag pairs as the one used in taggers.

In our previous work, we have described the hybrid approach combining unsupervised and supervised learning techniques for generation of word segmentation rules from a list of words. A bias for word segmentation [4] is reformulated as the fitness function of a simple genetic algorithm, which is used to search for the word list segmentation that corresponds to the best bias value. In the second phase, the list of segmented words obtained from the genetic algorithm is used as an input for CLOG [6], a first-order decision list learning algorithm. The result is a logic program in a decision list representation that can be used for segmentation of unseen words. Here an annotated lexicon of word-forms is used to assign morphosyntactic tags (or *descriptions*, MSDs) to each of the segments, and so build two annotated lexicons of stems and endings. The result is interpreted as a generative word grammar. The pertinence of this grammar is evaluated on the task of MSD prediction for unseen words, with and without the additional constraint of a single-word segmentation generated by the decision list learned in the previous step.

2 Overview of GA&ILP Learning of Segmentation Rules

This section provides a brief review of our hybrid GA&ILP approach, and for more details the reader should consult the paper in which the approach was first introduced [5].

2.1 Naïve Theory of Morphology as Word Segmentation Bias

Given a list of words segmented into stem-suffix pairs one can construct a pair of lexicons consisting of all stems, and suffixes, respectively.

The Naïve Theory of Morphology (NTM) bias [4] prefers segmentations which reduce the total number of characters N in the stem and suffix lexicons. The bias is based on the hypothesis that substrings composed out of real morphemes occur in the words with a frequency higher than any other left or right substrings.[1] In that way, a theory with a low N would produce lexicons where 'stems' and 'suffixes' correspond very often to single morphemes or their concatenation. Since

---

[1] This presumption is limited to the languages in which the main operator used to combine morphemes is `concatenation`.

the word list can be stored as a list of pairs of indices <stem,suffix> along with the two lexicons, the bias described can be seen as using Occam's razor to choose the simplest theory corresponding to the given dataset.

2.2 Genetic Algorithms

Genetic algorithms (GA) [3] are often used as an alternative approach to tasks with a large search space and multiple local maxima. A GA maintains a set of candidate solutions called *individuals* and applies the natural selection operators of *crossover* and *mutation* to generate, usually in several iterations, new candidate solutions from existing ones. A *fitness function* is employed to rank the individuals to determine their goodness. The individuals are represented as a sequence of characters of a given, often binary, alphabet. The *crossover* operation constructs two new child individuals by splicing two parent individuals at *n* points. The *mutation* operator creates a new individual from a single parent by randomly changing one of its characters. Individuals are mutated according to some mutation probability known as *mutation rate*.

The following algorithm, known as a *simple genetic algorithm*, has been used for the purposes of this research.

Procedure simple genetic algorithm

1. Initialisation
   (a) Create a random population of candidate solutions
       (*individuals*) of size *popsize*.
   (b) Evaluate all individuals using the fitness function.
   (c) Store the best evaluated individual as *best-ever* individual.
   (d) Set the number of generations to *NG*.
2. Generation and Selection
   For *NG* generations repeat:
   (a) Sample the individuals according to their fitness, so that
       in the resulting *mating pool* those with higher fitness
       appear repeatedly with a higher probability.
   (b) Apply crossover with probability *crossover_rate*.
   (c) Apply mutation with probability *mutation_rate*.
   (d) Evaluate all individuals using the fitness function.
   (e) Update the best-ever individual.
3. Provide the *best-ever* individual as a solution.

2.3 GA Search for Best NTM

The so described genetic algorithm is used to search the space of possible segmentations of given list of words and find a segmentation that is minimal with respect to the NTM bias.

The representation of the list of segmented words in the GA framework is straightforward. The position of the boundary between stem and suffix in a word is represented by an integer, equal to the number of characters in the stem. The segmentation of a list of words is represented as a vector of integers (see

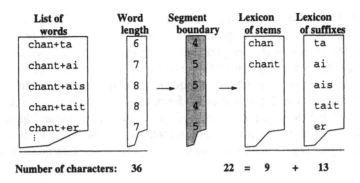

Fig. 1. Representing the segmentation of a list of words as a vector of integers, and creating lexicons of stems and suffixes

Figure 1). A randomly generated population of such segmentations is used as a starting point of the GA search. The *crossover* operator constructs two new child chromosomes by splicing two parent chromosomes at one point. The *mutation* operator modifies the split position of a single word either by incrementing or decrementing by one the corresponding integer, or by changing it randomly within the word length.

2.4 Segmentation Rule Learning Using CLOG

The GA produces for a given list of words their segmentation, along with a pair of lexicons of stems and suffixes. Typically for GAs, the segmentation is only near-optimal w.r.t. the bias, i.e. the change of some segmentations would result in a better bias value. The reusability of the GA output for unseen words is limited. Indeed, one could use the lexicons to segment an unseen word into a stem and suffix present in the lexicons. However, if there is more than one such segmentation, there is no way to choose among them. In the hybrid GA&ILP approach, the ILP system CLOG is applied to learn segmentation rules which produce better segmentations than the GA alone, and can be used to find the best segmentation of unseen words.

CLOG [6] is a system for learning of first-order decision lists. CLOG can learn from positive examples only using the *output completeness* assumption [7], only considering generalisations that are relevant to an example. In the current implementation these generalisations are supplied by a user-defined predicate which takes as input an example and generates a hard-coded list of generalisations that cover that example. The *gain* function currently used in CLOG is user-defined. For the segmentation problem we chose the following simple gain function: *gain* = $QP - SN - C$ where QP denotes the number of new examples covered positively, SN denotes the number of previously covered examples that are covered negatively and C is the number of literals in the clause body.

The words segmented with the GA are represented as clauses of the predicate seg(W,P,S), for instance: seg([a,n,t,o,n,i,m,i,h],[a,n,t,o,n,i,m],[i,h]).

Then `seg/3` is used as a target predicate with mode `seg(+,?,?)` of the inductive learning algorithm. Also, the predicate `append/3` is used as intentional background knowledge, and the range of the theory constants is limited to the set of stems and suffixes that appear in the predicate `seg/3`. In fact, either of the last two arguments of `seg/3` is redundant and the second of them was omitted in the real input dataset, which resulted in the format `seg([a,n,t,o,n,i,m,i,h],[i,h])`. The result of ILP learning is an ordered list of rules (non-ground logic clauses) preceded by a list of exceptions represented as ground facts, such as the following example: `seg([a,n,t,o,n,i,m,a], [i,m,a])`. The exceptions do not have

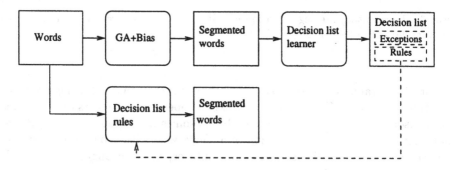

Fig. 2. GA&ILP word segmentation setting

any impact on the segmentation of unseen words, and they are removed from the decision list. In most cases, exceptions correspond to imperfectly segmented words. When the segmentation rules, with the exceptions removed, are applied on the GA input list of words, the result is, in general, a segmentation with a better bias value. Figure 2 summarises schematically the GA&ILP approach.

3 Dataset

For our experiments we used part of the lexicon of the Slovene language created within the EU Copernicus project MULTEXT-East [2]. The project developed a multi-lingual corpus of text and speech data, covering six languages, including Slovene, and lexical resources covering the corpus data. The Slovene lexicon contains the full inflectional paradigms for over 15,000 lemmas; it has over half a million entries, where each entry gives the word-form, its lemma and morphosyntactic description. These descriptions are constructed according to the MULTEXT-East grammar, which follows international recommendations and is harmonised for seven languages. The MSDs contain all morphosyntactic features which are relevant to a given PoS. For the 7 parts of speech actually represented in the data used here, the number of features is as follows: Noun–8 features, Verb–9, Adjective–9, Pronoun–13, Adverb–3, Numeral–10, Abbreviation–1.

The MULTEXT-East Slovene lexicon is freely available for research purposes. It includes a lexicon of neologisms from the Slovene translation of Orwell's *1984*. From that lexicon, we used a list of 4383 different word-forms, i.e. with homonyms represented only once.[2] The list was split at random into a training set of 3506 words and a test set containing 877 words. Next, the training set was divided into disjunctive lists of 100 words each and the genetic algorithm was separately run on each of them. Then those lists were merged again. This technique proves to be a feasible trade-off between the input data size and the time needed by the GA to find a segmentation of high quality. Task decomposition also makes the GA time complexity linear w.r.t. the input size. Indeed, if T is the time required to run the GA on a list of M words for a certain number of generations, then the time to apply the GA on a list of $K * M$ words will be approximately $K * T$ if the data set is divided into K separate chunks and the GA applied separately on each of them. The described decomposition also allows the individual GA runs to be run in parallel.

The list of segmentated words so obtained was used as input of CLOG. As a result, a first-order decision list was learned. The decision list contained 736 exceptions (Figure 3), and 242 rules (Figure 4). Only the rules were applied for the segmentation of the training list of words (cf. Figure 2), thus obtaining a segmentation with a better bias value.

```
%seg(Word,Suffix).
seg(['C',r,k,o,s,t,a,v,s,k,e], [k,o,s,t,a,v,s,k,e]) :- !.
seg(['C',i,t,a,m,o], [i,t,a,m,o]) :- !.
seg(['C',i,t,a,l], ['C',i,t,a,l]) :- !.
```

Fig. 3. Sample of decision list exceptions

Up to this point, no use whatsoever was made of the MSDs in the lexicon. In the final stage of data preparation, *all* MSDs which can be assigned to each word in the list were retrieved from the lexicon, and the 4-tuples word-stem-suffix-possible MSD were stored as clauses of the predicate msd_train/4:

```
msd_train([a,d,o,p,t,i,v,n,i],[a,d,o,p,t,i,v,n],[i],['A',f,p,m,s,a,y,-,n]).
```

There are 10477 such clauses, i.e. each word in the training set corresponds in average to 3 morphosyntactic descriptions. The latter are very detailed, ranging from part of speech to up to 12 more features. The MSDs are represented as lists of one-letter constants, where the lists for a given PoS have the same length.

Similarly, the 877 words in the test set were annotated with all possible MSDs, producing as a result 2531 word-tag pairs tagged_lex(['C',e,s,t,e,m,u], ['A',f,p,m,s,d]).

Given the predicate msd_train/4, the following two lexicons can be generated:

---

[2] For technical reasons, the characters č, š, and ž were replaced with 'C', 'S', and 'Z' respectively.

```
seg(A,B):-        append([s,u,p,e,r], B, A), !.
seg(A,B):-        append([s,u,g,e,r,i,r,a,j], B, A), !.
seg(A,B):-        append([s,u,g,e,r,i,r,a], B, A), !.
seg(A, [i]) :-
          append(_, [i], A),
             append(_, [i,t,e,t,i], A), !.
seg(A, B) :-
          append([p,o,z,i,v,a,j], B, A),
             append(_, [a], A), !.
seg(A,[]):-       append(_, [], A),
                     append(_, [u,j,o,'C'], A), !.
seg(A,[u]):-      append(_, [u], A),
                     append(_, [j,u], A), !.
seg(A,[e,m,a]):- append(_, [e,m,a], A), !.
seg(A,[e,m,u]):- append(_, [e,m,u], A), !.
seg(A,[i,t,a]):- append(_, [i,t,a], A), !.
seg(A,[i,m,o]):- append(_, [i,m,o], A), !.
```

Fig. 4. Sample of segmentation rules

- *stem-tag* lexicon containing all stem-MSD pairs contained in msd_train/4, *e.g.* stem_tag([a,d,o,p,t,i,v,n,i],['A',f,p,m,s,a,y,-,n]).
- *suffix-tag* lexicon containing all suffix-MSD pairs contained in msd_train/4, *e.g.* suffix_tag([i],['A',f,p,m,s,a,y,-,n]).

4 Tag Prediction

4.1 Method

The tag prediction task is to predict for a given word W the set of all possible MSDs (i.e. tags). This task is broken down into the following stages:

Segmentation Split W into stem Stm and suffix Suf by either method:
    Method 1 using the segmentation rules generated by CLOG
    Method 2 splitting the word into all possible stem-suffix pairs such that both the stem and suffix can be found in the *stem-tag* and *suffix-tag* lexicons.

Tag prediction Given a segmented word W = Stm + Suf, the prediction of the set of tags assigned to W is mainly based on the MSDs in suf-tag lexicon which match the suffix. When the stem is present in the stem-tag lexicon, it is used as an additional constraint, limiting the number of MSD candidates.
    PoS matching Produce the set of all MSDs selected by the suffix in the suf-tag lexicon, such that for each of them an MSD with the same PoS is selected by the stem in the stem-tag lexicon, i.e.:
        stem_tag(Stm,[PoS|_]),suffix_tag(Suf,MSD),MSD=[PoS|_].
    Suffix-based If the previous step produces an empty set of MSDs, then its second constraint is dropped, and the set of tags generated is the set of all MSDs matching the suffix in the suf-tag lexicon: suffix_tag(Suf, MSD).

4.2 Evaluation

A variant of the well-known statistics *precision* and *recall* have been employed to evaluate the performance of our approach for tag prediction. First, some metric should be adopted for the purposes of comparison between predicted and correct MSDs. The simplest, binary yes/no metric which would count only perfect matches was considered too rigorous for the comparison of MSDs with up to 13 features. Instead, we employ a finer-grain metric based on the similarity $sim(MSD_1, MSD_2)$ of two MSDs.

$$sim(MSD_1, MSD_2) = \#identical\ features \qquad (1)$$

We extend this to the similarity between an MSD and a tag-set (*i.e.* a set of MSDs):

$$sim(MSD, TagSet) = max\left(sim(MSD, MSD')\right), MSD' \in TagSet \qquad (2)$$

For a given word W, let the set of correct tags (MSDs) be $TagSet_c$, and the predicted set of tags $TagSet_p$. This similarity measure is incorporated in our definitions of precision and recall in the following way.

Let L denote the test set of words.
Let E denote the set of $(TagSet_c, TagSet_p)$ (correct-predicted) tagsets for every word W in L.
For any tagset $TagSet$, let $| TagSet |$ denote the total number of features in $TagSet$.
We define *precision* and *recall* as follows:

$$precision(E) = \frac{\sum\limits_{(TagSet_c, TagSet_p) \in E} \sum\limits_{MSD \in TagSet_p} sim(MSD, TagSet_c)}{\sum\limits_{(TagSet_c, TagSet_p) \in E} | TagSet_p |} \qquad (3)$$

$$recall(E) = \frac{\sum\limits_{(TagSet_c, TagSet_p) \in E} \sum\limits_{MSD \in TagSet_c} sim(MSD, TagSet_p)}{\sum\limits_{(TagSet_c, TagSet_p) \in E} | TagSet_c |} \qquad (4)$$

In other words, precision shows how closely the predicted tags match the gold standard. To compute precision, for each of the predicted MSDs the best match (the most similar MSD) is found in the set of correct tags, then the overall similarity for all predicted tags is found, and it is divided by the total number of features. Similarly, accuracy shows how well the correct tags are represented in the set of predicted tags.

4.3 Results

Using Segmentation Method 1 The segmentation rules learned with CLOG were applied on the test data. Out of 877 different words in the test set, 858 or 97.83% were covered by the rules. For the successfully segmented words, predictions were made for the set of corresponding MSDs. For each word in the test set, the set of predicted MSDs was in average 3.89 times larger than the set of correct MSDs (the set of correct MSDs contains in total 21742 features, as opposed to 84612 in the MSDs predicted). The figures for precision (82.35%) and recall (91.69%), as defined in Equations 3–4, can be interpreted as follows:

1. Precision can be seen as the correctness of the predictions made, whereas recall quantifies the ability to produce as many of the correct tags as possible. The result *precision* < *recall* means that our approach performs better on the latter task than on the former one, i.e. it is slightly over-general, more careful not to reject a correct MSD than not to generate an incorrect one. So, the metric used has a simple and plausible interpretation.
2. A high percentage of the MSDs predicted have a close match in the set of correct MSDs. Since $|MSD_p| > |MSD_c|$, that also means that many of the predicted MSDs are very similar to each other, differing only in a small percentage of features.

Using Segmentation Method 2 The results for this experiment are as follows: *precision = 48.28%, recall = 99.50%.*

5 Conclusions

This article introduces a method using a lexicon annotated with morphosyntactic features to learn rules for the prediction of those features for unseen words. The article also demonstrates the strength of the hybrid GA&ILP approach in learning segmentation rules from unnanotated words. The main advantages of the approach are threefold. Firstly, the lexicons of stems and suffixes produced by the segmentation rules learned can reliably capture the information relevant to the word morphosyntactic tags. This can be seen from the 99.50% recall for segmentation method 2, where all combinations of stems and suffixes with matching MSDs were used to predict word tags. The second contribution of the hybrid approach is that it learns rules assigning a single segmentation to each covered word. The additional information that this segmentation brings to the tag prediction task is reflected in the considerable increase in precision. Finally, the hybrid approach only requires a relatively small list of unnanotated words (10^3–10^4 as compared to the annotated corpora of 10^6 words used by Brill [1]) to learn segmentation rules, which can be used either for the segmentation of the words used for learning, or to segment unseen words. The unsupervised framework makes the application of the hybrid approach to word segmentation a possible way to apply corpus-based NLP methods requiring morphosyntactic tags to unannotated corpora. As the word constituents produced by the hybrid approach are closely related to the morphosyntactic features of the words, tagging the words in a corpus with their constituents produced by the segmentation rules could serve as a substitute for missing morphosyntactic tags.

6 Acknowledgements

The first author has been supported for this research by ESPRIT Projects 20237 ILP2, and 28623 ALADIN.

References

1. E. Brill. Some advances in transformation-based part of speech tagging. In *Proceedings of AAAI-94*, pages 748–753. AAAI Press/MIT Press, 1994.
2. Tomaž Erjavec. The MULTEXT-East Slovene Lexicon. In *Proceedings of the 7th Electrotechnical Conference ERK*, Volume B, pages 189–192, Portorož, Slovenia, 1998.
3. David E. Goldberg. *Genetic Algorithms in Search, Optimization, and Machine Learning*. Addison-Wesley, 1989.
4. Dimitar Kazakov. Unsupervised learning of naïve morphology with genetic algorithms. In W. Daelemans, A. van den Bosch, and A. Weijters, editors, *Workshop Notes of the ECML/MLnet Workshop on Empirical Learning of Natural Language Processing Tasks*, pages 105–112, Prague, April 1997.
5. Dimitar Kazakov, and Suresh Manandhar. A Hybrid Approach to Word Segmentation. In D. Page, editor, *Proc. of the 8th International Workshop on Inductive Logic Programming (ILP-98)*, pages 125–134. Berlin, 1998. Springer-Verlag.
6. Suresh Manandhar, Sašo Džeroski, and Tomaž Erjavec. Learning Multilingual Morphology with CLOG. In *The Eighth International Conference on Inductive Logic Programming (ILP'98)*, Madison, Wisconsin, USA, 1998.
7. Raymond J. Mooney and Mary Elaine Califf. Induction of first–order decision lists: Results on learning the past tense of English verbs. *Journal of Artificial Intelligence Research*, June 1995.

Approximate ILP Rules by Backpropagation Neural Network: A Result on Thai Character Recognition

Boonserm Kijsirikul and Sukree Sinthupinyo

Department of Computer Engineering, Chulalongkorn University,
Phayathai Rd., Phathumwan, Bangkok, 10330, Thailand
Email: Boonserm@cp.eng.chula.ac.th

Abstract. This paper presents an application of Inductive Logic Programming (ILP) and Backpropagation Neural Network (BNN) to the problem of Thai character recognition. In such a learning problem, there exist several different classes of examples; there are 77 different Thai characters. Using examples constructed from character images, ILP learns 77 rules each of which defines each character. However, some unseen character images, especially the noisy images, may not exactly match any learned rule, i.e., they may not be covered by any rule. Therefore, a method for approximating the rule that best matches the unseen data is needed. Here we employ BNN for finding such rules. Experimental results on noisy data show that the accuracy of rules learned by ILP without the help of BNN is comparable to other methods. Furthermore, combining BNN with ILP yields the significant improvement and surpasses the other methods tested in our experiment.

1 Introduction

Inductive Logic Programming (ILP) has been successfully applied to real-world tasks, such as drug design[11], traffic problem detection [4], etc. This paper presents an application of ILP to the task of Thai printed character recognition. Although this task has been widely researched for many years and there are some commercial products of Thai character recognition software available, the accuracies are not yet as high as those of English. This is due to the fact that Thai characters are comparatively more complex and some character is similar to others. Various approaches have been proposed to Thai character recognition such as the method of comparing the head of characters [6], backpropagation neural network [8,15], the method of combining fuzzy logic and syntactic method [13], the method of using cavity features [12], etc.

The reason for choosing ILP in the task of Thai printed character recognition is that ILP is able to employ domain-specific background knowledge that makes a better generalization performance on data. However, some problems arise when ILP is applied to our task where there are several classes of examples, i.e., 77 different Thai characters. Most ILP systems work with two classes of examples (positive and negative), and construct a set of rules for the positive class. Any example not covered by the rules is classified as negative. If we want to employ these systems to learn a multi-class concept, we could do this by first constructing a set of rules for the first class with its examples as positive and the other examples as negative, then constructing the sets of rules for other classes by the same process. The learned rules are then used to classify future data, and the rule that covers or exactly matches the data can be selected as the output. One major problem of this method is that some test data, especially noisy images in our task, may not be covered by any rule. Thus the method is unable to determine the correct rule. Dzeroski et al. [5] solved this problem by assigning the majority class recorded from training data to the test data that is not exactly matched against any rule.

We approach this problem directly by proposing a method to approximate the rule that provides the best match with the data. Here, we employ BNN for the approximation of ILP rules. First we tried to approximate the rule by using the number of *nonmatching* literals (literals whose truth values are false) and the number of *matching* literals (literals whose truth values are true) as the training input vector to the BNN. We found that the method is able to find the approximate rule that gives a higher accuracy than that of ILP alone. However, our first method did not take into account the significance or the weight of each literal. We then redesigned the structure of BNN to consider the weight of each literal. In our second method, instead of the numbers of nonmatching and matching literals, we use the truth values of all literals in the rules as the input vector, and design a new structure of BNN that can give a weight to each literal separately. Experimental result shows that the recognition accuracy of the new structure is further improved, and is higher than those of the other methods tested in our experiment.

2 Feature Extraction

In the literature of Thai printed character recognition, the method of combining fuzzy logic and syntactic (FLS) reported very high accuracy and was shown to be one of the most successful methods [13]. Therefore, in the following experiment FLS will be used to compare with our methods, and for the comparison purpose the feature extraction in FLS is employed.

After a character image is preprocessed by noise reduction and thinning processing, its features are extracted. Basically, the extracted feature is represented as a *primitive vector list*. A primitive vector list is composed of primitive vectors each of which represents the type of lines or circles in the original image. Therefore, the list represents the structure of lines and circles, and shows how these lines and circles are connected to form the character. Each primitive vector is defined to be one of 13 types shown in Figure 1.

The primitive vectors of type 0 to 7 represent lines and those of type 8 to 12 represent circles. The primitive vector of type 0 is the line whose angle is between 1 to 45 degrees, and the angle of the type 1 is between 46 to 90 degrees, and so on. The primitive vector of type 8 is the circle that does not connect to any line. The primitive vector of type 9 is the circle that connects to a line at the quadrant 1, etc.

In addition to the primitive vectors, other features are also extracted such as the starting and ending zone of a primitive vector, the level, and the ratio of the width and the height of characters, the list of zones containing junctions of lines, the list of zones

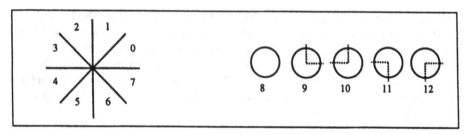

Fig. 1. Primitive Vectors

containing the 'ʌ' angles, and the list of zones containing 'v' angles. The level indicates the character position. Thai characters are written in 3 levels, i.e., level 1, level 2 and level 3. For example, in Figure 2, the word "กุ้ง(shrimp)" consists of four characters in the three levels; ' ̋ ',' ̣ ', 'ก' and 'ง' are in the level 1, the level 2, the level 3 and the level 3, respectively. The 'ʌ' and 'v' angles are helpful in distinguishing between a pair of similar characters except the angle; one of them contains such an angle and the other does not, such as ('ข','ช'), ('ก','ถ'), etc.

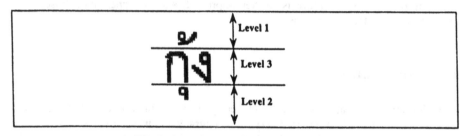

Fig. 2. Three levels of Thai writing system

An instance of the extracted features of the character image 'ก' is shown in Figure 3. This character image contains 8 primitive vectors whose numbers are indicated by 0, 1...7 in the figure. For instance, the vector no. 0 is of type 1, contains the end point (the point not connected to another which is indicated by -1), has the starting zone in zone 3 and the ending zone in zone 2. The image contains 'ʌ' angles in zone 1.

3 Applying Progol to Thai Character Recognition

The ILP system used in our experiment is Progol [10]. The inputs to Progol are positive examples, negative examples and background knowledge. The output is a set of rules defining the positive examples. The following subsection explains the inputs and output from Progol.

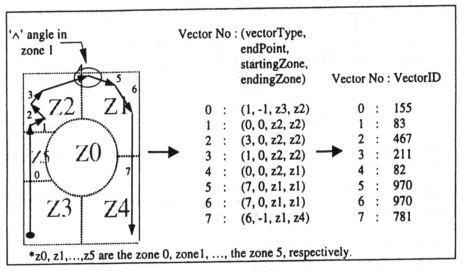

*z0, z1,...,z5 are the zone 0, zone1, ..., the zone 5, respectively.

Fig. 3. An instance of features extracted from a character image.

3.1 Example Representation & Background Knowledge

An example to Progol is a set of extracted features explained in the previous section. It is the same as one used by FLS, except that it is converted to the logical representation in the following form:

$$char(A,B,C,D,E,F)$$

where *char* is a character, A is the level of the character, B is the ratio of the width and the height, C is the list of numbers each of which represents a primitive vector, whether or not the primitive vector contains the end point, the starting zone and the ending zone of the vector, D is the list of zones that contain junctions of lines, E is the list of the zones that contain the '$\vee$' angles, and F is the list of the zones that contain the '$\wedge$' angles. For ease of writing definition of background knowledge, we map a tuple "(vectorType, endPoint, startingZone, endingZone)" into a number "VectorID", and used it in C. Figure 4 shows some examples of the character 'ก'.

n(3,0.78,[155,83,467,211,82,970,970,781],[],[],[z1]).

n(3,0.76,[155,339,339,211,83,83,978,970,781],[],[],[z2]).

n(3,0.72,[155,467,467,211,211,83,82,970,842,845,805,19],[z2],[z2],[z1]).

n(3,0.75,[155,467,211,83,83,978,842,842,714,653,19],[z2],[z2],[z2]).

n(3,0.75,[155,467,211,83,82,970,845,677,19],[z2],[z2],[z1]).

n(3,0.78,[155,467,211,83,82,970,970,781,83,979,19],[z2],[z2,z2],[z2,z1]).

Fig. 4. Examples of character 'ก'

The Thai character set consists of 77 different characters ('ก', 'ข', 'ฃ',..., 'ฮ'). We choose two types of fonts, i.e., Cordia and Eucrosia, each of which contains 7 different sizes (20,22,24,28,32,36 and 48 points). Therefore, the number of examples is 77 x 2 x 7 = 1078.

We have constructed background knowledge that describes our knowledge about the domain of Thai character recognition. The appropriate background knowledge will help Progol produce more accurate rules. For example, if we believe that the zone of the head of the character can be used to discriminate between the characters, we will add a predicate, such as head_zone(ListofPrimitiveVector,InZone) that examines this characteristic. The background knowledge used in our experiment contains 55 predicates. Some of them are shown in Figure 5. Note that some background predicates are complicated and defined by a recursive program. This is one reason of using Progol in our task.

```
head_zone(A,B) :- head(A,C), startZone(C,B).
head_primitive(A,B) :- head(A,C), primitive(C,B).
count_primitive_type4([],0).
count_primitive_type4([A|B],C) :-
    primitive(A,4), count_primitive_type4(B,D), C is D+1.
count_primitive_type4([A|B],C) :-
    not primitive(A,4), count_primitive_type4(B,C).
v_angle_at_head(A) :- member(z2,A).
endpoint_primitive(A,B) :-
    member(C,A),endpoint(C,-1),  primitive(C,B).
circle_at_endpoint_in_zone(A,B)  :-
    member(C,A), isCircleEndpoint(C), startZone(C,B).
count_circle_at_endpoint([],0).
count_circle_at_endpoint([A|B],C) :-
    isCircleEndpoint(A),count_circle_at_endpoint(B,D), C is D+1.
count_circle_at_endpoint([A|B],C) :-
    not isCircleEndpoint(A),count_circle_at_endpoint(B,D).
count_startZone5([],0).
count_startZone5([A|B],C) :-
    startZone(A,5), count_startZone5(B,D), C is D+1.
count_startZone5([A|B],C) :-
    not startZone(A,5), count_startZone5(B,C).
right_line(A) :-
    member(B,A), endPoint(B,-1),endZone(B,1), primitive(B,1).
right_line(A) :-
    member(B,A), endPoint(B,-1),endZone(B,1), primitive(B,2).
member_zone(A,B,C) :- member(E,A), startZone(E,B), endZone(E,C).
head_primitive_type9or10(A)  :- head_primitive(A,9).
head_primitive_type9or10(A)  :- head_primitive(A,10).
head_primitive_type10or11(A)  :- head_primitive(A,10).
head_primitive_type10or11(A)  :- head_primitive(A,11).
```

Fig. 5. Some of background knowledge used in the experiment.

3.2 The Output

We first train Progol to induce the rule for character 'n' by 14 examples of 'n' as positive examples and the rest (1,064 examples) as negative examples. The training process is then repeated for constructing the rules of all characters. The output of Progol is a set of 77 rules that are used to classify the future character images. Each rule defines the characteristics of each character. Note that we did not force Progol to learn one rule per class, but the output having one rule per class is just that obtained by Progol.

Figure 6 shows some of the learned rules. For instance, the first rule in Figure 6 defines the character 'n'; an input character image will be recognized as the character 'n' if that character is in level 3, has the head in zone 3, the head of character is the primitive vector of type 1, and the number of primitive vector of type 4 is equal to 0. These rules will be used to compare with the features of a future character image. The rule that exactly matches the image is selected as the output. However, in the case of noisy image or unseen data, a character image may not exactly match any rule in the rule set. In the next section, we will describe the methods of using BNN to approximately match the rule with the character image.

```
n(3,A,B,C,D,E)      :- head_zone(B,3), head_primitive(B,1),
                       count_primitive_type4(B,0).

u(3,A,B,C,D,E)      :- not v_angle_at_head(D), head_zone(B,2),
                       endpoint_primitive(B,1),
                       circle_at_endpoint_in_zone(B,2),
                       count_circle_at_endpoint(B,1),
                       right_line(B), member_zone(B,4,1),
                       head_primitive_type9or10(B),
                       count_startZone5(B,0).

u(3,A,B,C,D,E)      :- head_zone(B,2), head_primitive(B,10),
                       endpoint_zone(B,4),
                       begin_and_endzone(B,2,1),
                       member_zone(B,2,1), member_zone(B,4,1),
                       have_member(B,7,2,2),
                       head_primitive_type9or10(B),
                       head_primitive_type10or11(B).

n(3,A,B,[z3],C,D)   :- not ^_angle([z3]), not v_angle(C),
                       head_zone(B,0), endpoint_primitive(B,6).
```

Fig. 6. Some Rules learned by Progol.

4 Approximate ILP rules by BNN

Backpropagation neural network (BNN) [14] is widely applied to various recognition tasks. In this paper, BNNs are employed to select the rule that closely matches with the input image. The following subsections explain two types of BNNs, i.e., (1) BNN that uses *the number of nonmatching literals and the number of matching literals* of the rules as the input vector, and (2) BNN that uses *the truth values of literals* of the rules as the input vector.

4.1 Using Numbers of Nonmatching and Matching Literals (1st BNN)

There can be many ways to approximate the rule that best matches the data. A simple choice is based on the assumption that the best rule should be the rule that contains a small number of nonmatching literals but a large number of matching literals. We then first build a simple BNN to test this idea.

The structure of the first BNN is composed of three layers: (1) the input layer consisting of 154 neurons, (2) the hidden layer consisting of 154 neurons, and (3) the output neurons having 77 neurons. All neurons receive real values. The hidden and output neurons use the sigmoid function. The links from the input neurons to the hidden neurons, and from the hidden neurons to the output neurons are fully connected, as shown in Figure 7.

As described above, the training set in our experiment consists of 77 different characters ('ก', 'ข', 'ฃ', 'ค',...,'ฮ'). Each character has the corresponding rule produced by Progol. In the training process of BNN, for each training example, we evaluate the number of nonmatching and number of matching literals by comparing the example with all rules in the rule set. Therefore, 154 numbers from all 77 rules in the rule set are used as the training input vector for BNN. The hidden layer consists of 154 neurons, simply the same as the number of the input neurons. The output layer is composed of 77 neurons, each of which represents a character. When the BNN is trained by an example of the character 'ก', the first output neuron that corresponds to the character is activated to 1 and the other neurons are set to 0. In the recognition process, the neuron with the maximum activation will be turned on.

Figure 7 illustrates the input and output vectors of an example of character 'ก', First, the numbers of nonmatching and matching literals of the rule of character 'ก' are counted, that in our experiment are 0 and 4, respectively. Then the example is examined with the rule of the character 'ข', and numbers of nonmatching and matching literals are 5 and 5. After the example is checked with all 77 rules, the numbers of nonmatching and matching literals are then fed into the neuron network as an input vector of the character 'ก'. In the training mode, the first neuron in the output layer that corresponds to character 'ก' is set to 1. The training process is then repeated for the other examples of character 'ก' as well as the examples of the other characters.

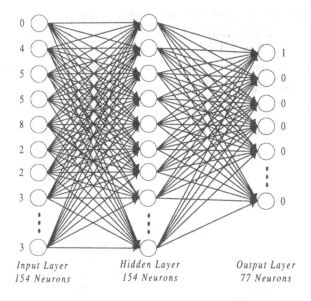

Fig. 7. The structure of the first BNN and the input & output vectors of character 'ŋ'

4.2 Using Truth Values of Literals (2nd BNN)

The disadvantage of the first BNN is that it takes each literal in a rule with equal significance. Thus it is unable to give important literals higher weights than others. We argue that literals in a rule have different levels of significance in classifying the characters. To capture this idea, instead of the numbers of nonmatching and matching literals, we design the structure of our second BNN by using the truth values of all literals for constructing the input vector. In the rules obtained in our experiment, no literal introduces a new variable which makes it easy to determine its truth value (true or false).

In this type of BNN, the value of matching literal is set to 1 (true) whereas the value of nonmatching literal is set to 0 (false) for an input neuron. Each hidden neuron represents each rule in the rule set. All input neurons corresponding to literals in the same rule are linked to one hidden neuron that represents the rule. Therefore the number of the hidden neurons is equal to the number of all rules; in our experiment, the number is 77, since only one rule per class is obtained by Progol. Nevertheless, if some class is defined by more than one rule, the additional hidden neurons together with their corresponding input neurons must be included, and this can be directly handled by the proposed BNN without any change.

Figure 8 shows the structure of our second BNN, and the input and output vectors for training the character 'ŋ'. When training the network with an example of character 'ŋ', the example is examined with all literals in all 77 rules. First, the truth values of four literals in the rule of the character 'ŋ' in Figure 6 are evaluated to 1, 1, 1 and 1.

Then the example is examined with the rule of the character 'ʋ', and the values of the literals are 1, 1, 0, 1, 0, 0, 1, 0, 0 and 1. After the image is checked with all 77 rules, these numbers are then fed into the neural network as the input vector for the character 'n'. In the training mode, the first neuron in the output layer that corresponds to the character 'n' is set to 1. This training process is then repeated for the other examples of the character 'n' as well as those of the other characters. In the recognition mode, the neuron with the highest-valued output will be taken as the prediction.

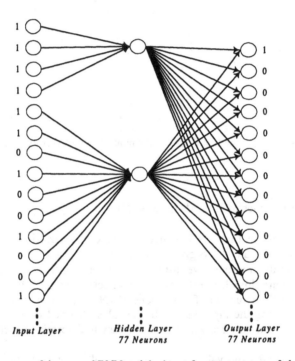

Fig. 8. The structure of the second BNN and the input & output vectors of character 'n'.

5 Experimental Results

The experiment was run to test our methods. The training character images in our experiment are printed by the laser printer with the resolution 300 dpi and scanned into the computer by the scanner with the same resolution. These images consists of 77 different characters ('n', 'ʋ', 'ʋ', 'ก',...,'ฮ'), 2 fonts (Cordia and Eucrosia), and 7 sizes (20, 22, 24, 28, 32, 36 and 48 points). These images are then fed into noise reduction and thinning processing for finding the structure of the images. Next, the important features are extracted for constructing the training examples. These examples are used to train FLS and our methods. For testing, the noise was added into an original image by copying the image by a photocopy machine twice; darker and lighter ones. The total number of test data was 2x2x7x7=2156. The experimental results on the test data are shown in Table 1. We did not report the accuracies of the methods on training set since they are almost the same and nearly 100%. We also include in Table 1 the result of using BNN alone with the same training examples.

Table 1. Accuracies of FLS, Progol, BNN and Progol & BNN on noisy images.

Font & Size	No. character	FLS	BNN	Progol	Progol& 1st BNN	Progol & 2nd BNN
C20*	154	86.54	80.52	80.52	93.47	94.77
C22	154	88.90	84.21	89.61	95.42	98.04
C24	154	89.20	90.91	87.01	93.54	94.77
C28	154	92.89	79.22	88.31	94.81	96.10
C32	154	88.23	85.71	88.31	95.42	98.04
C36	154	91.58	86.84	89.61	97.37	98.68
C48	154	87.95	72.73	85.06	92.84	93.46
E20*	154	68.19	81.82	68.18	75.99	78.57
E22	154	86.89	82.89	88.31	92.86	94.77
E24	154	87.86	93.51	83.77	90.92	92.86
E28	154	86.89	88.31	83.77	91.56	95.45
E32	154	93.51	92.21	89.61	95.46	95.45
E36	154	92.20	92.11	88.31	95.45	96.05
E48	154	85.90	68.42	79.22	90.76	92.72
Average	2156	87.62	84.25	84.97	92.55	94.26

* C and E are fonts Cordia and Eucrosia, respectively.

The results reveal that the accuracy of rules produced by Progol is comparable to BNN, and is lower than the accuracy of FLS. Since Progol can correctly recognize the input data only when the data is perfectly matched with the correct rule, it is not able to recognize some input data that is matched partly with the correct rule and partly with others. This is the reason for lower accuracy of Progol. On the other hand, FLS always chooses the most similar stored pattern as the matching character, even if there is no stored pattern that exactly matches the input data. After approximate match was performed by using the numbers of nonmatching and matching literals, the accuracy is improved to 92.55%. However, in the case of character that is similar to others, the first BNN may misclassify the character. For instance, in our experiment we found the case that the first BNN misclassified a character image 'n' as the character image 'ŋ'.

In this case, the second BNN that uses the truth values of literals correctly classified this character image. As shown in Table 1, the second BNN yields significant improvement by achieving 94.26% accuracy.

6 Related Works and Limitations

There are some ILP systems that are able to learn multi-class concepts represented in first-order rules, such as RTL [1], ICL[7], MULT_ICN[9]. Nevertheless, it is still possible that some unseen data may not exactly match the rules produced by these systems. We believe that our method for approximating rules can also be applied to these systems. TILDE [2] is a first-order extension of decision tree learning algorithm and it will assigns some class to a given unseen data. Therefore, TILDE can be applied to our task as well. Further study is required to compare our method and TILDE that is one of our ongoing work. KBANN [16] and FONN [3] are the systems that employ initial rules and training examples for learning neural networks. These systems showed that the performance is better than methods which learn purely from examples. FONN translates first-order rules possibly including literals with new variables into neural network. Its primary goal is to refine numerical literals of the rules. It first finds only substitutions for new variables that satisfy non-numerical literals and uses these substitutions for refining the numerical literals [3]. One limitation of our method is that the network deals only with rules which introduce no new variable. Though the rules with no new variable are sufficient for our current task, to be applied to other tasks where rules introduce new variables, the method should be further studied. The method like that of FONN may be helpful. In our task, we consider the method of approximation of ILP rules when there is no rule that exactly matches unseen data. Though it did not occur in our current task, a related problem when multiple rules fire will be studied in the near future.

7 Conclusions

We have proposed an improved method that combines ILP and BNN for the task of Thai printed character recognition. The experimental results show that our method gives a significant improvement on previous methods. The improved results come from the combination of ILP and BNN. ILP produces rules that accurately classify the training data, and BNN makes the rule more flexible for approximately matching with unseen or noisy data. Moreover, the results also demonstrate that to approximate the rule, each predicate in the rule should be weighted unequally; this is accomplished by using the truth values of literals as the input vector and separately assigning a weight to each literal.

Acknowledgements. We would like to thank Decha Rattanatarn for providing us the code of FLS, Apinya Supanwansa for helping us construct the background knowledge used in the work, and Apinetr Unakul for comments on the paper.

References

[1] C.Baroglio and M.Botta. Multiple Predicate Learning with RTL. *Topic in Artificial Intelligence, LNAI 992,* 1995.

[2] H.Blockeel and L.De Raedt. Experiments with Top-Down Induction of Logical Decision Trees. *Technical Report CW247*, Dept. of Computer Science, K.U.Leuven, 1997.

[3] M.Botta, A.Giordana and R.Piola. FONN: Combining First Order Logic with Connectionist Learning. *Proceedings of the 14th International Conference on Machine Learning*, 1997.

[4] S.Dzeroski, N.Jacobs, M.Molina, C.Moure, S.Muggleton and W.V.Laer. Detecting Traffic Problems with ILP. *Proceedings of the 8th International Workshop on Inductive Logic Programming*, 1998.

[5] S.Dzeroski, S.Schulze-Kremer, K.R.Heidtke, K.Siems and D.Wettschereck. Applying ILP to Diterpene Structure Elucidation from ^{13}C NMR Spectra. *Proceedings of 6th International Workshop on Inductive Logic Programming*, 1996.

[6] S.Eupiboon. Thai Handwritten Character Recognition by Considering the Character Head. *Master Thesis, KMIT*, Thailand, 1988 (in Thai).

[7] W.V.Laer, S.Dzeroski and L.D.Raedt. Multi-Class Problems and Discretization in ICL Extended Abstract. *Proceedings of the Mlnet Familiarization Workshop on Data Mining with Inductive Logic Programming*, pp.53-60, 1996.

[8] C.Lursinsap. Speeding Up Handwritten Character Neural Learning by Surface Projection. *Proceedings of the 2nd Symposium on Natural Language Processing*, pp. 198-205, 1995.

[9] L.Martin and C.Vrain. MULT_ICN: An Empirical Multiple Predicate Learner. *Proceedings of the 5th International Workshop on Inductive Logic Programming*, 1995.

[10] S.Muggleton. Inverse Entailment and PROGOL. *New Generation Computing*, 3:245-286, 1995.

[11] S.Muggleton, D.Page and A.Srinivasan. An Initial Experiment into Stereochemistry-Based Drug Design Using Inductive Logic Programming. *Proceedings of the 6th International Workshop on Inductive Logic Programming*, pp.25-40, 1996.

[12] P.Phokharatkul and C.Kimpan. Recognition of Handprinted Thai Characters Using the Cavity Features of Character Based on Neural Network. *Proceedings of the 1998 IEEE Asia-Pacific Conference on Circuits and Systems*, pp. 149-152. 1998.

[13] D. Rattanatarn and S. Jitapunkul. Thai Printed Characters Recognition Using the Fuzzy Logic Technique and Syntactic Method. *Proceedings of the 18th Conference of Electrical Engineering*, 1995 (in Thai)

[14] D.E.Rumelhart, G.E.Hinton and R.J.Williams. Learning internal representations by error propagation. In D. E. Rumelhart, & J. L. McClelland (Eds.), *Parallel distributed processing (Vol 1)*, Cambridge, MA:MIT Press, 1986.

[15] T.Tanprasert and C.Tanprasert, Variable Simulated Light Sensitive Model for Handwritten Thai Digit Recognition. *Proceedings of the 2nd Symposium on Natural Language Processing*, pp. 173-179, 1995.

[16] G.G.Towell and J.W.Shavlik. Knowledge-Based Artificial Neural Networks. *Artificial Intelligence*, 70 (4):119-116, 1994.

Rule Evaluation Measures: A Unifying View

Nada Lavrač[1], Peter Flach[2], Blaz Zupan[3,1]

[1] Department of Intelligent Systems
Jožef Stefan Institute, Ljubljana, Slovenia
[2] Department of Computer Science
University of Bristol, United Kingdom
[3] Faculty of Computer and Information Sciences
University of Ljubljana, Slovenia

Abstract. Numerous measures are used for performance evaluation in machine learning. In predictive knowledge discovery, the most frequently used measure is classification accuracy. With new tasks being addressed in knowledge discovery, new measures appear. In descriptive knowledge discovery, where induced rules are not primarily intended for classification, new measures used are novelty in clausal and subgroup discovery, and support and confidence in association rule learning. Additional measures are needed as many descriptive knowledge discovery tasks involve the induction of a large set of redundant rules and the problem is the ranking and filtering of the induced rule set. In this paper we develop a unifying view on some of the existing measures for predictive and descriptive induction. We provide a common terminology and notation by means of contingency tables. We demonstrate how to trade off these measures, by using what we call *weighted relative accuracy*. The paper furthermore demonstrates that many rule evaluation measures developed for predictive knowledge discovery can be adapted to descriptive knowledge discovery tasks.

1 Introduction

Numerous measures are used for performance evaluation in machine learning and knowledge discovery. In classification-oriented *predictive induction*, the most frequently used measure is classification accuracy. Other standard measures include precision and recall in information retrieval, and sensitivity and specificity in medical data analysis. With new tasks being addressed in knowledge discovery, new measures need to be defined, such as novelty in clausal and subgroup discovery, and support and confidence in association rule learning. These new knowledge discovery tasks belong to what is called *descriptive induction*. Descriptive induction also includes other knowledge discovery tasks, such as learning of properties, integrity constraints, and attribute dependencies.

This paper provides an analysis of selected rule evaluation measures. The analysis applies to cases where single rules have to be ranked according to how well they are supported by the data. It also applies to both predictive and descriptive induction. As we argue in this paper, the right way to use standard rule evaluation measures is relative to some threshold, e.g., relative to the trivial rule 'all instances belong to this class'. We thus introduce relative versions of these standard measures, e.g., relative accuracy. We then show that relative measures provide a link with descriptive measures estimating novelty. Furthermore, by taking a weighted variant of such relative measures we show that we in fact obtain a trade-off between several of them by maximizing a single measure called *weighted relative accuracy*.

The outline of the paper is as follows. In Section 2 we introduce the terminology and notation used in this paper. In particular, we introduce the contingency table notation that will be put to use in Section 3, where we formulate predictive and descriptive measures found in the literature in this framework. Our main results concerning unifications between different predictive measures, and between predictive and descriptive measures, are presented in Section 4. In Section 5 we support our theoretical analysis with some preliminary empirical evidence. Finally, in Section 6 we discuss the main contributions of this work.

2 Terminology and Notation

In this section we introduce a terminology and notation used throughout the paper. Since we are not restricted to predictive induction, the rules we consider have a more general format than the format of prediction rules that have a single classification literal in the conclusion of a rule. Below we only assume that induced rules are implications with a head and a body (Section 2.1). Due to this general rule form, the notions of positive and negative example have to be generalized: predicted positives/negatives are those instances for which the body is true/false, and actual positives/negatives are instances for which the head is true/false. In this framework, a contingency table, as explained in Section 2.2, is used as the basis for computing rule evaluation measures.

2.1 Rules

We restrict attention to learning systems that induce rules of the form

$$Head \leftarrow Body$$

Predictive induction deals with learning of rules aimed at prediction and/or classification tasks. The inputs to predictive learners are classified examples, and the outputs are prediction or classification rules. These rules can be induced by propositional or by first-order learners. In propositional predictive rules, *Body* is (typically) a conjunction of attribute-value pairs, and *Head* is a class assignment. In first-order learning, frequently referred to as *inductive logic programming*, predictive rules are Prolog clauses, where *Head* is a single positive literal and *Body* is a conjunction of positive and/or negative literals. The important difference with propositional predictive rules is that first-order rules contain variables that are shared between literals and between *Head* and *Body*.

Descriptive induction deals with learning of rules aimed at knowledge discovery tasks other than classification tasks. Those include learning of properties, integrity constraints, functional dependencies, as well as the discovery of interesting subgroups, association rule learning, etc. The input to descriptive learners are unclassified instances, i.e., descriptive induction is unsupervised. In comparison with propositional prediction rules, in which *Head* is a class assignment, *association rules* allow the *Head* to be a conjunction of attribute tests. Propositional association rules have recently been upgraded to the first-order case [2]. Descriptive first-order rules also include *general clauses*, which allow for a disjunction of literals to be used in the *Head*.

In the abstract framework of this paper, rules are binary objects consisting of *Head* and *Body*. Rule evaluation measures are intended to give an indication of the strength of the (hypothetical) association between *Body* and *Head* expressed by such a rule. We assume a certain unspecified language bias that determines all possible heads and bodies of rules. We also assume a given set of instances, i.e., classified or unclassified examples, and we assume a given procedure by which we can determine, for every possible *Head* and *Body*, whether or not it is true for that instance. We say that an instance is *covered* by a rule *Head* ← *Body* if *Body* is true for the instance. In the propositional case, an instance is covered when it satisfies the conditions of a rule (all the conditions of a rule are evaluated true given the instance description). In the first-order case, the atom(s) describing the instance are matched with the rule head, thus determining a substitution θ by which the variables in the rule head are replaced by the terms (constants) in the instance description. The rule covers the instance iff *Body*θ is evaluated as true.

2.2 Contingency Table

Given the above concepts, we can construct a *contingency table* for an arbitrary rule $H \leftarrow B$. In Table 1, B denotes the set of instances for which the body of the rule is true, and $\overline{B}$ denotes its complement (the set of instances for which the body is false); similarly for H and $\overline{H}$. HB then denotes $H \cap B$, $\overline{H}B$ denotes $\overline{H} \cap B$, and so on.

Table 1. A contingency table.

	B	$\overline{B}$	
H	$n(HB)$	$n(H\overline{B})$	$n(H)$
$\overline{H}$	$n(\overline{H}B)$	$n(\overline{H}\overline{B})$	$n(\overline{H})$
	$n(B)$	$n(\overline{B})$	N

We use $n(X)$ to denote the cardinality of set X, e.g., $n(\overline{H}B)$ is the number of instances for which H is false and B is true (i.e., the number of instances erroneously covered by the rule). N denotes the total number of instances in the sample. The relative frequency $\frac{n(X)}{N}$ associated with X is denoted by $p(X)$.[1] All rule evaluation measures considered in this paper are defined in terms of frequencies from the contingency table only.

Notice that a contingency table is a generalisation of a confusion matrix, which is the standard basis for computing rule evaluation measures in binary classification problems. In the confusion matrix notation, $n(H) = P_a$ – the number of positive examples, $n(\overline{H}) = N_a$ – the number of negative examples, $n(B) = P_p$ – the number of examples covered by the rule therefore predicted as positive, $n(\overline{B}) = N_p$ – the number of the examples not covered by the rule and therefore predicted as negative, $n(HB) = TP$ – the number of true positives, $n(\overline{H}\overline{B}) = TN$ – the number of true negatives, $n(\overline{H}B) = FP$ – the number of false positives, and $n(H\overline{B}) = FN$ – the number of false negatives.

3 Selected Rule Evaluation Measures

In this section, selected rule evaluation measures are formulated in the contingency table terminology, which is the first step towards the unifying view developed in Section 4. The definitions are given in terms of relative frequencies derived from the contingency table. Since our framework is not restricted to predictive induction, we also elaborate some novelty-based measures found in the knowledge discovery literature; see [9, 5] which discuss also other measures and the axioms that rule evaluation measures should satisfy. The usefulness of our unifying framework is demonstrated in Section 4, where we point out the many relations that exist between weighted and relative variants of these measures.

Definition 1 (Rule accuracy). $Acc(H \leftarrow B) = p(H|B)$.

Definition 2 (Negative reliability). $NegRel(H \leftarrow B) = p(\overline{H}|\overline{B})$.

Definition 3 (Sensitivity). $Sens(H \leftarrow B) = p(B|H)$.

Definition 4 (Specificity). $Spec(H \leftarrow B) = p(\overline{B}|\overline{H})$.

Accuracy of rule $R = H \leftarrow B$, here defined as the conditional probability that H is true given that B is true, measures the fraction of predicted positives that are true positives in the case of binary classification problems:

$$Acc(R) = \frac{TP}{TP + FP} = \frac{n(HB)}{n(HB) + n(\overline{H}B)} = \frac{n(HB)}{n(B)} = \frac{\frac{n(HB)}{N}}{\frac{n(B)}{N}} = \frac{p(HB)}{p(B)} = p(H|B).$$

Rule accuracy is also called precision in information retrieval. Furthermore, accuracy error $Err(H \leftarrow B) = 1 - Acc(H \leftarrow B) = p(\overline{H}|B)$.

Our definition of rule accuracy is intended for evaluating single rules, and therefore biased towards the accuracy of positive examples. As such, it is different from what we call rule set accuracy [6], defined as $Acc = \frac{TP+TN}{N} =$

---

[1] In this paper we are not really concerned with probability estimation, and we interpret the sample relative frequency as a probability.

$p(HB) + p(\overline{HB})$, which is standardly used for evaluation of hypotheses comprised of several rules.

Given our general knowledge discovery framework, it can now also be seen that rule accuracy is in fact the same as *confidence* in association rule learning. Rule accuracy can also be used to measure the *reliability* of the rule in the prediction of positive cases, since it measures the correctness of returned results.

The reliability of negative predictions is in binary classification problems computed as follows: $NegRel(R) = \frac{TN}{TN+FN} = \frac{TN}{N_p} = \frac{n(\overline{HB})}{n(\overline{B})} = \frac{p(\overline{HB})}{p(\overline{B})} = p(\overline{H}|\overline{B})$.

Sensitivity is identical to *recall* (of positive cases) used in information retrieval. Sensitivity, here defined as the conditional probability that B is true given that H is true, measures the fraction of true positives that are correctly classified in the case of binary classification problems: $Sens(R) = \frac{TP}{TP+FN} = \frac{TP}{P_a} = \frac{n(HB)}{n(HB)+n(\overline{H}B)} = \frac{n(HB)}{n(H)} = \frac{p(HB)}{p(H)} = p(B|H)$. Sensitivity can also be interpreted as the accuracy of the rule $B \leftarrow H$, which in logic programming terms is the *completion* of the rule $H \leftarrow B$.

Specificity is the conditional probability that B is false given that H is false. In binary classification problems, it is equal to the recall of negative cases in information retrieval: $Spec(R) = \frac{TN}{TN+FP} = \frac{TN}{N_a} = \frac{n(\overline{HB})}{n(\overline{H})} = p(\overline{B}|\overline{H})$.

We now introduce other measures that are used to develop our unifying view in the next section.

Definition 5 (Coverage). $Cov(H \leftarrow B) = p(B)$.

Definition 6 (Support). $Sup(H \leftarrow B) = p(HB)$.

Coverage measures the fraction of instances covered by the body of a rule. As such it is a measure of *generality* of a rule. *Support* of a rule is a related measure known from association rule learning, also called *frequency*. Notice that, unlike the previous measures, support is symmetric in H and B.

The next measure aims at assessing the novelty, interestingness or unusualness of a rule. Novelty measures are used, e.g., in the MIDOS system for subgroup discovery [8], and in the PRIMUS family of systems for clausal discovery [3]. Here we follow the elaboration of the PRIMUS novelty measure, because it is formulated in the more general setting of clausal discovery, and because it is clearly linked with the contingency table framework.

Consider again the contingency table in Table 1. We define a rule $H \leftarrow B$ to be *novel* if $n(HB)$ cannot be inferred from the marginal frequencies $n(H)$ and $n(B)$; in other words, if H and B are not statistically *independent*. We thus compare the *observed* $n(HB)$ with the *expected* value under independence $\mu(HB) = \frac{n(H)n(B)}{N}$. The more the observed value $n(HB)$ differs from the expected value $\mu(HB)$, the more likely it is that there exists a real and unexpected association between H and B, expressed by the rule $H \leftarrow B$. Novelty is thus defined as the relative difference between $n(HB)$ and $\mu(HB)$.

Definition 7 (Novelty). $Nov(H \leftarrow B) = p(HB) - p(H)p(B)$.

Notice that $p(HB)$ is what is called *support* in association rule learning. The definition of novelty states that we are only interested in high support if that couldn't be expected from the marginal probabilities, i.e., when $p(H)$ and/or $p(B)$ are relatively low. It can be demonstrated that $-0.25 \leq Nov(R) \leq 0.25$: a strongly positive value indicates a strong association between H and B, while a strongly negative value indicates a strong association between $\overline{H}$ and B.[2]

In the MIDOS subgroup discovery system this measure is used to detect unusual subgroups. For selected head H, indicating a property we are interested in, body B defines an unusual subgroup of the instances satisfying H if the distribution of H-instances among B-instances is sufficiently different from the distribution of H-instances in the sample. In situations like this, where H is selected, this definition of novelty is sufficient. However, notice that $Nov(H \leftarrow B)$ is symmetric in H and B, which means that $H \leftarrow B$ and $B \leftarrow H$ will always carry the same novelty, even though one of them may have many more counter-instances (satisfying the body but falsifying the head) than the other.

To distinguish between such cases, PRIMUS additionally employs the measure of satisfaction, which is the relative decrease in accuracy error between the rule $H \leftarrow true$ and the rule $H \leftarrow B$. It is a variant of rule accuracy which takes the whole of the contingency table into account — it is thus more suited towards knowledge discovery, being able trading off rules with different heads as well as bodies.

Definition 8 (Satisfaction). $Sat(H \leftarrow B) = \frac{p(\overline{H}) - p(\overline{H}|B)}{p(\overline{H})}$.[3]

It can be shown that $Sat(H \leftarrow B) = \frac{p(H|B) - p(H)}{1 - p(H)}$, since $p(\overline{H}) - p(\overline{H}|B) = (1 - p(H)) - (1 - p(H|B)) = p(H|B) - p(H)$. We thus see that $Sat(H \leftarrow B)$ is similar to rule accuracy $p(H|B)$, e.g., $Sat(R) = 1$ iff $Acc(R) = 1$. However, unlike rule accuracy, satisfaction takes the whole of the contingency table into account and is thus more suited towards knowledge discovery, trading off rules with different heads as well as bodies.

Finally, we mention that PRIMUS trades off novelty and satisfaction by multiplying them, resulting in a χ^2-like statistic:

$$Nov(H \leftarrow B) \times Sat(H \leftarrow B) = \frac{(Np(\overline{H}B) - \mu(\overline{H}B))^2}{\mu(\overline{H}B)}$$

This is one term in the χ^2 sum for the contingency table, corresponding to the lower left-hand cell (the counter-instances). We omit the details of the normalization.

---

[2] Since negative novelty can be transformed into positive novelty associated with the rule $\overline{H} \leftarrow B$, systems like MIDOS and PRIMUS set $Nov(H \leftarrow B) = 0$ if $p(HB) < p(H)p(B)$. The more general expression of Definition 7 is kept because it allows a more straightforward statement of our main results.

[3] Again, in practice we put $Sat(R) = 0$ if $p(\overline{H}) > p(\overline{H}|B)$.

4 A Unifying View

In the previous section we formulated selected rule evaluation measures in our more general knowledge discovery framework. In this section we show the usefulness of this framework by establishing a synthesis between these measures. The main inspiration for this synthesis comes from the novelty measure, which is *relative* in the sense that it compares the support of the rule with the expected support under the assumption of statistical independence (Definition 7).

Definition 9 (Relative accuracy). $RAcc(H \leftarrow B) = p(H|B) - p(H)$.

Relative accuracy of a rule $R = H \leftarrow B$ is the accuracy gain relative to the fixed rule $H \leftarrow true$. The latter rule predicts all instances to satisfy H; a rule is only interesting if it improves upon this 'default' accuracy. Another way of viewing relative accuracy is that it measures the utility of connecting body B with a given head H.

Similarly, we define relative versions of other rule evaluation measures.

Definition 10 (Relative negative reliability).

$$RNegRel(H \leftarrow B) = p(\overline{H}|\overline{B}) - p(\overline{H}).$$

Definition 11 (Relative sensitivity). $RSens(H \leftarrow B) = p(B|H) - p(B)$.

Definition 12 (Relative specificity). $RSpec(H \leftarrow B) = p(\overline{B}|\overline{H}) - p(\overline{B})$.

Like relative accuracy, relative negative reliability measures the utility of connecting body B with a given head H. The latter two measures can be interpreted as sensitivity/specificity gain relative to the rule $true \leftarrow B$, i.e., the utility of connecting a given body B with head H. Notice that this view is taken in rule construction by the CN2 algorithm [1], which first builds a rule body and subsequently assigns an appropriate rule head.

To repeat, the point about relative measures is that they give more information about the utility of a rule than absolute measures. For instance, if in a prediction task the accuracy of a rule is lower than the relative frequency of the class it predicts, then the rule actually performs badly, regardless of its absolute accuracy.

There is however a problem with relative accuracy as such: it is easy to obtain high relative accuracy with highly specific rules, i.e., rules with low generality $p(B)$. To this end, a weighted variant is introduced, which is the key notion in this paper.

Definition 13 (Weighted relative accuracy).

$$WRAcc(H \leftarrow B) = p(B)(p(H|B) - p(H)).$$

Weighted relative accuracy trades off generality and relative accuracy. It is known in the literature as a *gain* measure, used to evaluate the utility of a *literal L* considered for extending the body B of a rule: $\frac{p(BL)}{p(B)}(p(H|BL) - p(H|B))$.

We now come to a result, which — although technically trivial — provides a significant contribution to our understanding of rule evaluation measures.

Theorem 1. $WRAcc(R) = Nov(R)$.

Proof. $WRAcc(H \leftarrow B) = p(B)(p(H|B) - p(H)) = p(B)p(H|B) - p(H)p(B) = p(HB) - p(H)p(B) = Nov(H \leftarrow B)$. $\qquad\qquad\square$

Theorem 1 has the following implications.

1. Rules with high weighted relative accuracy also have high novelty, and *vice versa*.
2. High novelty is achieved by trading off generality and rule accuracy gained in comparison with a trivial rule $H \leftarrow true$. This also means that having high relative accuracy is not enough for considering a rule to be interesting, since the rule needs to be general enough as well.

This link between predictive and descriptive rule evaluation measures has — to the best of our knowledge — not been published before.

We proceed to show that weighted relative accuracy is one of the most fundamental rule evaluation measures, by showing that it also provides a trade-off between accuracy and other predictive measures such as sensitivity. To do so, we first define weighted versions of the other relative measures defined above.

Definition 14 (Weighted relative negative reliability).

$$WRNegRel(H \leftarrow B) = p(\overline{B})(p(\overline{H}|\overline{B}) - p(\overline{H})).$$

The weight $p(\overline{B})$ is motivated by the fact that overly general rules trivially have a high negative reliability.

Definition 15 (Weighted relative sensitivity).

$$WRSens(H \leftarrow B) = p(H)(p(B|H) - p(B)).$$

Definition 16 (Weighted relative specificity).

$$WRSpec(H \leftarrow B) = p(\overline{H})(p(\overline{B}|\overline{H}) - p(\overline{B})).$$

Again, the weights guard against trivial solutions.

This leads us to establishing a trade-off between the four standard predictive rule evaluation measures, by relating them through their weighted relative variants.

Theorem 2. $WRAcc(R) = WRSens(R) = WRSpec(R) = WRNegRel(R)$.

Proof. $WRAcc(H \leftarrow B) = p(B)(p(H|B) - p(H)) = p(HB) - p(H)p(B) = p(H)(p(B|H) - p(B)) = WRSens(H \leftarrow B)$.
$WRAcc(H \leftarrow B) = p(B)(p(H|B) - p(H)) = p(HB) - p(H)p(B) = (1 - p(\overline{H}\overline{B}) - p(H\overline{B}) - p(\overline{H}B)) - (1 - p(\overline{B}))(1 - p(\overline{H})) = (1 - p(\overline{H}) - p(\overline{B}) + p(\overline{H}\overline{B})) - (1 - p(\overline{H}) - p(\overline{B}) + p(\overline{H})p(\overline{B})) = p(\overline{H}\overline{B}) - p(\overline{H})p(\overline{B}) = p(\overline{H})(p(\overline{B}|\overline{H}) - p(\overline{B})) = WRSpec(H \leftarrow B)$.
$WRSpec(H \leftarrow B) = p(\overline{H})(p(\overline{B}|\overline{H}) - p(\overline{B})) = p(\overline{H}\overline{B}) - p(\overline{H})p(\overline{B}) = p(\overline{B})(p(\overline{H}|\overline{B}) - p(\overline{H})) = WRNegRel(H \leftarrow B)$. $\qquad\qquad\square$

We have thus established a complete synthesis between different predictive rule evaluation measures, and between these measures and the descriptive notion of novelty, by demonstrating that there is a single way in which all these measures can be combined and thus traded off in a principled way.

5 Rule Evaluation Measures in Practice

In the previous section we have shown that a single measure, weighted relative accuracy, can be used to trade off different evaluation measures such as accuracy, sensitivity, and novelty. In this section we further support this claim with some preliminary empirical evidence. First, we describe an experiment in which weighted relative accuracy correlates better with an expert's intuitive understanding of "reliability" and "interestingness" than standard rule evaluation measures. Secondly, we show the utility of weighted relative accuracy as a filtering measure in database dependency discovery.

5.1 An Experiment

The purpose of this experiment was to find out whether rule evaluation measures as discussed in this paper really measure what they are supposed to measure. To this end we compared an expert's ranking of a number of rules on two dimensions with the rankings given by four selected measures. We have used a CAR data set (see UCI Machine Learning Repository [7]), which includes 1728 instances that are described with six attributes and a corresponding four-valued class. The attributes are multi-valued and include buying price, price of maintenance, number of doors, capacity in terms of persons to carry, and estimated safety of the car.

An ML* Machine Learning environment was used to generate association rules from the CAR dataset. The designer of the experiment has semi-randomly chosen ten rules that he though may be of different quality in respect to the measures introduced in this text. Note that none of the rules, however, was explicitly measured at this stage.

The rules were then shown to the domain expert, who was asked to rank them according to their "reliability" and "interestingness". We chose these non-technical terms to avoid possible interference with any technical interpretation; neither term was in any way explained to the expert.[4] The domain expert first

---

[4] During the experiment, the expert expressed some of his intuitions regarding these terms: "reliability measures how reliable the rule is when applied for a classification"; "an interesting rule is the one that I never thought of when building a classification model, e.g., those without the class (car) in the head"; "an interesting rule has to tell me something new, but needs to be reliable as well (it would help me if I would somehow know the reliability first before ranking on interestingness)"; "a highly reliable rule which is at the same time unusual is interesting"; "a rule is interesting if it tells me something new, but it's not an outlier".

assigned qualitative grades to each rule (-,○,⊕,+), and then chose a final rank from these grades. The results of the ranking are shown in Table 2. Note that some rules are ranked equally (e.g., the first two rules for reliability), and in such cases a rank is represented as an interval. The correlation between the expert's rankings and ranks obtained from the rule evaluation measures are given in Table 3.

Table 2. Ten rules ranked by a domain expert on reliability (Rel) and interestingness (Int), and corresponding rule evaluation measures.

Rule	Expert				Rule evaluation measures			
	Rel	#	Int	#	Acc	Sens	Spec	WRAcc
buying=med car=good → maint=low	-	7-10	○	6	1.000	0.053	1.000	0.010
buying=low car=v-good → lugboot=big	-	7-10	-	7-10	0.615	0.042	0.987	0.006
safety=low → car=unacc	+	1	-	7-10	1.000	0.476	1.000	0.100
persons=2 car=unacc → lugboot=big	-	7-10	-	7-10	0.333	0.333	0.667	0.000
lugboot=big car=good → safety=med	○	5-6	○	5	1.000	0.042	1.000	0.009
car=v-good → lugboot=big	⊕	3	+	2	0.615	0.069	0.978	0.011
car=unacc → buying=v-high	⊕	4	+	3	0.298	0.833	0.344	0.033
car=v-good → safety=high	+	2	+	1	1.000	0.113	1.000	0.025
persons=4 → lugboot=big car=unacc	-	7-10	-	7-10	0.153	0.239	0.641	-0.020
persons=4 safety=high → car=acc	○	5-6	○	4	0.563	0.281	0.938	0.038

Although the correlations in Table 3 are quite low, the tentative conclusion is that *WRAcc* correlates best with *both* intuitive notions of reliability and interestingness. This provides some preliminary empirical support for the idea that *WRAcc* provides the right trade-off between predictive and descriptive rule evaluation measures.

Table 3. Rank correlations between two measures elicited from the expert and four rule evaluation measures.

	Acc	Sens	Spec	WRAcc
expert's Rel	0.150	0.152	0.116	0.323
expert's Int	0.067	-0.006	0.029	0.177

5.2 Rule Filtering

The measures discussed in this paper are primarily intended for ranking and filtering rules output by an induction algorithm. This is particularly important in descriptive induction tasks such as association rule learning and database dependency discovery, since descriptive induction algorithms typically output several thousands of rules. We briefly describe some preliminary experience with rule filtering using the functional dependency discovery tool fdep [4].

We ran fdep on some of the UCI datasets [7], and then used $WRAcc$ to rank the induced functional dependencies. Below we give some of the highest ranked rules in several domains. They have the form $A_1, \ldots, A_n \rightarrow A$, meaning "given the values of attributes $A_1, \ldots, A_n$, the value of attribute A is fixed"; see [4] for details of the transformation into $H \leftarrow B$ form.

Lymphography:

```
[block_lymph_c,regeneration,lym_nodes_enlar,no_nodes]->[block_lymph_s]
[lymphatics,by_pass,regeneration,lym_nodes_enlar]->[lym_nodes_dimin]
```

Primary tumor:

```
[class,histologic_type,degree_of_diffe,brain,skin,neck]->[axillar]
[class,histologic_type,degree_of_diffe,bone_marrow,skin,neck]->[axillar]
[class,histologic_type,degree_of_diffe,bone,bone_marrow,skin]->[axillar]
```

Hepatitis:

```
[liver_firm,spleen_palpable,spiders,ascites,bilirubin]->[class]
[liver_big,liver_firm,spiders,ascites,varices,bilirubin]->[class]
[anorexia,liver_firm,spiders,ascites,varices,bilirubin]->[class]
```

Wisconsin breast cancer:

```
[uni_cell_size,se_cell_size,bare_nuclei,normal_nucleoli,mitoses]->[class]
[uni_cell_shape,marginal_adhesion,bare_nuclei,normal_nucleoli]->[class]
[uni_cell_size,marginal_adhesion,se_cell_size,bare_nuclei,normal_nucleoli]
                                                             ->[class]
```

Our experience with rule filtering in these domains suggested that $WRAcc(R)$ would drop quite sharply after the first few rules. Notice that in the last two domains the induced functional dependencies determine the class attribute.

6   Summary and Discussion

In this paper we have provided an analysis of selected rule evaluation measures used in machine learning and knowledge discovery. We have argued that, generally speaking, these measures should be used relative to some threshold, e.g., relative to the situation where this particular rule head is *not* connected to this particular rule body. Furthermore, we have proposed a single measure that can be interpreted in at least 5 different ways: as weighted relative accuracy, as weighted relative sensitivity, as weighted relative precision, as weighted relative negative reliability, and as novelty. We believe this to be a significant contribution to the understanding of rule evaluation measures, which could be obtained because of our unifying contingency table framework.

Further work includes the generalization to rule *set* evaluation measures. These differ from rule evaluation measures in that they treat positive and negative examples symmetrically, e.g., $RuleSetAcc(H \leftarrow B) = p(HB) + p(\overline{HB})$.

Another extension of this work would be to investigate how some of these measures can be used as *search heuristics* rather than filtering measures. Finally, we would like to continue empirical evaluation of $WRAcc(R)$ as a filtering measure in various domains such as association rule learning and first-order knowledge discovery.

Acknowledgements

We are grateful to Dr. Marko Bohanec for his help in the expert evaluation of rules in the experimental rule evaluation, and to Dr. Iztok Savnik for his assistance in functional dependency filtering. We also acknowledge the useful comments of three anonymous reviewers. This work was partially supported by the Esprit Long Term Research Project 20237 (*Inductive Logic Programming 2*), a Joint Project with Central/Eastern Europe funded by the Royal Society, and the Slovenian Ministry of Science and Technology.

References

1. P. Clark and T. Niblett (1989). The CN2 induction algorithm. *Machine Learning* 3, pp. 261–284.
2. L. Dehaspe and L. De Raedt (1997). Mining association rules with multiple relations. In N. Lavrac and S. Džeroski (Eds.), *Proc. 7th Int. Workshop on Inductive Logic Programming (ILP'97)*, pp. 125–132, LNAI 1297, Springer-Verlag.
3. P.A. Flach and N. Lachiche (1999). A first-order approach to unsupervised learning. Submitted.
4. P.A. Flach and I. Savnik (1999). Database dependency discovery: a machine learning approach. *AI Communications*, to appear.
5. W. Klösgen (1996). Explora: A multipattern and multistrategy discovery assistant. In U.M. Fayyad, G. Piatetsky-Shapiro, P. Smyth and R. Uthurusamy (Eds.), *Advances in Knowledge Discovery and Data Mining*, 249–271, AAAI Press.
6. T. Mitchell (1997). *Machine Learning*, McGraw Hill.
7. P.M. Murphy and D.W. Aha (1994). UCI Repository of machine learning databases [http://www.ics.uci.edu/~mlearn/mlrepository.html]. Irvine, CA: University of California, Department of Information and Computer Science.
8. S. Wrobel (1997). An algorithm for multi-relational discovery of subgroups. In J. Komorowski and J. Zytkow (Eds.), *Proc. First European Symposium on Principles of Data Mining and Knowledge Discovery PKDD'97*, Springer-Verlag.
9. G. Piatetsky-Shapiro (1991). Discovery, analysis and presentation of strong rules. In G. Piatetsky-Shapiro and W. Frawley (Eds.), *Knowledge Discovery in Databases*, 229–249. AAAI Press.

Improving Part of Speech Disambiguation Rules by Adding Linguistic Knowledge

Nikolaj Lindberg[1] and Martin Eineborg[2]

[1] Centre for Speech Technology (CTT), Department of Speech, Music and Hearing, Royal Institute of Technology, Stockholm, Sweden, nikolaj@speech.kth.se

[2] Machine Learning Group, Department of Computer and Systems Sciences (DSV), Stockholm University/Royal Institute of Technology, Stockholm, Sweden, eineborg@dsv.su.se

Abstract. This paper reports the ongoing work of producing a state of the art part of speech tagger for unedited Swedish text. Rules eliminating faulty tags have been induced using Progol. In previously reported experiments, almost no linguistically motivated background knowledge was used [5, 8]. Still, the result was rather promising (recall 97.7%, with a pending average ambiguity of 1.13 tags/word). Compared to the previous study, a much richer, more linguistically motivated, background knowledge has been supplied, consisting of examples of noun phrases, verb chains, auxiliary verbs, and sets of part of speech categories. The aim has been to create the background knowledge rapidly, without laborious hand-coding of linguistic knowledge. In addition to the new background knowledge, new, more expressive rule types have been induced for two part of speech categories and compared to the corresponding rules of the previous bottom-line experiment. The new rules perform considerably better, with a recall of 99.4% for the new rules, compared to 97.6% for the old rules. Precision was slightly better for the new rules.

1 Introduction

The task of a part of speech (POS) tagger is to assign to each word in a text the contextually correct morphological analysis. POS tagging of unedited text is an interesting task because of several reasons: It is a well-known problem to which several different techniques have been applied, it is a hard task and it has real world applications (in text-to-speech conversion, information extraction/retrieval, corpus linguistics, and so on).

The current paper describes the ongoing work of creating a state of the art POS tagger for unrestricted Swedish text, based on ILP techniques. The rule based tagger is inspired by the Constraint Grammar approach to POS disambiguation [7], and the rules are induced with the help of the freely available Progol ILP system [10]. The training material is sampled from the 1 million word Stockholm-Umeå Corpus [6].

The experiments of this article build on previously reported bottom-line experiments [5, 8], in which only very limited background knowledge was supplied.

In the current work, Progol has been given a much richer, more linguistically motivated background knowledge. However, an important aspect when creating the background knowledge has been not to spend too much effort on hand-coding linguistic knowledge. The background knowledge has been produced using rather "quick and dirty" methods. In addition to the richer background knowledge, new, more expressive, rules have been induced. This study has been concentrated to the two most frequent POS categories of the training corpus, the verb and the noun, and the result is compared to the noun and verb rules of the previously reported bottom-line experiment.

The current experiment has not been focused on comparing the result to other (machine-learning) approaches. Rather, the purpose has been to investigate to what degree supplying a richer background knowledge would improve accuracy compared to the previous results of [8]. The result indicates that there is indeed quite a lot to gain: Comparing the new rules to those of the earlier experiment yields much better recall (99.4% v. 97.6%) and slightly better precision too.

The paper is organized as follows: Section 2 provides the necessary background on Constraint Grammar, the Stockholm-Umeå Corpus, and summarizes some previous work. The main features of the current work are presented in Sect. 3. The result is given in Sect. 4, in Sect. 5 there is a discussion of the results and finally in Sect. 6 some future work is presented.

2 Background

2.1 Constraint Grammar

Constraint Grammar (CG) is a successful approach to POS tagging (and shallow syntactic analysis), developed at Helsinki University [7]. After a lexicon look-up, rendering the text morphologically ambiguous, rules discarding contextually impossible readings are applied until the text is unambiguous or no more rules can fire. The rules are hand-coded by experts, and the CG developers report high figures of accuracy for unrestricted English text.

A nice feature of CG is that the rules can be thought of as independent of each other; new rules can be added, or old ones changed, without worrying about unexpected behaviour because of complex dependencies between existing rules or because of rule ordering.

2.2 The Stockholm-Umeå Corpus

The Stockholm-Umeå Corpus (SUC) is a POS tagged, balanced corpus of 1 000 000 words of Swedish text [6]. The SUC tag set has 146 unique tags, and the tags consist of a POS tag followed by a (possibly empty) set of morphological features. There are 24 different POS categories. The first edition is available on CD-ROM and a second, corrected edition is on its way.

2.3 Previous Work on the Induction of Constraint Grammars

Several experiments of inducing CGs have been reported [12, 4, 5, 8]—all with promising results. While [12] used n-gram statistics, the other authors used ILP (and Progol).

In [8], bottom-line experiments aimed at inducing rules for disambiguating the tag-set of the Swedish Stockholm-Umeå Corpus were reported. The intention was to investigate whether ILP and Progol were useful tools to apply to POS disambiguation. Rules discarding contextually incorrect readings were induced one POS category at a time, for all of the 24 POS categories of the corpus. The background knowledge given to Progol was extremely poor; it merely consisted of access predicates used to pull out features from the context words. Furthermore, the context of the focus word was limited to a window of only a few words. The disambiguation rules could refer to word tokens as well as morphological features of the context words and the target word. The following rule discards all verb tags (vb) in the imperative (imp), active voice (akt) if the word immediately to the left of the target word is *att* (which is the infinitive marker or a subordinating conjunction):

```
remove(vb, A) :-
    constr(A,left_target(word(att),feats([imp,akt]))).
```

The rules were tested on unseen test data of 42 925 known words (words in the lexicon), including punctuation marks. After lexicon look-up the words were assigned 93 810 readings, i.e., on average 2.19 readings per word. 41 926 words retained the correct reading after disambiguation, which means that the correct tag survived for 97.7% of the words. After tagging, there were 48 691 readings left, 1.13 readings per word. As a comparison to these results, a preliminary test of two different taggers [11] reports that the Brill tagger [1], also trained on SUC, tagged 96.9% of the words correctly, and Oliver Mason's HMM-based QTag [9] got 96.3% on the same data. Yet another Markov model tagger, trained on the same corpus, albeit with a slightly modified tag set, tagged 96.4% of the words correctly [2]. None of these taggers left ambiguities pending, and all handled unknown words (thus making a direct comparison of the results of [8] somewhat difficult).

3 Current Work

The current work investigates the possibility of increasing the tagging accuracy of [8] by adding more linguistic background knowledge and by extending the expressiveness of the rules in other respects as well. These are the four main novel contributions of the current work compared to the earlier reported experiments of [5, 8]:

- More extensive background knowledge
- New training example format, allowing for feature under-specification
- New rule types
- The possibility of feature unification
- Variable window size

3.1 Training Data

A lexicon was created from SUC, and each word in the training data was assigned an ambiguity class in which all possible morphological readings of the word were represented. Each tag was represented as a feature-value vector, where each feature had a name, e.g. 'POS'=vb, 'VFORM'=inf, 'VOICE'=akt, etc. The features were named to allow for the rules to refer to a feature without specifying its value. Negative and positive examples for the noun and the verb tags were generated for the different rule types to learn.

A positive training example in the new format for a select rule (see Sect. 3.3) can be found below. The format is *select(POSCategory, FocusWord, LHSContext, RHSContext)*.[1] The focus word as well as the context words are represented by a quadruple, where the first item is the actual word form; the second is the frequency of the word form in the training data; the third is a binary feature which says whether a word starts with a capital letter (*) or not (-). The fourth element representing a word is a morphological reading, *t/8*, in which the first argument is the base (look-up) form of the word, the second through seventh arguments are morphological feature-value pairs, and the last argument is a frequency figure for that particular reading of the word form.

```
% ''Affärsområden Plastic Systems 7 procent av faktureringen .''
select(nn,
[procent,488,-,t(procent,'POS'=nn,'GEN'=utr,'NUM'=plu,'DEF'=ind,
                'CASE'=nom,-,469)],
[
'7',132,-,t('7','POS'=rg,'CASE'=nom,-,-,-,-,124),
systems,6,*,t('Systems','POS'=pm,'CASE'=nom,
-,-,-,-,6),
plastic,4,*,t('Plastic','POS'=pm,'CASE'=nom,-,-,-,-,4),
affärsområden,1,*,t(affärsområde,'POS'=nn,'GEN'=neu,'NUM'=plu,
                'DEF'=ind,'CASE'=nom,-,1)
],
[
av,13973,-,t(av,'POS'=pp,-,-,-,-,-,13569),
faktureringen,12,-,t(fakturering,'POS'=nn,'GEN'=utr,'NUM'=sin,
                'DEF'=def,'CASE'=nom,-,12),
'.',57122,-,t('.','POS'=dl,'DEL'=mad,-,-,-,-,57122)
]).
```

The word frequency figures were used by the background predicates to avoid inducing rules referring to low-frequency word forms. The rules reported in this work were induced using the SICStus P-Progol implementation [13], version 2.7.4c. Due to rather long processing times (days in some cases), it was not feasible to perform a ten-fold cross validation of the induced theories.

---

[1] Following [4], the left hand side context (*LHSContext*) is reversed in order to make it easier for the background knowledge to refer to the words closest to the focus word.

3.2 Background Knowledge

One of the main goals of this paper has been to provide Progol with potentially useful linguistic knowledge, which hopefully would yield a better, more compact and interesting theory. However, writing a natural language grammar manually is a very complicated and time-consuming matter. The ambition has been to provide a happy medium between the two extremes of providing virtually no linguistic background knowledge at all, and spending a lot of time and effort on coding high-level linguistic knowledge (such as e.g. a phrase structure grammar).

Thus, the linguistic data added to the background knowledge consists of

- Examples of noun phrase (NP) tag sequences
- Auxiliary verbs
- Auxiliary verb sequences
- Examples of verb chains
- Sets of POS categories with similar distributional statistics
- Sets of 'barriers'

Noun Phrases. A collection of non-recursive base NPs was extracted manually from one of the corpus files (Table 1). These 196 noun phrases consist of the word tokens of the original text and a tag for each word. These noun phrases were reduced to 92 unique tag sequences where all word tokens have been removed. Examples of noun phrase tag sequences of the format $np\_tag\_seq(List)$ are found in Table 2, where $List$ is a sequence of morphological readings.

Table 1. Manually extracted noun phrases

```
% 'nuclear weapons'
NP: kärnvapen 'POS'=nn,'GEN'=neu,'NUM'=plu,'DEF'=ind,'CASE'=nom
% 'I'
NP: jag 'POS'=pn,'GEN'=utr,'NUM'=sin,'DEF'=def,'PFORM'=sub
% 'the Lithuanian member of parliament, Nikolaj Medvedjev'
NP: den 'POS'=dt,'GEN'=utr,'NUM'=sin,'DEF'=def
    litauiske 'POS'=jj,'DEG'=pos,'GEN'=mas,'NUM'=sin,'DEF'=def,'CASE'=nom
    parlamentsledamoten 'POS'=nn,'GEN'=utr,'NUM'=sin,'DEF'=def,'CASE'=nom
    nikolaj 'POS'=pm,'CASE'=nom
    medvedjev 'POS'=pm,'CASE'=nom
```

Verbs. Different sets of verbs and verb sequences ("verb chains") have been created by chopping off the top of frequency lists of verb sequences extracted automatically from the corpus. Auxiliary verb sequences of one or two consecutive auxiliaries are given by the aux/1 and aux/2 facts that can be seen

Table 2. NP tag sequences

```
% dt pc nn --- determiner, participle, noun
np_tag_seq([t('POS'=dt,'GEN'=utr/neu,'NUM'=plu,'DEF'=def),
    t('POS'=pc,'VFORM'=prf,'GEN'=utr/neu,'NUM'=plu,'DEF'=ind/def,
    'CASE'=gen),
    t('POS'=nn,'GEN'=utr,'NUM'=sin,'DEF'=ind,'CASE'=nom)]).
% dt jj nn --- determiner, adjective, noun
np_tag_seq([t('POS'=dt,'GEN'=utr,'NUM'=sin,'DEF'=def),
    t('POS'=jj,'DEG'=suv,'GEN'=utr/neu,'NUM'=sin/plu,'DEF'=def,
    'CASE'=nom),
    t('POS'=nn,'GEN'=utr,'NUM'=sin,'DEF'=def,'CASE'=nom)]).
```

in Table 3. Verb chains of one or more auxiliary verbs (possibly intervened by adverbs) followed by a full set of morphological features for the "content verb" which ends the verb chain are also supplied. The 126 most common verb chains are added to the background knowledge in the following format: $vb\_chain([token_1, ..., token_n, reading])$. A few examples are found in Table 4.

Table 3. Auxiliary verb sequences

```
%'have'    %'would have'    %'can'/'be able to'    %'would be able to'
aux(har). aux(skulle,ha). aux(kan).                aux(skulle,kunna).
```

Table 4. Verb chains

```
% skulle kunna...('would be able to...')
vb_chain([token(skulle),token(kunna),t('POS'=vb,'VFORM'=inf,
    'VOICE'=akt)]).
% att kunna... ('to be able to...')
vb_chain([token(att),token(kunna),t('POS'=vb,'VFORM'=inf,'VOICE'=akt)]).
```

Sets of POS Categories with Similar Distributional Statistics. Twenty-four different sets of two or three POS categories have been extracted from the training data semi-automatically. These sets of POS categories have been produced from tables of trigrams of the tags of the training corpus. Sets of POS categories that seemed to have a similar distribution were created by inspecting bigram frequency lists of tag pairs of words separated by one word in between. For each such tag pair, a frequency list of the tags occurring between the bigram tags was used to find tags which might have a similar distribution. In addition to raw frequency, an association ratio score (or mutual information, see e.g. [3]) was computed for each bigram and the tags which occurred in between, and the most frequent tags with the highest association ratio were lumped together to form a POS set. Association ratio indicates the extent to which items co-occur, and was computed using

$$I(x,y) = \log \frac{P(x,y)}{P(x)P(y)}$$

where $P(x,y)$ is the probability of the POS bigram x occurring with the category y in between; $P(x)$ is the probability of the bigram x and $P(y)$ the probability of the category y. Examples of the resulting sets are found in Table 5.

Table 5. Examples of sets of POS categories

```
pos_set([sn,hp,pc]). pos_set([rg,nn,ro]). pos_set([pm,pn]).
pos_set([ab,jj]).    pos_set([ab,ha,ps]). pos_set([ab,ha]).
pos_set([dt,ab,ha]). pos_set([ab,pl]).    pos_set([ab,jj,ps]).
pos_set([ps,ha]).    pos_set([pl,ha,jj]).
```

Barriers. The sets of POS categories used in the barrier rules have been collected in an even simpler manner: By the help of frequency lists of POS bigrams, the categories which occur most frequently before the category that the barrier rule was intended for have been put into a set. For instance, the categories most frequently occurring immediately before the verb are {nn,pn,ab,hp,ie} (noun, pronoun, adverb, WH-pronoun, infinitive marker), and can be used by barrier rules for discarding faulty verbal readings. Barrier rules are explained in Sect. 3.3.

3.3 The Rule Types: Remove, Barrier and Select

Remove rules, barrier rules and select rules have been induced. These rule types are all presented in [12]. Sets of "lexical" rules have also been induced. Each of the rule types will be described in the next four sections.

The window size of the select and remove rules is not fixed, but depends on the size of a potential background knowledge noun phrase or verb sequence (see Sect. 3.2).

Different numbers of training examples have been used for the different rule types, depending on the complexity of the background knowledge. For the barrier rules, 2 000 positive and 6 000 negative examples have been used. The other rule types had up to 10 000 positive and 20 000 negative examples.

The format of the rules presented below is not the actual Progol output format, but a common intermediate format, which the Progol rules have been translated into.

Remove Rules. Remove rules are used to remove unwanted readings of a word. The remove rule can look at specific features of words and also take advantage of the linguistic background knowledge (described in Sect. 3.2).

The rule below is an example of a remove rule that removes every noun reading (nn) of the word *för*[2] ('for', 'to', 'prow', 'of' ...) if the first word to the right is an auxiliary verb (aux).

```
nn remove
    target: token=för,
    right 1: sequence=aux.
```

Barrier Rules. Barrier rules allow for an arbitrarily long context, given that certain features are not present in the context. The features not allowed are called *barriers* (which in this case consist of POS categories) and block out exceptions to the rule which would otherwise have made it invalid.

The barrier rules of the current work consist of at most three parts: a constraint on a word on an unspecified position to the left of the target, a barrier, and a constraint on the target word.

Below, an example of an induced rule which removes the noun (nn) reading of the word *man* ('man', 'one' (pronoun), 'mane') if there is a verb (vb) somewhere (*) to the left, and no determiner (dt) or adjective (jj) occur between the verb and the target word.

```
nn barrier
    left *: pos=vb,
    barrier: {dt,jj},
    target: token=man.
```

Select Rules. In a sense, the select rule contradicts the philosophy of Constraint Grammar, in that it says which reading is the correct one and should be kept, discarding every other reading. In some contexts, it might be easier to identify the correct reading rather than the faulty ones, and it is in these cases the select rule is useful.

The following rule says that if the word to the left is *alla* ('all', 'everyone'), the plural noun reading(s) should be selected, and every other reading discarded.

```
nn select
    left 1: token=alla,
    target: num=plu.
```

---

[2] The word *för* appears more than 11 000 times in the training data and has an ambiguity class of size eight.

Lexical Rules. In the current work, the term "lexical rule" is used somewhat differently from how it is used in [12], where a lexical rule discards a given reading for a specific word form without any contextual constraints at all.

The lexical rules of the current work are allowed to look at context word forms and they have a fixed window of maximally two words to the left and two words to the right, plus the focus word. An advantage of using lexical rules is that they can be applied even if the context is ambiguous. They take care of frequent, easy cases of ambiguities, making it possible for other rules, which demand an unambiguous context, to trigger.

Below are two lexical rules, the first one discarding the noun (nn) reading of the word *var* ('was', 'pus', '(pillow) case') if it is preceded by the word *det* ('it').

The second rule says that a specific noun reading should be selected, if the target word is preceded by the two-word sequence *ett bra* ('a good').

```
nn remove
    left 1: token=det,
    target: token=var.

nn select
    left 1: {token=ett | token=bra},
    target: {pos=nn,gen=neu,num=sin,def=ind,case=nom}.
```

3.4 Under-specification and Feature Unification

The format of the examples has been changed to allow for more powerful rules, e.g. by making it possible to induce rules which have under-specified feature values.

A benefit of using a rich language such as Horn clauses, compared to for example n-gram statistics, is that it is easier to make use of feature unification.

Under-specified Feature Values. In the previous work ([5, 8]), only feature *values* were extracted. In other words, the rules could not refer to a feature without having to specify its value. This is an unnecessary restriction which could make the resulting theory larger than it has to be. Separating the feature name from its value allows for constraints that, for example, cover both nouns and adjectives in the singular and the plural.

The following select rule is an example of a rule with an under-specified feature value (select rules are described in Sect. 3.3). It says that the plural noun reading should be kept and every other reading should be removed if the target word is *folk* ('people', 'folk'—singular or plural), and the word to the left has the feature VFORM, but that its value is of no importance (thus covering both the verb and the participle which have this feature in common).

```
nn select
    left 1: vform=_,
    target: {token=folk, num=plu}.
```

Feature Unification. Given the proper Progol mode declarations, it is possible for a feature to take a variable as its value. In fact, two features can share the same variable, forcing the values of the two features to unify. This makes it possible to induce more compact rules. Feature unification has, to our knowledge, not been used in the original Constraint Grammar.

In Swedish, adjectives show number (and gender) agreement with the noun on which they are dependent. An example of a rule that makes use of feature unification can be seen below. The rule forces the number (num) of the target word *stora* ('big', adjective, plural or singular) and the first word to the right to unify, and selects the agreeing adjective (jj) analysis of the target word.

```
jj select
    target: {token=stora, num=V},
    right: num=V.
```

The above rule would for instance select the singular reading of *stora* in the phrase *den stora fågeln* ('the big bird'), but select the plural reading of *stora* in *de stora fåglarna* ('the big birds').

4 Results

The rule types described above were induced for the two most frequent POS categories of the training data, the noun (nn) and the verb (vb). The corpus was split into a 90% training set and a 10% test set, in which the different files were evenly distributed over the different text genres. The training set was further split into a training set proper and an evaluation set. The evaluation set was used to identify and remove bad rules. The surviving rules were tested on 8 780 ambiguous words from the unseen test data. The test words all had at least one verb and/or noun reading, in all 35 678 readings ($\approx$ 4 readings/word). The exact same data was also disambiguated with the help of the old noun and verb rules of [8]. The old rules made 210 mistakes (discarding the correct reading), and there were 28 601 readings left after disambiguation (obviously leaving readings which belong to POS categories other than the noun or verb). The new rules made 57 mistakes and left 28 546 tags pending. This means that the new rules show a significant improvement in recall, 99.4% compared to 97.6%, while keeping the ambiguity at about the same level as in the bottom-line experiment. This appears to be a promising result. If it holds for the rest of the POS categories, there will be space for applying less reliable rules to reduce the pending ambiguities to a more acceptable level than the 1.13 tags/word reported in [8].

Table 6. Result

	OLD RULES	NEW RULES
READINGS PENDING	28601	28546
RECALL	97.6%	99.4%

5 Discussion

As mentioned in Sect. 2.3, a state of the art tagger trained on the Stockholm-Umeå Corpus typically has a recall of 96.3–96.9%, with no remaining ambiguities.

There are no results reported for these taggers for the individual POS categories. The rules induced in the work reported in this paper should primarily be compared with the rules induced in [8], rather than to other taggers. However, a small experiment of running the QTag on nouns and verbs yields a recall of 95.2%, with no remaining ambiguities. How this result should be compared in a fair way to the result reported in this paper is unfortunately not obvious.

Some of the rules induced in the current work refer to sets of POS categories, which makes these less dependent on a disambiguated context. This is also true for the rules which make use of under-specified feature values. We believe that when rules for all POS categories have been induced this will result in not only better recall, but also better overall precision, compared to the rules of [8].

In an early stage of the work described here, a class of verbs of "saying", denoting things like "say", "propose", etc, was added to the background knowledge. However, it turned out that this (semantic) category was quite useless for the task at hand, and was never used in any rules.

6 Future Work

When collecting the noun phrases used in the current investigation, they were initially divided into six different categories, which were lumped together in the background knowledge finally used in the rule induction. Perhaps it would be worth while to split the NP example base into these categories, and see if there are some NP categories that are more useful than others.

An important task of a useful tagger is that of handling unknown words (words not in the lexicon); however big a lexicon might be, new words will always turn up. Just consider proper nouns or foreign (loan) words. In Swedish, which has a much richer morphology than English, new words can for instance be created by concatenating two or more existing words—possibly by infixing a "glue *s*". For example, *rusdrycksförsäljningsförordning* ('law governing the sale of liquor and wine') consists of the concatenated words *rus-dryck-s-försäljning-s-förordning*. This way of extending the lexicon is a productive process, not at all unusual.

Replacing the previously induced rules (with minimal background knowledge) with the rules reported in this paper would increase recall without increasing the ambiguity. If the results of the current investigation holds for the rest of the POS categories it means that the performance of the tagger will increase considerably. We consider the results of this study to be good news, and will continue by producing rules for all the 24 POS categories of the corpus.

Acknowledgments

We are very grateful to James Cussens for providing the SICStus Prolog Progol implementation. We would also like to thank Henrik Boström for stimulating discussions. The second author has been supported by the European Community ESPRIT Long Term Research Project no. 20237 *Inductive Logic Programming II*.

References

1. Eric Brill. Some advances in transformation-based part of speech tagging. In *Proceedings of the Twelfth National Conference on Artificial Intelligence (AAAI-94)*, 1994.
2. Johan Carlberg and Viggo Kann. Implementing an efficient part-of-speech tagger. To appear. Available at http://www.nada.kth.se/theory/projects/granska/, 1999.
3. Kenneth Ward Church and Patrick Hanks. Word association norms, mutual information, and lexicography. In *Proceedings from the 27th Meeting of the ACL*, pages 76–83, 1989.
4. James Cussens. Part of speech tagging using Progol. In *Proceedings of the 7th International Workshop on Inductive Logic Programming (ILP-97)*, pages 93–108, Prague, Czech Republic, September 1997.
5. Martin Eineborg and Nikolaj Lindberg. Induction of Constraint Grammar-rules using Progol. In *Proceedings of The Eighth International Conference on Inductive Logic Programming (ILP'98)*, Madison, Wisconsin, 1998.
6. Eva Ejerhed, Gunnel Källgren, Wennstedt Ola, and Magnus Åström. *The Linguistic Annotation System of the Stockholm-Umeå Project*. Department of General Linguistics, University of Umeå, 1992.
7. Fred Karlsson, Atro Voutilainen, Juha Heikkilä, and Arto Anttila, editors. *Constraint Grammar: A language-independent system for parsing unrestricted text*. Mouton de Gruyter, Berlin and New York, 1995.
8. Nikolaj Lindberg and Martin Eineborg. Learning Constraint Grammar-style disambiguation rules using Inductive Logic Programming. In *Proceedings of COLING/ACL'98*, volume II, pages 775–779, Montreal, Canada, 1998.
9. Oliver Mason. *QTAG—A portable probabilistic tagger*. Corpus Research, The University of Birmingham, U.K., 1997.
10. Stephen Muggleton. Inverse entailment and Progol. *New Generation Computing Journal*, 13:245–286, 1995.
11. Daniel Ridings. SUC and the Brill tagger. GU-ISS-98-1 (Research Reports from the Department of Swedish, Göteborg University), 1998.
12. Christer Samuelsson, Pasi Tapanainen, and Atro Voutilainen. Inducing Constraint Grammars. In Miclet Laurent and de la Higuera Colin, editors, *Grammatical Inference: Learning Syntax from Sentences*, pages 146–155. Springer-Verlag, 1996.
13. Ashwin Srinivasan. *P-Progol User and Reference Manual*. http://www.comlab.ox.ac.uk/oucl/groups/machlearn/PProgol/, 1998.

On Sufficient Conditions for Learnability of Logic Programs from Positive Data*

Eric Martin and Arun Sharma

School of Computer Science and Engineering, The University of New South Wales,
Sydney, NSW 2052, Australia
E-mail: emartin@cse.unsw.edu.au, arun@cse.unsw.edu.au

Abstract. Shinohara, Arimura, and Krishna Rao have shown learnability in the limit of minimal models of classes of logic programs from positive only data. In most cases, these results involve logic programs in which the "size" of the head yields a bound on the size of the body literals. However, when local variables are present, such a bound on body literal size cannot directly be ensured. The above authors achieve such a restriction using technical notions like mode and linear inequalities.

The present paper develops a conceptually clean framework where the behavior of local variables is controlled by nonlocal ones. It is shown that for certain classes of logic programs, learnablity from positive data is equivalent to limiting identification of bounds for the number of clauses and the number of local variables. This reduces the learning problem finding two integers. This cleaner framework generalizes all the known results and establishes learnability of new classes.

1 Introduction

Recently, there has been considerable interest in deriving theoretical learnability results for Inductive Logic Programming. A lot of this work has been in the framework of *Probably Approximately Correct* (PAC) learning. The reader is referred to Dzeroski, Muggleton, and Russell [7, 8], Cohen [4, 5], De Raedt and Dzeroski [6], Frisch and Page [9], Yamamoto [19], Kietz [12], and Maass and Turán [15] for a sample.

Unfortunately, most of the positive results in the PAC setting are for very restricted classes of logic programs. PAC is a very strict learning criterion more suited to learnability analyses of less expressive concepts representable in propositional logic. This necessitates exploring less strict learnability criteria like identification in the limit for learnability analyses of logic programs.[1]

---

* Supported by the Australian Research Council Grant A49803051.

[1] The learnability analyses for ILP in the learning by query model overcomes some of the restrictive nature of the PAC model by allowing the learner queries to an oracle. However, these oracles may sometimes be noncomputable. For examples of such analyses, see Khardon [11] and Krishna-Rao and Sattar [14]. Also, it may be argued that concrete learning models proposed for ILP (like Muggleton and Page's [16] U-learnability) have an identification in the limit flavor.

The first identification in the limit result about learnability of logic programs is due to Shapiro [17]. He showed that the class of h-easy models is identifiable in the limit from both positive and negative facts. *In this paper we are mainly concerned with learnability from only positive facts.* Shinohara [18] showed that the class of minimal models of *linear* Prolog programs consisting of at most m clauses is identifiable in the limit from only positive facts. Unfortunately, linear logic programs are very restricted as they do not even allow local variables (i.e., each variable in the body must appear in the head). Arimura and Shinohara [3] introduced the class of *linearly-covering* logic programs that allows local variables in a restricted sense. They showed that the class of minimal models of linearly-covering Prolog programs consisting of at most m clauses of bounded body length is identifiable in the limit from only positive facts. Krishna Rao [13] noted that the class of linearly-covering programs is very restrictive as it did not even include the standard programs for `reverse`, `merge`, `split`, `partition`, `quick-sort`, and `merge-sort`. He proposed the class of *linearly-moded* programs that included all these standard programs and showed the class of minimal models of such programs consisting of at most m clauses of bounded body length to be identifiable in the limit from positive facts.

In this paper, we present a general framework for learnability of minimal models of definite logic programs from positive facts that covers all the above-mentioned cases and more. In the rest of this section, we give an informal discussion of our results.

A *frame* is a pair consisting of a class C of Herbrand structures and a recursive enumeration $(T_i)_{i \in N}$ of definite logic programs such that:

1. the minimal Herbrand model of each program in $\{T_i \mid i \in N\}$ belongs to C and each structure in C is the minimal Herbrand model of a program in $\{T_i \mid i \in N\}$;
2. the class of structures represented by the sequence of programs is an indexed family of recursive structures[2]; and
3. all nonempty subsets of a program (viewed as a set of definite clauses) in the sequence $(T_i)_{i \in N}$ are also in the sequence.

Intuitively, C is the *concept class* of the frame and the sequence $(T_i)_{i \in N}$ is its *hypothesis space*.

The positive data about a structure is modeled as a text. A *text* for a structure is any enumeration of all atomic sentences in the language true in the structure.

In the sequel, let $\mathcal{F} = (C, \mathcal{H})$ be a frame.

We say that C *is learnable in* $\mathcal{F}$ just in case for any structure S in C, a program for S in $\mathcal{H}$ can be determined in the limit from any text for S.

In the present paper we tie the learnability of concepts to the learnability of bounds for the number of clauses and bounds for the number of local variables. We informally introduce these latter notions next.

We say that *bounds for the number of clauses are learnable* in $\mathcal{F}$ if for any structure S in C, a bound for the number of clauses of a program for S in $\mathcal{H}$ can

---

[2] This means that some effective procedure decides whether α is a logical consequence of T_i, for all atomic sentences α and $i \in N$.

be determined in the limit from any text for S. Similarly, we say that *bounds for the number of local variables are learnable* in $\mathcal{F}$ if for any structure S in $\mathcal{C}$, a bound for the number of local variables for all clauses of a program for S in $\mathcal{H}$ can be determined in the limit from any text for S.

We show that $\mathcal{C}$ is learnable in $\mathcal{F}$ just in case:

1. bounds for the number of clauses in $\mathcal{F}$ are learnable;
2. bounds for the number of local variables in $\mathcal{F}$ are learnable; and
3. for natural numbers n_1 and n_2 and for each atomic sentence α, there are only finitely many programs with no more than n_1 clauses each of which have no more than n_2 local variables that entail α.[3]

The above may be viewed as an extension of Shinohara's [18] framework and condition (c) is very similar to Shinohara's notion of finite bounded thickness. However, to simplify the application of the above sufficient condition, we consider special cases of hypotheses spaces.

In Sect. 4 we introduce the semantic notion of *admissible programs* such that if the hypothesis space $\mathcal{H}$ of frame $\mathcal{F}$ consists only of admissible programs, then the concept class $\mathcal{C}$ is learnable in $\mathcal{F}$ if and only if bounds for number of clauses and bounds for number of local variables are learnable in $\mathcal{F}$.

The notion of admissible programs however is semantic and it cannot be determined from syntax whether a definite program is admissible. Also, all admissible programs in a language cannot be cast in a frame as the class of all admissible programs is not recursively enumerable.

Hence, the next two sections address frames whose hypothesis spaces consist of programs whose admissibility can be determined syntactically. Section 5 introduces the notion of *strongly admissible* programs that generalize the class of linear programs due to Shinohara [18] and reductive programs due to Krishna Rao [13]. Strongly admissible programs, however, do not allow local variables. Section 6 considers the interesting case of *safe* programs that allow local variables. The main idea in their definition is to "bound" all atomic formulas in which local variables occur by atomic formulas without local variables in such a way that the resulting program is strongly admissible. This idea may be viewed as a generalization of the very technical approaches taken by Arimura and Shinohara [3] in lineraly-covering programs and by Krishna Rao [13] in linearly-moded programs.

In Sect. 7, we give examples of safe programs, including `exponentiation`, an example that cannot be shown to be learnable according to Krishna Rao's [13] linearly-moded programs. We now proceed formally.

2 General notation and terminology

Let $\mathcal{L}$ be a finite first-order language without equality, whose set of variables is $\{v_i \mid i \in N\}$. Let $\kappa \geq 1$ and $\{\iota_k \mid k < \kappa\}$ be such that $\{p_k \mid k < \kappa\}$ enumerates the predicates of $\mathcal{L}$ and for all $k < \kappa$, ι_k is the arity of p_k. $\mathcal{L}_{term}$ denotes the set of

---

[3] More precisely, the programs have to be mimimal with respect to inclusion, which means that none of their strict subsets implies α.

$\mathcal{L}$-terms, $\mathcal{L}_{cterm}$ the set of closed $\mathcal{L}$-terms (ground terms), $\mathcal{L}_{at}$ the set of atomic $\mathcal{L}$-formulas, $\mathcal{L}_{atsen}$ the set of atomic $\mathcal{L}$-sentences (*i.e.* closed atomic $\mathcal{L}$-formulas, or ground facts), $\mathcal{L}^*_{atsen}$ the set of finite sequences of atomic $\mathcal{L}$-sentences, $\mathcal{L}_{at[k]}$, $k < \kappa$, the set of atomic $\mathcal{L}$-formulas of form $p_k(t_1 \ldots t_{\iota_k})$, $t_1 \ldots t_{\iota_k} \in \mathcal{L}_{term}$. Given $k < \kappa$, $t_1 \ldots t_{\iota_k} \in \mathcal{L}_{term}$, and $1 \le i \le \iota_k$, if φ denotes the formula $p_k(t_1 \ldots t_{\iota_k})$ then $\varphi(i)$ denotes the term t_i. Given clause C, $Var_{loc}(C)$ denotes the set of local variables of C (*i.e.* variables that appear in the body of C, but not in its head). Without loss of generality, we assume that for every clause C and $i > 0$, if v_i occurs in C then all of $v_0 \ldots v_{i-1}$ occur in C before each occurrence of v_i in C. Given u which is either a term or an atomic formula, and given partial function $h : Var \to \mathcal{L}_{term}$, $u[h]$ denotes the result of substituting in u every occurrence of every x in the domain of h by $h(x)$. We always write "program" instead of "definite program." For all programs T, $\mathcal{H}_T$ denotes the minimal Herbrand model of T. If e denotes a sequence whose index set is N then for all $k \in N$, $e[k]$ denotes the initial segment of length $(k + 1)$ of e (e.g., if $e = (e_0, e_1, e_2 \ldots)$ then $e[3] = (e_0, e_1, e_2)$ and $e[0] = ()$). The cardinality of a set X is denoted $card(X)$. Given set X of sets and property P on X, a *minimal member of X that satisfies P* is any $E \in X$ such that E satisfies P and no $F \in X$ which is strictly included in E satisfies P. By *cofinitely many*, we mean all but a finite number of.

3   Frames

Definition 1. *Given class C of Herbrand structures and recursive enumeration $(T_i)_{i \in N}$ of programs, we say that the pair $(C, (T_i)_{i \in N})$ is a frame just in case:*

1. *$C = \{\mathcal{H}_{T_i} \mid i \in N\}$;*
2. *$(\mathcal{H}_{T_i})_{i \in N}$ is an indexed family of recursive Herbrand structures;*
3. *every nonempty subset of a program in $\{T_i \mid i \in N\}$ belongs to $\{T_i \mid i \in N\}$.*

Definition 2. *A text for a Herbrand structure S is an enumeration of all atomic sentences α such that $S \models \alpha$.*

Definition 3. *Let frame $\mathcal{F} = (C, (T_i)_{i \in N})$ be given.*

We say that bounds for the number of clauses are learnable in $\mathcal{F}$ *just in case there is partial recursive function $\Xi : \mathcal{L}^*_{atsen} \to N$ with the following property. For all $S \in C$ and texts e for S, there is $n \in N$ such that:*

i) *$\Xi(e[k]) = n$ for cofinitely many $k \in N$;*
ii) *there is $i \in N$ such that $\mathcal{H}_{T_i} = S$ and $card(T_i) \le n$.*

We say that bounds for the number of local variables are learnable in $\mathcal{F}$ *just in case there is partial recursive function $\Lambda : \mathcal{L}^*_{atsen} \to N$ with the following property. For all $S \in C$ and texts e for S, there is $n \in N$ such that:*

iii) *$\Lambda(e[k]) = n$ for cofinitely many $k \in N$;*
iv) *there is $i \in N$ such that $\mathcal{H}_{T_i} = S$ and $card(Var_{loc}(C)) \le n$ for all $C \in T_i$.*

We say that C is learnable in $\mathcal{F}$ *just in case there is partial recursive function $\Psi : \mathcal{L}^*_{atsen} \to \{T_i \mid i \in N\}$ with the following property. For all $S \in C$ and texts e for S, there is $i \in N$ such that:*

v) $\Psi(e[k]) = i$ *for cofinitely many* $k \in N$;

vi) $\mathcal{H}_{T_i} = S$.

Proposition 1. *Let frame* $\mathcal{F} = (\mathcal{C}, (T_i)_{i \in N})$ *be such that the following holds:*

1. *bounds for the number of clauses are learnable in* $\mathcal{F}$;
2. *bounds for the number of local variables are learnable in* $\mathcal{F}$;
3. *for every* $n_1, n_2 \in N$ *and* $\alpha \in \mathcal{L}_{atsen}$, *the set of all minimal* $T \in \{T_i \,|\, i \in N\}$ *such that* $T \models \alpha$, $\mathrm{card}(T) \leq n_1$, *and* $\mathrm{card}(\mathrm{Var}_{loc}(C)) \leq n_2$ *for all* $C \in T$, *is finite.*

Then $\mathcal{C}$ *is learnable in* $\mathcal{F}$.

Proof. We first define a partial recursive function Φ whose domain is $\mathcal{L}^*_{atsen}$ and whose codomain is the set of all finite subsets of $\{T_i \,|\, i \in N\}$. Since bounds for the number of clauses (respect. local variables) are learnable in $\mathcal{F}$, choose partial recursive $\Xi : \mathcal{L}^*_{atsen} \to N$ (respect. $\Lambda : \mathcal{L}^*_{atsen} \to N$) that satisfies conditions i) and ii) (respect. iii) and iv)) of Definition 3. Let $k \in N$ and $\alpha_0 \ldots \alpha_k \in \mathcal{L}_{atsen}$ be given. We define $\Phi(\alpha_0 \ldots \alpha_k)$. Towards this aim, we construct by induction a sequence $(F_0 \ldots F_k)$ of finite subsets of $\{T_i \,|\, i \in N\}$. Let F_0 be the set of all T_j, $j \leq k$, such that T_j is a minimal member of $\{T_i \,|\, i \in N\}$ with $T_j \models \alpha_0$, $\mathrm{card}(T_j) \leq \Xi(\alpha_0 \ldots \alpha_k)$, and $\mathrm{card}(\mathrm{Var}_{loc}(C)) \leq \Lambda(\alpha_0 \ldots \alpha_k)$ for all $C \in T_j$. Let $p < k$ be given, and suppose that F_p has been defined. We define F_{p+1}. Given $X \in F_p$, let G_X be the set of all T_j, $j \leq k$, such that T_j is a minimal member of $\{T_i \,|\, i \in N\}$ with $T_j \models \alpha_{p+1}$, $\mathrm{card}(X \cup T_j) \leq \Xi(\alpha_0 \ldots \alpha_k)$, and $\mathrm{card}(\mathrm{Var}_{loc}(C)) \leq \Lambda(\alpha_0 \ldots \alpha_k)$ for all $C \in T_j$. Set:
$$F_{p+1} = F_p \cup \{X \cup Y \,|\, X \in F_p, \; X \not\models \alpha_{p+1}, \; Y \in G_X\}.$$
Then set $\Phi(\alpha_0 \ldots \alpha_k) = F_k$. This completes the definition of Φ. Now we define from Φ a partial recursive function $\Psi : \mathcal{L}^*_{atsen} \to \{T_i \,|\, i \in N\}$. Fix an enumeration $(\beta_i)_{i \in N}$ of $\mathcal{L}_{atsen}$. Let computable function Θ whose domain is the cartesian product of N with the set of all finite subsets of $\{T_i \,|\, i \in N\}$, whose codomain is the set of all finite sequences of members of $\{T_i \,|\, i \in N\}$, satisfy the following. For all $k, n \in N$ and members $X_0 \ldots X_n$ of $\{T_i \,|\, i \in N\}$, $\Theta(k, \{X_0 \ldots X_n\})$ orders $X_0 \ldots X_n$ in such a way that:

1. for all $r, s \leq n$, X_r occurs before X_s in $\Theta(k, \{X_0 \ldots X_n\})$ whenever $\{i \leq k \,|\, X_r \models \beta_i\} \subset \{i \leq k \,|\, X_s \models \beta_i\}$;
2. for all $k' \in N$, if $\{i \leq k \,|\, X_r \models \beta_i\} \subseteq \{i \leq k \,|\, X_s \models \beta_i\}$ and $\{i \leq k' \,|\, X_r \models \beta_i\} \subseteq \{i \leq k' \,|\, X_s \models \beta_i\}$ are equivalent for all $r, s \leq n$, then $\Theta(k, \{X_0 \ldots X_n\}) = \Theta(k', \{X_0 \ldots X_n\})$.

Let $k \in N$ and $\alpha_0 \ldots \alpha_k \in \mathcal{L}_{atsen}$ be given. We define $\Psi(\alpha_0 \ldots \alpha_k)$. Suppose there is $n \in N$, $X_0 \ldots X_n \in \{T_i \,|\, i \in N\}$, and least $i \leq n$ such that $\Theta(k, \Phi(\alpha_0 \ldots \alpha_k)) = (X_0 \ldots X_n)$ and $\{\alpha_0 \ldots \alpha_k\} \subseteq \{\alpha \in \mathcal{L}_{atsen} \,|\, X_i \models \alpha\}$. Then set $\Psi(\alpha_0 \ldots \alpha_k) = X_i$. Otherwise $\Psi(\alpha_0 \ldots \alpha_k)$ is undefined. This completes the definition of Ψ.

Let $S \in \mathcal{C}$ and text $e = (\alpha_k)_{k \in N}$ for S be given. To finish the proof it suffices to show that there is $i \in N$ such that Ψ satisfies conditions v) and vi) of Definition 3. By the definitions of Ξ and Λ, let $K, n_1, n_2 \in N$ be such that $\Xi(e[k]) = n_1$ and $\Lambda(e[k]) = n_2$ for all $k \geq K$, and let $j \in N$ be such that $\mathcal{H}_{T_j} = S$, $\mathrm{card}(T_j) \leq n_1$, and $\mathrm{card}(\mathrm{Var}_{loc}(C)) \leq n_2$ for all $C \in T_j$. We define by induction sequences $(k_0 \ldots k_{n_1})$ and $(i_0 \ldots i_{n_1})$ of integers. Set $k_0 = 0$. Let $i_0 \in N$ be such that T_{i_0} is a minimal member of $\{T_i \,|\, i \in N\}$ with $T_{i_0} \models \alpha_0$, and $T_{i_0} \subseteq T_j$. Let $p < n_1$ be given, and suppose that k_p and i_p have been defined. We define k_{p+1} and i_{p+1}. If $\bigcup_{q \leq p} T_{i_q}$ and T_j are logically equivalent then set $k_{p+1} = k_p$ and $i_{p+1} = i_p$. Suppose otherwise. Let $k_{p+1} > k_p$ be least such that $\bigcup_{q \leq p} T_{i_q} \not\models \alpha_{k_{p+1}}$. Let $i_{p+1} \in N$ be such that $T_{i_{p+1}}$ is a minimal member of $\{T_i \,|\, i \in N\}$ with $T_{i_{p+1}} \models \alpha_{k_{p+1}}$, and $T_{i_{p+1}} \subseteq T_j$. Trivially, $\bigcup_{p \leq n_1} T_{i_p}$ is a subset of T_j which is logically equivalent to T_j. Fix $K' \geq K, k_{n_1}, i_0 \ldots i_{n_1}$. It is easy to verify that $\bigcup_{p \leq n_1} T_{i_p}$ belongs to $\Phi(\alpha_0 \ldots \alpha_k)$ for all $k \geq K'$. Moreover, it is easy to show that there is finite $E \subseteq \{T_i \,|\, i \in N\}$ such that $\Phi(\alpha_0 \ldots \alpha_k) = E$ for cofinitely many $k \in N$. With the definition of Θ, we infer that there is $K'' \geq K'$, $n \in N$, and $X_0 \ldots X_n \in \{T_i \,|\, i \in N\}$ such that $\Theta(k, \Psi(\alpha_0 \ldots \alpha_k)) = (X_0 \ldots X_n)$ for all $k \geq K''$, and there is least $p \leq n$ such that $\mathcal{H}_{X_p} = S$. By the definition of Θ again, $\mathcal{H}_{X_p} - \mathcal{H}_{X_q} \neq \emptyset$ for all $q < p$. Let $K''' \geq K''$ be such that for all $q < p$, $\{\alpha_0 \ldots \alpha_{K'''}\} - \mathcal{H}_{X_q} \neq \emptyset$. It follows immediately from the definition of Ψ that for all $k \geq K'''$, $\Psi(\alpha_0 \ldots \alpha_k) = X_p$. So $i \in N$ with $X_p = T_i$ satisfies conditions v) and vi) of Definition 3, as required. □

An immediate modification in the proof of Proposition 1 shows the following result, due to Shinohara [18].

Proposition 2. *Let frame $\mathcal{F} = (\mathcal{C}, (T_i)_{i \in N})$ be such that the following holds:*

1. *bounds for the number of clauses are learnable in $\mathcal{F}$;*
2. *for every $n \in N$ and $\alpha \in \mathcal{L}_{atsen}$, the set of all minimal $T \in \{T_i \,|\, i \in N\}$ such that $T \models \alpha$ and $card(T) \leq n$, is finite.*

Then $\mathcal{C}$ is learnable in $\mathcal{F}$.

4 Admissible programs

To apply Proposition 1, we have to consider frames which satisfy the condition expressed in (3). Towards this aim, it suffices to consider frames built from programs T such that:

1. to any atomic sentence α is associated a complexity measure such that only finitely many atomic sentences are at most as complex as α;
2. all sentences that are derived thanks to any clause in T are at least as complex as the premises.

The following notation is used for the remainder of the paper; it captures the abstract notion of complexity measure we need.

Definition 4. $\preceq$ *denotes a pre-order on $\mathcal{L}_{atsen}$ such that for all $\alpha \in \mathcal{L}_{atsen}$, $E_\alpha = \{\beta \in \mathcal{L}_{atsen} \,|\, \beta \preceq \alpha\}$ is finite, and $\{(\alpha, E_\alpha) \,|\, \alpha \in \mathcal{L}_{atsen}\}$ is computable.*

Here are two natural examples of such pre-orders.

Example 1. Given $t \in \mathcal{L}_{cterm}$, denote by $size(t)$ the total number of occurrences of constants and function symbols occurring in t. Let $k, k' < \kappa$ and $t_1 \ldots t_{\iota_k}, t'_1 \ldots t'_{\iota_{k'}} \in \mathcal{L}_{cterm}$ be given. Set $p_k(t_1 \ldots t_{\iota_k}) \preceq p_{k'}(t'_1 \ldots t'_{\iota_{k'}})$ just in case $\max_{1 \leq i \leq \iota_k} size(t_i) \leq \max_{1 \leq i \leq \iota_{k'}} size(t'_i)$.

Example 2. We define inductively the *heigth* of a closed term t and denote it by $height(t)$. All constants have a heigth of 0. Let $n \geq 1$, $t_1 \ldots t_n \in \mathcal{L}_{cterm}$, and $k \in N$ be least such that the height of all t_p is at most equal to k. Then for all n-ary function symbols f, the height of $f(t_1 \ldots t_n)$ is equal to $k+1$. Let $k, k' < \kappa$ and $t_1 \ldots t_{\iota_k}, t_1' \ldots t_{\iota_{k'}}' \in \mathcal{L}_{cterm}$ be given. Set $p_k(t_1 \ldots t_{\iota_k}) \preceq p_{k'}(t_1' \ldots t_{\iota_{k'}}')$ just in case $\max_{1 \leq i \leq \iota_k} height(t_i) \leq \max_{1 \leq i \leq \iota_{k'}} height(t_i')$.

Relying on $\preceq$, we can now define a set of programs that fulfill the former requirements.

Definition 5. *Let Herbrand structure S and clause $C = A_0 \leftarrow A_1 \ldots A_\ell$ be given. We say that C is admissible with respect to S just in case for every $h : \text{Var} \to \mathcal{L}_{cterm}$, if $A_n[h] \in S$ for all $n \leq \ell$ then $A_n[h] \preceq A_0[h]$ for all $n \leq \ell$.*

A program is admissible if all its clauses are admissible with respect to its least Herbrand model.[4]

Lemma 1. *For every recursive enumeration $(T_i)_{i \in N}$ of admissible programs, $(\mathcal{H}_{T_i})_{i \in N}$ is an indexed family of recursive Herbrand structures.*

Proof. It suffices to show that there exists a partial recursive function Φ such that for all admissible programs T and atomic sentences α, $\Phi(T, \alpha) = 1$ if $\mathcal{H}_T \models \alpha$, and $\Phi(T, \alpha) = 0$ otherwise. We describe informally how Φ reacts faced with program T and atomic sentence α. By Definition 4 let E be the finite set of all $\psi \in \mathcal{L}_{atsen}$ such that $\psi \preceq \alpha$. Let F_0 be the set of all closed instances of members of T which belong to E. Let $i \in N$ be given, and suppose that F_i has been defined. Let F_{i+1} be the union of F_i with the set of all $\psi \in E$ such that for some clause $C = A_0 \leftarrow A_1 \ldots A_\ell$ in T and sequence $(\psi_1 \ldots \psi_\ell)$ of members of F_i, $\psi \leftarrow \psi_1 \ldots \psi_\ell$ is a closed instance of C. Let $i \in N$ be least such that $F_i = F_{i+1}$. Set $\Phi(T, \alpha) = 1$ if $\alpha \in F_i$, and $\Phi(T, \alpha) = 0$ otherwise. It follows easily from Definition 5 that if T is admissible, then $\Phi(T, \alpha) = 1$ whenever $\mathcal{H}_T \models \alpha$, and $\Phi(T, \alpha) = 0$ otherwise. $\square$

Proposition 3. *Let frame $\mathcal{F} = (\mathcal{C}, (T_i)_{i \in N})$ be such that for all $i \in N$, T_i is an admissible program. Then the following conditions are equivalent.*

(a) *Bounds for the number of clauses and bounds for the number of local variables are learnable in $\mathcal{F}$.*

(b) *$\mathcal{C}$ is learnable in $\mathcal{F}$.*

Proof. Trivially, (b) implies (a). Suppose that (a) holds. Let $\alpha \in \mathcal{L}_{atsen}$ and $n \in N$ be given. Let E be the set of admissible programs T such that: (1) $T \models \alpha$, (2) for all $T' \subset T$, $T' \not\models \alpha$, and (3) all members of T contain no more than n local variables.

By Proposition 1 it suffices to show that E is finite. Let $T \in E$ be given. By (1) let $i \in N$ and sequence $(\alpha_0 \ldots \alpha_i)$ of atomic sentences be a proof of α from T, i.e., $\alpha_i = \alpha$ and for all $j \leq i$, there is a clause $C = A_0 \leftarrow A_1 \ldots A_\ell$ in

---

[4] It should be noted that the class of admissible programs is more general than the class of acyclic programs defined in [2].

$T, j_1 \ldots j_\ell < j$, and $h : \text{Var} \to \mathcal{L}_{cterm}$ with $A_0[h] = \alpha_j$ and $A_n[h] = \alpha_{j_n}$ for all $1 \le n \le \ell$. Without loss of generality, we can suppose that $(\alpha_0 \ldots \alpha_i)$ is minimal, i.e., there is no $i' \in N$ and sequence $(\alpha'_0 \ldots \alpha'_{i'})$ of atomic sentences which is a proof of α from T with $\{\alpha'_j \mid j \le i'\} \subset \{\alpha_j \mid j \le i\}$. Since T is admissible, $\alpha_j \preceq \alpha_i$ for all $j \le i$. Hence $\{\alpha_j \mid j \le i\}$ is a subset of the finite set Y_1 of all $\beta \in \mathcal{L}_{atsen}$ such that $\beta \preceq \alpha$. Let Y_2 be the set of all atomic formulas χ such that for some $\psi \in Y_1$, ψ is an instance of χ, and let Z be the set of clauses built from Y_2. Note that for every $t \in \mathcal{L}_{cterm}$ there are, up to a renaming of variables, only finitely many $t' \in \mathcal{L}_{term}$ such that t is an instance of t'. Since Y_1 is finite, this implies that Z is finite (recall the convention on the variables appearing in a clause). By (2), for every atomic formula A occurring in T, there is $j \le i$ such that α_j is an instance of A. Hence every atomic formula that occurs in T belongs to Y_2. This, (3), and the fact that Z is finite imply immediately that E is finite, as required. □

Corollary 1. *Let $\mu, \nu \in N$ and frame $\mathcal{F} = (\mathcal{C}, (T_i)_{i \in N})$ be such that for all $i \in N$, T_i is an admissible program which contains at most μ clauses, each of them containing at most ν distinct local variables. Then $\mathcal{C}$ is learnable in $\mathcal{F}$.*

5 Strongly admissible programs

The notion of admissible program has a semantic character since it relies on least Herbrand models. Unfortunately, all admissible programs cannot be cast in a frame. We will now consider two kinds of frames built from programs whose admissibility is established thanks to a syntactic examination. The first kind of frames are limited to programs without local variables (provided that $\mathcal{L}_{cterm}$ is infinite, which is the interesting case). This is achieved technically as follows.

Definition 6. *Let binary relation R on $\mathcal{L}_{at}$ be defined as follows: for all $\psi, \varphi \in \mathcal{L}_{at}$, $\psi R \varphi$ just in case for all $h : \text{Var} \to \mathcal{L}_{cterm}$, $\psi[h] \preceq \varphi[h]$. It is easy to verify that R is a pre-order on $\mathcal{L}_{at}$ which extends $\preceq$. It will also be denoted $\preceq$. Moreover, we now suppose that $\{(\psi, \varphi) \mid \psi \preceq \varphi, \ \psi, \varphi \in \mathcal{L}_{at}\}$ is computable.*

Definition 7. *A program is* strongly admissible *just in case for every clause $A_0 \leftarrow A_1 \ldots A_\ell$ in T and $n \le \ell$, $A_n \preceq A_0$.*

Example 3. Examples 1 and 2 define pre-orders on $\mathcal{L}_{cterm}$ whose extensions to $\mathcal{L}_{term}$ satisfy the condition expressed in Definition 6. Hence all reductive programs are strongly admissible (for the notion of reductive program, see [13]).

In case $\mathcal{L}_{cterm}$ is infinite, it is easy to verify that for all $\psi, \varphi \in \mathcal{L}_{at}$ with $\psi \preceq \varphi$, every variable that occurs in ψ also occurs in φ. Hence:

Lemma 2. *Suppose that $\mathcal{L}_{cterm}$ is infinite. Then all strongly admissible programs have no local variables.*

Directly from Definitions 5, 6, and 7 we have Lemmas 3 and 4:

Lemma 3. *The set of strongly admissible programs is computable.*

Lemma 4. *Every strongly admissible program is admissible.*

Directly from Lemma 1, Proposition 3, and Lemmas 3 and 4:

Proposition 4. *Let $(T_i)_{i\in N}$ be a computable enumeration of all strongly admissible programs. Then the following conditions are equivalent.*

1. *Bounds for the number of clauses are learnable in $(\{\mathcal{H}_{T_i} \mid i \in N\}, (T_i)_{i\in N})$.*
2. *$\{\mathcal{H}_{T_i} \mid i \in N\}$ is learnable in $(\{\mathcal{H}_{T_i} \mid i \in N\}, (T_i)_{i\in N})$.*

6 Safe programs

Now we investigate the interesting case of programs with local variables. The key idea is to "bound" all atomic formulas in which local variables occur with atomic formulas without local variables, in such a way that the resulting program is strongly admissible. To this aim, we generalise the partial pre-order $\preceq$ to a partial pre-order on the set of $\mathcal{L}$-terms.

Definition 8. $\preceq$ *now also denotes a pre-order on $\mathcal{L}_{term}$ with these properties:*

1. *For all $t, t' \in \mathcal{L}_{term}$, $t \preceq t'$ iff $t[h] \preceq t'[h]$ for all $h : Var \to \mathcal{L}_{cterm}$.*
2. *Given $k, k' < \kappa$ and $t_1 \ldots t_{\iota_k}, t'_1 \ldots t'_{\iota_{k'}} \in \mathcal{L}_{term}$, $p_k(t_1 \ldots t_{\iota_k}) \preceq p_{k'}(t'_1 \ldots t'_{\iota_{k'}})$ just in case for all $1 \le i \le \iota_k$, there is $1 \le j \le \iota_{k'}$ with $t_i \preceq t_j$.*
3. *Let X be the set of all $(t_0 \ldots t_n, t'_0 \ldots t'_n) \in \mathcal{L}_{term}^{2n+2}$, $n \in N$, that satisfy the following. For all $h : Var \to \mathcal{L}_{term}$, if $t_m[h] \preceq t'_m[h]$ for all $m < n$ then $t_n[h] \preceq t'_n[h]$. Then X is computable.*

Example 4. Consider the pre-order $\preceq$ on $\mathcal{L}_{at}$ defined in example 1 (respect. example 2). Given $t, t' \in \mathcal{L}_{cterm}$, set $t \preceq t'$ just in case $size(t) \preceq size(t')$ (respect. $height(t) \preceq height(t')$). The conditions expressed in Definition 8 are satisfied.

Definition 9. *Let program T be given. A subset X of $\bigcup_{k<\kappa}(\mathcal{L}_{at[k]} \times \{1 \ldots \iota_k\}^2)$ is a bound kit for T just in case for all clauses $A_0 \leftarrow A_1 \ldots A_\ell$ in T and $h : Var \to \mathcal{L}_{cterm}$, (*) below implies (†) below.*

(*) For all $1 \le j \le \ell$ and $(\varphi, p, q) \in X$ with $\varphi \models A_j$, $A_j\langle p\rangle[h] \preceq A_j\langle q\rangle[h]$.
(†) For all $(\varphi, p, q) \in X$ such that $\varphi[h'] = A_0[h']$ for some $h' : Var \to \mathcal{L}_{term}$, $A_0\langle p\rangle[h] \preceq A_0\langle q\rangle[h]$.

It is easy to verify the following, by induction on the length of proofs.

Lemma 5. *Let program T, $\alpha \in \mathcal{L}_{atsen}$ with $T \models \alpha$, and bound kit X for T be given. Then for all $(\varphi, p, q) \in X$ with $\varphi \models \alpha$, $\alpha\langle p\rangle \preceq \alpha\langle q\rangle$.*

Definition 10. *A program T is safe just in case for all clauses $A_0 \leftarrow A_1 \ldots A_\ell$ in T, $1 \le j \le \ell$, and $p \ge 1$ no greater than the arity of A_0, there exists $q \ge 1$ no greater than the arity of A_j, $s \in N$, sequence $((\varphi_r, p_r, q_r))_{r\le s}$ of members of a bound kit for T, and $1 \le k_0 \ldots k_s \le \ell$ such that:*

1. *for all $r \le s$, $\varphi_r \models A_{k_r}$;*
2. *$A_j\langle p\rangle \preceq A_{k_0}\langle p_0\rangle$;*
3. *for all $r < s$, $A_{k_r}\langle q_r\rangle \preceq A_{k_{r+1}}\langle p_{r+1}\rangle$;*
4. *$A_{k_s}\langle q_s\rangle \preceq A_0\langle q\rangle$.*

Directly from Definitions 7, 8 and 10:

Lemma 6. *Every strongly admissible program is safe.*

The third condition in Definition 8 implies that the set of pairs (T, X) where X is a bound kit for T, is computable. With Definition 10, we conclude that:

Lemma 7. *The set of safe programs is computable.*

Lemma 8. *Every safe program is admissible.*

Proof. Let safe program T be given. Let clause $A_0 \leftarrow A_1 \ldots A_\ell$ in T and $h :$ $Var \to \mathcal{L}_{cterm}$ be such that for all $n \leq \ell$, $T \models A_n[h]$. Let $1 \leq j \leq \ell$ be given. Let $p \geq 1$ be no greater than the arity of A_j. Then there exists $q \geq 1$ no greater than the arity of A_0, $s \in N$, sequence $((\varphi_r, p_r, q_r))_{r \leq s}$ of members of a bound kit for T, and $1 \leq k_0 \ldots k_s \leq \ell$ which satisfy the four conditions expressed in Definition 10. Hence $\varphi_r \models A_{k_r}[h]$ for all $r \leq s$, which with Lemma 5 and the fact that $T \models A_n[h]$ for all $1 \leq n \leq \ell$, implies that $A_{k_r}\langle p_r \rangle[h] \preceq A_{k_r}\langle q_r \rangle[h]$ for all $r \leq s$. Moreover, the first condition in Definition 8 implies that $A_j\langle p \rangle[h] \preceq A_{k_0}\langle p_0 \rangle[h]$, $A_{k_r}\langle q_r \rangle[h] \preceq A_{k_{r+1}}\langle p_{r+1} \rangle[h]$ for all $r < s$, and $A_{k_s}\langle q_s \rangle[h] \preceq A_0\langle q \rangle[h]$. It follows that $A_j\langle p \rangle[h] \preceq A_0\langle q \rangle[h]$. By the second condition in Definition 8, we infer that $A_j[h] \preceq A_0[h]$. Hence T is admissible. $\square$

Directly from Lemma 1, Proposition 3, and Lemmas 7 and 8:

Proposition 5. *Let $(T_i)_{i \in N}$ be a computable enumeration of all safe programs. Then the following conditions are equivalent.*

1. *Bounds for the number of clauses and bounds for the number of local variables are learnable in $(\{\mathcal{H}_{T_i} \mid i \in N\}, (T_i)_{i \in N})$.*
2. *$\{\mathcal{H}_{T_i} \mid i \in N\}$ is learnable in $(\{\mathcal{H}_{T_i} \mid i \in N\}, (T_i)_{i \in N})$.*

7 Examples

We now give a few examples of safe programs, among which *linearly-moded programs* in the sense of [13]. They are safe on the basis of a wide class of preorders $\preceq$, among which those given as examples.

Example 5. The reverse program:

```
app([ ],Ys,Ys) ←
app([X|Xs],Ys,[X|Zs]) ← app(Xs,Ys,Zs)
rev([ ],[ ]) ←
rev([X|Xs],Zs) ← rev(Xs,Ys), app(Ys,[X],Zs)
```

$\{(app(X,Y,Z),1,3)\}$ is a bound-kit for the reverse program, because for all $h : Var \to \mathcal{L}_{cterm}$, $[\ ][h] \preceq Ys[h]$ (see first clause) and $Xs[h] \preceq Zs[h]$ implies $[X|Xs][h] \preceq [X|Zs][h]$ (see second clause). So $rev(Xs,Ys)$ and $app(Ys,[X],Zs)$ in the fourth clause can be "bounded" by $rev(Xs,Zs)$ and $app(Zs,[X],Zs)$ respectively. We conclude easily that the reverse program is safe.

Example 6. The quick-sort program:

```
ap([ ],Ys,Ys) ←
ap([X|Xs],Ys,[X|Zs]) ← ap(Xs,Ys,Zs)
par([ ],H,[ ],[ ]) ←
par([X|Xs],H,[X|Ls],Bs) ← X≤H, par(Xs,H,Ls,Bs)
par([X|Xs],H,Ls,[X|Bs]) ← X>H, par(Xs,H,Ls,Bs)
qs([ ],[ ]) ←
qs([H|L],S) ← par(L,H,A,B), qs(A,A1), qs(B,B1), ap(A1,[H|B1],S)
```

It is easily verified that the set consisting of $(ap(X,Y,Z),1,3)$, $(ap(X,Y,Z),2,3)$, $(par(X,H,L,B),3,1)$ and $(par(X,H,L,B),4,1)$ is a bound-kit for the quick-sort program. Hence par(L,H,A,B), qs(A,A1), qs(B,B1) and ap(A1,[H|B1],S) in the definition of qs can be "bounded" by par(L,H,L,L), qs(L,S), qs(L,S) and ap(S,S,S) respectively. We conclude immediately that quick-sort is a safe program.

Example 7. The exponential program:

```
adminus1(s(X),0,X) ←
adminus1(s(X),s(Y),s(Z)) ← adminus1(s(X),Y,Z)
mult(0,Y,0) ←
mult(s(X),0,0) ←
mult(s(X),s(Y),s(Z)) ← mult(s(X),Y,U), adminus1(s(X),U,Z)
exp(X,0,1) ←
exp(0,s(Y),0) ←
exp(s(X),s(Y),Z) ← exp(s(X),Y,U), mult(s(X),U,Z)
```

It is easy to verify that $\{(\text{adminus1}(X,Y,Z),2,3),(\text{mult}(s(X),Y,Z),2,3)\}$ is a bound-kit for the exponential program. Therefore the atoms mult(s(X),Y,U) and adminus1(s(X),U,Z) (respect. exp(s(X),Y,U) and mult(s(X),U,Z)) in the definition of mult (respect. exp) can be "bounded" by mult(s(X),Y,Z) and adminus1(s(X),Z,Z) (respect. by exp(s(X),Y,Z) and mult(s(X),Z,Z)). We conclude immediately that exponential is a safe program.

8 Conclusion

The results in this paper give a generalized framework for proving convergence results for learnability of logic programs from positive data. Clearly, the next step is explore more concrete models by introducing resource-boundedness and probabilistic data settings in the above model. These issues are topics for our future work. We would also like to note that the results presented here can be extended to include ordinal bounds on the number of mind changes in the spirit of [10]. This issue will be included in the journal version of the paper.

References

1. Arimura, H.: Completeness of depth-bounded resolution in logic programming. In: Proceedings of the 6th Conference, Japan Soc. Software Sci. Tech. (1989) 61–64

2. Arimura, H.: Learning Acyclic First-Order Horn Sentences from Entailment In: Li, M., Maruoka, A. (eds.): Algorithmic Learning Theory: Eighth International Workshop (ALT '97). LNAI, Vol. 1316. Springer-Verlag (1997) 432–445
3. Arimura, H., Shinohara, T.: Inductive inference of Prolog programs with linear data dependency from positive data. In: Jaakkola, H., Kangassalo, H., Kitahashi, T., Markus, A. (eds.): Proc. Information Modelling and Knowledge Bases V. IOS Press (1994) 365–375
4. Cohen, W.W.: PAC-Learning non-recursive Prolog clauses. Artificial Intelligence **79** (1995) 1–38
5. Cohen, W.W.: PAC-Learning Recursive Logic Programs: Efficient Algorithms. Journal of Artificial Intelligence Research **2** (1995) 501–539
6. De Raedt, L., Dzeroski, S.: First-order jk-clausal theories are PAC-learnable. Artificial Intelligence **70** (1994) 375–392
7. Dzeroski, S., Muggleton, S., Russell, S.: PAC-Learnability of constrained nonrecursive logic programs. In: Proc. of the 3rd International Workshop on Computational Learning Theory and Natural Learning Systems. Wisconsin, Madison (1992)
8. Dzeroski, S., Muggleton, S., Russell, S.: PAC-Learnability of determinate logic programs. In: Proceedings of the Fifth Annual Workshop on Computational Learning Theory. ACM Press (1992) 128–135
9. Frisch, A., Page, C.D.: Learning constrained atoms. In: Proceedings of the Eighth International Workshop on Machine Learning. Morgan Kaufmann (1991)
10. Jain, S., Sharma, A.: Mind Change Complexity of Learning Logic Programs. In: Proceedings of the 1999 European Conference on Computational Learning Theory. Lecture Notes in Artificial Intelligence. Springer-Verlag (1999) (to appear)
11. Khardon, R.: Learning first-order universal Horn expressions. In: Proceedings of the Eleventh Annual Conference on Computational Learning Theory. ACM Press (1998) 154–165
12. Kietz, J.-U.: Some computational lower bounds for the computational complexity of inductive logic programming. In: Proceedings of the 1993 European Conference on Machine Learning. Vienna (1993)
13. Krishna Rao, M.: A class of Prolog programs inferable from positive data. In: Arikawa, A., Sharma, A. (eds.): Algorithmic Learning Theory: Seventh International Workshop (ALT '96). Lecture Notes in Artificial Intelligence, Vol. 1160. Springer-Verlag (1996) 272–284
14. Krishna Rao, M., Sattar, A.: Learning from entailment of logic programs with local variables. In: Richter, M., Smith, C., Wiehagen, R., Zeugmann, T. (eds.): Algorithmic Learning Theory: Ninth International Workshop (ALT '97). Lecture Notes in Artificial Intelligence. Springer-Verlag (1998) (to appear)
15. Maass, W., Turán, Gy.: On learnability and predicate logic. NeuroCOLT Technical Report NC-TR-96-023 (1996)
16. Muggleton, S., Page, C.D.: A Learnability Model for Universal Representations. Technical Report PRG-TR-3-94. Oxford University Computing Laboratory, Oxford (1994)
17. Shapiro, E.: Inductive Inference of Theories from Facts. Technical Report 192. Computer Science Department, Yale University (1981)
18. Shinohara, T.: Inductive Inference of Monotonic Formal Systems From Positive Data. New Generation Computing **8** (1991) 371–384
19. Generalized unification as background knowledge in learning logic programs. In: Jantke, K., Kobayashi, S., Tomita, E., Yokomori, T. (eds.): Algorithmic Learning Theory: Fourth International Workshop (ALT '93). Lecture Notes in Artificial Intelligence, Vol. 744. Springer-Verlag (1993) 111–122

A Bounded Search Space of Clausal Theories

Herman Midelfart

Department of Computer and Information Science,
Norwegian University of Science and Technology,
N-7491 TRONDHEIM,
Norway,
herman@idi.ntnu.no

Abstract. In this paper the problem of induction of clausal theories through a search space consisting of theories is studied. We order the search space by an extension of θ-subsumption for theories, and find a least generalization and a greatest specialization of theories. A most specific theory is introduced, and we develop a refinement operator bounded by this theory.

1 Introduction

In the normal setting of ILP, the goal is to find a hypothesis theory which explains a set of examples given some background theory. This is done iteratively such that one single clause is found at the time. Each clause is usually found by searching some ordering of clauses. When a clause is found, it is added to the hypothesis theory, and the examples it explains are removed from the example set.

This approach poses a problem since the clauses may depend on each other. So the sequence in which they are found may be critical. A strategy such as selecting the clause that explains the most examples or seems the best given some measure, is often used. But this does not mean that the best theory is found. This is really a greedy strategy and the search is by no means complete.

One way to overcome this problem would be to a use a search space consisting of theories rather than clauses. The best theory will obviously be in this search space. A drawback is of course that this search space is much larger, but it has the benefit that we can control the search more directly. So even if we cannot search it completely, it might be easier to define good heuristics for this search space.

In this paper we study this search space of theories. Section 2 recaptures some preliminaries. Section 3 mentions some related work. In section 4, we find a least generalization and a greatest specialization and show that this search space has no ideal refinement operator. We introduce a most specific theory which a can be used to bound the search space in section 5. Finally, in section 6 we construct a refinement operator for this search space which is bounded by this most specific theory.

2 Preliminaries

First-order logic We assume that the reader is familiar with basic logic programming concepts and recapture just a few that are necessary for this paper.

As in [7], a clausal language $\mathcal{C}$ given by an alphabet is the set of all clauses. A Horn language $\mathcal{H}$ given by an alphabet is the set of all Horn clauses. A (Horn) theory is a set finite of (Horn) clauses. A clause or a theory is *function-free* if it does not contain functions with arity ≥ 1. Two clauses are *standardized apart* if they have no variables in common. Let T be a theory. Then $HB(T)$ denotes the *Herbrand base* of T, and $M(B)$ denotes the *least Herbrand model* of T. $HB_P(T)$ is the subset of $HB(T)$ containing only the ground instances of the predicate P. If e is a clause and B a theory then e^+ and e^- designate the head and the body of e. $\bar{e}$ denotes $(\neg e^+ \wedge e^-)\sigma$ where σ is a Skolem substitution wrt. B. Let E be a theory where $E = \{e_1, \ldots, e_m\}$ and each e_i is a clause. Then $\overline{E}$ denotes $\bar{e}_1 \vee \cdots \vee \bar{e}_m = (\neg e_1^+ \wedge e_1^-)\sigma_1 \vee \cdots \vee (\neg e_m^+ \wedge e_m^-)\sigma_m$ such that for all $1 \leq i \leq m$, σ_i is a Skolem substitution wrt. B and $(\neg e_j^+ \wedge e_j^-)\sigma_j$ for all $j \neq i$.

Quasi-orders. A *quasi-ordered set* $\langle G, R \rangle$ is a set G ordered by a relation R where R is reflexive ($\forall x \in G \; xRx$) and transitive ($\forall x, y, z \in G$, xRy and $yRz \Rightarrow xRz$). Let $\langle G, \geq \rangle$ be a quasi-ordered set and let $x, y \in G$. If $x > y$ and there is no z such that $x > z > y$, then x is an *upward cover* of y, and y is a *downward cover* of x. θ-subsumption is a quasi-order that is usually defined between clauses, but has also been defined between theories [1, 3]:

Definition 1. *(θ-subsumption) A clause c_1 θ-subsumes a clause c_2 ($c_1 \succeq c_2$) iff $c_1\theta \subseteq c_2$. Two clauses c_1 and c_2 are θ-equivalent ($c_1 \sim c_2$) iff $c_1 \succeq c_2$ and $c_2 \succeq c_1$. A clause c_1 is θ-reduced iff there is no proper subset c_2 of c_1 ($c_2 \subset c_1$) such that $c_1 \sim c_2$. A theory T_1 θ-subsumes a theory T_2 ($T_1 \succeq T_2$) iff $\forall c_2 \in T_2 \exists c_1 \in T_1 \; c_1 \succeq c_2$. Two theories T_1 and T_2 are θ-equivalent ($T_1 \sim T_2$) iff $T_1 \succeq T_2$ and $T_2 \succeq T_1$. A theory T_1 is θ-reduced iff all the clauses in the theory are θ-reduced and there is no proper subset of T_2 of T_1 such that $T_1 \sim T_2$.*

Partial order. A partially ordered set $\langle G, R \rangle$ is a set G ordered by a relation R where R is reflexive, anti-symmetric ($\forall x, y \in G$, xRy and $yRx \Rightarrow x = y$), and transitive. A quasi-order may $\langle G, \geq \rangle$ may induce an equivalence-relation $\approx$ such that $x \approx y$ iff $x \geq y$ and $y \geq x$. Let $[x]$ denote the equivalence class of x, i.e., $[x] = \{x \mid x \approx y\}$. Then we can define a relation $\hat{\geq}$ on the quotient set $G/\approx$ such that $[x]\hat{\geq}[y]$ iff $x \geq y$. Then $\langle G/\approx, \hat{\geq} \rangle$ is a partial order. θ-equivalence is such an equivalence-relation, and θ-subsumption becomes a partial order when it is defined on the equivalence classes induced by $\sim$.

Lattice. If $\langle G, \geq \rangle$ is a quasi-ordered set and $S \subseteq G$. $x \in G$ is a *generalization* (upper bound) if $x \geq y$ for all $y \in S$ and a *least generalization* (least upper bound) if $z \geq x$ for all generalizations $z \in G$ of S. Similarly, $x \in G$ is a *specialization* (lower bound) of S if $y \geq x$ for all $y \in S$ and a *greatest specialization* (greatest lower bound) if $x \geq z$ for all specializations of $z \in G$ of S. $\langle G, \geq \rangle$ is called a *lattice* if for all $x, y \in G$ a least generalization and a greatest specialization of $\{x, y\}$ exists.

A lattice is usually defined on a partial order, but as in [7], we define it on a quasi-order. This does not really matter since if $\langle G, \geq \rangle$ is a lattice defined on a quasi-order, $\langle G/\approx, \hat{\geq} \rangle$ will be a lattice defined on a partial order.

Refinement operators. Let $\langle G, \geq \rangle$ be a quasi-ordered set G. A *downward refinement operator* for $\langle G, \geq \rangle$ is a function $\rho(C) \subseteq \{D \mid C \geq D\}$, and an *upward refinement operator* for $\langle G, \geq \rangle$ is a function $\delta(C) \subseteq \{D \mid D \geq C\}$, for all $C \in G$.

A refinement operator may be characterized by a number of properties. These are given for a downward operator ρ below, but can easily be changed to fit an upward refinement operator.

Definition 2. *Let $\langle G, \geq \rangle$ be a quasi-ordered set.*

1. *The* refinement closure $\rho^*(C)$ *for some $C \in G$ is:*

   $$\rho^0(C) = \{C\}$$
   $$\rho^n(C) = \{D \mid \text{ there is an } E \in \rho^{n-1}(C) \text{ such that } D \in \rho(E)\}, n \geq 1$$
   $$\rho^*(C) = \rho^0(C) \cup \rho^1(C) \cup \cdots$$

2. *A ρ-chain from C to D is a sequence $C = C_0, C_1, \ldots, C_n = D$, such that $C_i \in \rho(C_{i-1})$ for every $1 \leq i \leq n$.*
3. *ρ is locally finite iff for every $C \in G$, $\rho(C)$ is finite and computable.*
4. *ρ is proper iff for every $C \in G$, $\rho(C) \subseteq \{D \mid C > D\}$.*
5. *ρ is complete iff for every $C, D \in G$ such that $C > D$, there is an $E \in \rho^*(C)$ such that D and E are equivalent in the $\geq$-order.*
6. *ρ is ideal iff it is locally finite, complete, and proper.*

If a refinement operator is applied on a lattice we may define completeness with respect to a bottom element.

Definition 3. *Let $\langle G, \geq \rangle$ be a lattice with a top element, $\top$, and a bottom element, $\bot$. ρ is complete wrt. to a bottom element $\bot$ iff for every $C, D \in G$ such that $C > D \geq \bot$ there is an $E \in \rho^*(C)$ such that D and E are equivalent in the $\geq$-order.*

3 Related work

Plotkin [8] and Reynolds [9] both proved that the language of literals forms a lattice ordered by either θ-subsumption or entailment. Plotkin proved also that a clausal language C ordered by θ-subsumption forms an lattice and gave an algorithm to compute least generalization of clauses. He showed that this lattice contained infinite ascending and descending chains. Some examples of such chains (taken from [7]) are:

An infinite ascending chain: $c \succ \ldots \succ e_{k+1} \succ e_k \succ \ldots \succ e_2 \succ e_1$, where
$c = \{P(x_1, x_2), P(x_2, x_1)\}, d_n = \{P(y_1, y_2), P(y_2, y_3), \ldots, P(y_{n_1}, y_n)\}, n \geq 2$,
$c_n = c \cup d_n, n \geq 3$, and $e_k = c_{3^k}, k \geq 1$

An infinite descending chain: $c_2 \succ c_3 \succ \ldots \succ c_n \succ c_{n+1} \succ \ldots \succ c$, where $c = P(x_1, x_1)$ and $c_n = \{P(x_i, x_j) | 1 \leq i, j \leq n\}, n \geq 2$

Laag and Nienhuys-Cheng [4] used such chains to prove that there is no ideal refinement operator for clauses. For any quasi-order the following lemmas hold:

Lemma 1. *[7] Let $\langle G, \geq \rangle$ be a quasi-ordered set. If there exists an ideal downward (upward) refinement operator for $\langle G, \geq \rangle$, then every $C \in G$ has a finite complete set of downward (upward) covers.*

Because of the chains, there is a clause that has no finite complete set of downward covers, and there is a clause that has no upward cover at all.

Proposition 1. *[7] Let C be a clausal language containing a binary predicate symbol P. Then $c = \{P(x_1, x_2), P(x_2, x_1)\}$ has no finite complete set of downward covers in $\langle C, \succeq \rangle$.*

Proposition 2. *[7] Let C be a clausal language containing a binary predicate symbol P. Then $c = \{P(x_1, x_1)\}$ has no upward cover in $\langle C, \succeq \rangle$*

Thus there is no ideal downward or upward refinement operator for $\langle C, \succeq \rangle$. Similar results holds also for Horn clauses. Nevertheless, there are locally finite and complete refinement operators which are not proper. One of those will be extended in section 6.

In [5, 6], Muggleton introduced the concept of a *most specific clause*, which is also called a *bottom clause*. This clause is induced from an example e relative to a background theory B, and is defined as follows.

Definition 4. *[6] Let B be a Horn theory, e a clause such that $F = (B \cup \bar{e})$ is satisfiable (i.e. $B \not\models e$). The bottom clause of e under B is denoted $BOT(B, e)$ and is defined as follows.*

$$BOT^+(B, e) = \{a \mid a \in HB(F) \backslash M(F)\}, \qquad BOT^-(B, e) = \{\neg a \mid a \in M(F)\}$$
$$BOT(B, e) = BOT^+(B, e) \cup BOT^-(B, e)$$

The bottom clause is infinite if B and e contains functions, but finite if they are function-free. A clause containing functions can be made function-free by flattening. In Progol, the bottom clause $BOT(B, e)$ is used for bounding the search space so only the sub-lattice, consisting of the clauses θ-subsuming $BOT(B, e)$, is searched.

4 Properties of θ-subsumption on theories

Lattice. The least generalization of clauses is important since it can be used for generalizing clauses. In the next lemma we find a least generalization of theories.

Lemma 2. *Let S be $\{T_1, \ldots, T_n\}$ where each T_i is a theory (i.e., T_i a finite subset C). Then $T = \cup_{i=1}^{n} T_i$ is a least generalization (least upper bound) of S.*

Proof.

1. T is a generalization of S, i.e., for all T_i in S we have $T \succeq T_i$. This holds since any clause c_i in T_i is also in T.

2. T is a least generalization of S, i.e., for all U if $U \succeq T_i$ holds for all T_i then $U \succeq T$. Assume that U is an arbitrary theory such that $U \succeq T_i$ for all T_i. For each $c \in T$ there is a T_i and a $c_i \in T_i$ such that $c = c_i$ (since T is the union of the T_i). For this c_i there is a $d \in U$ (since $U \succeq T_i$) such that $d \succeq c_i$. So $d \succeq c$. Thus for each $c \in T$ there must be at least one $d \in U$ such that $d \succeq c$, and therefore $U \succeq T$. Since U is an arbitrary theory this must hold generally as well. Thus for all U for which $U \succeq T_i$ holds for all T_i, we have $U \succeq T$.

So $T = \cup_{i=1}^{n} T_i$ is a least generalizations of $S = \{T_1, \ldots, T_n\}$. S may actually have several least generalizations, but all them belong to the same equivalence class induced by θ-equivalence.

Example 1. Let $T_1 = \{P(x_1, x_2) \vee P(x_2, x_1), Q(x, x)\}$ and $T_2 = \{P(x_1, a) \vee P(a, x_1), Q(a, a)\}$. Then $T = T_1 \cup T_2 = \{P(x_1, x_2) \vee P(x_2, x_1), P(x_1, a) \vee P(a, x_1), Q(x, x), Q(a, a)\}$ is a least generalization of T_1 and T_2. Since $T_1 \succeq T_2$, T_1 is also a least generalization of T_1 and T_2. But T_1 and T belong to the same equivalence class since $T_1 \sim T$.

We can also find a greatest specialization of a arbitrary set of theories as the next lemma shows. It builds directly on a greatest specialization of clauses given by [8, p. 88] and [7]: If $c_1, \ldots, c_n$ are standardized apart then $c_1 \cup \cdots \cup c_n$ is a greatest specialization. Using this greatest specialization of clauses the lemma follows quite easily. Thus the proof will not be given here.

Lemma 3. *Let S be $\{T_1, \ldots, T_n\}$ where each T_i is a theory. Then a greatest specialization (greatest lower bound) of $T_1, \ldots,$ and T_n is*

$$T = \left\{ c_1' \cup \cdots \cup c_n' \;\middle|\; \begin{array}{l} \langle c_1, \ldots, c_n \rangle \in T_1 \times T_2 \times \cdots \times T_n \text{ and } c_1', \ldots, c_n' \\ \text{are variants of } c_1, \ldots, c_n \text{ and standardized apart} \end{array} \right\}$$

Like the least generalization, the greatest specialization presented here is one of several, but all of them belong to the same equivalence classes induce by θ-equivalence.

Thus the set of all theories, $\mathcal{S}$, ordered by $\succeq$ has a least upper bound and a greatest lower bound for each subset of $\mathcal{S}$. The theory containing only the empty clause (i.e., $\{\Box\}$) is the top element in this order since for all $T \in \mathcal{S}$ $\{\Box\} \succeq T$ (all clauses in T are θ-subsumed by $\Box$). The bottom element is the empty theory $\{\}$ which contains no clauses, since for all $T \in \mathcal{S}$ $T \succeq \{\}$ (there are no clauses in $\{\}$ that have to be θ-subsumed by a clause in T). Thus $\langle \mathcal{S}, \succeq \rangle$ is a lattice.

The set of all Horn theories has the same least generalization as the set of all theories, but a greatest specialization of the set of all Horn theories must be based on a greatest specialization of a set of Horn clauses which is [7]:

$$gs_{\mathcal{H}}(c_1, \ldots, c_n) = \begin{cases} c_1 \cup \cdots \cup c_n & \text{if } c_1, \ldots, c_n \text{ are headless} \\ c_1\theta \cup \cdots \cup c_n\theta & \text{if } \theta = mgu(c_1^+, \ldots, c_n^+) \\ \bot & \text{if } c_1^+, \ldots, c_n^+ \text{ do not unify} \end{cases}$$

$\perp$ is the bottom clause in the lattice formed by $\langle \mathcal{H}, \succeq \rangle$. A Horn language does not really have a bottom clause, but $\perp$ is an artificial bottom clause inserted into the language in order to complete the lattice. This bottom clause is also necessary when considering Horn theories. A greatest specialization of a set of Horn theories is the found by replacing $c_1 \cup \cdots \cup c_n$ with $gs_{\mathcal{H}}(c_1', c_2', \ldots, c_n')$ in lemma 3. Consequently, the set of all Horn theories order by θ-subsumption is a lattice.

Notice that the least generalization of clauses can be used as an inductive operator to perform an inductive leap beyond what is already known. This is not true for the least generalization of theories. The reason is that theories is such a general representation that given a set of examples (e.g. ground atoms) we can represent them directly. There is no bias in the representation. Thus we must rely on refinement operators to perform induction. Next, we show that there is no ideal refinement operator for theories.

Covers. The problem of infinite ascending chains carry over to theories, but we can prove more directly that there is no finite downward cover for theories ordered by θ-subsumption.

Lemma 4. *Let $c = \{P(x_1, x_2), P(x_2, x_1)\}$ be a clause in C and S be the set of all finite subsets of C. Then $\{c\} \in S$ has no finite complete set of downward covers ordered by $\succeq$.*

Proof. Assume that $F = \{T_1, \ldots, T_n\}$ is a finite complete set of downward covers of $\{c\}$ according to the $\succeq$-order, where each T_i is finite. Now let T be the union of the T_i's. If we can show that T is a finite complete set of downward covers of c, we will have a contradiction with proposition 1. Thus F cannot be finite and complete. Since both the number of T_i's and the T_i's themselves are finite, T must be finite. Thus just proving that T is a complete set of covers for c, remains.

For each T_i in F we have that $\{c\} \succeq T_i$ since F is a set of downward covers of $\{c\}$. Thus for all T_i and for all $e_i \in T_i$ $c \succeq e_i$. Since each $e \in T$ is also in a T_i, we must have $c \succeq e$ for each e in T. At the same time we have $T_i \not\succeq \{c\}$ for all T_i's, or else they would not be covers of $\{c\}$. Thus none of e in the T_i's θ-subsume c. So, each member e of T is a proper specialization of c, i.e., for all e in T $c \succ e$.

For each d such that $c \succ d$, we have also $\{c\} \succ \{d\}$. Since F is a complete set of downward covers of $\{c\}$, there must be a $T_i \in F$ such that $\{c\} \succ T_i \succeq \{d\}$ for each d. $T_i \succeq \{d\}$ means there is an $e \in T_i$ such that $e \succeq d$. c must also θ-subsume this e since $\{c\} \succ T_i$ means that $c \succ e_i$, for all $e_i \in T_i$. Thus there is an $e \in T_i$ such that $c \succ e \succeq d$. Since T is union of the T_i's, it must include e as well. Thus for all d such that $c \succ d$, we have an $e \in T$ such that $c \succ e \succeq d$. So T is a finite complete set of covers of c. But as mentioned above, this contradicts proposition 1. So there is no finite complete set of covers for $\{c\}$.

Also, the descending chain for clauses given in section 3 reappears for theories: $\{c_2\} \succ \ldots \succ \{c_n\} \succ \{c_{n+1}\} \succ \ldots \succ \{c\}$ (where $c = P(x, x)$). The proofs will not be presented here, but it is possible to prove that there is no finite upward cover E of $\{c\}$ such that $\{c_k\} \succ E$, for all $k \geq 2$. Then it follows that $\{c\}$ has no finite complete set of covers.

So if the language contains a predicate or a function with arity ≥ 2, there are theories that do not have a finite and complete set of downward or upward covers. Then by lemma 1, there is no ideal downward or upward refinement operator for $\langle S, \succeq \rangle$ where S is the set of all finite subsets of C. This holds also if S is set of all finite subsets of $\mathcal{H}$.

5   A most specific theory

One problem when extending the most specific clause to theories lies in the difference between θ-subsumption on clauses and θ-subsumption on theories. θ-subsumption on clauses is a generalization of the *subset* relation between sets of literals, but θ-subsumption on theories is a generalization of the *superset* relation on sets of clauses. We can create a generalization S of a theory T by adding a clause to T that is not θ-equivalent to any other clause in T. Thus a theory that θ-subsumes a bottom theory, can contain a clause that does not θ-subsume any clause in the bottom theory. This means that a bottom theory is not a sufficient condition (as the bottom clause) telling what kind of clauses there can be in a theory θ-subsuming it. The bottom theory is rather a necessary condition telling which clauses there must be in a theory θ-subsuming it.

The most specific clause corresponds to the least Herbrand model $M(B \cup \{\bar{e}\})$ of $B \cup \{\bar{e}\}$. Given the prior necessity $((B \cup \{\bar{e}\}) \not\models \Box)$ and posterior sufficiency $((B \cup h \cup \{\bar{e}\}) \models \Box)$ requirements, it follows that $M(B \cup \{\bar{e}\})$ cannot be a model of h. Thus there must be a substitution θ such that $h^+\theta \subseteq HB(B \cup \{\bar{e}\}) \backslash M(B \cup \{\bar{e}\})$ and $h^-\theta \subseteq M(B \cup \{\bar{e}\})$. If we let $HB(B \cup \{\bar{e}\}) \backslash M(B \cup \{\bar{e}\})$ and $M(B \cup \{\bar{e}\})$ be the head and body of the bottom clause, we see that h must θ-subsume it. If we assume that B and e are function-free, this clause will also be finite since in that case $M(B \cup \{\bar{e}\})$ and $HB(B \cup \{\bar{e}\})$ are finite.

We can extend this approach to theories. Then the requirements are that $K = (B \cup \overline{E}) \not\models \Box$ and $L = (B \cup H \cup \overline{E}) \models \Box$ where $E = \{e_1, \ldots, e_m\}$, and the heads of all the examples e_i are instances of a single *learning predicate* P (i.e., the predicate we want to learn). Now, each model M of K corresponds to a distinct bottom clause that a h in H must θ-subsume. The bottom theory could include just one such clause or them all. H must θ-subsume it in any case, but the more of them it contains, the tighter bound it will be. Selecting all of them is not practically feasible. So we have selected just some. The choice made here is related to the next section and will be made more apparent there.

Definition 5. *Let B be a background Horn theory, E be a set of example Horn clauses where the head of each clause is an instance of the learning predicate P. Then the most specific theory $BOT_T(B, E)$ is defined as:*

$$BOT_T(B, E) = \{BOT_C(B, e) \mid e \in E \text{ and } (B \cup HB_P^{-e}(B \cup \overline{E}) \cup \{\bar{e}\}) \not\models \Box\}$$
$$BOT_C(B, e) = BOT_C^+(B, e) \cup BOT_C^-(B, e)$$

$$BOT_C^+(B,e) = \{a \mid a \in HB(B \cup \overline{E}) \backslash M\}, \qquad BOT_C^-(B,e) = \{\neg a \mid a \in M\}$$

where $M = M(B \cup HB_P^{-e}(B \cup \overline{E}) \cup \{\overline{e}\})$. $HB_P^{-e}(B \cup \overline{E}) = HB_P(B \cup \overline{E}) \backslash \{e^+\sigma\})$ where $\overline{e}$ is in $\overline{E}$ and σ is the Skolem substitution for $\overline{e}$ such that $\overline{e} = (\neg e^+ \wedge e^-)\sigma$. ($HB_P^{-e}(B \cup \overline{E})$ is the set of all ground instances of P expect the Skolemized head of e).

Now, we will show that $BOT_T(B,E)$ is a bottom theory such that any H satisfying $B \cup H \models E$ must θ-subsume it.

Theorem 1. *(Completeness wrt. the bottom theory) Let H be a Horn theory, and let B, E, and P be as in definition 5. H satisfies $L = (B \cup H \cup \overline{E}) \models \Box$ and $K = (B \cup \overline{E}) \not\models \Box$ and $HB(K) = HB(L)$ only if $H \succeq BOT_T(B,E)$*

Proof. Let $F = (B \cup HB_P^{-e}(B \cup \overline{E}) \cup \{\overline{e}\})$ where $e \in E$, and $(B \cup HB_P^{-e}(B \cup \overline{E}) \cup \{\overline{e}\}) \not\models \Box$. Then $M(F)$ is a model of K since:

1. $F \models B$. So $M(F) \models B$.
2. $F \models \overline{e}$. So $M(F) \models \overline{e}$. Since $\overline{E}$ is disjunction of negated Skolemized clauses where $\overline{e}$ is in this disjunction, $M(F) \models \overline{E}$.

$M(F)$ is an interpretation of L, but $M(F)$ cannot be a model of L. Thus there is a $h \in H$ such that $M(F) \not\models h$. Then there is a substitution θ such that $h^+\theta \subseteq HB(K) \backslash M(F)$ (since $HB(K) = HB(L)$) and $h^-\theta \subseteq M(F)$ which is similar to $h \succeq BOT_C(B,e)$. This holds for any examples in E. So for all $e \in E$ there is a $h \in H$ such that $h \succeq BOT_C(B,e)$. This is again the same as $H \succeq BOT_T(B,E)$.

5.1 Relevance

An ILP system such as FOIL and Progol finds clauses iteratively by adding a clause at the time to a resulting theory. A common feature of these clauses is that they explain at least one previously unexplained example given the background theory and previously discovered hypothesis clauses. It is not necessary that a clause explains any examples directly. The clause can imply some ground instance of the learning predicate[1] which again imply an example through another (recursive) clause, provided that this clause has already been found. In this case the clause explains the example indirectly.

Since the search space of theories is quite large, we need to set some restrictions. We will use the restriction that all clauses in a theory must explain some examples directly. We call such clauses (theories) relevant. This leads to incompleteness, since we will no longer consider all possible hypotheses H that satisfy $B \cup H \models E$. But this restriction is not that severe. If the example set includes at least an example for each of the clauses in the theory that we want to learn, we will be able to find it. Also, it seems natural that the examples should give some evidence of which clauses there should be in the hypothesis theory. Relevance is defined as:

---

[1] Consider examples as just ground atoms.

Definition 6. *Let H be a Horn theory, and let B, E, and P be as in definition 5. A clause A clause h in H is relevant iff there is an example e in E such that $(B \cup HB_P^{-e}(B \cup \overline{E}) \cup h \cup \{\overline{e}\}) \models \Box$, but $(B \cup HB_P^{-e}(B \cup \overline{E}) \cup \{\overline{e}\}) \not\models \Box$. A theory H is relevant iff every clause in H is relevant.*

Example 2. Let $B = \{A(a,b), A(b,c), A(b,d), B(d,c)\}$, $H = \{h_1, h_2, h_3\}$, $E = \{P(a,b), P(a,c), P(d,c)\}$, $h_1 = P(x,y) \leftarrow A(x,y)$, $h_2 = P(x,y) \leftarrow B(x,y)$, and $h_3 = P(x,y) \leftarrow A(x,z) \wedge P(z,y)$. Then H is a relevant theory since $(B \cup HB_P^{-e}(B \cup \overline{E}) \cup h \cup \{\overline{e}\}) \models \Box$ holds for h_1 and $P(a,b)$, h_2 and $P(d,c)$, and h_3 and $P(a,b)$ or $P(a,c)$. If $P(d,c)$ were removed from E, h_2 would no longer be relevant even though it explains $P(a,c)$ indirectly through h_3.

If we apply this restriction to our learning problem, the most specific theory becomes more useful since each clause in the hypothesis has to θ-subsume some clause in the most specific theory.

Theorem 2. *(Completeness wrt. relevance) Let B, E, H, and P be as in definition 6. H satisfies $\forall h \in H \ \exists e \in E \ K = (B \cup HB_P^{-e}(B \cup \overline{E}) \cup \{\overline{e}\}) \not\models \Box$ and $L = (B \cup HB_P^{-e}(B \cup \overline{E}) \cup h \cup \{\overline{e}\}) \models \Box$ (i.e., H is relevant) and $HB(L) = HB(K) = HB(B \cup \overline{E})$ only if $\forall h \in H \ \exists b \in BOT_T(B, E) \ h \succeq b$.*

Proof. For each h in H there is an example $e \in E$ such that K is satisfiable while L is inconsistent. Then $M(K)$ is a model of K, but not of L since L is inconsistent. This means that h must be false in $M(K)$. Thus there must be a substitution θ such that $h^+\theta \subseteq HB(K)\backslash M(K)$ (since $HB(L) = HB(K)$) and $h^-\theta \subseteq M(K)$. This is exactly the same condition as $h \succeq BOT_C(B, e)$ (since $HB(K) = HB(B \cup \overline{E})$) which is in $BOT_T(B, E)$.

Thus for each h in H there is an example e and for this example $h \succeq BOT_C(B, e)$. So we have $\forall h \in H \ \exists b \in BOT_T(B, E) \ h \succeq b$.

6   Bounded refinement operators

Having defined that the most specific theory, we are ready to define a refinement operator that can be applied on a search space bounded by this theory. We only consider downward operators, and find a bounded operator for theories. This operator applies a bounded operator for clauses as a sub-operator. Since there already exists a bounded downward operator for clauses such as the one in Progol [5], we could have used it as a sub-operator. But it relies on mode declarations of the each predicate in the language. These mode declarations are a syntactic bias that restricts the language, and we wanted rather to consider an unrestricted language. So we have chosen to base our operator on Laird's operator.

6.1   A bounded downward operator for clauses

Laird's refinement operator (denoted ρ_L as in [7]) is a downward refinement operator for $\langle C, \succeq \rangle$. It is locally finite and complete for a clausal language if the language contains only a finite number of constants, functions and predicates [4]. We define a bounded version of this refinement operator such that it works with a bottom clause.

Definition 7. *Let c be a clause. Then $\rho_L(c)$ is a downward refinement operator and is defined as:*

1. *For every variable z in c and every n-ary function symbol f in the language, $c\{z/f(x_1,\ldots,x_n)\} \in \rho_L(c)$ where $x_1,\ldots,x_n$ are distinct variables not appearing in c.*
2. *For every two distinct variables x and z in c, $c\{z/x\} \in \rho_L(c)$.*
3. *For every n-ary predicate symbol P in the language, both $c \cup \{p(x_1,\ldots,x_n)\}$ and $c \cup \{\neg p(x_1,\ldots,x_n)\}$ are in $\rho_L(c)$ where $x_1,\ldots,x_n$ are distinct variables not appearing in c.*

Definition 8. *Let c be a clause and $\perp$ a bottom clause such that $c \succeq \perp$. Then $\rho_B(c,\perp)$ is downward refinement operator bounded by $\perp$ and is defined as:*

$$\rho_B(c,\perp) = \{c \in \rho_L(c) \mid c \succeq \perp\}$$

This refinement operator might be inefficient since it requires θ-subsumption testing which is NP-complete[2]. We can prove that this bounded refinement operator is locally finite and complete wrt. a bottom clause.

Theorem 3. *Let C be a clausal language, containing only a finite number of constants, function symbols and predicate symbols. Let $\perp$ be a bottom clause. Then ρ_B is downward refinement operator which is locally finite and complete wrt. $\perp$.*

Proof. First, ρ_B is also locally finite since ρ_L is locally finite, and $\rho_B(c) \subseteq \rho_L(c)$. Second, We will show that if $c \succ d \succeq \perp$ holds for any two clauses c and d then any ρ_L-chain between c and d is also a ρ_B-chain. We already know that ρ_L is complete. So for any two clause c and d satisfying $c \succ d \succeq \perp$, there is a ρ_L-chain between them. Then there must be a ρ_B-chain as well. So ρ_B is complete wrt. $\perp$.

Now, let c and d be two clauses such that $c \succ d \succeq \perp$, and let $c = c_1, c_2, \ldots, c_n$ $= d'$ where $d' \sim d$ be a ρ_L-chain between them. For ρ_L (and ρ_B) we have that $d \in \rho_L(c)$ implies $c \succeq d$. This follow directly from the definition. Thus we have $(c =)c_1 \succeq c_2 \succeq \cdots \succeq c_n(= d') \succeq d$. Since $d \succeq \perp$, it follows that all c_i must θ-subsume $\perp$. $\rho_B(c_i, \perp)$ contains the subset of $\rho_L(c_i)$ where each clause θ-subsumes $\perp$. So c_{i+1} must be in $\rho_B(c_i, \perp)$, since it is in $\rho_L(c_i)$ and θ-subsumes $\perp$. Therefore this chain is also a ρ_B-chain.

Remark 1. Functions of any arity are allowed in refinement operator presented here. But since a bottom clause is infinite for a clausal language with functions, only bottom clauses for a function-free language can be used in practice. So in a practical application, flattening must be used to remove functions, and the refinement operator will only add functions of arity $= 0$ (i.e., constants).

6.2 A bounded downward operator for theories

Nienhuys-Cheng and Wolf [7, p. 317] defined a complete and locally finite refinement operator for $\langle \mathcal{S}, \models \rangle$ where $\mathcal{S}$ is the set of all finite subsets of C. This operator used Laird's operator as a sub-operator. We define a similar, but bounded refinement operator for $\succeq$ where ρ_B is applied as a sub-operator. Since we are only constructing an operator for θ-subsumption and not entailment, this operator has an advantage. It does not need to save every clause produced in order to resolve them with later refinements.

Definition 9. *Let S be the set of all finite subsets of C, $T = \{c_1, \ldots, c_n\}$ a theory in S, and $\perp = \{\perp_1, \ldots, \perp_m\} \in S$ a bottom theory such that $T \succeq \perp$. Then $\rho_{BT}(T, \perp)$ is a bounded downward refinement operator and is defined as:*

1. *$((T\backslash\{c_i\}) \cup \rho_B(c_i, \perp)) \in \rho_{BT}(T, \perp)$ for all $\perp \in f(c_i)$ and $1 \leq i \leq n$.*
2. *if $f(c_i) \subseteq \cup_{j \neq i} f(c_j)$ then $(T\backslash\{c_i\}) \in \rho_{BT}(T, \perp)$, for $1 \leq i \leq n$.*

where $f(c_i) = \{\perp \in \perp \mid c_i \succeq \perp\}$, for $1 \leq i \leq n$

The refinement operator is complete wrt. a bottom theory, $BOT_T(B, E)$, if the set of theories is restricted so only relevant theories are allowed.

Theorem 4. *Let C be a language, containing only a finite number of constants, functions, and predicates. Let $\perp$ be a finite bottom theory consisting of clauses from C. Let R be the set of all finite subsets of C such that each theory $T \in R$ satisfies $\forall c \in T \exists \perp \in \perp\ c \succeq \perp$. Then ρ_{BT} is a locally finite and complete downwards refinement operator wrt. $\perp$ for $\langle R, \succeq \rangle$.*

Proof. ρ_{BT} is locally finite. This follows from the facts that ρ_B is locally finite and that there is a finite number of clauses in each theory. Thus item 1 and 2 are applied only a finite number of times on a theory and each application creates another finite theory.

To prove the completeness of ρ_{BT}, assume that there are two theories $S = \{c_1, \ldots, c_n\}$ and T such that $S \succ T \succeq \perp$. Let $T' = \{d_1, \ldots, d_m\}$ be a minimal subset of T such that $T \sim T'$ and there are no proper subset U of T' such that $U \sim T'$. Then no $d_i \in T'$ θ-subsume another $d_j \in T'$ (or a proper subset U would exists). Since $S \succ T \sim T'$, we must have $\forall j \exists i\ c_i \succeq d_j$. For each c_i let $T'_i = \{d^i_1, \ldots, d^i_{m_i}\}$ be a subset of T' with all the clauses in T' that are θ-subsumed by c_i (i.e., $T'_i = \{d \in T' \mid c_i \succeq d\}$). Now we know that each of the clauses in T'_i θ-subsumes a clause in $\perp$ since $\forall d \in T \exists \perp \in \perp\ d \succeq \perp$. Thus if $d^i_r \in T'_i$, it must θ-subsume some clause $\perp_j \in \perp$, and by the completeness of ρ_B, there must be a ρ_B-chain $c_i = e_1, e_2, \ldots, e_{k^i_r} \sim d^i_r$ with length k^i_r from c_i.

Let $k^i = max\{k^i_1, \ldots, k^i_{m_i}\}$. Using item 1 of the definition in a breadth-first manner, there must be ρ_{BT}-chain $\{c_i\} = R^i_0, \ldots, R^i_1, \ldots, \ldots R^i_{k^i}$ where for each $d \in T_i$ there is a θ-equivalent $d' \in R^i_{k^i}$. We stop unfolding a branch when it reaches a clause that is θ-equivalent to one in T'_i. So each R^i_j contains the refinement of all the clauses in R^i_{j-1} expect those that are θ-equivalent to one in T'_i, i.e., $R^i_j = X^i_j \cup Y^i_j$ where $X^i_j = \{e \in R^i_{j-1} \mid e \sim d \in T_i\}$ and $Y^i_j = \{f \mid f \in \rho_B(e, \perp)$ and $\perp \in f(e)$ and $e \in R^i_{j-1}\backslash X^i_j\}$. Between each R^i_{j-1} and R^i_j there is a ρ_{BT}-subchain $R^i_{j-1} = Q_0, Q_1 \ldots Q_l = R^i_j$ where $Q_k = (Q_{k-1}\backslash\{e_k\}) \cup \{f \mid f \in \rho_B(e_k, \perp)$ and $\perp \in f(e_k)\}$ if $R^i_{j-1}\backslash X^i_j = \{e_1, \ldots e_l\}$.

Thus for each c_i we have a ρ_{BT}-chain between R_0^i and $R_{k_i}^i$. Handling each c_i sequentially, we get a ρ_{BT}-chain $S = S_0, \ldots, S_1, \ldots, S_2, \ldots, \ldots, S_n$ where $S_i = (S_{i-1} \backslash \{c_i\}) \cup R_{k_i}^i$. Then we must have $T'' \subset S_n$ where $T'' = \{d_1', \ldots, d_m'\}$ and $d_l' \sim d_l$ for all $1 \leq l \leq m$.

Now $T \succeq \perp$ and $T \sim T' \sim T''$. So $T'' \succeq \perp$ and $f(T'') = \cup_{c \in T''} f(c) = \perp$. Thus for each clause $d \in (S_n \backslash T'')$ we have $\bar{f}(d) \subseteq f(T'')$. So these clauses can be deleted by item 2, and there is a ρ_{BT}-chain from S_n to T'' This means that there is a complete ρ_{BT}-chain from S to T'' where $T \sim T''$. So ρ_{BT} is complete.

7 Conclusion and future work

In this paper, we studied the search space ordered by θ-subsumption on theories. We found a least generalization and a greatest specialization of theories and showed that the search space is a lattice. We proved also that there is no ideal refinement operator for this search space, and introduced a most specific theory for a restricted set of theories, called relevant theories. Finally, a downward refinement operator for theories ordered by θ-subsumption was given. It was bounded by a most specific theory, and we proved it complete with some restrictions.

This refinement operator was not very efficient since it requires θ-subsumption testing. So a more efficient operator should be developed. Future work should also include an actual implementation.

Acknowledgments. I would like to thank Stephen Muggleton for letting me to visit his group in York and for suggesting this area of clausal theories. I wish also to thank my supervisor Øystein Nytrø for discussions on this topic.

References

1. H. Arimura. Learning acyclic first-order horn sentences from entailment. In *Proc. of ALT-97*, LNAI 1316, pp. 432–445. Springer-Verlag, 1997.
2. M. R. Garey and D. S. Johnson. *Computers and Intractability - A Guide to Theory of NP-completeness*. Freeman, 1997.
3. M. Krishna Rao and A. Satter. Learning from entailment of logic programs with local variables. *Proc. of ALT-98*, LNAI 1501, pp. 143–157. Springer-Verlag, 1998.
4. P. R. J. van der Laag and S.-H. Nienhuys-Cheng. Existence and nonexistence of complete refinement operators. In *Proc. of ECML-94*, LNAI 784, pp. 307–322. Springer-Verlag, 1994.
5. S. Muggleton. Inverse entailment and Progol. *New Generation Computing*, 13(3/4):245–286, 1995.
6. S. Muggleton. Completing inverse entailment. In *Proc. of ILP-98*, LNAI 1446, pp. 245–249. Springer-Verlag, 1998.
7. S.-H. Nienhuys-Cheng and R. de Wolf. *Foundations of Inductive Logic Programming*. LNAI 1228. Springer-Verlag, 1997.
8. G. D. Plotkin. *Automatic Methods of Inductive Inference*. PhD thesis, Edinburgh University, 1971.
9. J. C. Reynolds. Transformational systems and the algebraic structure of atomic formulas. In *Machine Intelligence*, vol. 5, pp. 135–151. Edinburgh University Press, 1970.

Discovering New Knowledge from Graph Data Using Inductive Logic Programming

Tetsuhiro Miyahara[1], Takayoshi Shoudai[2], Tomoyuki Uchida[1],
Tetsuji Kuboyama[3], Kenichi Takahashi[1], and Hiroaki Ueda[1]

[1] Faculty of Information Sciences,
Hiroshima City University, Hiroshima 731-3194, Japan
{miyahara@its, uchida@cs, takahasi@its, ueda@its}.hiroshima-cu.ac.jp
[2] Department of Informatics, Kyushu University 39, Kasuga 816-8580, Japan
shoudai@i.kyushu-u.ac.jp
[3] Center for Collaborative Research, University of Tokyo, Tokyo 153-0041, Japan
kuboyama@ccr.u-tokyo.ac.jp

Abstract. We present a method for discovering new knowledge from structural data which are represented by graphs in the framework of inductive logic programming. A graph, or network, is widely used for representing relations between various data and expressing a small and easily understandable hypothesis. Formal Graph System (FGS) is a kind of logic programming system which directly deals with graphs just like first order terms. By employing refutably inductive inference algorithms and graph algorithmic techniques, we are developing a knowledge discovery system KD-FGS, which acquires knowledge directly from graph data by using FGS as a knowledge representation language.
In this paper we develop a logical foundation of our knowledge discovery system. A term tree is a pattern which consists of variables and tree-like structures. We give a polynomial-time algorithm for finding a unifier of a term tree and a tree in order to make consistency checks efficiently. Moreover we give experimental results on some graph theoretical notions with the system. The experiments show that the system is useful for finding new knowledge.

1 Introduction

The aim of knowledge discovery is to find a small and easily understandable hypothesis explaining given data. Many machine learning and data mining technologies for discovering knowledge have been proposed in many fields. Especially Inductive Logic Programming (ILP) techniques have been applied to discover knowledge from "real-world" data [4]. A graph is one of the most common abstract structures and is widely used for representing relations between various data. In many "real-world" domains such as vision, pattern recognition and organic chemistry, data are naturally represented by graphs.

Formal Graph System (FGS, [12]) is a kind of logic programming system which uses graphs, called term graphs, instead of terms in first-order logic. FGS can represent naturally logical knowledge explaining data represented by graphs. When we try to discover new knowledge from given data, we can not assume that a given hypothesis space contains a hypothesis explaining given data from the beginning. Hence, when we know that the hypothesis is not in the hypothesis space, it is necessary to change the hypothesis space to another space. In [9], the method of refutably inductive inference is proposed. If a correct hypothesis dose not exist in a hypothesis space, we can refute the hypothesis space and change it to another one by using this method. Refuting a hypothesis space is a quite important suggestion for us.

With the above motivations, in [8], we implemented a prototype of a knowledge discovery system KD-FGS (see Fig. 1). As inputs, the system receives positive and negative examples of graph data. As an output, the system produces an FGS program which is consistent with the positive and negative examples if such a hypothesis exists. Otherwise, the system refutes the hypothesis space. KD-FGS consists of an FGS interpreter and a refutably inductive inference algorithm of FGS programs. The FGS interpreter is used to check whether a hypothesis is consistent with the given graph data or not. The refutably inductive inference algorithm is a special type of inductive inference algorithm with refutability of hypothesis spaces and is based on [9]. When the hypothesis space is refuted, KD-FGS chooses another hypothesis space and tries to make a discovery in the new hypothesis space. By refuting the hypothesis space, the algorithm gives important suggestions to achieve the goal of knowledge discovery. Thus, KD-FGS is useful for knowledge discovery from graph data.

In this paper, we also consider a restricted term graph g, called a term tree, such that the term graph obtained by applying any substitution θ to g is a tree, where each graph in θ is a tree. A term tree can represent a tree structure which has variables at internal nodes. But we can not represent such a tree structure in the standard representation of a first order term. In [1, 3], a tree pattern was considered, and learning algorithms for tree patterns from queries were presented, where a tree pattern has constants at its internal nodes, but only its leaves may be variables. Since KD-FGS is a system directly dealing with graphs, the running time is long, in general. Especially, KD-FGS must solve the subgraph isomorphism problem, which is NP-complete, in the component of the FGS interpreter. However, a polynomial-time algorithm solving the subgraph isomorphism problem for trees was proposed in [10]. The FGS interpreter must find a unifier of an input graph and a term graph. Since there exists no mgu (most general unifier) of two term trees in general, we can not apply the standard term algorithms to finding a unifier of a term tree and a tree. Then we give a polynomial-time algorithm for finding a unifier of a term tree and a tree by using graph theoretical techniques. By employing this algorithm, if input data have tree structures, KD-FGS may output a hypothesis within a practical time. There are many "real-world" data having tree structures [13]. This algorithm enables the application of KD-FGS for those data.

This paper is organized as follows. In Section 2, we introduce FGS as a new knowledge representation language for graph data. In Section 3, by giving a

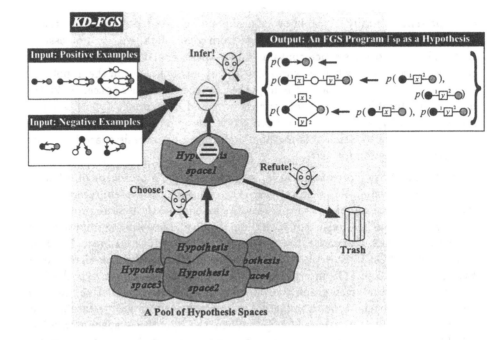

Fig. 1. KD-FGS: a knowledge discovery system from graph data using FGS.

framework of refutably inductive inference of FGS programs, we develop a logical foundation of KD-FGS. In Section 4, we give a polynomial-time algorithm for finding a unifier of a term tree and a tree. In Section 5, we give some examples for graph theoretical notions to our system in order to show the usefulness of our system.

2 FGS as a New Knowledge Representation Language

Formal Graph System (FGS, [12]) is a kind of logic programming system which directly deals with graphs just like first order terms. In [11, 12], we have shown that a class of graphs is generated by a hyperedge replacement grammar (HRG) [5] if and only if it is defined by an FGS of a special form called a regular FGS, and that for a node-label controlled graph grammar (NLC grammar) G introduced in [6], there exists an FGS Γ such that the language generated by G can be definable by Γ. These show that FGS is more powerful than HRG or NLC grammar.

Let Σ and Λ be finite alphabets, and let X be an alphabet, whose element is called a *variable label*. Assume that $(\Sigma \cup \Lambda) \cap X = \emptyset$. A *term graph* $g = (V, E, H)$ consists of a vertex set V, an edge set E and a multi-set H where each element is a list of distinct vertices in V and is called a *variable*. And a term graph g has a vertex labeling $\varphi_g : V \to \Sigma$, an edge labeling $\psi_g : E \to \Lambda$ and a variable

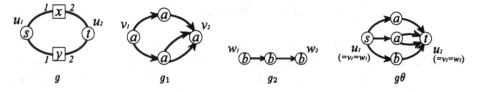

Fig. 2. Term graphs g and $g\theta$ obtained by applying a substitution $\theta = \{x :=[g_1, (v_1, v_2)], y := [g_2, (w_1, w_2)]\}$ to g.

labeling $\lambda_g : H \to X$. A term graph $g = (V, E, H)$ is called *ground* and simply denoted by $g = (V, E)$ if $H = \emptyset$. For example, a term graph $g = (V, E, H)$ is shown in Fig. 2, where $V = \{u_1, u_2\}$, $E = \emptyset$, $H = \{e_1 = (u_1, u_2), e_2 = (u_1, u_2)\}$, $\varphi_g(u_1) = s$, $\varphi_g(u_2) = t$, $\lambda_g(e_1) = x$, and $\lambda_g(e_2) = y$. A variable is represented by a box with lines to its elements and the order of its elements is indicated by the numbers at these lines. An *atom* is an expression of the form $p(g_1, \ldots, g_n)$, where p is a predicate symbol with arity n and $g_1, \ldots, g_n$ are term graphs. Let $A, B_1, \ldots, B_m$ be atoms with $m \geq 0$. Then, a *graph rewriting rule* is a clause of the form $A \leftarrow B_1, \ldots, B_m$. An *FGS program* is a finite set of graph rewriting rules. For example, the FGS program Γ_{SP} in Fig. 1 generates the family of all two-terminal series parallel (TTSP) graphs.

Let g be a term graph and σ be a list of distinct vertices in g. We call the form $x := [g, \sigma]$ a *binding* for a variable label $x \in X$. A *substitution* θ is a finite collection of bindings $\{x_1 := [g_1, \sigma_1], \ldots, x_n := [g_n, \sigma_n]\}$, where x_i's are mutually distinct variable labels in X and each g_i $(1 \leq i \leq n)$ has no variable labeled with an element in $\{x_1, \ldots, x_n\}$. For a set or a list S, the number of elements in S is denoted by $|S|$. In the same way as logic programming system, we obtain a new term graph f by applying a substitution $\theta = \{x_1 := [g_1, \sigma_1], \cdots, x_n := [g_n, \sigma_n]\}$ to a term graph $g = (V, E, H)$ in the following way. For each binding $x_i :=[g_i, \sigma_i] \in \theta$ $(1 \leq i \leq n)$ in parallel, we attach g_i to g by removing the all variables $t_1, \cdots, t_k$ labeled with x_i from H, and by identifying the m-th element t_j^m of t_j and the m-th element σ_i^m of σ_i for each $1 \leq j \leq k$ and each $1 \leq m \leq |t_j| = |\sigma_i|$, respectively. We remark that the label of each vertex t_j^m of g is used for the resulting term graph which is denoted by $g\theta$. Namely, the label of σ_i^m is ignored in $g\theta$. In Fig. 2, for example, we draw the term graph $g\theta$ which is obtained by applying a substitution $\theta = \{x := [g_1, (v_1, v_2)], y := [g_2, (w_1, w_2)]\}$ to the term graph g. A *unifier* of two term graphs g_1 and g_2 is a substitution θ such that $g_1\theta$ and $g_2\theta$ are isomorphic. In general, there exists no mgu (most general unifier) of two term graphs. Therefore, in FGS a derivation is based on an enumeration of unifiers and only ground goal is considered in this paper. A graph rewriting rule C is *provable from* an FGS program Γ if C is obtained from Γ by finitely many applications of graph rewriting rules and modus ponens. An FGS interpreter as a component of KD-FGS is used to check whether a hypothesis, which is an FGS program, is consistent with the given graph data or not.

3 Refutably Inductive Inference of FGS Programs

In this section we introduce refutably inductive inference of FGS programs. And we give two interesting hypothesis spaces of FGS programs, weakly reducing and size-bounded FGS programs, which are refutably inferable. Moreover, we present refutably inductive inference algorithms for the hypothesis spaces. We give our framework of refutably inductive inference of FGS programs according to [2, 9, 14]. Mukouchi and Arikawa [9] originated a computational learning theory of machine discovery from facts. They showed that refutably inductive inference is essential in machine discovery from facts and the sufficiently large hypothesis spaces for language learning are refutably inferable.

We give our hypothesis spaces of FGS programs. Let $g = (V, E, H)$ be a term graph. Then we denote the *size* of g by $|g|$ and define $|g| = |V| + |E| + |H|$. For example, $|g| = |V| + |E| + |H| = 2 + 0 + 2 = 4$ for the term graph $g = (V, E, H)$ in Fig. 2. For an atom $p(g_1, \ldots, g_n)$, we define $\|p(g_1, \ldots, g_n)\| = |g_1| + \cdots + |g_n|$. An *erasing binding* is a binding $x := [g, \sigma]$ such that g consists of all vertices in σ, no edge and no variable. An *erasing substitution* is a substitution which contains an erasing binding. In this paper, we disallow an erasing substitution. Then $\|g\theta\| \geq \|g\|$ for any term graph g and any substitution θ (Size Non-decreasing Property). A graph rewriting rule $A \leftarrow B_1, \ldots, B_m$ is said to be *weakly reducing* (resp., *size-bounded*) if $\|A\theta\| \geq \|B_i\theta\|$ for any $i = 1, \ldots, m$ and any substitution θ (resp., $\|A\theta\| \geq \|B_1\theta\| + \cdots + \|B_m\theta\|$ for any substitution θ). An FGS program Γ is *weakly-reducing* (resp., *size-bounded*) if every graph rewriting rule in Γ is weakly reducing (resp., size-bounded). A size-bounded FGS program is also weakly reducing. For example, the FGS program Γ_{SP} in Fig. 1 is weakly reducing but not size-bounded. Let $g = (V, E, H)$ be a term graph. For a variable label $x \in X$, the number of variables in H labeled with x is denoted by $o(x, g)$. For example, $o(x, g) = 1$ and $o(y, g) = 1$ for the term graph $g = (V, E, H)$ in Fig. 2. For an atom $p(g_1, \ldots, g_n)$ and a variable label $x \in X$, we define $o(x, p(g_1, \ldots, g_n)) = o(x, g_1) + \cdots + o(x, g_n)$.

We consider the two properties of hypothesis spaces for machine discovery from facts. Firstly, the hypothesis space for machine discovery must be recursively enumerable. Secondly, whether a hypothesis is consistent with examples or not must be recursively decidable. The following Lemma 1 and 2 show that our target hypothesis spaces have the first and second properties, respectively. The proofs of Lemma 1 and 2 are based on [2, 14]. In case a hypothesis space dose not have Size Non-decreasing Property, Lemma 1 does not hold. The set of all ground atoms with ground term graphs as arguments is called the Herbrand base and denoted by HB. For an FGS program Γ, M_Γ denotes the least Herbrand model of Γ.

Lemma 1. *A graph rewriting rule $A \leftarrow B_1, \ldots, B_m$ is weakly reducing (resp., size-bounded) if and only if $\|A\| \geq \|B_i\|$ and $o(x, A) \geq o(x, B_i)$ for any $i = 1, \ldots, m$ and any variable label x (resp., $\|A\| \geq \|B_1\| + \cdots + \|B_m\|$ and $o(x, A) \geq o(x, B_1) + \cdots + o(x, B_m)$ for any variable label x).*

Lemma 2. *Let Γ be a weakly reducing or size-bounded FGS program. Then the least Herbrand model M_Γ of Γ is a recursively decidable set.*

We explain the refutably inductive inference of FGS programs. Let Π be a finite set of predicate symbols. For an atom A, $pred(A)$ denotes the predicate symbol of A. For a set $\Pi_0 \subseteq \Pi$ and a set S of atoms, $S\mid_{\Pi_0}$ denotes the set of all atoms in S whose predicate symbols are in Π_0. That is $S\mid_{\Pi_0} = \{A \in S \mid pred(A) \in \Pi_0\}$. A *predicate-restricted complete presentation* of a set $I \subseteq HB$ w.r.t. $\Pi_0 \subseteq \Pi$ is an infinite sequence $(A_1, t_1), (A_2, t_2), \ldots$ of elements in $HB\mid_{\Pi_0} \times \{+, -\}$ such that $\{A_i \mid t_i = +, i \geq 1\} = I\mid_{\Pi_0}$ and $\{A_i \mid t_i = -, i \geq 1\} = HB\mid_{\Pi_0} \setminus I\mid_{\Pi_0}$. A *refutably inductive inference algorithm* ($RIIA$) is a special type of algorithm that receives a predicate-restricted complete presentation as an input. An RIIA $\mathcal{A}$ is said to *refute* a hypothesis space, if $\mathcal{A}$ produces the sign "refute" as an output and stops. An RIIA either produces infinitely many FGS programs as outputs or refutes a hypothesis space. For an RIIA $\mathcal{A}$ and a presentation δ, $\mathcal{A}(\delta[n])$ denotes the last output produced by $\mathcal{A}$ which is successively presented the first n elements in δ. An RIIA $\mathcal{A}$ is said to *converge* to an FGS program Γ for a presentation δ, if there is a positive integer m_0 such that for any $m \geq m_0$, $\mathcal{A}(\delta[m])$ is defined and equal to Γ. Let $\mathcal{HS}$ be a hypothesis space of FGS programs. For an FGS program $\Gamma \in \mathcal{HS}$ and a predicate-restricted complete presentation δ of M_Γ w.r.t. $\Pi_0 \subseteq \Pi$, an RIIA $\mathcal{A}$ is said to be *infer* the FGS program Γ w.r.t. $\mathcal{HS}$ *in the limit from δ*, if $\mathcal{A}$ converges to an FGS program $\Gamma' \in \mathcal{HS}$ with $M_{\Gamma'}\mid_{\Pi_0} = M_\Gamma\mid_{\Pi_0}$ for δ.

A hypothesis space $\mathcal{HS}$ is said to be *theoretical-term-freely and refutably inferable from complete data*, if for any nonempty finite subset Π_0 of Π, there is an RIIA $\mathcal{A}$ which satisfies the following condition: For any set $I \subseteq HB$ and any predicate-restricted complete presentation δ of I w.r.t. Π_0, (i) if there is an FGS program $\Gamma \in \mathcal{HS}$ such that $M_\Gamma\mid_{\Pi_0} = I\mid_{\Pi_0}$, then $\mathcal{A}$ infers Γ w.r.t. $\mathcal{HS}$ in the limit from δ, (ii) otherwise $\mathcal{A}$ refutes the hypothesis space $\mathcal{HS}$ from δ.

Theoretical terms are supllementary predicates that are necessary for defining some goal predicates. In the above definition, the phrase "theoretical-term-freely inferable" means that using only facts on the goal predicates an RIIA can generates some suppllementary predicates. $\mathcal{WR}^{[\leq n]}$ (resp., $\mathcal{SB}^{[\leq n]}$) denotes the set of all weakly reducing (resp., size-bounded) FGS programs with at most n graph rewriting rules. There are many FGS programs which have the same least Herbrand model. We can assume a canonical form of such FGS programs by fixing predicate symbols in $\Pi \setminus \Pi_0$ and variable labels. $\mathcal{CWR}^{[m]}[\Pi_0]$ denotes the set of all such canonical weakly reducing FGS programs with just m graph rewriting rules. We define $\mathcal{CWR}^{[m]}[\Pi_0](s) = \{\Gamma \in \mathcal{CWR}^{[m]}[\Pi_0] \mid$ the head's size of each rule of Γ is not greater than $s\}$. The proof of Theorem 1 is based on [9].

Theorem 1. *For any $n \geq 1$, the hypothesis space $\mathcal{WR}^{[\leq n]}$ (resp., $\mathcal{SB}^{[\leq n]}$) of all weakly reducing (resp., size-bounded) FGS programs with at most n graph rewriting rules has infinitely many hypotheses. And $\mathcal{WR}^{[\leq n]}$ (resp., $\mathcal{SB}^{[\leq n]}$) is theoretical-term-freely and refutably inferable from complete data.*

```
procedure RIIA_WR(integer n, set of predicate symbols Π₀ ⊆ Π);
begin
    T := ∅; F := ∅;
    read_store(T, F);
    while T = ∅ do begin
        output the empty FGS program;
        read_store(T, F);
    end;
    T₀ := T; F₀ := F;
    for m = 1 to n do begin
        sₘ := max{||A|| | A ∈ Tₘ₋₁};
        recursively generate CWR[m][Π₀](sₘ), and set it to S;
        for each Γ ∈ S do
            while (T, F) is consistent with MΓ do begin
                output Γ;
                read_store(T, F);
            end;
            Tₘ := T; Fₘ := F;
    end;
    output "refute" and stop;
end;

procedure read_store(T, F);
begin
    read the next fact (w, t);
    if t =' +' then T := T ∪ {w} else F := F ∪ {w};
end.
```

Fig. 3. RIIA_WR: a refutably inductive inference algorithm for the hypothesis space $WR^{[\le n]}$ of all weakly reducing FGS programs with at most n graph rewriting rules.

Proof. (Sketch of proof) We feed a predicate-restricted complete presentation of a set $I \subseteq HB$ w.r.t. Π_0 to the procedure RIIA_WR in Fig. 3. (i) In case there is an FGS program $\Gamma \in WR^{[\le n]}$ such that $M_\Gamma |_{\Pi_0} = I |_{\Pi_0}$. It follows by Size Non-decreasing Property that a graph rewriting rule whose head has greater size than a ground atom A is not used to derive the atom A. Thus, in the procedure, for any $0 \le m \le n$, if T_m and F_m are defined, then $M(\Gamma) |_{\Pi_0}$ is not consistent with T_m and F_m for any $\Gamma \in CWR^{[m]}[\Pi_0]$. Therefore T_n and F_n are never defined and the procedure never terminates the first or second while-loop. (ii) Otherwise. For any $1 \le m \le n$, all FGS programs in $CWR^{[m]}[\Pi_0](s_m)$ are discarded.

By simple enumeration of hypotheses, the hypothesis spaces $WR^{[\le n]}$ and $SB^{[\le n]}$ are inferable but not refutably inferable. If the number of graph rewriting rules is not bounded by a constant, then these hypothesis spaces are not refutably inferable. We can construct a machine discovery system for a refutably inferable hypothesis space. Thus Theorem 1 gives a theoretical foundation of KD-FGS.

procedure Unification(regular term tree t_1, tree T_2);
begin
    Let r_1 be one of leaves of t_1;
    Construct the set of all labeling rules R_{r_1};
    foreach leaf r_2 of T_2 **do begin**
        Label each leaf of T_2 except r_2 with the set of all leaves of T_1 except r_1;
        while there exists a vertex v of T_2
                such that v is not labeled and all children of v are labeled
            do Labeling(v, R_{r_1});
        if the label of r_2 includes r_1 **then** t_1 and T_2 are unifiable **and exit**
    end;
    t_1 and T_2 are not unifiable
end.

Fig. 4. Unification: an algorithm for deciding whether t_1 and T_2 are unifiable or not.

4   An Efficient Algorithm for Finding a Unifier of a Term Tree and a Tree

In this section, we give a polynomial-time algorithm for finding a unifier of a term tree and a tree in order to achieve speedup of KD-FGS.

A term graph g is called a *term tree* if each variable in g is a list of two distinct vertices and, for any substitution $\theta = \{x_1 := [g_1, \sigma_1], \cdots, x_n := [g_n, \sigma_n]\}$ such that each term graph g_i is a tree, $g\theta$ is also a tree. A term tree g is called *regular* if each variable label in g occurs exactly once [7]. For example, a term tree $g = (\{r, s, t, u, v, w\}, \{\{r, s\}, \{u, v\}\}, \{(s, t), (s, u), (u, w)\})$ is shown in Fig. 6. As stated in the section 2, in general, there exists no mgu of two regular term trees. Therefore, even if the input data for KD-FGS is restricted to trees, a derivation in FGS is based on an enumeration of unifiers and only ground goal is considered. From a simple observation we can show that the FGS interpreter must solve the subgraph isomorphism problem, which is NP-complete. For certain special subclasses of graphs, the subgraph isomorphism problem is efficiently solvable [10]. But we should note that even if a subclass of graphs has an efficient algorithm for the subgraph isomorphism problem, we can not construct a unification algorithm straightforwardly from the algorithm.

In this section, we assume that a tree which is an input to our unification algorithm is an unrooted tree without a vertex label and an edge label, since we can easily construct a unification algorithm for a tree having a vertex label and an edge label. Let $t_1 = (V_1, E_1, H_1)$ and $T_2 = (V_2, E_2)$ be a regular term tree and a tree, respectively. Then, we give the algorithm Unification (Fig. 4) for finding a unifier of a regular term tree and a tree. First we specify one of leaves of t_1. Let the leaf be r_1. We define the rooted tree T_1 as $T_1 = (V_1, E_1 \cup \{\{u_1, u_2\} \mid (u_1, u_2) \in H_1 \text{ or } (u_2, u_1) \in H_1\})$ with the root r_1. For a vertex $u \in V_1$, let $w_1, \cdots, w_k$ be all children of u in T_1 such that each $\{u, w_i\}$ is an edge in t_1 for $i = 1, \ldots, k$ and let $w_{k+1}, \cdots, w_m$ be all children of u in T_1 such that either (u, w_i) or (w_i, u) is

procedure Labeling(vertex $v \in V_2$, set of labeling rules R);
begin
    $L := \emptyset$;
    Let d be the number of children of v and $L_1, \cdots, L_d$ be labels of the children;
    foreach $u \leftarrow w_1, \cdots, w_d$ in R **do begin**
        Let $E := \{\{w_i, L_j\} \mid w_i \in L_j (1 \le i \le d, 1 \le j \le d)\}$
        if there is a perfect matching
            for the bipartite graph $(\{w_1, \cdots, w_d\}, \{L_1, \cdots, L_d\}, E)$
        then $L := L \cup \{u\}$
    end;
    foreach $u \Leftarrow w_1, \cdots, w_k, (w_{k+1}), \cdots, (w_m)$ in R with $m \le d$ **do begin**
        Let $E_1 := \{\{w_i, L_j\} \mid w_i \in L_j \ (1 \le i \le k, 1 \le j \le d)\}$,
        $E_2 := \{\{w_i, L_j\} \mid w_i \in L_j$ or $(w_i) \in L_j \ (k+1 \le i \le m, 1 \le j \le d)\}$ and
        if for the bipartite graph $(\{w_1, \cdots, w_m\}, \{L_1, \cdots, L_d\}, E_1 \cup E_2)$
            there is a maximum matching which contains all vertices $w_1, \cdots, w_m$
        then $L := L \cup \{u\}$
    end;
    foreach $(w) \Leftarrow (w)$ in R **do begin**
        if there is a set among $L_1, \cdots, L_d$ which includes w or (w) **then**
            $L := L \cup \{(w)\}$
    end;
    Label v with L
end.

Fig. 5. Labeling: a procedure for labeling a vertex in T_2 with a set of vertices in t_1.

a variable in t_1 for $i = k+1, \ldots, m$. We let v be the parent of u in T_1 if u is not a root of T_1. We define labeling rules for u as follows: If there is no variable which has u as a its element, i.e. $k = m$ and both (v, u) and (u, v) are not variables in t_1, then we simply add the following rule to the set of labeling rules:
$$u \leftarrow w_1, w_2, \cdots, w_m.$$
If $k = m$ but either (v, u) or (u, v) is a variable in t_1, we add the following rule:
$$u \Leftarrow w_1, w_2, \cdots, w_m.$$
Otherwise, we add the following rules:
$$u \Leftarrow w_1, \cdots, w_k, (w_{k+1}), \cdots, (w_m)$$
and for $k+1 \le i \le m$,
$$(w_i) \Leftarrow (w_i).$$
Let R_{r_1} be the set of all labeling rules obtained by applying the above process to all vertices in V_1. We specify one of leaves r_2 of T_2 and consider T_2 as the rooted tree with root r_2. Then, we label all vertices of T_2 with sets of vertices of T_1 using the procedure Labeling (Fig. 5). First we label each leaf of T_2 except r_2 with the set of all leaves of T_1 except r_1. For each vertex u in T_2 such that u itself is not labeled yet but all children of u have been already labeled, we repeat the procedure Labeling until r_2 is labeled. After the procedure Labeling for a vertex $v \in V_2$ terminates , if v has u as an element of the label of v, it shows that v possibly corresponds to u. If v has (u) as an element of the label

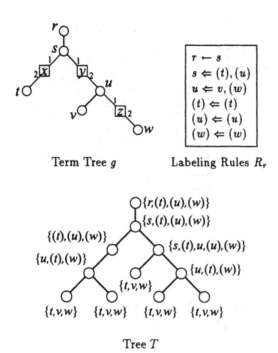

Term Tree g Labeling Rules R_r

Tree T

Fig. 6. An example: the labeling rule constructed from a term tree g and the labels of a tree T after the Unification algorithm terminates.

of v, it shows that v possibly corresponds to u or v has a descendant which possibly corresponds to u. In the procedure Labeling, a labeling rule of the form $u \leftarrow w_1, w_2, \cdots, w_m$ can be applied to $v \in V_2$ only when v has exactly m children $c_1, c_2, \cdots, c_m$ such that each child c_i has w_{ℓ_i} as an element of the label of c_i for $i = 1, \ldots, m$, where $\{w_{\ell_1}, w_{\ell_2}, \cdots, w_{\ell_m}\} = \{w_1, w_2, \cdots, w_m\}$. On the other hand, $u \Leftarrow w_1, \cdots, w_k, (w_{k+1}), \cdots, (w_m)$ can be applied to $v \in V_2$ when v has at least m children $c_1, \cdots, c_k, c_{k+1}, \cdots, c_m$ such that for $i = 1, \ldots, k$, c_i has w_{ℓ_i} as an element of the label of c_i where $\{w_{\ell_1}, w_{\ell_2}, \cdots, w_{\ell_k}\} = \{w_1, w_2, \cdots, w_k\}$ and for $i = k + 1, \ldots, m$, c_i has w_{ℓ_i} or (w_{ℓ_i}) as an element of the label of c_i where $\{w_{\ell_{k+1}}, \cdots, w_{\ell_m}\} = \{w_{k+1}, \cdots, w_m\}$. The rules of the form $(w) \Leftarrow (w)$ are used to define the descendant relation. If r_2 is labeled with a set including r_1, the Unification algorithm reports the fact that there is a unifier of t_1 and T_2, and terminates. Otherwise, the Unification algorithm applies the above process to the other leaves of T_2. In Fig. 6, for example, we give the labeling rules R_r constructing in the Unification algorithm and show the label assigned to each vertex of T in the Labeling procedure when the term tree g and the tree T shown in Fig. 6 are given as inputs.

If the algorithm declares that t_1 and T_2 are unifiable, we can easily find a unifier from labels of T_2. Since the number of vertices contained in each label is $O(|V_1|)$, we show the following theorem:

Table 1. Experimental results on the KD-FGS system.

No.	Examples	Hypothesis Space	Result
1	TTSP graph	weakly reducing, #atom≤ 2, #rule≤ 2	refute
2		weakly reducing, #atom≤ 2, #rule≤ 3	infer
3		size-bounded, #atom≤ 6, #rule≤ 2	refute
4		size-bounded, #atom≤ 6, #rule≤ 3	refute
5	undirected tree	weakly reducing, #atom≤ 1, #rule≤ 2	refute
6		weakly reducing, #atom≤ 1, #rule≤ 3	infer
7		size-bounded, #atom≤ 6, #rule≤ 2	refute
8		size-bounded, #atom≤ 6, #rule≤ 3	infer

Theorem 2. *A unifier of a regular term tree and a tree can be found in polynomial time.*

5 Experimental Results: Obtaining Some New Knowledge about Graph Theoretical Notions

In order to show that the KD-FGS system is useful for knowledge discovery from graph data, we have preparatory experiments of running the system (see Table 1). We give examples for graph theoretical notions to the system and obtain some new knowledge about representability in FGS programs. For example, in Exp. 2 and 4, input data are positive and negative examples of TTSP graphs (see Fig. 1). In Exp. 2 (resp., 4), the hypothesis space C_2 (resp., C_4) is the set of all restricted weakly reducing (resp., size-bounded) FGS programs with at most 2 (resp., 6) atoms in each body and at most 3 (resp., 3) rules in each program. After the system receives some positive and negative examples, it infers a correct FGS program in C_2 for TTSP graphs in Exp. 2 (resp., it refutes C_4 in Exp. 4). No one knows whether there exists a size-bounded FGS program for TTSP graphs. So we have interests in the experiment of finding such an FGS program. The new results of inferring an FGS program or refuting a hypothesis space are new knowledge about graph theoretical notions. Thus, we confirm that the system is useful for knowledge discovery from graph data.

6 Concluding Remarks

We have given a logical foundation for discovering new knowledge from graph data by employing a refutably inductive inference algorithm, which is one of ILP methods. And we have presented a polynomial-time algorithm for finding a unifier of a term tree and a tree. This algorithm leads us to discover new knowledge from "real-world" data having tree structures.

In order to apply our system to huge "real-world" data, we must achieve practical speedup of the KD-FGS system. We are implementing another FGS interpreter, which is based on a bottom-up theorem proving method, in a parallel logic programming language KLIC.

Acknowledgments

We are grateful to anonymous referees for their valuable comments. The first author would like to thank Akihiro Yamamoto and Hiroki Arimura for their helpful suggestions. This work is partly supported by Grant-in-Aid for Scientific Research No.09780356 from the Ministry of Education, Science, Sports and Culture, Japan and Grant for Special Academic Research No.9870 from Hiroshima City University.

References

1. T. R. Amoth, P. Cull, and P. Tadepalli. Exact learning of tree patterns from queries and counterexamples. *Proc. COLT-98, ACM Press*, pages 175–186, 1998.
2. S. Arikawa, T. Shinohara, and A. Yamamoto. Learning elementary formal systems. *Theoretical Computer Science*, 95:97–113, 1992.
3. H. Arimura, H. Ishizaka, and T. Shinohara. Learning unions of tree patterns using queries. *Proc. ALT-95, Springer-Verlag, LNAI 997*, pages 66–79, 1995.
4. S. Džeroski, N. Jacobs, M. Molina, C. Moure, S. Muggleton, and W. V. Laer. Detecting traffic problems with ILP. *Proc. ILP-98, Springer-Verlag, LNAI 1446*, pages 281–290, 1998.
5. A. Habel and H.-J. Kreowski. May we introduce to you: hyperedge replacement. *Proc. 3rd Graph-Grammars and Their Application to Computer Science, Springer-Verlag, LNCS 291*, pages 15–26, 1987.
6. D. Janssens and G. Rozenberg. On the structure of node-label-controlled graph languages. *Information Sciences*, 20:191–216, 1980.
7. S. Matsumoto, Y. Hayashi, and T. Shoudai. Polynomial time inductive inference of regular term tree languages from positive dat. *Proc. ALT-97, Springer-Verlag, LNAI 1316*, pages 212–227, 1997.
8. T. Miyahara, T. Uchida, T. Kuboyama, T. Yamamoto, K. Takahashi, and H. Ueda. KD-FGS: a knowledge discovery system from graph data using formal graph system. *Proc. PAKDD-99, Springer-Verlag, LNAI 1574, (to appear)*, 1999.
9. Y. Mukouchi and S. Arikawa. Towards a mathematical theory of machine discovery from facts. *Theoretical Computer Science*, 137:53–84, 1995.
10. S. Reyner. An analysis of a good algorithm for the subtree problem. *SIAM Journal on Computing*, 6(4):730–732, 1977.
11. T. Uchida, T. Miyahara, and Y. Nakamura. Formal graph systems and node-label controlled graph grammars. *Proc. 41th Inst. Syst. Control and Inf. Eng.*, pages 105–106, 1997.
12. T. Uchida, T. Shoudai, and S. Miyano. Parallel algorithm for refutation tree problem on formal graph systems. *IEICE Trans. Inf. Syst.*, E78-D(2):99–112, 1995.
13. J. T.-L. Wang, K. Zhang, K. Jeong, and D. Shasha. A system for approximate tree matching. *IEEE Trans. on Knowledge and Data Engineering*, 6(4):559–571, 1994.
14. A. Yamamoto. Procedural semantics and negative information of elementary formal system. *Journal of Logic Programming*, 13:89–98, 1992.

Analogical Prediction

Stephen Muggleton,
Michael Bain*

Department of Computer Science,
University of York,
YO10 5DD,
United Kingdom.

Abstract. Inductive Logic Programming (ILP) involves constructing an hypothesis H on the basis of background knowledge B and training examples E. An independent test set is used to evaluate the accuracy of H. This paper concerns an alternative approach called Analogical Prediction (AP). AP takes B, E and then for each test example $\langle x, y \rangle$ forms an hypothesis H_x from B, E, x. Evaluation of AP is based on estimating the probability that $H_x(x) = y$ for a randomly chosen $\langle x, y \rangle$. AP has been implemented within CProgol4.4. Experiments in the paper show that on English past tense data AP has significantly higher predictive accuracy on this data than both previously reported results and CProgol in inductive mode. However, on KRK illegal AP does not outperform CProgol in inductive mode. We conjecture that AP has advantages for domains in which a large proportion of the examples must be treated as exceptions with respect to the hypothesis vocabulary. The relationship of AP to analogy and instance-based learning is discussed. Limitations of the given implementation of AP are discussed and improvements suggested.

1 Introduction

1.1 Analogical prediction (AP)

Suppose that you are trying to make taxonomic predictions about animals. You might already have seen various animals and know some of their properties. Now you meet a platypus. You could try and predict whether the platypus was a mammal, fish, reptile or bird by forming analogies between the platypus and other animals for which you already know the classifications. Thus you could reason that a platypus is like other mammals since it suckles its young. In doing so you are making an assumption which could be represented as the following clause.

```
class(A,mammal) :- has_milk(A).
```

---

* Current address: Department of Artificial Intelligence, School of Computer Science and Engineering, University of New South Wales, Sydney 2052, Australia.

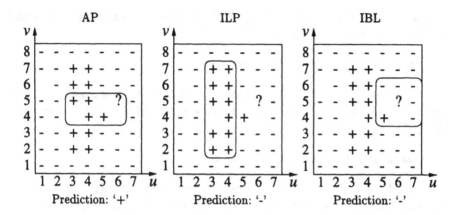

Fig. 1. Comparison of AP, ILP and IBL. Instances x are pairs $\langle u, v \rangle$ from $\{1, .., 7\} \times \{1, .., 8\}$. Each x can have a classification $y \in \{+, -\}$. The test instance x to be classified is denoted by '?'. The rounded box in each case defines the extension of the hypothesis H. Below each box the corresponding prediction for x is given.

It might be difficult to find a consistent assumption similar to the above which allowed a platypus to be predicted as being a fish or a reptile. However, you could reason that a platypus is similar to various birds you have encountered since it is both warm blooded and lays eggs. Again this would be represented as follows.

```
class(A,bird) :- homeothermic(A), has_eggs(A).
```

Note that the hypotheses above are related to a particular test instance, the platypus, for which the class value (mammal, bird, etc.) is to be predicted. We will call this form of reasoning *Analogical Prediction* (AP).

1.2 AP, induction and instance-based learning

In the above AP is given a *test instance* x, a training set E and background knowledge B. It then constructs an hypotheses H_x which not only covers some of the training set but also predicts the class y of x. This can be contrasted with the normal semantics of ILP [10], in which hypotheses H are constructed on the basis of B and E alone. In this case x is presented as part of the test procedure after H has been constructed.

AP is in some ways more similar to Instance-Based Learning (IBL) (see for example [3]), in which the class y would be attributed to x on the basis of its proximity to various elements of E. However, in the case of IBL, instead of constructing H, a similarity measure is used to determine proximity.

Figure 1 illustrates the differences in prediction between AP, standard ILP and IBL on a 2D binary classification problem. The test concept, 'insign', is actually a picture of the symbol '⊢' made out of +'s. If AP is restricted to making a single clause maximally general hypothesis, it would predicts x to be positive based on the following.

```
insign(U,V) :- 3=<U=<6, 4=<V=<5.
```

Assuming the closed world assumption is used for prediction, normal ILP will predict x to be negative based on the following hypothesis (note the exception at $\langle 5, 4 \rangle$).

```
insign(U,V) :- 3=<U=<4, 2=<V=<7.
```

Finally IBL will predict x to be negative based on the fact that 5/6 of the surrounding instances are negative. Note that IBL's implicit hypothesis in this case could be denoted by the following denial.

```
:- insign(U,V), near(U,V,6,5).
```

The background predicate *near/4* in the above encodes the notion of 'nearness' used in a k-nearest neighbour type algorithm.

1.3 Motivation

AP can be viewed as a half-way house between IBL and ILP. IBL has a number of advantages over ILP. These include ease of updating the knowledge-base and the fact that theory revision is unnecessary after the addition of new examples. AP shares both these advantages with IBL. On the other hand IBL has a number of disadvantages with respect to ILP. Notably, IBL predictions lack explanation, and there is a need to define a metric to describe similarity between instances. Generally, similarity metrics are hard to justify, even when they can be shown to have desirable properties (eg. [5, 11, 12]). In comparison AP predictions are directly associated with an explicit hypothesis, which provides explanation. Also AP does not require a similarity measure since predictions are made on the basis of the hypothesis.

This paper has the following structure. A formal framework for AP is provided in Section 2. Section 3 describes an implementation of AP within CProgol4.4 (ftp://ftp.cs.york.ac.uk/pub/ML_GROUP/progol4.4). This implementation is restricted to the special case of binary classification. Experiments using this implementation of AP are described in Section 4. On the standard English past tense data set [7] AP has higher predictive accuracy than FOIDL, FOIL and CProgol in inductive mode. By contrast, on KRK illegal AP performs slightly worse than CProgol in inductive mode. In the discussion (Section 5) we conjecture that AP has advantages for domains in which a large proportion of the examples must be treated as exceptions with respect to the hypothesis vocabulary. We also compare AP to analogical reasoning. The results are summarised in Section 6, and further improvements in the existing implementation are suggested.

```
Aleave(B,E)
    Let AP=Ap=aP=ap=0
    For each e = ⟨x, y⟩ in E
(a)    Construct ⊥_{B,x}
       E' := E \ e
(b)    Using E' find most compressive H_x ⪰ ⊥_{B,x}
       if y = H_x(x) then
           if y = True then AP := AP + 1
           else ap := ap + 1
       else
           if y = True then Ap := Ap + 1
           else aP := aP + 1
    Print-contingency-table(AP,Ap,aP,ap)
```

Fig. 2. Aleave algorithm. Algorithms from CProgol4.1 are used to (a) construct the bottom clause and (b) search the refinement graph.

2 Definitions

We assume denumerable sets X, Y representing the instance and prediction spaces respectively and a probability distribution $\mathcal{D}$ on X. The target theory is a function $f : X \to Y$. An AP learning algorithm L takes background knowledge B together with a set of training examples $E \subseteq \{\langle x', f(x') \rangle : x' \in X\}$. For any given B, E and test instance $x \in X$ the output of L is an hypothesised function H_x. Error is now defined as follows.

$$error(L, B, E) = Pr_{x \in \mathcal{D}}[h_x(x) \neq f(x)] \tag{1}$$

3 Implementation

AP has been implemented as a built-in predicate *aleave* in CProgol4.4 (available from ftp://ftp.cs.york.ac.uk/pub/ML_GROUP/progol4.4). The algorithm, shown in Figure 3, carries out a leave-one-out procedure which estimates AP error as defined in Equation (1). In terms of Section 2 each left out example e is viewed as a pair $\langle x, y \rangle$ where x is a ground atom and $y = $ True if e is positive and $y = $ False if e is negative.

AP error (see Equation 1) is estimated using the counters AP, Ap, aP and ap ('a' and 'p' stand for actual and predicted, and capitalisation/non-capitalisation stands for the value being True/False). For each example $e = \langle x, y \rangle$ left out, a bottom clause $\perp_{B,x}$ is constructed which predicts $y := $ True. A refinement graph search of the type described in [8] is carried out to find a maximally compressive single clause H_x which subsumes $\perp_{B,x}$. In doing so compression is computed relative to $E \setminus e$. If no compressive clause is found then the prediction is False. Otherwise it is True.

English past tense	KRK illegality
past([w,o,r,r,y],[w,o,r,r,i,e,d]).	illegal(3,5,6,7,6,2).
past([c,l,u,t,c,h],[c,l,u,t,c,h,e,d]).	illegal(3,6,7,6,7,4).
past([w,h,i,z],[w,h,i,z,z,e,d]).	:- illegal(2,5,5,2,4,1).
past([g,r,i,n,d],[g,r,o,u,n,d]).	:- illegal(5,7,1,2,0,0).

Fig. 3. Form of examples for both domains

English past tense	KRK illegality
	illegal(A,B,A,B,_,_).
past(A,B) :- split(A,C,[r,r,y]), split(B,C,[r,r,i,e,d]).	illegal(A,B,_,_,C,D) :- adj(A,C), adj(B,D).
	illegal(A,_,B,_,B,_) :- not A=B.
	illegal(_,A,B,C,B,D) :- A<C, A<D.

Fig. 4. Form of hypothesised clauses

The procedure Print-contingency-table(AP,Ap,aP,ap) prints a two-by-two table of the 4 values together with the accuracy estimate, standard error of estimation and χ^2 probability.

4 Experiments

The experiments were aimed at determining whether AP could provide increased predictive accuracy over other ILP algorithms. Two standard ILP data sets were chosen for comparison (described in Section 4.2 below).

4.1 Experimental hypotheses

The following null hypotheses were tested in the first and second experiments respectively.

Null hypothesis 1. AP does not have higher predictive accuracy than any other ILP system on any standard data set.

Null hypothesis 2. AP has higher predictive accuracy than any other ILP system on all standard data sets.

Note that hypothesis 1 is not the negation of hypothesis 2. If both are rejected then it means simply that AP is better for some domains but not others.

4.2 Materials

The following data sets were used for testing the experimental hypotheses.

English past tense. This is described in [15, 6, 7]). The available example set E_{past} has size 1390.

KRK illegality. This was originally described in [9]. The total instance space size is $8^6 = 262144$.

For both domains the form of examples are shown in Figure 3 and the form of hypothesised clauses in Figure 4. Note that in the KRK illegality domain negative examples are those preceded by a ':-', while the English past tense domain has no negative examples. The absence of negative examples in the English past tense domain is compensated for by a constraint on hypothesised clauses which Mooney and Califf [7] call output completeness. In the experiments output completeness is enforced in CProgol4.4 by including the following user defined constraint which requires that *past/2* is a function.

```
:- hypothesis(past(X,Y),Body,_), clause(past(X,Z),true), Body, not(Y==Z).
```

4.3 Method

English past tense Mooney and Califf [7] compared the predictive accuracy of FOIL, IFOIL and FOIL on the alphabetic English past tense task. We interpret the description of their training regime as follows. Training sets of sizes 25, 50, 100, 250 and 500 were randomly sampled without replacement from E_{past}, with 10 sets of each size. For each training set E a test set of size 500 was randomly sampled without replacement from $E_{past} \setminus E$. Each learning system was applied to each training set and the predictive accuracy assessed on the corresponding test set. Results were averaged for each training set size and reported as a learning curve.

For the purposes of comparison we followed the above training regime for CProgol4.4 in inductive mode. We also ran AP with the *aleave* predicate built-in to CProgol4.4 (Section 3) on each of the training sets and then for each training set size averaged the results over the 10 sets.

KRK illegality Predictive accuracies were compared for CProgol4.4 using AP with leave-one-out (*aleave*) against induction with leave-one-out (*leave*). Training sets of sizes 5, 10, 20, 30, 40, 60, 80, 100, 200 were randomly sampled with replacement from the total example space, with 10 sets of each size. For each of the training sets both *aleave* and *leave* were run. The resulting predictive accuracies were averaged for each training set size.

4.4 Results

English past tense The five learning curves are shown in Figure 5. The horizontal line labelled "Default rules" represents the following simple Prolog program which adds a 'd' to verbs ending in 'e' and otherwise adds 'ed'.

```
past(A,B) :- split(A,B,[e]), split(B,A,[d]), !.
past(A,B) :- split(B,A,[e,d]).
```

The differences between AP and all other systems are significant at the 0.0001 level with 250 and 500 examples. Thus null hypothesis 1 is clearly rejected.

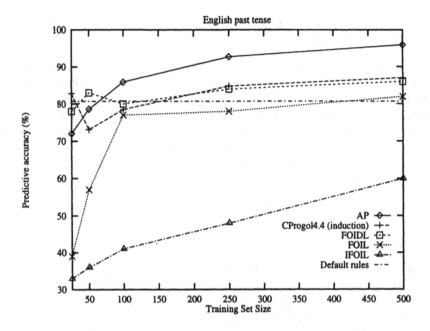

Fig. 5. Learning curves for alphabetic English past tense.

KRK illegality The two learning curves are shown in Figure 6. The horizontal line labelled "Majority class" shows the percentage of negative examples in the domain. Only the accuracy difference between induction and AP for 200 examples is significant at the 0.05 level, though taken together the differences are significant at the 0.0001 level. Thus null hypothesis 2 can be rejected.

5 Discussion and related work

The strong rejection of the two null hypotheses indicate that the advantages of AP relative to induction are domain dependent. The authors believe that AP has advantages for domains, like the English past tense, in which a large proportion of the examples must be treated as exceptions with respect to the hypothesis vocabulary. Note that KRK illegal contains exceptions, though they fall into a relatively small number of classes, and have relatively low frequency (a 2 clause approximation of KRK illegal has over 90% accuracy). By contrast, around 20% of the verbs in the past tense data are irregular.

It should be noted that our implementation of AP has a tendency to overgeneralise. This stems from the assymetry in constructing only clauses which make positive predictions in the *aleave* algorithm (Section 3). The tendency to overgeneralise decreases accuracy in the KRK illegal domain but increases accuracy in the past tense domain, due to the lack of negative examples. Even when negative examples are added to the past tense training set, predictive accuracy is unaffected due to the output completeness constraint.

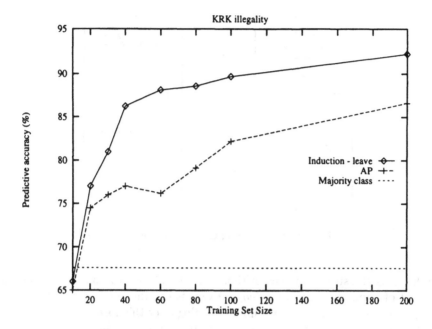

Fig. 6. Learning curves for KRK illegality.

The AP accuracies on English past tense data shown in Figure 5 are the highest on this data set in the literature. However, it is interesting to note that CProgol's induction mode results are as good as FOIDL. This contradicts Mooney and Califf's claim that FOIDL's decision list representation gives FOIDL strong advantages in this domain.

5.1 Relationship of AP to analogy

Evans' [4] early studies of analogy concentrated on IQ tests of the form shown in Figure 7. Evans in was the first to implement a program for solving geometric analogy problems. These are problems of the form "A is to B as C is to ?" where the answer is one of five possible solutions, i.e. a multiple-choice format. The problems solved by his program were taken from actual high-school level test papers. The program, called ANALOGY, comprised two parts. Part 1 is given two line drawings A and B as input and calculates a set of properties, relations and "similarities" such as rotations and reflections which take A into B and relate C to each of the five possible answers. Part 2 forms a set of theories or transformation rules taking A into B. It then attempts to generalize these theories to cover additional data (C and the answer figures). This results in a subset of the admissible theories, i.e. transformation rules which take A into B and C into exactly one answer figure. Finally, the program chooses the most specific theory from these admissible theories.

Evans notes that the program does very little search, which indicates that the hypothesis space of ANALOGY is highly constrained. The solution is chosen

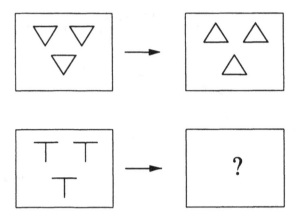

Fig. 7. IQ test problem of the type studied by Evans.

on the basis of a specificity bias. Although Part 1 of the program includes a large amount of domain-specific knowledge, Evans is careful to point out that Part 2 is a general purpose method for finding analogies of this form.

Analogical reasoning is often viewed as having a close relationship to induction. For instance, both Peirce and Polya suggested that analogical conclusions could be deduced via an inductive hypothesis [13, 14]. Similar views are expressed in the Artificial Intelligence literature [2]. For instance, Arima [1] formalises the problem of analogy as involving a comparison of a *base* B and *target* T. When B and T are found to share a similarity property S analogical reasoning predicts that they will also share a projected property P. This is formalised in the following analogical inference rule.

$$\frac{P(B)}{S(T) \wedge S(B)}{P(T)}$$

The rule above can be viewed as involving the construction of the following inductive hypothesis.

$$\forall x.S(x) \rightarrow P(x)$$

From this $P(T)$ can be inferred deductively. Note that S and P can obviously be extended to take more than one argument. For instance, given the Evans' type problem in Figure 7 we might formulate the following hypothesis as a Prolog clause.

```
is_to(X,Y) :- invertall(X,Y).
```

In this way we can view analogical reasoning as a special case of AP, in which the example set contains a single *base* example and the test instance relates to the *target*. According to Arima the following issues are seen as being central in the discussion of analogy.

1. What object (or case) should be selected as a base with respect to a target,

2. which property is significant in analogy among properties shared by two objects and
3. what property is to be projected w.r.t. a certain similarity.

These three issues are handled in the CProgol4.4 AP implementation as follows.

1. A set of base cases is used from the example set based on maximising compression over the hypothesis space,
2. relevant properties are found by constructing the bottom clause relative to the test instance and
3. the relevant projection properties are decided on the basis of modeh declarations given to CProgol.

6 Conclusions and further work

In this paper we have introduced the notion of AP as a half-way house between induction and instance-based learning. An implementation of AP has been incorporated into CProgol4.4 (ftp://ftp.cs.york.ac.uk/pub/ML_GROUP/progol4.4). In experiments AP produced the best predictive accuracy results to date on the English past tense data, outstripping FOIDL by around 10% after 500 examples. However, on KRK illegal AP performs consistently worse than CProgol4.4 in inductive mode. We believe that AP works best with domains in which a large proportion of the examples must be treated as exceptions with respect to the hypothesis vocabulary.

The present implementation of AP is limited in a number of ways. For instance, for any test instance x predictions must be binary, i.e. $y \in \{\text{True}, \text{False}\}$. Also, because no constructed hypotheses are ever stored, AP cannot deal with recursion. It is envisaged that a strategy which mixed both induction and AP might work better than either. Thus some, or all, of the AP hypotheses could be stored for later use. However, it is not yet clear to the authors which strategy would operate best.

Acknowledgements

The first author would like to thank Thirza and Clare for their good-natured support during the writing of this paper. This work was supported partly by the Esprit Long Term Research Action ILP II (project 20237), EPSRC grant GR/K57985 on Experiments with Distribution-based Machine Learning.

References

1. J. Arima. *Logical Foundations of Induction and Analogy*. PhD thesis, Kyoto University, 1998.

2. T. Davies and S.J. Russell. A logical approach to reasoning by analogy. In *IJCAI-87*, pages 264–270. Morgan Kaufmann, 1987.

3. W. Emde and D. Wettschereck. Relational Instance-Based Learning. In L. Saitta, editor, *Proceedings of the 13th International Machine Learning Conference*, pages 122–130, Los Altos, 1996. Morgan Kaufmann.

4. T.G. Evans. A program for the solution of a class of geoemtric analogy intellgence test questions. In M. Minsky, editor, *Semantic Information Processing*. MIT Press, Cambridge, MA, 1968.

5. A. Hutchinson. Metrics on terms and clauses. In M. Someren and G. Widmer, editors, *Proceedings of the Ninth European Conference on Machine Learning*, pages 138–145, Berlin, 1997. Springer.

6. C.X. Ling. Learning the past tense of english verbs: the symbolic pattern associators vs. connectionist models. *Journal of Artificial Intelligence Research*, 1:209–229, 1994.

7. R.J. Mooney and M.E. Califf. Induction of first-order decision lists: Results on learning the past tense of english verbs. *Journal of Artificial Intelligence Research*, 3:1–24, 1995.

8. S. Muggleton. Inverse entailment and Progol. *New Generation Computing*, 13:245–286, 1995.

9. S. Muggleton, M.E. Bain, J. Hayes-Michie, and D. Michie. An experimental comparison of human and machine learning formalisms. In *Proceedings of the Sixth International Workshop on Machine Learning*, Los Altos, CA, 1989. Kaufmann.

10. S. Muggleton and L. De Raedt. Inductive logic programming: Theory and methods. *Journal of Logic Programming*, 19,20:629–679, 1994.

11. S.H. Nienhuys-Cheng. Distance between Herbrand interpretations: a measure for approximations to a target concept. In N. Lavrač and S. Džeroski, editors, *Proceedings of the Seventh International Workshop on Inductive Logic Programming (ILP97)*, pages 321–226, Berlin, 1997. Springer-Verlag. LNAI 1297.

12. S.H. Nienhuys-Cheng. Distances and limits on Herbrand interpretations. In C.D. Page, editor, *Proceedings of the Eighth International Conference on Inductive Logic Programming (ILP98)*, pages 250–260, Berlin, 1998. Springer. LNAI 1446.

13. C.S. Peirce. Elements of logic. In C. Hartshorne and P. Weiss, editors, *Collected Papers of Charles Sanders Peirce*, volume 2. Harvard University Press, Cambridge, MA, 1932.

14. G. Polya. Induction and analogy in mathematics. In *Mathematics and Plausible Reasoning*, volume 1. Princeton University Press, Princeton, 1954.

15. D.E. Rumelhart and J.L. McClelland. On learning the past tense of english verbs. In *Explorations in the Micro-Structure of Cognition Vol. II*, pages 216–271. MIT Press, Cambridge, MA, 1986.

Generalizing Refinement Operators
to Learn Prenex Conjunctive Normal Forms

Shan-Hwei Nienhuys-Cheng, Wim Van Laer
Jan Ramon, Luc De Raedt
cheng@few.eur.nl, {wimv,lucdr}@cs.kuleuven.ac.be

Department of Computer Science, Katholieke Universiteit Leuven
Celestijnenlaan 200A, B-3001 Heverlee, Belgium

Abstract. Inductive Logic Programming considers almost exclusively universally quantified theories. To add expressiveness we should consider general prenex conjunctive normal forms (PCNF) with existential variables. ILP mostly uses learning with refinement operators. To extend refinement operators to PCNF, we should first extend substitutions to PCNF. If one substitutes an existential variable in a formula, one often obtains a specializtion rather than a generalization. In this article we define substitutions to specialize a given PCNF and a *weakly complete* downward refinement operator. Based on this operator, we have implemented a simple learning system PCL on some type of PCNF.

1 Introduction

Inductive Logic Programming learns a *correct* logic formula with respect to examples. The definition of correctness has to do with the way examples are presented. Suppose some interpretations are given as examples, formulas with these examples as models should be found. A *downward* refinement operator ρ can be used to search for such a formula. If a searching process begins with $\top = \{\Box\}$, it should be replaced by the set of its refinements in $\rho(\top)$ because $\Box$ has no models. A refinement $\phi \in \rho(\top)$ may have to be replaced by its refinements again because some given interpretations are not its models. This process can go on until correct formulas are found.

Refinement operators have often been used ([S81,RD97]) to learn a correct universally quantified theory incrementally. If clause C subsumes clause D, then a *refinement chain* exists from C to D using *elementary substitutions* and adding literals. Let $C = p(x,y)$ and $D = p(x,x) \vee \neg q(f(x))$. Then a chain may be $p(x,y), p(x,y) \vee \neg q(z), \ p(x,y) \vee \neg q(f(u)), \ p(x,x) \vee \neg q(f(u)), \ p(x,x) \vee \neg q(f(x))$. If a correct universally quantified theory does exist, then a refinement chain from $\Box$ to every clause in this theory exists because $\Box$ subsumes every clause.

Until now almost all ILP researchers are only interested in universally quantified clauses, especially definite program clauses. However, we may want to learn a concept expressed by a formula ϕ with existential variables such as a prenex conjunctive normal form (PCNF). To solve such problems, one considers the universally quantified Skolem standard form ψ of ϕ. It is well known that $\psi \models \phi$ but often $\phi \not\models \psi$. For instance, let the 3-ary predicate p be interpreted in the set of real numbers $\mathbf{R}$ as $p(x, y, z)$ is true iff $xy = z$. The concept that for an arbitrary $z \in \mathbf{R}$, there are x, y such that $xy = z^2$ can be expressed by $\phi = \forall z \exists x \exists y\, p(x, y, z^2)$. A standard form of the formula ϕ is $\psi = \forall z\, p(f(z), g(z), z^2)$ for new function symbols f, g. A model of ϕ is also a model of ψ only when f and g are interpreted in certain ways, e.g. $f(z) = 2z$ and $g(z) = z/2$, but we would like to check the truth value of ϕ directly. In a database we may have an integrity constraint $\forall x \forall y \exists z \neg sell(x, y) \vee supply(x, y, z)$: if a shop x sells an item y, there must be a company z which supplies x with y. Of course we can define one particular supplier as $f(x, y)$ but we have to change f when we consider another supplier. To add expressiveness we should consider learning PCNF in general.

We would also like to use (elementary) substitutions to refine a PCNF. The usual substitutions often generalize a formula instead of specializing it because of the existential variables. Let $\phi = \forall x \exists y p(x, y)$ and $\psi = \forall x p(x, x)$. Then $\psi \models \phi$ but $\phi \not\models \psi$. Therefore we will define a new type of substitutions to specialize a PCNF. Based on our substitutions and adding literals, we can define a *downward* refinement operator ρ which is *weakly complete*: For every ϕ there is a refinement chain from $\top$ to ϕ, i.e., there is an n such that $\phi \in \rho^n(\top)$.

Generalizing and specializing a formula with existential quantifiers have also been considered in [GF96]. A formula there involves only one clause (actually a clause presented in a special form). The variables in the head of a clause are universally quantified. The variables not in the head are quantified separately in the body by existential and universal quantifiers. Some rules are given to manipulate the variables only in the body. It seems that the rules are motivated by the following principle: if the body is generalized, then the formula is specialized and vice versa. [GF96] adopts neither PCNF in general nor a uniform approach with substitutions.

In this article we begin with establishing some properties of PCNF. We then define (elementary) substitutions and a downward refinement operator. We use a refinement operator to search in the set of theories expressed in PCNF. This differs from a classic refinement opertor which is defined in a serach space of universally quantified clauses. Most proofs will be omited (see [NLR99]). We explain then briefly our first step in implementation. If $I_1, I_2, \ldots, I_n$ is a set of interpretations, the system PCL finds a PCNF ϕ such that every I_j is a model of ϕ. Hence we have generalized the Claudien system[RD97] which only deals with the standard forms.

2 Prenex Conjunctive Normal Forms

In the first subsection we give some well known basic definitions and results in logic (see [NW97]). In the second subsection we state two important lemmas of ours. In the last subsection we consider the effects of adding literals to a clause in a PCNF.

2.1 Preliminaries

Definition 1. *An* interpretation I *with domain* D *of a first-order language* L *consists of the following: (a) Each n-ary function symbol* f *in* L *is assigned a mapping from* D^n *to* D. *(b) Each n-ary predicate symbol* p *in* L *is assigned a mapping from* D^n *to* $\{true, false\}$.

Definition 2. *Let* I *be an interpretation of the first-order language* L *with domain* D. *Let* V *be a set of variables, then a mapping* $\theta : V \to D$ *is called a* variable assignment *from* V. *Given a variable assignment* θ *from the set of variables in a formula* ϕ, *we can check if* ϕ *is true or false under* I *and* θ. *If* ϕ *is a closed formula, then the truth value of* ϕ *is independent of the variable assignment we choose.* I *is a* model *of the closed formula* ϕ *if* ϕ *is true in* I. *Formula* ψ logically implies *formula* ϕ, *denoted by* $\psi \models \phi$, *if every model of* ψ *is also a model of* ϕ. ψ *and* ϕ *are called* logically equivalent, *denoted by* $\psi \Leftrightarrow \phi$, *if they have the same models.*

Definition 3. *A* clause *is a disjunction of a finite number of literals. A* prenex conjunctive normal form *(PCNF)* ψ *is a closed formula* $q_1 x_1 q_2 x_2 \ldots q_n x_n (C_1 \wedge C_2 \wedge \ldots \wedge C_m)$ *where* q_i *is a quantifier (*$\exists$ *or* $\forall$*),* $x_i \neq x_j$ *if* $i \neq j$ *and* C_j *is a clause.* $q_1 x_1 q_2 x_2 \ldots q_n x_n$ *is the* prenex *of* ψ *and* $C_1 \wedge C_2 \wedge \ldots \wedge C_m$ *is the* matrix *of* ψ. *We denote* ψ *often by* $q_1 x_1 q_2 x_2 \ldots q_n x_n M(x_1, \ldots, x_n)$ *or* $Q(x_1, \ldots, x_n) M(x_1, \ldots, x_n)$ *or* $Q(\overline{x}) M(\overline{x})$ *or* $Q(\psi) M(\psi)$ *or* QM. *We call variables in* $Q(\psi)$ universal *or* existential; *depending on how they are bound; the set of existential and universal variables are denoted by* $eVar(\psi)$ *and* $uVar(\psi)$, *respectively. We have* $Var(\psi) = uVar(\psi) \cup eVar(\psi)$.

Note that if $\{y_1, \ldots, y_m\} \supseteq \{x_1, \ldots, x_n\}$, *then* $Q(\overline{y}) M(\overline{x}) \Leftrightarrow Q(\overline{x}) M(\overline{x})$.

Theorem 1. *Let* ϕ *be a closed formula. Then there exists a PCNF* ψ *such that* ϕ *and* ψ *are logically equivalent.*

2.2 Some properties of PCNF

We often need to check if some interpretation I is a model of a formula ψ. Lemma 1 in this subsection gives a necessary and sufficient condition for I to be a model of ψ. Lemma 2 tells that the truth value of a formula has often to do with the positions of variables in the prenex. Both lemmas will often be used for proving other results. We will often use variable assignments the same way as they are usual substitutions.

Example 1. Let $\psi = \exists x \forall y p(x, f(y))$ and $\phi = \forall y \exists x p(x, f(y))$. Then $\psi \models \phi$: Let I be an interpretation with domain D. Then ψ is true in I iff there is a $d \in D$ such that the formula $\forall y p(d, f(y)))$ is true in I iff there is $d \in D$ such that for every $e \in D$, $p(d, f(e))$ is true. On the other hand, ϕ is true in I iff for every $e \in D$, $\exists x p(x, f(e))$ is true iff for every $e \in D$, there is $d \in D$ such that $p(d, f(e))$ is true. Notice that the choice of d here may depend on e. Since I is a model of ψ, for every $e \in D$, we can choose the same $d \in D$ such that $p(d, f(e))$ is true in I. Consider the Herbrand interpretation $I = \{p(t, f(t)) | t \text{ ground}\}$. Then I is a model of ϕ. For an assignment $\sigma = \{x/t\}$, let $\gamma = \{y/t\}$ then $\phi(\sigma \cup \gamma)$ is true. We can not say I is a model of ψ because γ depends on σ. We can generalize this example to the following lemmas

Lemma 1. *Let $\phi = q_1 x_1 \ldots q_n x_n M(x_1, \ldots, x_n)$. An interpretation I with domain D is a model of ϕ iff for every $\sigma : \mathrm{uVar}(\phi) \to D$ there is a $\gamma : \mathrm{eVar}(\phi) \to D$ such that the following two conditions are satisfied: (a) $M(\sigma \cup \gamma)$ is true in I. (b) the definition of γ on x_i depends only on how σ and γ are defined on $\{x_1, x_2, \ldots, x_{i-1}\}$, i.e., an element in D can be assigned to x_i after the assignment of all $x_j, j < i$ has been done.*

It is possible to extend the next lemma to some other situations. We prove only the case which is need for defining our refinement operator.

Lemma 2. *Let*
$$\psi = q_1 x_1 \ldots \exists x_i \ldots \forall x_j \ldots q_n x_n M, \quad \phi = q_1 x_1 \ldots \forall x_j \ldots \exists x_i \ldots q_n x_n M$$
and suppose there is no other existential variable between x_i and x_j in the prenexes of these two formulas. Then $\psi \models \phi$.

Proof . Suppose I is a model of ψ. We want to prove that I is also a model of ϕ. Let $\sigma : \mathrm{uVar}(\phi) \to D$. By Lemma 1, there is a variable assignment γ of $\mathrm{eVar}(\psi)$ such that $M(\psi)(\sigma \cup \gamma)$ is true under I. The assignment of $x_k \in \mathrm{eVar}(\psi)$ may depend on the definition of σ and γ on variables before x_k in $Q(\psi)$. Since $\mathrm{uVar}(\psi) = \mathrm{uVar}(\phi)$ and $M(\psi) = M(\phi)$, we have $M(\phi)(\sigma \cup \gamma)$ true under I. By Lemma 1, we can say I is a model of ϕ if γ in $x_k \in \mathrm{eVar}(\phi)$ depends on the assignment of variables before x_k in $Q(\phi)$. Note that $Q(\phi)$ interchanges only the order of $\exists x_i$ and $\forall x_j$ in $Q(\psi)$. The assignment of x_i in γ depends only on the assignment of σ, γ on $x_1, \ldots, x_{i-1}$ which appear before $\exists x_i$ in $Q(\phi)$. If $x_k \in \mathrm{eVar}(\phi)$ is another existential variable, then it is not between x_i and x_j so $x_1, \ldots, x_{k-1}$ are still before x_k in $Q(\phi)$. That means I is a model of ϕ.

2.3 Adding literals

A classic refinement step for a universal quantified PCNF extends a clause in the matrix with an extra literal containing new variables. This will also be done for our refinement operator for PCNF. For this we need the the following results which are based on the fact that the disjunctions of formulas is true if at least one of them is true.

Lemma 3. *Let $\psi = q_1 x_1 \ldots q_n x_n C_1 \wedge C_2 \ldots \wedge C_m$ where every C_i is a clause. Let L be a literal which contains only variables $y_1, \ldots, y_k$ that are new w.r.t. ψ. If $\phi = q_1 x_1 \ldots q_n x_n \forall y_1 \ldots \forall y_k \ C_1 \wedge \ldots \wedge (C_j \vee L) \ldots \wedge C_m$, then $\psi \models \phi$.*

We call the action in Lemma 3 *adding a u-literal*. Similarly we can prove the following lemma which *adds an e-literal* to a formula.

Lemma 4. *Let $\psi = q_1 x_1 \ldots q_n x_n C_1 \wedge C_2 \ldots \wedge C_m$ where every C_i is a clause. Let L be a literal which contains only new variables $y_1, \ldots, y_k$ that are new w.r.t. ψ. If $\phi = \exists y_1 \ldots \exists y_k q_1 x_1 \ldots q_n x_n \ C_1 \wedge \ldots \wedge (C_j \vee L) \ldots \wedge C_m$, then $\psi \models \phi$.*

3 Substitutions and Specializations

We are used to that a substitution θ replaces some variables with terms. For a universally quantified clause C we have always $C \models C\theta$. This is not valid for PCNF as the following examples show. Thus we are motivated to define a new type of substitutions which specialize PCNF.

Example 2. Consider the following implications:

$\forall x\, p(x) \models p(a)$ and $p(a) \not\models \forall x\, p(x)$

$p(a) \models \exists x\, p(x)$ and $\exists x\, p(x) \not\models p(a)$

$\exists x\, p(x,x) \models \exists x \exists y\, p(x,y)$ and $\exists x \exists y\, p(x,y) \not\models \exists x\, p(x,x)$

A unification of two universally quantified variables does not always specialize a PCNF. Let $\psi = \forall x \exists y \forall z p(x,y,z)$, $\phi = \forall x \exists y p(x,y,x)$, $\phi' = \exists y \forall z p(z,y,z)$, and $I = \{p(t,f(t),t') \mid t,t' \text{ ground}\}$. Then I is a model of ψ and ϕ but not a model of ϕ'. For ϕ' true in I, we need an s such that $p(t,s,t)$ true for every t.

3.1 Elementary substitutions for PCNF

A matrix can be pictured as a tree, with the root on top. At each node, number downgoing branches 1, 2, 3, etc. from left to right. Each node and the tree hanging from it is given by the path that leads to it from the top. For example, let $M = p(x,y) \wedge (p(x,x) \vee \neg q(f(x)))$. The second clause has position $\langle 2 \rangle$. $\neg q(f(x))$ has position $\langle 2, 2 \rangle$, $f(x)$ has position $\langle 2, 2, 1 \rangle$, etc.

Definition 4. *An substitution for a matrix M has the form $\theta = \{(t_1/s_1, p_1), \ldots, (t_n/s_n, p_n)\}$. $M\theta$ is a matrix formed by using M and θ: for every i, the term at position p_i in M is t_i and t_i should be replaced by s_i. For example, if $M = p(x,y) \wedge (p(x,x) \vee \neg q(f(x)))$ and $\theta = \{(x/f(z), \langle 1, 1 \rangle), (f(x)/g(z), \langle 2, 2, 1 \rangle)\}$, then $M\theta = p(f(z), y) \wedge (p(x,x) \vee \neg q(g(z)))$. It is easy to see that the old definition of a substitution is a special case of the new kind of substitutions. In such a case we use the old notation where the positions are not needed.*

Definition 5. *Let $\psi = q_1 x_1 \ldots q_n x_n C_1 \wedge \ldots \wedge C_m = Q(\psi) M(\psi)$ be a PCNF. There are the following 5 types of elementary substitutions for ψ:*

The first two types have to do with universal variables:

- *Let $x_i, x_j \in \mathrm{uVar}(\psi)$ and $i < j$. An elementary u-unification $\theta = \{x_j/x_i\}$ can be applied to ψ such that $\psi\theta = q_1 x_1 \ldots q_n x_n (M(\psi)\theta)$. For example let $\psi = \forall x \forall y p(f(x), y)$ and $\theta = \{y/x\}$. Then $\psi\theta = \forall x \forall y p(f(x), x)$ which is equivalent to $\forall x p(f(x), x)$.*
- *Let $x_i \in \mathrm{uVar}(\psi)$. If $t = f(y_1, \ldots, y_k)$, where $y_1, \ldots, y_k$ are new distinct variables w.r.t. ψ, then $\theta = \{x_i/t\}$ is called an elementary u-substitution. Let $\psi\theta$ be the new formula constructed as follows. All x_i-occurrences in the matrix of ψ are replaced by t simultaneously, i.e. $M(\psi\theta) = M(\psi)\theta$. Moreover, the $\forall x_i$ in the prenex of ψ is replaced by $\forall y_1 \forall y_2 \ldots \forall y_k$. For example, let $\psi = \forall x \exists y p(x,y)$ and $\theta = \{x/f(u,v)\}$. Then $\psi\theta = \forall u \forall v \exists y p(f(u,v), y)$.*

The next two types have to do with existential variables:

- *Let $x_i \in \mathrm{eVar}(\psi)$ and let $\{(x_i, p_1), \ldots, (x_i, p_k)\}$ be a proper subset of the x_i-occurrences in $M(\psi)$. If z is a new variable, then $\theta = \{(x_i/z, p_1), \ldots, (x_i/z, p_k)\}$ is called an elementary e-antiunification and $\psi\theta$ is the PCNF $q_1 x_1 \ldots \exists x_i \exists z q_{i+1} x_{i+1} \ldots q_n x_n (M\theta)$. For example, let $\psi = \exists x p(x, x)$ and $\theta = \{x/z, \langle 2 \rangle\}$. Then $\psi\theta = \exists x \exists z p(x, z)$.*

- *Let $t = f(x_{i_1}, \ldots, x_{i_m})$ which contains only distinct existential variables. Let $i_j = \max\{i_1, \ldots, i_m\}$. Let $\{(t, p_1), \ldots, (t, p_k)\}$ be occurrences in $M(\psi)$. If z is a new variable, then $\theta = \{(t/z, p_1), \ldots, (t/z, p_k)\}$ is called an elementary e-substitution for ψ. We define $\psi\theta = q_1 x_1 \ldots q_{i_j} x_{i_j} \exists z q_{i_j+1} x_{i_j+1} \ldots q_n x_n (M\theta)$. For example, let $\psi = \forall x \exists y \exists u \exists v\, p(x, u) \wedge (p(x, y) \vee \neg q(f(u, v)))$. If $\theta = \{(f(u, v)/z, \langle 2, 2, 1 \rangle)\}$, then $\psi\theta = \forall x \exists y \exists u \exists v \exists z\ p(x, u) \wedge (p(x, x) \vee \neg q(z))$.*

The last type has to do with interchanging the places of an existential and a universal variable in $Q(\psi)$:

- *Suppose $x_i \in \mathrm{eVar}(\psi)$, $x_j \in \mathrm{uVar}(\psi)$ and $i < j$. If there is no other existential variable between x_i and x_j in $Q(\psi)$, then $\{(x_i, x_j)\}$ denotes an elementary eu-substitution. It interchanges the positions of x_i and x_j in $Q(\psi)$. For example, let $\theta = \{(x, y)\}$. Then $(\exists x \forall y\, p(x, y))\theta = \forall y \exists x\, p(x, y)$.*

3.2 Substitutions and specializations

For every elementary substitutions θ w.r.t. ψ we can prove that $\psi \models \psi\theta$. For instance,

Lemma 5. *Let $\psi = Q(\psi) M(\psi)$ be a PCNF. Let $\theta = \{(t/z, p_1), \ldots, (t/z, p_m)\}$ be an elementary e-substitution. Then $\psi \models \psi\theta$.*

Proof . Let I be a model of ψ. Let t contain only the existential variables $x_{i_1}, \ldots, x_{i_k}$ where $i_1 < i_2 \ldots < i_k$. Then $\psi\theta = q_1 x_1 \ldots q_{i_k} x_{i_k} \exists z q_{i_k+1} x_{i_k+1} \ldots q_n x_n M\theta$. $M(\psi)$ differs from $M(\psi\theta)$ only at position $p_1, p_2, \ldots, p_k$. Clearly, $\mathrm{uVar}(\psi\theta) = \mathrm{uVar}(\psi)$ and $\mathrm{eVar}(\psi\theta) = \mathrm{eVar}(\psi) \cup \{z\}$. Since I is a model of ψ, and the assignment σ is also an assignment of $\mathrm{uVar}(\psi)$, by Lemma 1 there is a variable assignment γ of $\mathrm{eVar}(\psi)$ to D such that $M(\psi)(\sigma \cup \gamma)$ is true under I. Moreover, if $x_i \in \mathrm{eVar}(\psi)$, then $\gamma(x_i)$ depends only on how σ and γ beheave on variables before x_i in $P(\psi)$. Notice that at every position p_j in $M(\psi)(\sigma \cup \gamma)$ we have in fact $t\gamma$. We consider the subsitution $\gamma' = \gamma \cup \{z/t\gamma\}$. Then $M(\psi)(\sigma \cup \gamma) = M(\psi)\theta(\sigma \cup \gamma')$. Notice z is behind all variables $x_1, \ldots, x_{i_k}$ in $P(\psi\theta)$. Thus z depends also only on how σ and γ' defined on the variables before it. By applying Lemma 1, we have I is a model of $\psi\theta$.

We can combine the elementary substitutions to get the following definition and theorem.

Definition 6. *Let ψ be a PCNF. Suppose θ_1 is an elementary substitution w.r.t. ψ and θ_i is elementary w.r.t. $(\ldots (\psi\theta_1)\theta_2 \ldots)\theta_{i-1}$ for every $i = 2, \ldots, n$. Let $\theta = \theta_1 \ldots \theta_n$ be the composition of these θ_i, i.e. $\psi\theta = (\ldots (\psi\theta_1)\theta_2) \ldots)\theta_n$. Then θ is called a substitution w.r.t. ψ.*

Theorem 2. *For a PCNF ψ and a substitution θ defined as above, $\psi \models \psi\theta$.*

4 Downward Refinement Operator

Let the search space S be the set of all PCNF of a first order logical language which has a finite number of function and predicate symbols. Let the top $\top \in S$ be the conjunction of a positive number of empty clauses, i.e. $\top = \Box \wedge \Box \ldots \wedge \Box$. The number of $\Box$ is irrelevant because they are all equivalent to *false*. A *refinement operator* on S is a function $\rho : S \to 2^S$ (the set of all subsets of S). A refinement operator ρ is *downward* if for every ψ and $\phi \in \rho(\psi)$, we have $\psi \models \phi$. A *refinement chain* from ψ to ϕ is a sequence $\psi_0, \psi_1, \ldots, \psi_k$ in S such that $\psi_0 \Leftrightarrow \psi$, $\psi_k \Leftrightarrow \phi$ and $\psi_i \in \rho(\psi_{i-1})$.

Definition 7. *Let $\psi = q_1 x_1 \ldots q_n x_n C_1 \wedge C_2 \ldots \wedge C_m$. Let ρ be a refinement operator on S defined by the following items.*
Note that there are only a finite number of non-alphabetical variants in $\rho(\psi)$.

The first three items have to do with universal variables:

- *1. For an elementary u-unification $\theta = \{y/x\}$, where $x, y \in \text{uVar}(\psi)$ and x comes before y in $Q(\psi)$, let $\psi\theta \in \rho(\psi)$.*
- *2. Let $x \in \text{uVar}(\psi)$ and an elementary u-substitution $\theta = \{x/f(y_1, \ldots, y_k)\}$, let $\psi\theta \in \rho(\psi)$.*
- *3. Let $L = p(y_1, \ldots, y_k)$ or $\neg p(y_1, \ldots, y_k)$ where $y_1, \ldots, y_k$ are distinct variables new w.r.t. ψ. For an arbitrary $j = 1, \ldots, m$, let ϕ_j be defined by adding a u-literal to ψ: $\phi_j = q_1 x_1 \ldots q_n x_n \forall y_1 \ldots \forall y_k \, C_1 \wedge \ldots \wedge (C_j \vee L) \wedge \ldots \wedge C_m$. Let $\phi_j \in \rho(\psi)$.*

The next 3 items have to do with existential variables:

- *4. Let $x \in \text{eVar}(\psi)$ and $\{(x, p_1), \ldots, (x, p_k)\}$ be some (not all) x-occurrences in $M(\psi)$. For a new variable y and an elementary e-antiunification $\theta = \{(x/y, p_1), \ldots, (x/y, p_k)\}$, let $\psi\theta \in \rho(\psi)$.*
- *5. Let $(t, p_i) = (f(y_1, \ldots, y_s), p_i), i = 1, \ldots, k$ be term occurrences in $M(\psi)$ such that all y_j are distinct and in $\text{eVar}(\psi)$. Then for the elementary e-substitution $\theta = \{(t/y, p_1), \ldots, (t/y, p_k)\}$, let $\psi\theta \in \rho(\psi)$.*
- *6. Let $L = p(y, \ldots, y)$ or $L = \neg p(y, \ldots, y)$ be a literal with new variable y. Then for $j = 1, \ldots, m$, let $\phi_j \in \rho(\psi)$ be defined by adding an e-literal, i.e. $\phi_j = \exists y q_1 x_1 \ldots q_n x_n \, C_1 \wedge \ldots \wedge (C_j \vee L) \ldots \wedge C_m$.*

The last item has to do with eu-substitutions:

- *7. Let $x \in \text{eVar}(\psi)$ and $y \in \text{uVar}(\psi)$ and suppose x comes before y in $Q(\psi)$. For the elementary eu-substitution $\theta = \{(x, y)\}$, let $\psi\theta \in \rho(\psi)$*

Theorem 3. *If $\phi \in \rho(\psi)$, then $\psi \models \phi$, i.e. ρ is a downward refinement operator.*

5 The Completeness of the Refinement Operator ρ

In this section we will show that the refinement operator ρ is *weakly complete* in S. That is to say, for every ϕ in S, there is a finite refinement chain from $\top$ to ϕ. We show this by the following steps. Example 3 will illustrate these steps more concretely.

1. Replace every existential variable in $M(\phi)$ by a new constant not in ϕ and remove all the existential variables from $Q(\phi)$. Let the new PCNF be ψ. Then the variables in ψ are universally quantified. Let $M(\psi) = C_1 \wedge C_2 \dots \wedge C_m$. We have then $\square$ subsumes C_i ($\square \succeq C_i$) for all i.
2. Similar to a result about the classic refinement refinement operator [S81,NW97], we can prove that there is a chain from $\square$ to every C_i. The combination of these chains will give a chain from $\top$ to ψ.
3. By using the elementary e-substitutions (item 4 of ρ) we can change the constant occurrences in ψ back to existential variables. This establishes a refinement chain from ψ to ϕ' which looks almost like ϕ but all existential variables appear before the universal variables.
4. Using eu-substitutions (item 7 of ρ) we can move the existential variables to the right places in the prenex. This means there is a chain from ϕ' to ϕ. Thus we have the weak completeness of ρ.

Example 3. We will give an example to show what a concrete finite chain from $\top$ to a given $\phi = \forall x \exists y ((\neg p(x) \vee q(f(x)) \vee q(y)) \wedge r(y, a))$ looks like. Note that the chain is not unique. Such a chain exists for a general ϕ (Theorem 4) because of the following lemmas. We use an arrow $\xrightarrow{n}$ to denote a refinement step which uses the n-th item of ρ.

$$\square \xrightarrow{3} \forall x \neg p(x) \xrightarrow{3,3,3}$$
$$\forall x \forall u \forall v \forall w \forall w'((\neg p(x) \vee p(u) \vee q(v)) \wedge r(w, w') \xrightarrow{2}$$
$$\forall x \forall u_1 \forall v \forall w \forall w'((\neg p(x) \vee p(f(u_1)) \vee q(v)) \wedge r(w, w') \xrightarrow{1,1}$$
$$\forall x \forall v \forall w'(\neg p(x) \vee p(f(x)) \vee q(v)) \wedge r(v, w') \xrightarrow{2,2}$$
$$\psi = \forall x(\neg p(x) \vee p(f(x)) \vee q(b)) \wedge r(b, a)) \xrightarrow{5}$$
$$\phi' = \exists y \forall x(\neg(p(x) \vee p(f(x)) \vee q(y)) \wedge r(y, a) \xrightarrow{7}$$
$$\phi = \forall x \exists y(\neg p(x) \vee p(f(x)) \vee q(y)) \wedge r(y, a)$$

Lemma 6. *Let C be a universally quantified clause. Then there is a finite chain of refinements from $\square$ to C.*

Lemma 7. *Let $\psi = Q(\psi)M(\psi)$ be a universally quantified PCNF. Then there is a finite ρ-chain from $\top$ to ψ.*

Lemma 8. *Let $\phi = \exists y_1 \dots \exists y_n \forall x_1 \dots \forall x_m M(\phi)$ whose existential variables in the prenex appear before the universal variables. Let $b_1, \dots, b_n$ be different constants which do not appear in ϕ. Let the universally quantified ψ be ϕ after replacing variable y_i by b_i. Then there is a finite ρ-chain from ψ to ϕ.*

Theorem 4. *Given $\phi = Q(\phi)M(\phi)$, there is a finite ρ-chain from $\top$ to ϕ.*

6 Learning PCNF in Practice

Based on the refinement operator given in the previous sections, we have extended a simple version of the Claudien system (see [RD97]) to a learning system PCL (abbreviation of *PCNF Claudien*), and implemented it in Prolog. These two systems use *learning by interpretations*[R97]. They learn actually a set of regularities such that they are true in the interpretations. For instance, the integrity constraint about the suppliers in section 1 can be considered as a regularity in the database although these clauses of regularities do not imply any ground atom (see Introduction for examples which are presented as ground atoms).

Claudien learns a universal clausal theory w.r.t. a set of positive examples (interpretations), such that each example is a model of the theory. This clausal theory can be considered as a set of regularities (or integrity constraints) satisfied by these examples. PCL is able to learn a PCNF which is more expressive.

Consider a finite set of scenes (*bongard interpretations*) as positive examples. A scene contains several figures: each figure has properties like *shape, size,...* and these figures are related to each other indicated by *in, above, left_of,....* Claudien is able to find things like: $\forall x \forall y (shape(y, circle) \leftarrow figure(x), figure(y), in(x, y))$, i.e., for every figure x and y in a scene, when x is inside y, then y must be a circle. The following rule cannot be found by Claudien, but PCL can: $\forall x \exists y ((in(x, y) \leftarrow shape(x, triangle)) \wedge shape(y, circle))$, each triangle is in at least one circle.

To extend Claudien towards PCL, several issues have to be addressed. In the following subsections we discuss the most important ones.

6.1 Testing interpretation in a search space

In Claudien, a clause *head ← body* is true for an example if the Prolog query $? - body, not(head)$ fails for that example. This works only if the clauses are *range restricted*, meaning that all variables in the head should also occur in the body. Indeed, consider a Herbrand interpretation $I = \{p(a, b), q(a)\}$ and $\phi = \forall x \forall y (p(x, y) \leftarrow q(x))$. ϕ is false because $p(a, a) \leftarrow q(a)$ is false. We get *No* as the answer of the query because there is a refutation of $false \leftarrow p(x, y)$ and $p(x, y) \leftarrow q(x)$.

For PCL, we also consider range restricted PCNFs. The following definition can be found in [N82]: a PCNF ϕ in S is *range restricted* iff

- If $x \in uVar(\phi)$ and x is in a positive literal of a clause C (in $head(C)$) in $M(\phi)$, then x must also appear in a negative literal of C (in $body(C)$).
- If $x \in eVar(\phi)$ and x is in a negative literal of a clause C (in $body(C)$) in $M(\phi)$, then there is a clause D in $M(\phi)$ with only positive literals (no body) such that x appears in every literal in D (in every atom of $head(D)$).

Intuitively, a range restricted formula is structured in such a way that for an interpretation, the range of a variable is restricted to the elements defined by some other relations in the same formula. For example, $\exists x (false \leftarrow p(x)))$ is not range restricted. To test this kind of rule, we need an explicit domain for the variable x. Let $\phi = \forall x \exists y (r(y) \wedge (q(x) \leftarrow p(x,y)))$ and $I = \{q(a), r(a), p(b,a)\}$. Then ϕ is range restricted. To check if I is a model of ϕ, we need only to consider y where $r(y)$ is true, i.e. $\{y/a\}$.

A **search space** S for PCL consists of range restricted, function free PCNFs (the only functions are constants). Moreover, in a PCNF there are upper bounds for clauses in a matrix, literals in each clause, constants and variables, hence S is a finite set. The search space is further restricted by some language bias. For instance, the types of the arguments of each predicate must be declared. Also, a declaration is necessary for each type for which constants must be generated. This allows for example to specify some types where no constants should be generated,

6.2 The downward refinement operator

For the implementation of the refinement operator ρ, several issues must be addressed.

First, for efficiency it is necessary to optimize the refinement operator. We should try to avoid deriving equivalent PCNF. One way to do this is to define an order in which literals occur in each clause and an order of the clauses. This removes equivalencies obtained by applying assiociativity and commutativity rules. e.g. we can obtain $false \leftarrow p \wedge q$ in two ways: We can start from the empty clause $false$, first add p to obtain $false \leftarrow p$ and then add q to obtain $false \leftarrow p \wedge q$. We could also first add q to obtain $false \leftarrow q$ and then add p to obtain $false \leftarrow q \wedge p$ but the latter is not allowed because p comes alphabetically before q. Such orders are also considered in Claudien using the DLAB language bias.

Second, we need to address the following problem: For every i-th clause in a matrix with $n(\geq i)$ clauses, we can start from the conjunction of i empty clauses Thus we have to search n trees. The computational cost of searching in the i-th tree grows very fast as i increases. We can solve this problem partially by reusing the formulas we have found. If $q_1 x_1 ... q_k x_k C_1 \wedge .. \wedge C_{i-1} \wedge C_i$ is a PCNF with i clauses which is correct w.r.t. the examples, then $q_1 x_1 ... q_k x_k C_1 \wedge .. \wedge C_{i-1}$ must also be a correct PCNF. To find the correct PCNF with i clauses, we can start from a correct PCNF containing $i-1$ clauses with an extra empty clause added. The refinement operator can be applied again and again until good PCNFs are found.

7 Experiments

In this section we present some experiments which illustrate PCL and show that PCL can learn rules which can not be learned by existing systems that only learn single clauses.

Experiment 1 We considered a set of undirected graphs as positive examples. A possible example:

```
r(a,b).    r(b,a).   r(a,c).   r(c,a).
r(a,d).    r(d,a).   r(e,a).   r(a,e).
```

Every graph had the property that each point was connected to at least one other point. PCL found this and also some other rules:

$$\forall x\forall y(r(x,y) \leftarrow r(y,x)), \quad \forall x\exists y(r(x,y) \leftarrow \text{point}(x))$$

Note that the last PCNF is made range restricted by adding a predicate *point*. PCL automatically makes PCNF formulas range restricted by using the language bias and the definitions of the domain predicates.

Experiment 2 We also did an experiment on some *bongard-like* examples mentioned at the beginning of last section. These are scenes of figures (in this case triangles and circles) which are related to each another. One example is

```
figure(a).  figure(b).   figure(c).   figure(d),
in(a,b).     in(c,b),
shape(a,triangle). shape(c,triangle). shape(b,circle). shape(d,circle).
```

The search space is large and many correct formulas are possible. This means that, even more than the case of Claudien, many trivial rules are found which do not give much new knowledge:

$$\exists x(\text{shape}(x,\text{triangle})), \quad \exists x\exists y(\text{in}(x,y)),$$
$$\exists y(\text{figure}(y) \wedge (\text{false} \leftarrow \text{shape}(y,\text{triangle}))).$$

After the search continued for some time, more interesting results were given, such as:

$$\forall x\exists y(\text{shape}(y,\text{circle})\wedge (\text{in}(x,y) \leftarrow \text{shape}(x,\text{triangle})).$$

8   Conclusion and Future Work

As we know, every closed formula is equivalent to a PCNF but not necessarily its Skolem standard form. Until now we consider in ILP almost exclusively conjunctions of universally quantified clauses, especially Horn clauses. To add expressiveness we should consider PCNF in general.

If we want to extend refinement operators from sets of clauses to sets of PCNF, we should first extend substitutions to PCNF. In this article we have defined the substitutions which specialize a given PCNF. Elementary substitutions and adding literals can be used to define a refinement operator ρ which is weakly complete. Notice that we have not used items 5 and 6 in ρ for weak completeness. In a set of formulas ordered by some kind of generalization, a refinement operator is *complete* if there is a refinement chain from ψ to ϕ whenever ψ is more general than ϕ. For example, item 5 is needed when we consider $\psi = \exists x\, p(x,x)$ and $\phi = \exists x\exists y\, p(x,y)$. We would like to know more about the search spaces where ρ is complete and the relation between item 5, 6 and the completeness.

This article not only lays a theoretical foundation for PCNF learning systems but also demonstrates a simple system PCL which is already implemented. This system deals with a finite search space of function free and range restricted PCNF.

References

[R97]   L. De Raedt, Logical settings for concept learning, AI Journal, 95:187-201, 1997.

[RD97]   L. De Raedt and L. Dehaspe, Clausal discovery, *Machine Learning*, 26:99-146, 1997.

[GF96]   M. Goncalves and C. Froidevaux, A new formalism to integrate quantification in inductive processes, *Proceedings of ILP96*, S. Muggleton (ed.) Vol. 1314 of LNAI series, 1997, Springer, Berlin.

[LN94]   P. van der Laag and S. H. Nienhuys-Cheng, Existence and nonexistence of complete refinement operators, *Proceedings of ECML94*, Vol. 784 of LNAI series, F. Bergadano and L. De Raedt (eds.). Springer-Verlag, Berlin, 1994.

[N82]   J.-M. Nicolas, Logic for Improving Integrity Checking in Relational Data Bases, *Informatica*, 1982, Springer-Verlag.

[NLR99]   S. H. Nienhuys-Cheng, W. Van Laer, L. De Raedt, *Substitutions and Refinement operator for PCNF*, Work Report, EUR-FEW-CS-99-03.

[NW97]   S. H. Nienhuys-Cheng and R. de Wolf, *Foundations of Inductive Logic Programming*, LNAI Tutorial 1228, Springer-Verlag, 1997.

[S81]   E. Y. Shapiro, *Inductive inference of theories from facts*. Research Report 192, Yale University, 1981.

Theory Recovery

Rupert Parson[1], Khalid Khan[1], and Stephen Muggleton[2]

[1] Oxford University Computing Laboratory, UK
[rupert.parson,khalid.khan]@comlab.ox.ac.uk
[2] Department of Computer Science, University of York, UK
stephen@cs.york.ac.uk

Abstract. In this paper we examine the problem of repairing incomplete background knowledge using *Theory Recovery*. Repeat Learning under ILP considers the problem of updating background knowledge in order to progressively increase the performance of an ILP algorithm as it tackles a sequence of related learning problems. Theory recovery is suggested as a suitable mechanism. A bound is derived for the performance of theory recovery in terms of the information content of the missing predicate definitions. Experiments are described that use the *logical back-propagation* ability of Progol 5.0 to perform theory recovery. The experimental results are consistent with the derived bound.

1 Introduction

In a previous paper [1], the authors described an extension of the standard machine learning framework, called *repeat learning*. In this framework, the learner is not trying to learn a single concept, but a series of related concepts, all drawn independently from the same distribution $\mathcal{D}$. A finite sequence of examples is provided for each concept in the series. The learner does not initially know $\mathcal{D}$, but progressively updates a posterior estimation of $\mathcal{D}$ as the series progresses.

Under Inductive Logic Programming (ILP) [6], the learner's estimation of $\mathcal{D}$ depends on the linguistic bias conveyed by his hypothesis language. The ILP learner can therefore alter the estimation of $\mathcal{D}$ by making changes to the hypothesis language. The previous paper [1] discussed a mechanism for this process that adjusted the background knowledge using predicate invention.

One can quantify the expected performance of an ILP algorithm by bounding the expected error of a hypothesis formed given the number of examples seen. Previous bounds for Progol [3, 4] have only considered the situation in which the learner knows the distribution $\mathcal{D}$. In this paper, we construct a bound for the case when the learner's estimate is incorrect. Significantly, this bound describes the difference between the estimate and the true distribution $\mathcal{D}$ in terms of the missing information content in the hypothesis language used by the learner.

Theory recovery is the process of adjusting, or completing background knowledge. In theory recovery, an incomplete logic program is reconstructed on the basis of examples. The examples indicate the desired behaviour of a particular predicate in the program, defined in terms of the background knowledge. A new version of the ILP algorithm Progol, version 5.0, uses *logical back-propagation* to perform theory recovery.

The paper is structured as follows. Section 2 describes the formulation of the new expected error bound, with its proof given in Appendix C. Section 3 describes experiments that give results that are consistent with this bound. A complete set of results is given in Appendix A. Finally, our conclusions are drawn in Section 4. Appendix B briefly describes the mechanics of logical back-propagation in Progol 5.0.

2 A Theory Recovery Error Bound

It was shown in [5] that under suitable assumptions the class of all polynomial time-bounded logic programs is (U-)learnable. In [4] explicit upper bounds were given for the error of a Progol-like learning algorithm. The paper considered the case of positive-only learning compared to the more traditional positive and negative setting. In both cases upper bounds on expected error were derived showing that learning could be efficiently achieved. However under both models a strong assumption was made: that the learner knows the prior distribution (used by the teacher) over hypotheses. Clearly there is no reason why this should in general be true. In particular, in the following result we assume that the background knowledge of the learner is missing some predicate(s) contained in the target concept. In Subsection 2.1 we review the average case Bayesian model of learning used in [4] to analyse the expected error of a Progol-like learner. In Subsection 2.2 we modify the model by assuming that the learner is not in command of the correct prior distribution and derive adjusted upper bounds.

2.1 Known Prior

The following is a version of the U-learnability framework presented in [5] and restated in [4].

The Model X is taken to be a countable class of instances and $\mathcal{H} \subseteq 2^X$ to be a countable class of concepts. D_X and $D_{\mathcal{H}}$ are probability distributions over X and $\mathcal{H}$ respectively. The teacher randomly chooses a target theory T from $D_{\mathcal{H}}$ then randomly and independently chooses a series of examples $E = \langle x_1, \ldots, x_m \rangle$ from D_X and classifies them according to T.

Given E, $D_{\mathcal{H}}$ and D_X a learner L outputs a hypothesis $H \in \mathcal{H}$. The error of the hypothesis is measured as $D_X(H \setminus T) + D_X(T \setminus H)$.

The hypotheses in $\mathcal{H}$ are assumed to be ordered according to decreasing prior probability as $H_1, H_2, \ldots$. The distribution $D_{\mathcal{H}}(H_i) = \frac{a}{i^2}$ is assumed, where $a = 6/\pi^2$ is a normalising constant. This is similar to the prior probability assumptions used in Progol 4.1 [3]. This distribution is a smoothed version of the *universal distribution*[1] which assigns equal probability to the 2^b hypotheses describable in b bits, where the sum of the probabilities of such hypotheses is 2^{-b}.

Expected Error The following theorem (stated and proved in [4]) gives an upper bound on the expected error of an algorithm which learns by maximising the Bayes' posterior probability over the initial am hypotheses within the space.

Theorem 1. *Let X be a countable instance space and $\mathcal{H} \subseteq 2^X$ be a countable hypothesis space containing at least all finite subsets of X. Let $D_{\mathcal{H}}$, D_X be probability distributions over $\mathcal{H}$ and X. Assume that $\mathcal{H}$ has an ordering $H_1, H_2, \ldots$ such that $D_{\mathcal{H}}(H_i) \geq D_{\mathcal{H}}(H_j)$ for all $j > i$. Let $D_{\mathcal{H}}(H_i) = \frac{a}{i^2}$ where $\frac{1}{a} = \sum_{i=1}^{\infty} \frac{1}{i^2} = \frac{\pi^2}{6}$. Let $\mathcal{H}_n = \{H_i : H_i \in \mathcal{H} \text{ and } i \leq n\}$. T is chosen randomly from $D_{\mathcal{H}}$. Let $ex(x, H) = \langle x, v \rangle$ where $v = \text{True}$ if $x \in H$ and $v = \text{False}$ otherwise. Let $E = \langle ex(x_1, T), \ldots, ex(x_m, T) \rangle$ where each x_i is chosen randomly and independently from D_X. $H_E = \{x : \langle x, \text{True} \rangle \in E\}$. Hypothesis H is said to be consistent with E if and only if $x_i \in H$ for each $\langle x_i, \text{True} \rangle$ in E and $x_j \notin H$ for each $\langle x_j, \text{False} \rangle$ in E. Let $n = am$. L is the following learning algorithm. If there are no hypotheses $H \in \mathcal{H}_n$ consistent with E then $L(E) = H_E$. Otherwise $L(E) = H_n(E) = H$ only if $H \in \mathcal{H}_n$, H consistent with E and for all $H' \in \mathcal{H}_n$ consistent with E it is the case that $D_{\mathcal{H}}(H) \geq D_{\mathcal{H}}(H')$. The error of a hypothesis H is defined as $Error(H, T) = D_X(T \setminus H) + D_X(H \setminus T)$. The expected error of L after m examples, $EE(m)$, satisfies:*

$$EE(m) \leq \frac{1.51 + 2\ln m}{m} \tag{1}$$

2.2 Unknown Prior

We consider an extension of the above model. Previously it was assumed that the learner knew precisely the distribution $D_{\mathcal{H}}$ from which the target concepts were drawn. Clearly there is no reason why this should hold in practical machine learning situations. We now relax this assumption and consider what happens to the expected error of learning when the learner does not know the exact distribution $D_{\mathcal{H}}$. In particular we consider an incorrect prior over hypotheses induced by incomplete background knowledge.

The Modified Model We assume the existence of a universal linguistic bias generator G that, given a target space $\mathcal{H}$, and an hypothesis language B for it, returns a probability distribution $D_{\mathcal{H}} = G(\mathcal{H}, B)$ over the target space. Occam's razor can be taken as an example of such a generator, that always gives a distribution that assigns a higher probability to hypotheses that can be expressed more simply in the hypothesis language.

---

[1] If we take the universal distribution to be $u(\mathcal{H}_n) = 2^{-2\lfloor \log_2(n+1) \rfloor}$ then the probability of the 2^nth hypothesis is $u(\mathcal{H}_{2^n}) = 2^{-2n} = \frac{1}{(2^n)^2}$. So $\frac{a}{i^2}$ is a smoothed and renormalised version of u.

The teacher selects the target concept from $\mathcal{H}$ according to the distribution D_T. The learner's imperfect hypothesis language $B_{\mathcal{L}}$ induces an incorrect probability distribution $D_{\mathcal{L}} = G(\mathcal{H}, B_{\mathcal{L}})$. We assume the existence of some set of predicate definitions P such that $G(\mathcal{H}, (B_{\mathcal{L}} \cup P)) = D_T$. In other words a set of "missing" predicates, that, if added to the background knowledge of the learning algorithm, would mean that the the learner's induced distribution $D_{\mathcal{L}}$ would be the correct one. The hypotheses in $\mathcal{H}$ are ordered by the teacher according to decreasing prior probability $D_T(H_i) = \frac{a}{i^2}$ as $H_1, H_2, \ldots, H_i, \ldots$. The learner only has partial information about this ordering in that its prior is a corrupted version of the teachers distribution. In particular, there is a set of hypotheses $\mathcal{H}_P \subseteq \mathcal{H}$ for which $H \in \mathcal{H}_P \Leftrightarrow D_T(H) > D_{\mathcal{L}}(H)$. Let the information content in bits (see, for example [8]) of an hypothesis relative to a distribution D be given by $\mathrm{info}_D(H) = -\log_2(D(H))$. The information content of $H \in \mathcal{H}_P$ under the learner's distribution $D_{\mathcal{L}}$ is more (in bits) than the information that would be assigned under the teacher's distribution D_T.

Lemma 1. $H \in \mathcal{H}_P$ *is given different indices H_i and H_j under the orderings induced by D_T and $D_{\mathcal{L}}$. Assume that the learner's prior distribution satisfies $D_{\mathcal{L}}(H_j) = \frac{a}{j^2}$. If the information content of the "missing" predicates in P is at most k bits, then for any hypothesis $H \in \mathcal{H}$ the indices i and j satisfy $j \leq 2^{k/2} i$.*

Proof. If $H \in \mathcal{H}_P$, then

$$k \geq \mathrm{info}_{D_{\mathcal{L}}}(H) - \mathrm{info}_{D_T}(H) = -\log_2 D_{\mathcal{L}}(H) + \log_2 D_T(H)$$

$$= -\log_2 \frac{a}{j^2} + \log_2 \frac{a}{i^2} = 2\log_2 j - 2\log_2 i = 2\log_2 \frac{j}{i}$$

Therefore $j \leq 2^{k/2} i$. Clearly, if $H \notin \mathcal{H}_P$, then $j \leq i \leq 2^{k/2} i$.

Expected Error

Theorem 2. *Let X be a countable instance space and $\mathcal{H} \subseteq 2^X$ be a countable hypothesis space containing at least all finite subsets of X. Assume the existence of a universal linguistic bias generator G that, given a target space $\mathcal{H}$, and an hypothesis language B for it, returns a probability distribution $D_{\mathcal{H}} = G(\mathcal{H}, B)$ over the target space. Let D_X be a probability distribution over X. Let D_T, $D_{\mathcal{L}}$ be probability distributions over $\mathcal{H}$, where $D_{\mathcal{L}} = G(\mathcal{H}, B_{\mathcal{L}})$ is the probability distribution induced by the learners hypothesis language. Assume the existence of some set of predicate definitions P such that $G(\mathcal{H}, (B_{\mathcal{L}} \cup P)) = D_T$. Let the information content of the predicate definitions P be at most k bits. Assume that $\mathcal{H}$ has an ordering $H_1, H_2, \ldots, H_i, \ldots$ such that $D_T(H_i) \geq D_T(H_{i+1})$ for all i and an ordering $H'_1, H'_2, \ldots, H'_j, \ldots$ such that $D_{\mathcal{L}}(H'_j) \geq D_{\mathcal{L}}(H'_{j+1})$ for all j. Assume $D_T(H_i) = \frac{a}{i^2}$, and $D_{\mathcal{L}}(H'_j) = \frac{a}{j^2}$, where $\frac{1}{a} = \sum_{i=1}^{\infty} \frac{1}{i^2} = \pi^2/6$. Let $\mathcal{H}'_n = \{H'_i : H'_i \in \mathcal{H} \text{ and } i \leq n\}$. T is chosen randomly from D_T. Let $ex(x, H) = \langle x, v \rangle$ where $v = True$ if $x \in H$ and $v = False$ otherwise. Let $E = \langle ex(x_1, T), \ldots, ex(x_m, T) \rangle$ where each x_i is chosen randomly and independently* from D_X. $H_E = \{x : \langle x, True \rangle \in E\}$. Hypothesis H is said to be consistent with E if and only if $x_i \in H$ for each $\langle x_i, True \rangle$ in E and $x_j \notin H$ for each $\langle x_j, False \rangle$ in E. Let $n = am$. L is the following learning algorithm. If there are no hypotheses $H \in \mathcal{H}'_n$ consistent with E then $L(E) = H_E$. Otherwise $L(E) = H_n(E) = H$ only if $H \in \mathcal{H}'_n$, H consistent with E and for all $H' \in \mathcal{H}'_n$ consistent with E it is the case that $D_{\mathcal{L}}(H) \geq D_{\mathcal{L}}(H')$. The error of an hypothesis H is defined as $Error(H,T) = D_X(T \setminus H) + D_X(H \setminus T)$. The expected error of L after m examples, $EE(m)$, satisfies:

$$EE(m) \leq \frac{1.51 + 2\ln m + k\ln 2}{m} \tag{2}$$

Proof. Given in Appendix C

3 Experiments

To confirm the assumptions given to derive the bound given in Equation 2, the following experiments were devised and run. The experiments made use of the *logical back-propagation* abilities of Progol 5.0. This ILP algorithm uses an augmented version of Inverse entailment that includes the completion of background knowledge in the generalisation process. The mechanism is described in Appendix B.

The aim of the experiments were to determine how the accuracy of the logic program would be affected by having a percentage of the clauses of the program removed, and then using Progol 5.0 to repair the program, given a varying number of examples.

3.1 The Experimental Domain

The experiments are conducted in an artificial domain, called the *base-n-string* domain. The elements of the domain are strings in base n, where $n \in \{2, 3, 4, 5\}$, of length up to a maximum value l.

The target program has a distinct predicate for each distinct length of string. The predicate that defines strings of length m is defined in terms of the predicate that defines strings of length $m - 1$. This means that a missing clause definition for a predicate defining strings of length m will affect the definition of all strings of length greater than m. Table 1.1 shows the program for the binary case - that is, $n = 2$ where $l = 10$.

The maximum string length l was determined by restricting the total number of clauses in the logic program to be 20. For the cases $n = 2, 4, 5$, this gave values $l = 10, 5, 4$ respectively. For the case $n = 3$, the value $l = 7$ was chosen, and then one of the definitions for p7/1 was excluded from the program.

3.2 Method

In order to be able to encapsulate the entire success set of the logic program, a *meta*-predicate ss/1 was defined. For every predicate pred(X) defined, the

```
p1(zero).
p1(one).
p2(zero(A)) :- p1(A).
p2(one(A)) :- p1(A).
   . . .
p10(zero(A)) :- p9(A).
p10(one(A)) :- p9(A).
```

Base		Clause
n	l	information
2	10	7.64
3	7	7.20
4	5	6.64
5	4	6.32

Table 1.1: The program for base $n = 2$, $l = 10$.

Table 1.2: Information content (in bits, to 2 d.p.) of a single clause in each base.

clause `ss(pred(X)) :- pred(X).` was added to the program. This meant that calling `ss/1` would then return all the ground facts provable in the original logic program.

In the learning sessions under Progol 5.0, `ss/1` was the target to be learned, and the incomplete logic program is given as background knowledge for `ss/1`. The examples given were of the form `ss(fact)` where `fact` is a ground fact that should be provable by the original complete logic program. Logical back-propagation in Progol 5.0 uses these examples to complete any missing predicates in the background knowledge. Notice that only positive examples were used.

A complete program can be used to generate the set of all base-n-strings up to a certain length. An incomplete or partially repaired program will generate only a subset of these strings. Therefore at each stage we were measuring the *coverage* accuracy of the program.

Each run of the experiment was parameterised by two parameters: p, the percentage of the logic program that was deleted, and m, the number of examples seen by Progol 5.0 in order to reconstruct the missing predicates.

A run proceeded as follows:

- The original program (defined in the background knowledge) has p percent of its clauses deleted.
- Measure the accuracy of the program with depleted background knowledge.
- Generate m random examples of the success set of the complete program.
- Run Progol 5.0 with the incomplete program as background knowledge using the generated examples.
- Measure the accuracy of the repaired program.

Each run was repeated 10 times, for each of the possible combinations of values of $p \in \{10, 20, 30, 40, 50, 60, 70, 80, 90, 100\}$ and $m \in \{10, 20, 40, 80, 120, 160\}$, for each of the original logic programs in base $n \in \{2, 3, 4, 5\}$.

3.3 Theoretical Results for the Domain

The theoretical bound 2 requires that one estimates the size in bits of the information content of the missing predicates.

In reconstructing a background clause in base n, Progol 5.0 has a choice of a certain number, l, of predicate symbols for the head, and a choice of the same l

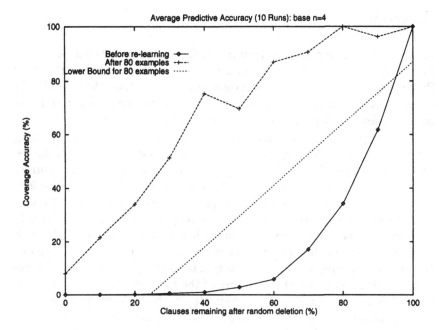

Fig. 1. Experimental result for the case $n = 4, m = 80$. Complete results are shown in appendix A.

predicate symbols for the one atom in the body. It also has a choice of n function symbols to add to the string. (**one**, **two**, etc).

If it is assumed that all of the possible choices are assigned equal probability, then the information content of a single clause of this kind is therefore $\mathrm{info}(n) = \log_2(nl^2)$. The values of this function for the different possible values of n are given in Table 1.2.

The bound on the expected experimental error is then:

$$\mathrm{EE}(m) \leq \frac{1.51 + 2\ln(m) + c.\mathrm{info}(n)\ln(2)}{m}$$

where c is the number of missing clauses.

3.4 Results

A typical result is shown in Figure 1. This graph shows the case that $n = 4, m = 80$. The lower curve is the accuracy of the incomplete logic program before theory recovery. The upper curve is the accuracy of the logic program after theory recovery using m examples. The straight line is the theoretical bound.

As the graph shows, the bound fits the results well, and runs parallel to the observed experimental accuracy. The results for other values of n (the base), and m (the number of examples) are similar. Results for all the values of n and m are given in Appendix A.

The experiments are consistent with the theoretical bound, and the calculation of the information content of clauses in this domain (see Table 1.2).

4 Conclusions

This paper has introduced a theoretical model for analysing learning when performing theory recovery. We derived an average case error bound for the error of a Progol-like learner in such a situation and showed that the bound held and was reasonably tight under experiment. The experiments used logical back-propagation, a feature of Progol 5.0, to perform theory recovery.

This work is part of a wider programme to analyse multiple-task learning within a relational (ILP) setting. In particular, we analyse an issue raised by the *repeat learning* framework introduced in [1], that of learning under an incorrect prior distribution. The experiments differ from those conducted in the previous paper in that theory recovery, rather than predicate invention, is used to alter background knowledge. However the repeat learning framework does not specify the particulars of how the linguistic bias of the learner is to be altered. Although there is no multiple-task learning in this work - we are only ever learning one concept - the link with repeat learning comes in the form of the updating of background knowledge and hence the updating of the linguistic bias of the learner. In both models the learner is missing predicates in the background knowledge. The analysis could easily be extended to the case when one is learning more than one task. This would be the natural direction in which to extend the research.

Acknowledgements

Rupert Parson would like to thank the William Esson Bequest Fund, by whom he is partially funded. Khalid Khan would like to thank his parents. This work was supported partly by the Esprit Long Term Research Action ILP II (project 20237) and EPSRC grant GR/K57985 on Experiments with Distribution-based Machine Learning.

References

1. K. M. Khan, S. H. Muggleton, and R. D. G. Parson. Repeat learning using predicate invention. In David Page, editor, *Proceedings of the Eighth International Conference on Inductive Logic Programming*, volume 1446 of *LNAI*, pages 165–174, Madison, Wisconsin, USA, 1998. Springer.
2. S. Moyle and S. H. Muggleton. Learning programs in the event calculus. In Nada Lavrač and Sašo Džeroski, editors, *Proceedings of the Seventh International Conference on Inductive Logic Programming*, volume 1297 of *LNAI*, pages 205–212, Prague, Czech Republic, September 1997. Springer.
3. S. H. Muggleton. Inverse entailment and progol. *New Generation Computing*, 13:245–286, 1995.
4. S. H. Muggleton. Learning from positive data. In *Proceedings of the Sixth Workshop on Inductive Logic Programming*, Stockholm, 1996.
5. S. H. Muggleton and C. D. Page. A learnability model for universal representations. Technical report, Oxford University Computing Laboratory, Oxford, UK, 1997.

6. S. H. Muggleton and L. De Raedt. Inductive logic programming: theory and methods. *Journal of Logic Programming*, 19,20:629–679, 1994.
7. M. E. Stickel. A prolog technology theorem prover: a new exposition and implementation in prolo. *Theoretical Computer Science*, 104(1):109–128, 1992.
8. D. Welsh. *Codes and Cryptography*. Oxford Science Publications. Oxford University Press, 1989.

A Experimental Results

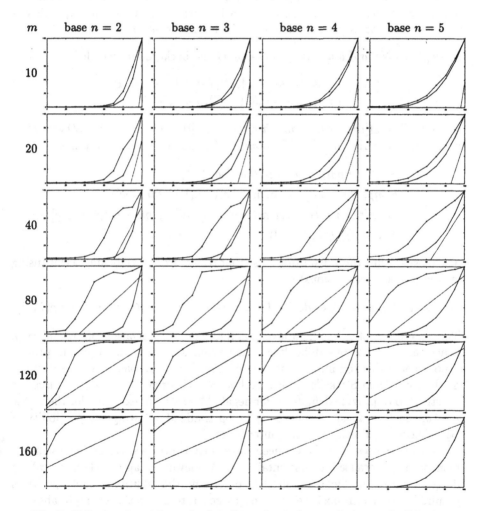

Fig. 2. Full experimental results for all numbers of examples m, and all bases n

B Progol 5.0: Theory recovery by Logical Back-propagation

The theory recovery mechanism that is applied to the experiments in the paper is provided by *logical back-propagation* [2], a form of generalised inverse entailment [3]. The problem specification for ILP is: *given* background knowledge B and examples E; *find* the simplest consistent hypothesis H s.t. $B \wedge H \models E$. In the case that both E and H are single Horn clauses then by inverse entailment it is possible to generate the conjunction of all ground literals that are true in all models of $B \wedge \overline{E}$, denoted by $\overline{\bot}$ (i.e. $B \wedge \overline{E} \models \overline{\bot} \models \overline{H}$). In logical back-propagation examples of an observational predicate are used to augment the definition of a related theoretical predicate. In the following, examples of sentences (predicates for s) are used to augment a definition for noun phrase (np).

Example 1. Natural language processing. Given background knowledge

$$B = \begin{cases} s(A,B) \leftarrow np(A,C), vp(C,D), np(D,B) \\ np(A,B) \leftarrow det(A,C), noun(C,B) \end{cases}$$

example $E = s([the, nasty, man, hit, the, dog], [])$, and a prior hypothesis $H = np(A,D) \leftarrow det(A,B), adj(B,C), noun(C,D)$ then by inverse entailment

$$\overline{\bot} = \neg s([the, nasty, man, hit, the, dog], [])$$
$$\wedge \neg np([the, nasty, man, hit, the, dog], [hit, the, dog])$$
$$\wedge det([the, nasty, man, hit, the, dog], [nasty, man, hit, the, dog])$$
$$\wedge \ldots \wedge np([the, dog], [])$$

The most specific (non-definite) clause that results from variablising terms (using guided y mode declarations) is

$$\bot = s(A,B); np(A,C) \leftarrow det(A,D), adj(D,E), noun(E,C), vp(C,F), np(F,B)$$

The generation of $\overline{\bot}$ in the above example requires derivation of $\neg s$ and $\neg vp$, which leads to obvious difficulties when using a Horn clause theorem prover. To overcome this the implementation of logical back-propagation makes use of mechanisms from Stickel's Prolog Technology Theorem Prover [7]. Clauses are constructed to provide definitions for negated literals. For example, for the clause $p \leftarrow q$, the *contrapositive* clause $\neg q \leftarrow \neg p$ is added, allowing the possibility of $\neg q$ being derived using a Prolog interpreter.

Not all clauses of a theory need have their contrapositive added when implementing generalised inverse entailment. A relevance map based on the calling diagram among predicates is used to determine the additional contrapositives required. The contrapositive required to generate $\bot$ for the example above is $\neg np(A,C) \leftarrow \neg s(A,B), vp(C,D), np(D,B)$. This enables the derivation of $\neg np$ for the generalisation of $\bot$. The theoretical and observational predicates involved in the generalisations are communicated by the user to Progol 5.0 by way of mode declarations.

C   Proof of Theorem 2

Proof. For all $H_i \in \mathcal{H}_P$,

$$D_T(H_i) = \frac{a}{i^2} \leq \frac{a}{(j^2/2^k)} = \frac{a2^k}{j^2} \text{ Since } j \leq 2^{k/2} i.$$

So for the learner's ordering over hypotheses :

$$\sum_{j \geq n+1}^{\infty} D_T(H'_j) \leq \sum_{j \geq n+1}^{\infty} \frac{a2^k}{j^2} \leq \int_{j \geq n}^{\infty} \frac{a2^k}{j^2} \, dj = \left[-\frac{a2^k}{j} \right]_{j=n}^{\infty} = \frac{a2^k}{n}$$

The proof now proceeds in a similar manner to the proof of Theorem 1 given in [4].

$$EE(m) = \sum_{T \in \mathcal{H}} D_T(T) \sum_{E \in T^m} D_X(E|T) Error(L(E), T)$$

$$\leq \sum_{T \in \mathcal{H}'_n} D_T(T) \sum_{E \in T^m} D_X(E|T) Error(H'_n(E), T) + \sum_{T \in \mathcal{H} \backslash \mathcal{H}'_n} D_T(T).1$$

$$\leq \sum_{T \in \mathcal{H}'_n} D_T(T) \sum_{E \in T^m} D_X(E|T) Error(H'_n(E), T) + \frac{a2^k}{n}$$

Let $\tau_{mn}(\epsilon) = \{E' : E' \in T^m \text{ and } Error(H'_n(E'), T) \leq \epsilon\}$. Then:

$$\sum_{T \in \mathcal{H}'_n} D_T(T) \sum_{E \in T^m} D_X(E|T) Error(H'_n(E), T)$$

$$= \sum_{T \in \mathcal{H}'_n} D_T(T) \sum_{E \in \tau_{mn}(\epsilon)} D_X(E|T) Error(H'_n(E), T)$$

$$+ \sum_{T \in \mathcal{H}'_n} D_T(T) \sum_{E \in T^m \backslash \tau_{mn}(\epsilon)} D_X(E|T) Error(H'_n(E), T)$$

$$\leq \epsilon + Pr(\exists H \in \mathcal{H}'_n : Error(H, T) > \epsilon \text{ and } x_1, \ldots, x_m \in T \cap H)$$

$$\leq \epsilon + n e^{-\epsilon m}$$

Thus,

$$EE(m) = \epsilon + n e^{-\epsilon m} + \frac{a2^k}{n}$$

Optimal values of n and ϵ are found by successively setting to zero the partial derivatives of n, ϵ and solving. This gives $\epsilon = \frac{\ln mn}{m}$ and $n = 2^k am$. Substituting gives

$$EE(m) \leq \frac{2 + k \ln 2 + 2 \ln m + \ln a}{m} < \frac{1.51 + 2 \ln m + k \ln 2}{m}$$

Instance Based Function Learning

Jan Ramon and Luc De Raedt

Katholieke Universiteit Leuven, Department of Computer Science
Celestijnenlaan 200A, B-3001 Heverlee, Belgium
{janr,lucdr}@cs.kuleuven.ac.be

Abstract. The principles of instance based function learning are presented. In IBFL one is given a set of positive examples of a functional predicate. These examples are true ground facts that illustrate the input output behaviour of the predicate. The purpose is then to predict the output of the predicate given a new input. Further assumptions are that there is no background theory and that the inputs and outputs of the predicate consist of structured terms. IBFL is a novel technique that addresses this problem and that combines ideas from instance based learning, first order distances and analogical or case based reasoning. We also argue that IBFL is especially useful when there is a need for handling complex and deeply nested terms. Though we present the technique in isolation, it might be more useful as a component of a larger system to deal e.g. with the logic, language and learning challenge.

1 Introduction

Within the field of machine learning, both instance based learning [1] and inductive logic programming (or relational learning) [10,9] are important subfields. In instance based learning one tries to predict classes of examples by comparing these examples to other examples from a training set. Most often there is only a finite and small set of discrete classes, and the class can be regarded as a discrete attribute of the examples. Instance based learning (and concept-learning) can be regarded as function learning, where the function takes as input the example description and produces as output the value for the class attribute.

In recent work within the field of inductive logic programming classical propositional instance based learning techniques have been upgraded towards a first order framework. A prominent example of this approach is the RIBL system [2]. RIBL (and other approaches along this line) take as input a first order description of an example and predict the value for the corresponding class attribute. In terms of function learning, RIBL maps complex inputs (example descriptions in first order logic) to simple outputs (the value of the class attribute). From the viewpoint of function learning, one may wonder whether it would be possible to extend this framework to learn more complex functions that would map complex inputs onto complex outputs. Within the framework of computational logic, the inputs and outputs would then naturally correspond to deeply structured terms (cf. e.g. [4]). The technique of IBFL, presented in this paper, addresses precisely this problem. IBFL starts from a set of positive examples of a functional predicate p. The examples are thus of the form $p(in, out)$ where in represents a possibly complex input term and out the corresponding output terms. IBFL is then given a new input terms in' for which it has to compute the corresponding output out' such that $p(in', out')$ holds. IBFL is not given any other information and thus operates with an empty background theory.

This IBFL setting extends the classical first order instance based learning framework. It also provides a framework for studying the issues involved in handling deeply structured terms, which is known to be one of the hard problems in inductive logic programming (cf. e.g. the Project Programme of the ESPRIT IV project on Inductive Logic Programming II). The hardness of this problem is illustrated by the fact that well-known ILP systems are unable to produce good results on the setting mentioned above due to 1) the combinatorics involved in handling deeply structured terms, and 2) the fact that the background theory in IBFL is empty, which makes it necessary to induce recursive hypotheses for defining p. Recursion (and program synthesis) is one of the other known hard problems in ILP. Despite the difficulties involved, many potential applications need to deal with structured terms. One such application is the recent Logic, Language and Learning challenge (cf. [8]) issued by Kazakov, Pulman and Muggleton. We hope that the IBFL framework and its techniques will contribute to a better understanding and possible solutions of these problems. IBFL will therefore also be illustrated on (simple) tasks that are relevant to the LLL challenge as well as to program synthesis.

This paper is organized as follows. In section 2, we review some important aspects of inductive logic programming and instance based learning. In section 3, we state the problem specification. In section 4, we present the base idea of instance based function learning. In section 5, we extend this method with a recursive component that allows to learn the translations of parts of terms. In section 6, we present some experiments, and finally, in section 7, we give some conclusions and possibilities for further work.

2 Preliminaries

A substitution $\theta = \{X_1/Y_1, \ldots, X_n/Y_n\}$ is a set of elements X_i/Y_i such that X_i are variables and Y_i are terms. If t is a term and θ is a substitution, then we can apply θ to t: $t\theta$ is the term t in which each occurrence X_i is simultanuously replaced by Y_i. e.g. if $\theta = \{X/f(a), Y/X\}$ and $t = f(X, Y, g(X))$, then $t\theta = f(f(a), X, g(f(a)))$. If an inverse substitution θ^{-1} is applied to a term s, the result is the set of terms t such that $t\theta = s$. e.g. if $\theta = \{X/a, Y/f(a), Z/a\}$ and $t = g(f(f(a)), a)$, $t\theta^{-1} = \{g(f(f(X)), X), g(f(f(X)), Z), g(f(f(Z)), X),$ $g(f(f(Z)), Z), g(f(Y), X), g(f(Y), Z)\}$. We will use the notion of least general generalization [12]: a term t_1 subsumes (or is more general than) a term t_2 iff there is a substitution θ such that $t_1\theta = t_2$. The subsumes relation induces a partial order on the set of terms. The least upper bound under subsumption is called the least general generalization (lgg).

We also use the notion of *position* as defined in [6]. *Positions* are sequences of positive integers (e.g. [2,3,2]). ϵ denotes the empty position, and $\cdot$ the concatenation operation on positions. With t a term or atom the sub-term of t at position u, t/u is defined as follows:

- If t is a term, then $t/\epsilon = t$.
- if $t = f(t_1, \ldots, t_n)$, then $t/(i \cdot u) = t_i/u$.

In instance based learning a distance is needed between the examples. As we work with structured terms as examples, we must use a distance between terms such as the distances defined in [11], [7], [13], [14]. In this paper we use the simple distance defined in [11]:

Definition 1 (distance d_{nc} between terms). *If t_1 and t_2 are terms, then*

- *if $t_1 = t_2$, $d_{nc}(t_1, t_2) = 0$.*
- *if $t_1 = p(x_1, \ldots, x_n)$ and $t_2 = q(y_1, \ldots, y_m)$ with $p \neq q$ or $n \neq m$, then $d_{nc}(t_1, t_2) = 1$.*
- *if $t_1 = p(x_1, \ldots, x_n)$ and $t_2 = p(y_1, \ldots, y_n)$, then $d_{nc}(t_1, t_2) = \frac{1}{2n} \sum_{i=1}^{n} d_{nc}(x_i, y_i)$.*

e.g. we can compute $d_{nc}(p(f(a), g(h(c), d)), p(f(b), h(e, d))) = \frac{1}{4}(d_{nc}(f(a), f(b)) + d_{nc}(g(h(c), d), h(e, d))) = \frac{1}{4}(\frac{1}{2}d_{nc}(a, b) + 1) = \frac{1}{4}(\frac{1}{2}.1 + 1) = \frac{3}{8}$

3 Problem specification

In this section we state the problem we want to solve. The unknown target predicate represents a function. This means that the examples are ground facts about the input-output behaviour of the predicate. In terms of ILP we have the following problem setting:

Given is:

- an unknown functional target predicate p.
- a set of positive examples (ground facts) for p. In the following we will denote the training examples with $E_i = p(E_{i,in}, E_{i,out})$ with $E_{i,in}$ the input term and $E_{i,out}$ the output term.
- an empty background theory.
- an input term N_{in}.

Find:

- an unknown output N_{out} such that $p(N_{in}, N_{out})$.

Suppose e.g. we have an example $p(in(circle, square), in(square, circle))$, and have to find the output of $in(circle, triangle)$ (see figure 1). The program could then answer $in(triangle, circle)$. This is also an example of learning by analogy (cf. [3]).

4 Instance based function learning

In the attribute-value setting, the process of predicting a class for an example with the k-nearest neighbours method can be divided in three important steps. First, the example input is compared using a distance with all the training example inputs and the k nearest examples are selected. Second, from each of these k nearest examples the class information is extracted. Third, from these k classes the most frequent class is selected and used to predict the example.

Predicting a whole term at once is difficult. For this reason we will only predict one functor at a time. Algorithm 1 is the basic algorithm for this.

We start with a variable (a completely uninstantiated term) as predicted output and we repeatedly apply a substitution of the form $Var/f(Var_1, ..., Var_n)$ to add functors (with variable arguments) until we obtain a ground term. In practice, since it is not always guaranteed that all positions will eventually become ground (by filling them with functors with arity 0 (constants)), a stopping criterion could be used. A good stopping criterion is restricting the maximum number of functors in the predicted output term.

Functors are added using the instance based learning component whose three components we discuss below. We know that algorithm 1 provides a partially instantiated term N_{out}^{tmp} and a position pos such that the sub-term N_{out}^{tmp}/pos at position pos of N_{out}^{tmp} is a variable. Thus the task of this instance based learning component is to (partially) instantiate N_{out}^{tmp}/pos, so we get a better approximation N_{out}^{better} of our prediction N_{out}^* of N_{out}.

First we need to measure the distance between the new example and the training examples. We can use for this the distance d_{nc} given in section 2.

After measuring the distances between the input of the new example and the inputs of all training examples, we can select the k nearest relevant training examples. Whether an example is relevant or not is determined by the possibility of the second step to extract useful information (functors) from that example, as will soon become clear.

In the second step, we must extract information about which functor to predict from the k nearest (relevant) examples. The way this is done is important as this causes the method to be able to transform the structure of terms.

Suppose we must extract information from training example E_i. First the least general generalization under subsumption $G_{in} = \text{lgg}(E_{i,in}, N_{in})$ of the input terms $E_{i,in}$ and N_{in} is computed, together with substitutions θ_e and θ_n such that $G_{in}\theta_e = E_{i,in}$ and $G_{in}\theta_n = N_{in}$ (see also figure 2). Then, we con-

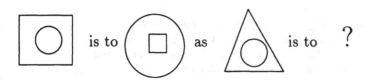

Fig. 1. An example where IBFL could be used to learn by analogy

sider the set $S = E_{i,out}\theta_e^{-1}\theta_n$. Because of the inverse substitution this set can contain several elements. Let then S_1 be the subset of S of all terms t of S such that the functors along the path from the top functor to pos of t and N_{out} are identical. E.g. if $pos = [2, 1, 1]$ and $N_{out} = a(b, c(d(f, g), e))$ and $S = \{a(x, c(d(g, z), e)), a(b, q(d(h, g), e))\}$, then $S_1 = \{a(x, c(d(g, z), e))\}$ (see fig. 3).

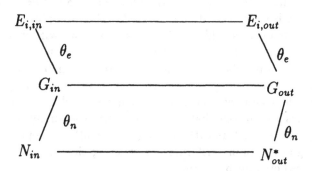

Fig. 2. Step 2 of the instance based learning process

Let then $S_2 = \{t/pos | t \in S_1\}$. In the above example with $pos = [2, 1, 1]$, $S_1 = \{a(x, c(d(g, z), e))\}$, $S_2 = \{g\}$. Note that if t/pos is a variable (which will be possible after the extensions of section 5), this does not add functors to S_2. If S_2 is not empty, then the example is relevant.

So for each relevant example a multi-set of functors is obtained. In the third step then the most frequent occurring functor is predicted.

We illustrate this with a small example. We suppose 1-nearest neighbours is used for simplicity.

Example 1. Suppose we have the following training examples:

```
p(swap(a,b),swapped(b,a)).
p(dontswap(c,d),notswapped(c,d)).
```

We want to know the output of $swap(g, h)$. First set the prediction $N_{out}^* = Var$. We first measure the distances $d_{nc}(swap(g, h), swap(a, b)) = \frac{1}{2}$ and $d_{nc}(swap(g, h),$

Algorithm 1 Base iteration

---

predict_term(N_{in})
    Let $N_{out}^* = A\_New\_Variable$,
    while not(ground(N_{out}^*)) and not(*stoppingcriterion*) do
        Let Pos be a position such that $V = N_{Out}^*/Pos$ is a variable,
        predict_best_functor_at_pos($N_{in}, N_{out}^*, pos, Functor/Arity$),
        $V \leftarrow V\theta$ with $\theta = \{V/Functor(Newvar_1, ..., Newvar_{Arity})\}$
    return N_{out}^*.

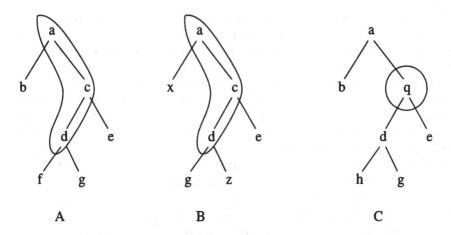

Fig. 3. A and B have equal functors along the path to $[2, 1, 1]$

$dontswap(c, d)) = 1$. So $p(swap(a, b), swapped(b, a))$ is the nearest example. Then the lgg is $G_{in} = swap(X, Y)$ and $\theta_e = \{X/a, Y/b\}$ and $\theta_n = \{X/g, Y/h\}$. Next, $swapped(b, a)\theta_e^{-1}\theta_n = swapped(Y, X)\theta_n = swapped(h, g)$. The main functor of N_{out} is predicted to be $swapped/2$ and we get a more instantiated prediction $N_{out}^* = swapped(\_, \_)$. This is not yet ground: In $swapped(\_, \_)$ positions [1] and [2] are still variables. For this select [1] as the position to be instantiated and again select the nearest training example, recompute G_{in}, θ_e, θ_n which in this case all obtain the same result. Again $swapped(b, a)\theta_e^{-1}\theta_n = swapped(h, g)$, so we predict $N_{out}^*/[1] = h$ and $N_{out}^* = swapped(h, \_)$. Iterating a third time we get $N_{out}^* = swapped(h, g)$. This is fully instantiated, so we predict $swapped(h, g)$ as the output term.

5 Recursive IBFL

The method described in the previous section works fine when the main problem is to transform structure. However, we also want to do more complex things. It can happen that too many examples become irrelevant as the predicted output term becomes more and more instantiated. Consider following training examples:

Example 2.
```
p(dog,chien).     p(house,maison).          p(near,pres).
p(cat,chat).      p(school,ecole).          p(in,dans).
p(place(near,school)              ,lieu(pres,ecole)).
p(walks(dog,place(in,school))     ,court(lieu(dans,ecole),chien)).
p(walks(cat,place(near,school))   ,court(lieu(pres,ecole),chat)).
p(walks(cat,place(in,house))      ,court(lieu(dans,maison),chat)).
p(sleeps(cat,place(near,school)),dort(lieu(pres,ecole),chat)).
```

This example concerns a small translation problem. We would like to predict (i.e. translate) the output of $sleeps(dog, place(in, house))$. However, if we apply the method from the previous section, at some point we get $N_{out}^* = dort(lieu(\_,\_),\_)$ and $pos = [1, 2]$. Now there are no good and relevant examples: e.g. for $p(walks(dog, place(in, school)), court(lieu(dans, ecole), chien))$, we get $G = X$, $\theta_e = \{X/walks(dog, place(in, school))\}$, $\theta_n = \{X/sleeps(dog, place(in, house))\}$ and $court(lieu(dans, ecole), chien)\theta_e^{-1}\theta_n = court(lieu(dans, ecole), chien)$, the main functor is here $court$ while the main functor of N_{out}^* is $dort$, so we can't use this to predict the first argument of $dort$. On the other hand, for the example $p(sleeps(cat, place(in, school)), dort(lieu(dans, ecole), chat))$, we have $G = sleeps(X, place(in, Y))$, $\theta_e = \{X/cat, Y/school\}$, $\theta_n = \{X/dog, Y/house\}$, and $dort(lieu(dans, ecole), chien)\theta_e^{-1}\theta_n = dort(lieu(dans, ecole), chien)$, and so $ecole$ would be predicted.

This is not what is intended as we can intuitively see that the result of the prediction should optimally be $dort(lieu(dans, maison), chien)$.

One solution to this problem is to allow the system to learn from the solution of subproblems (subterms). In the above example, this would mean that we let the system use the 'lexicon' that gives the translations for sub-terms.

To achieve this, we will, before using the instance based learning system of the previous section, add information to the input terms of the examples. An example is given in figure 4. This causes the substitutions that are essential in the prediction process to contain as much information as possible. The algorithm translates now all the subterms of the input term before translating the input term. The translation thus proceeds in a bottom-up fashion, starting at the leaves of the tree and gradually working on larger terms.

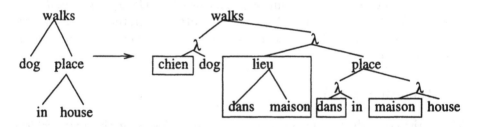

Fig. 4. Additional information for the input term to improve the substitutions

Example 3. What is the effect on example 2?

We can now translate $sleeps(dog, place(in, house))$: First, the input term $sleeps(dog, place(in, house))$ is extended with info on the sub-terms: we therefore first need to solve two other problems: Given input term dog, what is the output term? Given input term $place(in, house)$, what is the output term? We have a training example which gives the translation for dog. We translate $place(in, house)$ recursively: we have training examples for $p(in, dans)$ and $p(house, maison)$, so we get $p(place(in, house), lieu(dans, maison))$. So in our original problem, the extended input term is $(sleeps(dog, house), sleeps(\lambda(chien, dog), \lambda(lieu(dans, maison), place(\lambda(dans, in), \lambda(maison, house)))))$. Now the instance based algorithm is applied. In the first step we get as preliminary prediction $dort(\_,\_)$. Suppose we now fill in the first argument. $p(sleeps(cat, place(in, house)), dort(lieu(dans, maison), chat))$ is a near and relevant example for this. We extend the input term of this training example. We get $(sleeps(cat, place(in, house)), sleeps(\lambda(chat, cat), \lambda(lieu(dans, ecole), place(\lambda(dans, in), \lambda(maison, house)))))$. We get as generalization of the input terms $G = (sleeps(X, house), sleeps(\lambda(V, X), \lambda(lieu(dans, maison), place(\lambda(dans, in), \lambda(maison, house)))))$ with $\theta_e = \{X/cat, V/chat\}$ and $\theta_n = \{X/dog, V/chien\}$. Finally, applying these same substitutions to $dort(lieu(dans, ecole), chat)$, we get $dort(lieu(dans, ecole), chat)\theta_e^{-1}\theta_n = dort(lieu(dans, W), V)\theta_n = dort(lieu(dans, maison), chien)$ which was the correct translation.

This kind of experiment is difficult for classical ILP systems such as Progol. We tried to run this example with Progol but ran into problems of too large search space due to the exponential number of terms (in the size of the examples) in the bottom clause[1].

6 Experiments

We implemented the method described in the previous sections. In this section, we summarize the result of some experiments.

Experiment 1 *Another application where IBFL could be useful is the learning of parsers. e.g. Given an expression such as $+(2, *(4, 5))$, we would like to be able to execute it (compute the result) on a stack-machine. Therefore we need a program such as $[push(2), push(4), push(5), *, +]$ which computes the expression. The IBFL system can learn to do this conversion. Given the following examples:*

```
p(3+(4*2),[push(3),[push(4),push(2),*],+]).
p(5*6,[push(5),push(6),*]).
p(8+9,[push(8),push(9),+]).
p(11,push(11)).
```

The system can correctly predict

```
p((11+12)*(13+14),[[push(11),push(12),+],[push(13),push(14),+],*]).
```

Then after removing the redundant brackets in the output we obtain the desired program. This is possible independently of the complexity of the expressions to convert, as long as sufficient training examples are given, including simple cases (from which the system can learn most unambiguously).

Experiment 2 *We want to learn the induction step of the predicate reverse (see algorithm 2). We can learn this from partial execution traces. The system was given a set of training examples:*

---

[1] James Cussens, personal communication

```
p(reverse([c,d,e],[b,a],Result),reverse([d,e],[c,b,a],Result)).
p(reverse([a,b],[],Result),reverse([b],[a],Result)).
p(reverse([],[z,y,x],Result),Result=[z,y,x]).
p(reverse([r,s,t,u,v],[q,p],Result),
                 reverse([s,t,u,v],[r,q,p],Result)).
```

The p predicate has as first (input) argument the predicate to be executed. The second (output) argument represents what must be done for that. There are two kinds of execution steps: If the output term of p is a simple operation (a unification of the output term with the correct result), this can be done at once. This is the case if the first argument in the call of reverse is []. If the output term of p is a new call to reverse, we can again execute this call by predicting the output of p when this new call is given as input, and so on.

The input of some other steps were given. The system predicted the following outputs correctly:

```
p(reverse([f,g,h,i],[e,d,c],Result),
                 reverse([g,h,i],[f,e,d,c],Result)).
p(reverse([x,y,z],[],Result),reverse([y,z],[x],Result)).
p(reverse([],[z,y,x,w],Result),Result=[z,y,x,w]).
```

The following observations can be made: first, the system could correctly distinguish between the base case (where the first argument is []) and other cases. Second, the only test examples whose output term was predicted incorrectly were the examples with a first argument at least as large as the largest first argument in the training examples. e.g.

```
p(reverse([r,s,t,u,v],[q],Result),reverse([s,t,u,[]],[r,q],Result)).
```

One can conclude from this that the system can learn the induction step of the reverse predicate, but that further work could make it possible to generalize to larger inputs.

When an induction step is learned, this induction step can be applied several times (i.e. the predicted output can be used as input of the next step). If we do this until the result does not contain any further call to reverse, we can compute for all inputs the result of the reverse predicate. This means we can learn the reverse predicate from partial execution traces..

7 Conclusions

We have presented an approach that extends instance based learning to the learning of complex functions from terms to terms, we have argued that IBFL is

---

Algorithm 2 Reverse

```
reverse([X|Y],Z,Result) :-
        reverse(Y,[X|Z],Result).
reverse([],Z,Result) :- Z=Result.
```

---

relevant to the problem of handling deeply structured terms and recursion, and we have illustrated the potential use of IBFL in natural language applications and program synthesis.

We expect that the approach can best be used as a component of a larger system that might use IBFL to compute e.g. the output structure of a clause in a program synthesis application. One current limitation of the technique is its inability to incorporate background knowledge. It may be possible to incorporate background knowledge in the process in similar ways as in RIBL and the framework by Flach et al [4]. This framework encodes examples (and background theory) as structured terms and may therefore be well-suited for IBFL.

IBFL is related to the instance based learning work in ILP (see [1]) it can be considered a form of analogical reasoning (see [3],[5],[15]). Indeed, in analogical and case based reasoning one maps a target problem onto a target solution by using similarities with a source problem with known solution. In IBFL the target problem is the new input term, and the source problems and solutions correspond to the examples of the input-output behaviour of the function.

8 Acknowledgements

Jan Ramon is supported by the Flemish Institute for the Promotion of Science and Technological Research in Industry (IWT). Luc De Raedt is supported by the Fund for Scientific Research (FWO), Flanders. This work is supported by the European community Esprit project no. 20237, Inductive Logic Programming 2. We also thank James Cussens for the many helpful mails about progol.

References

1. D. W. Aha, D. Kibler, and M. K. Albert. Instance-based learning algorithms. *Machine Learning*, 6(1):37–66, January 1991.
2. W. Emde and D. Wettschereck. Relational instance-based learning. In L. Saitta, editor, *Proceedings of the 13th International Conference on Machine Learning*, pages 122–130. Morgan Kaufmann, 1996.
3. Thomas G. Evans. A program for the solution of a class of geometric-analogy intelligence-test questions. In Marvin L. Minsky, editor, *Semantic Information Processing*, pages 271–353. MIT Press, Cambridge, Massachusetts, 1968.
4. P.A. Flach. Strongly typed inductive concept learning. In D. Page, editor, *Proceedings of the 8th International Conference on Inductive Logic Programming*, volume 1446, pages 185–194. Springer-Verlag, 1998.
5. E. Hirowatari and S. Arikawa. Explanation based generalisation by analogical reasoning. In *Proceedings of the 2nd International Workshop on Inductive Logic Programming*. Institute for New Generation Computer Technology, 1992.
6. G. Huet. Confluent reductions: Abstract properties and applications to term rewriting systems. *Journal of the Association for Computing Machinery*, 27(4):797–821, 1980.
7. A. Hutchinson. Metrics on terms and clauses. In *Proceedings of the 9th European Conference on Machine Learning*, Lecture Notes in Artificial Intelligence, pages 138–145. Springer-Verlag, 1997.

8. D. Kazakov, S. Pulman, and S. Muggleton. The fracas dataset and the lll challenge. Technical report, 1998.

9. N. Lavrač and S. Džeroski. *Inductive Logic Programming: Techniques and Applications*. Ellis Horwood, 1994.

10. S. Muggleton and L. De Raedt. Inductive logic programming : Theory and methods. *Journal of Logic Programming*, 19,20:629–679, 1994.

11. Shan-Hwei Nienhuys-Cheng. Distance between herbrand interpretations: A measure for approximations to a target concept. In *Proceedings of the 7th International Workshop on Inductive Logic Programming*, Lecture Notes in Artificial Intelligence. Springer-Verlag, 1997.

12. G. Plotkin. A note on inductive generalization. In *Machine Intelligence*, volume 5, pages 153–163. Edinburgh University Press, 1970.

13. J. Ramon and M. Bruynooghe. A framework for defining distances between first-order logic objects. In *Proceedings of the 8th International Conference on Inductive Logic Programming*, Lecture Notes in Artificial Intelligence, pages 271–280. Springer-Verlag, 1998.

14. J. Ramon, M. Bruynooghe, and W. Van Laer. Distance measures between atoms. In *Proceedings of the CompulogNet Area Meeting on 'Computational Logic and Machine Learning'*, pages 35–41, 1998.

15. K. Sadohara and M. Haraguchi. Analogical logic program synthesis from examples. In N. Lavrač and S. Wrobel, editors, *Proceedings of the 8th European Conference on Machine Learning*, volume 912 of *Lecture Notes in Artificial Intelligence*, pages 232–244, Berlin, Heidelberg, New York, 1995. Springer-Verlag.

Some Properties of Inverse Resolution in Normal Logic Programs

Chiaki Sakama

Department of Computer and Communication Sciences
Wakayama University
Sakaedani, Wakayama 640 8510, Japan
sakama@sys.wakayama-u.ac.jp
http://www.sys.wakayama-u.ac.jp/~sakama

Abstract. This paper studies the properties of inverse resolution in normal logic programs. The V-operators are known as operations for inductive generalization in definite logic programs. In the presence of negation as failure in a program, however, the V-operators do not work as generalization operations in general and often make a consistent program inconsistent. Moreover, they may destroy the syntactic structure of logic programs such as acyclicity and local stratification. On the procedural side, unrestricted application of the V-operators may lose answers computed in the original program and make queries flounder. We provide sufficient conditions for the V-operators to avoid these problems.

1 Introduction

Inverse resolution introduced in [13] is known as operations which perform inductive generalization in definite logic programs. There are two operators that carry out inverse resolution, *absorption* and *identification*, which are called the *V-operators* together. Each operator builds one of the two parent clauses given the other parent clause and the resolvent. More precisely, absorption constructs C_2 from C_1 and C_3, while identification constructs C_1 from C_2 and C_3 in the figure (where lower-case letters are atoms and upper-case letters are conjunction of atoms).

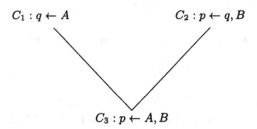

Absorption and identification are realized in Duce [10, 11] for propositional Horn theories, and a restricted version of absorption is implemented in CIGOL [13] for predicate Horn theories.

The V-operators are considered as program transformation rules. That is, absorption transforms the set of clauses $\{C_1, C_3\}$ to $\{C_1, C_2\}$, while identification transforms $\{C_2, C_3\}$ to $\{C_1, C_2\}$. In logic programming, program transformation is an important technique for program development, especially for deriving an efficient program preserving the meaning of the original program. In the context of *inductive logic programming* (ILP), program transformation is used for a different purpose. In ILP the original program represents an imperfect background theory, and it is transformed to a more general/specific program which covers given positive/negative evidences. The V-operators are used as program transformation rules which generalize definite Horn logic programs.

When a program is *nonmonotonic*, however, the behavior of the V-operators is not clear. The importance of nonmonotonic reasoning in commonsense inference is widely recognized, and many studies have been done to formalize nonmonotonic reasoning in logic programming [6]. In logic programming, nonmonotonic reasoning is realized using *negation as failure*, and a program with negation as failure is called a *normal logic program*. Then, our primary interest is the semantic nature of the V-operators in normal logic programs.

This paper investigates the properties of inverse resolution in normal logic programs. In the presence of negation as failure, we show that the V-operators do not work as generalization operators in general and often make a consistent program inconsistent. Moreover, the V-operators destroy the structures of logic programs such as acyclicity and local stratification. On the procedural side, it is shown that unrestricted application of the V-operators may lose answers computed in the original program and make queries flounder. We provide sufficient conditions for the V-operators to avoid these problems.

The paper is organized as follows. Section 2 reviews the logic programming framework considered in this paper. Section 3 shows the declarative properties of inverse resolution in normal logic programs. Section 4 argues the effects of the V-operators on query-answering. Section 5 presents related issues and Section 6 concludes the paper.

2 Normal Logic Programs

A *normal logic program* is a set of rules of the form:

$$p \leftarrow q_1, \ldots, q_m, \neg q_{m+1}, \ldots, \neg q_n \tag{1}$$

where p and q_i $(1 \leq i \leq n)$ are atoms and $\neg$ presents *negation as failure*. Throughout the paper a program means a normal logic program unless stated otherwise. The left-hand side of the rule is the *head*, and the right-hand side is the *body*. A rule with an empty body is a *fact*. A program P is *definite* if no rule in P contains negation as failure. A program, a rule or an atom is *ground* if it contains no variable. A program P is semantically identified with its ground instantiation, i.e., the set of ground rules obtained from P by substituting variables in P by elements of its Herbrand universe in every possible way.

A partial order relation $\geq$ is defined over the Herbrand base HB of a program such that: if $p \geq q$ then p is in a level higher than or equal to q. A program P is *locally stratified* [15] if (i) for any ground rule of the form (1) from P, $p \geq q_i$ $(i = 1, \ldots, m)$ and $p > q_j$ $(j = m + 1, \ldots, n)$; and (ii) there is no infinite sequence such as $p_1 > p_2 > \cdots$. Here, $p > q$ if $p \geq q$ and $q \not\geq p$. A program P is *acyclic* [2] if (i) for any ground rule of the form (1) from P, $p > q_i$ $(i = 1, \ldots, n)$; and (ii) the same condition as above. By definition, the class of acyclic programs is strictly included in the class of locally stratified programs.

An interpretation I $(\subseteq HB)$ *satisfies* the conjunction $C = q_1, \ldots, q_m, \neg q_{m+1}, \ldots, \neg q_n$ if $\{q_1, \ldots, q_m\} \subseteq I$ and $\{q_{m+1}, \ldots, q_n\} \cap I = \emptyset$ (written as $I \models C$). I satisfies the rule (1) if $\{q_1, \ldots, q_m\} \subseteq I$ and $\{q_{m+1}, \ldots, q_n\} \cap I = \emptyset$ imply $p \in I$. An interpretation I which satisfies every rule in a program P is a *model* of the program (written as $I \models P$). A model I of a program P is called *supported* [1] if for each atom p in I, there is a ground rule (1) from P such that I satisfies its body. A model I of P is *minimal* if there is no model J of P such that $J \subset I$. A definite program P has the unique minimal model which is the *least model* (denoted by LM_P).

For the semantics of normal logic programs, we consider the *stable model semantics* of [8] and Clark's *completion* [7]. Given a program P and an interpretation I, the ground definite program P^I is defined as follows: a ground rule $p \leftarrow q_1, \ldots, q_m$ is in P^I iff there is a ground rule of the form (1) in the ground instantiation of P such that $\{q_{m+1}, \ldots, q_n\} \cap I = \emptyset$. If the least model of P^I is identical to I, I is called a *stable model* of P. A program may have none, one, or multiple stable models in general. In a definite program, a stable model coincides with the least model. A locally stratified program has the unique stable model which is called the *perfect model*. A program is *consistent* (under the stable model semantics) if it has a stable model; otherwise it is *inconsistent*. For a consistent program P and an atom a, if a is included in every stable model of P, it is written as $P \models a$; otherwise $P \not\models a$.

On the other hand, suppose that a ground program P has k rules $p \leftarrow B_1; \ldots; p \leftarrow B_k$ defining the predicate p. Then, the completion of a program P (written as $comp(P)$) includes the first-order formula $p \leftrightarrow B_1 \vee \cdots \vee B_k$.[1] In particular, when P has no definition of p, $p \leftrightarrow false$ is in $comp(P)$. We say that an interpretation I is a *completion model* of P if I is a minimal model of $comp(P)$. The (in)consistency of a program under the completion semantics is defined in the same way as the stable model semantics.

3 Declarative Properties

This section investigates the declarative properties of inverse resolution, and programs and rules are assumed to be ground.

---

[1] In this paper we consider the completion of a ground program. $\neg$ is interpreted as classical negation in $comp(P)$.

3.1 Semantic Properties

Absorption and *identification* are operations such that

Absorption:

$$Input : C_1 : q \leftarrow A \text{ and } C_3 : p \leftarrow A, B \qquad (2)$$
$$Output : C_2 : p \leftarrow q, B \text{ and } C_1$$

Identification:

$$Input : C_2 : p \leftarrow q, B \text{ and } C_3 : p \leftarrow A, B \qquad (3)$$
$$Output : C_1 : q \leftarrow A \text{ and } C_2$$

where p and q are atoms, and A and B are conjunctions in the body. Throughout the paper, we use the symbols C_1, C_2, and C_3 which refer to rules of the above forms. Absorption and identification are called the *V-operators* together. Note that in [13] these operations are introduced to definite programs. Here we consider the V-operators in normal logic programs.

In the ILP literature, there are two cases in the usage of these operations. The first case is that the input rule C_1 in absorption or C_2 in identification is included in the background theory P, while the input rule C_3 is given as an example aside from P (e.g. [13, 16, 17]). In this case, the output rule C_2 in (2) or C_1 in (3) is just added to the original theory P. The second case is that the input rule C_3 is also included in the background theory P as well as the input rule C_1 or C_2 (e.g. [5, 10, 11]). In this case, the input rule C_3 in P is replaced by the output rule C_2 in (2) or C_1 in (3).[2]

In this section, the distinction of two cases is not important. In fact, the properties presented in Sections 3.1 and 3.2 hold in either case. Then, we do not distinguish the locations of the input rules and consider the second case in this section.[3] Given a program P containing the rules C_1 and C_3, absorption produces the program $A(P)$ such that

$$A(P) = (P \setminus \{C_3\}) \cup \{C_2\}.$$

On the other hand, given a program P containing the rules C_2 and C_3, identification produces the program $I(P)$ such that

$$I(P) = (P \setminus \{C_3\}) \cup \{C_1\}.$$

Note that there are multiple $A(P)$ or $I(P)$ exist in general according to the choice of the input rules in P.

For notational convenience, we use $V(P)$ which means either $A(P)$ or $I(P)$. With this setting, absorption (resp. identification) is captured as a program transformation from P to $A(P)$ (resp. $I(P)$). Then, we first investigate semantical relations between the original program P and the produced program $V(P)$.

---

[2] C_3 is derived from C_1 and C_2, hence it is redundant.

[3] The distinction between two cases makes sense in Section 4. We will notice this point in Section 4.

Proposition 3.1. *Let P be a normal logic program. If M is a stable model of $V(P)$, M is a model of P.*

Proof. When M is a stable model of $V(P)$, M satisfies C_1 and C_2 in $V(P)$. If $M \not\models A$, M satisfies C_3. Else if $M \models A$, $q \in M$ by C_1. As M satisfies C_2, $M \models B$ implies $p \in M$. Hence, M satisfies C_3. Therefore, M is a model of P. $\qquad\square$

Corollary 3.2 *Let P be a definite program and $LM_{V(P)}$ a least model of $V(P)$. Then, $LM_P \subseteq LM_{V(P)} \subseteq HB$.*

Proof. Since $LM_{V(P)}$ is a model of P by Proposition 3.1, the result follows immediately. $\qquad\square$

In the above corollary, when $LM_{V(P)} \setminus LM_P \neq \emptyset$, any atom $p \in LM_{V(P)} \setminus LM_P$ is often called an *inductive leap* in the literature.

Proposition 3.1 presents that any stable model M of the produced program $V(P)$ satisfies the original program P (i.e., $M \models P$). Clearly, a stable model M of $V(P)$ is not necessarily a stable model of P. Indeed, M is neither minimal nor supported in P in general.

Proposition 3.3. *A stable model M of $V(P)$ is generally neither minimal nor supported in P.*

Example 3.1. Let P_1 be the program

$$p \leftarrow q, \quad r \leftarrow q, \quad r \leftarrow .$$

Using the first rule and the second rule, absorption produces $A(P_1)$:

$$p \leftarrow r, \quad r \leftarrow q, \quad r \leftarrow .$$

Here, $A(P_1)$ has the stable model $\{p, r\}$, which it is neither minimal nor supported in P_1. Next, let P_2 be the program

$$p \leftarrow q, r, \quad p \leftarrow s, r, \quad s \leftarrow .$$

Using the first rule and the second rule, identification produces $I(P_2)$:

$$p \leftarrow q, r, \quad q \leftarrow s, \quad s \leftarrow .$$

Here, $I(P_2)$ has the stable model $\{q, s\}$, which is neither minimal nor supported in P_2.

The V-operators may increase proven facts hence a stable model of $V(P)$ is not a minimal model of P in general. On the other hand, absorption generalizes the condition of a rule, so that the body of the original rule may not be requested to be true for implying the head of the rule in $A(P)$. Also, identification may produce a rule having the head with an atom that does not appear in the head of any rule in the original program. When a stable model of $I(P)$ contains such an atom, it may not be supported in P.

Next we consider the completion semantics. It is shown that a completion model of $V(P)$ is a model of P.

Proposition 3.4. *Let P be a normal logic program. When M is a completion model of $V(P)$, M is a model of P.*

Proof. Suppose that C_1 and C_2 are respectively completed as $C_1' : q \leftrightarrow A \vee \Gamma_1$ and $C_2' : p \leftrightarrow q, B \vee \Gamma_2$ in $V(P)$, where Γ_1 and Γ_2 are formulas in disjunctive normal forms. When M is a completion model of $V(P)$, M satisfies C_1' and C_2'. Then, M satisfies $p \leftrightarrow ((A \vee \Gamma_1) \wedge B) \vee \Gamma_2 = p \leftrightarrow (A \wedge B) \vee (\Gamma_1 \wedge B) \vee \Gamma_2$. Hence, M satisfies $C_3 : p \leftarrow A, B$. Therefore, M is a model of P. $\qquad\square$

A completion model of $V(P)$ is not necessarily a completion model of P, and vice versa.

Example 3.2. Let P be the program

$$p \leftarrow r, s, \quad q \leftarrow r, \quad q \leftarrow t, \quad s \leftarrow, \quad t \leftarrow .$$

Then $comp(P)$ becomes

$$p \leftrightarrow r, s, \quad q \leftrightarrow r \vee t, \quad r \leftrightarrow false, \quad s \leftrightarrow true, \quad t \leftrightarrow true,$$

which has the completion model $\{q, s, t\}$. On the other hand, using the first rule and the second rule in P, absorption produces $A(P)$:

$$p \leftarrow q, s, \quad q \leftarrow r, \quad q \leftarrow t, \quad s \leftarrow, \quad t \leftarrow .$$

Then $comp(V(P))$ becomes

$$p \leftrightarrow q, s, \quad q \leftrightarrow r \vee t, \quad r \leftrightarrow false, \quad s \leftrightarrow true, \quad t \leftrightarrow true,$$

which has the completion model $\{p, q, s, t\}$.

From a consistent program P, the V-operators may produce an inconsistent program $V(P)$.

Example 3.3. Let P_1 be the program

$$p \leftarrow q, \neg p, \quad q \leftarrow r, \quad s \leftarrow r, \quad s \leftarrow,$$

which has the stable model $\{s\}$. Using the second rule and the third rule, absorption produces $A(P_1)$:

$$p \leftarrow q, \neg p, \quad q \leftarrow s, \quad s \leftarrow r, \quad s \leftarrow,$$

which has no stable model. Next, let P_2 be the program

$$p \leftarrow q, \neg p, \quad r \leftarrow q, \quad r \leftarrow s, \quad s \leftarrow,$$

which has the stable model $\{r, s\}$. Using the second rule and the third rule, identification produces $I(P_2)$:

$$p \leftarrow q, \neg p, \quad r \leftarrow q, \quad q \leftarrow s, \quad s \leftarrow,$$

which has no stable model.

The same problem happens under the completion semantics, e.g.,

$$comp(P_1) = \{p \leftrightarrow q, \neg p, \quad q \leftrightarrow r, \quad r \leftrightarrow false, \quad s \leftrightarrow r \vee true\}$$

is consistent, while

$$comp(A(P_1)) = \{p \leftrightarrow q, \neg p, \quad q \leftrightarrow s, \quad r \leftrightarrow false, \quad s \leftrightarrow r \vee true\}$$

is inconsistent. Therefore, it is concluded that:

Proposition 3.5. *The V-operators may turn a consistent normal logic program into inconsistent under both the stable model semantics and the completion semantics.*

This problem does not arise in definite programs since a definite program is always consistent. A sufficient condition for guaranteeing the consistency of the produced program $V(P)$ is given in the next section.

Next we consider the use of the V-operators as generalization operators. We say that a program P_1 *generalizes* a program P_2 if $P_2 \models a$ implies $P_1 \models a$ for any atom a. The V-operators generalize a program P when P is definite, but this is not the case in the presence of negation as failure in general.

Example 3.4. Let P_1 be the program

$$p \leftarrow \neg q, \quad q \leftarrow r, \quad s \leftarrow r, \quad s \leftarrow,$$

which has the stable model $\{p, s\}$. Using the second rule and the third rule, absorption produces $A(P_1)$:

$$p \leftarrow \neg q, \quad q \leftarrow s, \quad s \leftarrow r, \quad s \leftarrow,$$

which has the stable model $\{q, s\}$. Then, $P_1 \models p$ but $A(P_1) \not\models p$.

Next, let P_2 be the program

$$p \leftarrow \neg r, \quad q \leftarrow r, \quad q \leftarrow s, \quad s \leftarrow,$$

which has the stable model $\{p, q, s\}$. Using the second rule and the third rule, identification produces $I(P_2)$:

$$p \leftarrow \neg r, \quad q \leftarrow r, \quad r \leftarrow s, \quad s \leftarrow,$$

which has the stable model $\{q, r, s\}$. Then, $P_2 \models p$ but $I(P_2) \not\models p$.

The same phenomenon is observed under the completion semantics. In nonmonotonic theories, newly proven facts may block the derivation of other facts which are proven beforehand. As a result, the V-operators may not generalize the original program. Note that the above two programs P_1 and P_2 are (locally) stratified, which are the simplest extension of definite programs.

Proposition 3.6. *The V-operators do not generalize a normal logic program in general. This is the case even if a program is locally stratified.*

A simple condition for absorption (resp. identification) to generalize a normal logic program P is that for any negative literal $\neg a$ in P, a does not depend on p of C_3 (resp. q of C_2) in P.[4]

3.2 Syntactic Properties

In normal logic programs, syntactic restrictions on a program often introduce some nice properties in both the declarative and the procedural aspects. For instance, a locally stratified program always has a unique stable model, and an acyclic program guarantees termination of a top-down proof procedure. Therefore, when considering any program transformation, the preservation of such syntactic structures is particularly important to keep those nice properties in the transformed program. Unfortunately, the V-operators may destroy the structure of both acyclicity and local stratification.

Example 3.5. Let P_1 be the locally stratified (and also acyclic) program

$$p \leftarrow q, \quad r \leftarrow q, \quad r \leftarrow \neg p,$$

where $p \geq q$, $r \geq q$, $r > p$. Using the first rule and the second rule, absorption produces $A(P_1)$:

$$p \leftarrow r, \quad r \leftarrow q, \quad r \leftarrow \neg p,$$

where $p \geq r$, $r \geq q$, $r > p$. Here $p \geq r$ conflicts with $r > p$, hence $A(P_1)$ is neither acyclic nor locally stratified.

Next, let P_2 be the locally stratified (and also acyclic) program

$$p \leftarrow q, r, \quad p \leftarrow q, \neg s, \quad s \leftarrow \neg r,$$

where $p \geq q$, $p \geq r$, $p > s$, $s > r$. Using the first rule and the second rule, identification produces $I(P_2)$:

$$p \leftarrow q, r, \quad r \leftarrow \neg s, \quad s \leftarrow \neg r,$$

where $p \geq q$, $p \geq r$, $r > s$, $s > r$. Here $r > s$ conflicts with $s > r$, hence $I(P_2)$ is neither acyclic nor locally stratified.

Proposition 3.7. *Given a locally stratified (resp. acyclic) program P, $V(P)$ is not locally stratified (resp. acyclic) in general.*

We give a sufficient condition for the V-operators to preserve such syntactic structures of the original program.

Proposition 3.8. *Let P be a locally stratified (resp. acyclic) program.*

(i) Suppose that the rule C_2 is produced from C_1 and C_3 by absorption of (2). If the relation $p \geq q$ (resp. $p > q$) holds in P, $A(P)$ is also locally stratified (resp. acyclic).

---

[4] Here, *depends on* is a transitive relation defined as: p depends on q if there is a ground rule from P s.t. p appears in the head and q appears in the body of the rule.

(ii) Suppose that the rule C_1 is produced from C_2 and C_3 by identification of (3). For any positive literal a_i in A and any negative literal $\neg a_j$ in A, if the relations $q \geq a_i$ (resp. $q > a_i$) and $q > a_j$ hold in P, $I(P)$ is also locally stratified (resp. acyclic).

Proof. (i) When P is locally stratified (resp. acyclic), for any positive literal b_i in B of C_3 and any negative literal $\neg b_j$ in B of C_3, the relations $p \geq b_i$ (resp. $p > b_i$) and $p > b_j$ hold. In addition, the relation $p \geq q$ (resp. $p > q$) holds in P by assumption, then the rule C_2 produced by absorption satisfies the condition of local stratification (resp. acyclicity).

(ii) Since the relations $q \geq a_i$ (resp. $q > a_i$) and $q > a_j$ hold in P, the rule C_1 produced by identification satisfies the condition of local stratification (resp. acyclicity). Hence, the result follows. □

The above proposition implies a sufficient condition which guarantees the consistency of $V(P)$ for a locally stratified program P.

Corollary 3.9 *Let P be a locally stratified program. If P satisfies the condition (i) (resp. (ii)) of Proposition 3.8, $A(P)$ (resp. $I(P)$) is consistent under both the stable model semantics and the completion semantics.*

Proof. When P satisfies the condition (i) (resp. (ii)), $A(P)$ (resp. $I(P)$) is locally stratified. Since any locally stratified program is consistent under both the stable model semantics and the completion semantics, the result holds. □

4 Procedural Properties

In the previous section, we observed that the V-operators may introduce cycles to a program. This means that given an acyclic program P, the completeness of SLDNF-resolution in the produced program $V(P)$ is not guaranteed in general. The conditions of Proposition 3.8 are useful for keeping $V(P)$ acyclic. This problem does not happen when a program is definite. When a definite program contains variables, however, an application of the V-operators may lose answers which are computed using SLD-resolution in the original program.

Example 4.1. Let P_1 be the program

$$p(x,y) \leftarrow q(x,y), \quad r(y) \leftarrow q(x,y), \quad q(a,b) \leftarrow,$$

and $A(P_1)$ the program

$$p(x,y) \leftarrow r(y), \quad r(y) \leftarrow q(x,y), \quad q(a,b) \leftarrow .$$

Using SLD-resolution, the query $\leftarrow p(x,b)$ computes the answer $x = a$ in P_1, but the answer is not obtained in $A(P_1)$. Next, let P_2 be the program

$$p(x,y) \leftarrow r(y), \quad p(x,y) \leftarrow q(x,y), \quad q(a,b) \leftarrow,$$

and $I(P_2)$ the program

$$p(x,y) \leftarrow r(y), \quad r(y) \leftarrow q(x,y), \quad q(a,b) \leftarrow .$$

Using SLD-resolution, the query $\leftarrow p(x,b)$ computes the answer $x = a$ in P_2, but the answer is not obtained in $I(P_2)$.

Thus, unrestricted application of the V-operators does not always extend the set of computed answers even in a definite program. Note that such phenomena happen only when the input rule C_3 is included in the original program P in (2) and (3). When C_3 is given aside from P, the relation $P \subseteq V(P)$ holds hence every computed answer in P is obtained in $V(P)$. Hence, the following arguments are meaningful when C_3 is in P.

We first define the notion of generalization wrt computed answers. Given a definite program P and a goal $\leftarrow G$, we write $P \models_{SLD} G\theta$ if the goal has an SLD-refutation with a computed answer θ.[5]

Definition 4.1. Let P_1 and P_2 be definite programs. Then, P_1 is a *generalization of P_2 wrt computed answers* if $P_2 \models_{SLD} G$ implies $P_1 \models_{SLD} G$ for any atom G.

The next proposition presents sufficient conditions for the V-operators to generalize a program wrt computed answers.

Proposition 4.1. *Let P be a definite program.*

(i) $A(P)$ is a generalization of P wrt computed answers if in the rule $C_1 : q \leftarrow A$, every variable in A appears in q.

(ii) $I(P)$ is a generalization of P wrt computed answers if in the rule $C_2 : p \leftarrow q, B$, every variable in p appears in either q or B.

Proof. (i) Without loss of generality, we can put $C_1 : q(x,y) \leftarrow A(x)$ and $C_3 : p(z) \leftarrow A(x), B(w)$, where x, y, z, w are vectors of terms. Suppose that $C_2 : p(z) \leftarrow q(x,y), B(w)$ is produced by absorption. Resolving C_2 with C_1, we get the original rule C_3 in $A(P)$. Hence, if a query has a computed answer in P, the same answer is computed by SLD-resolution in $A(P)$.

(ii) Put $C_2 : p(x,y) \leftarrow q(x,z), B(y,w)$ and $C_3 : p(x,y) \leftarrow A(u), B(y,w)$, where x, y, z, w, u are vectors of terms. Suppose that $C_1 : q(x,z) \leftarrow A(u)$ is produced by identification. Resolving C_2 with C_1, we get the rule $C_3' : p(x,y) \leftarrow A(u'), B(y,w)$ where u' is possibly different from u. For variables in x, two cases are considered. (a) When x and u share no variable in C_3, x and u' also share no variable in C_3'. (b) When x and u share variables in C_3, the same variables are shared in x and u in C_1 and thereby shared in x and u' in C_3'. In either case, any binding for the variables in x, that is computed using C_3 in P, is also computed using C_3' in $I(P)$. Next, for variables in y, two cases are considered. (c) When y and u share no variable in C_3, y and u' also share no variable in C_3'.

---

[5] We assume familiarity with basic terminologies wrt SLD-resolution given in [9].

(d) When y and u share variables in C_3, the variables are possibly renamed in u' in C_3' but any binding for the variables in y is computed by $B(y, w)$ in C_3'. In either case, any binding for the variables in y, that is computed using C_3 in P, is also computed using C_3' in $I(P)$. Therefore, if a query has a computed answer in P, the same answer is computed by SLD-resolution in $I(P)$. □

The V-operators do not preserve the condition of *allowedness*[6] in general. For instance, the program P_1 of Example 4.1 is allowed but $A(P_1)$ is not. In normal logic programs, the condition of allowedness provides a sufficient condition to prevent a query from *floundering* [9]. Thus, given an allowed normal logic program P, a query may flounder in $V(P)$. The condition (i) of Proposition 4.1 prevents the decrease of variables in the body of C_3, hence it guarantees that $A(P)$ is allowed if P is allowed. On the other hand, the condition (ii) is insufficient to keep $I(P)$ allowed. Suppose that a program P has the rules

$$C_2 : p(x, y) \leftarrow q(x, y), s(y), \quad C_3 : p(x, y) \leftarrow r(x), s(y),$$

which are allowed and C_2 satisfies the condition (ii) of Proposition 4.1. But identification produces $C_1 : q(x, y) \leftarrow r(x)$ which is not allowed. Then, the query $\leftarrow q(x, y), \neg t(x, y)$ may flounder in $I(P)$. To keep $I(P)$ allowed, it is sufficient that every variable in q of C_2 appears in a positive literal in A of C_3 in P.

5 Discussion

There are variants of the V-operators. Muggleton [12] introduces the *most specific* version of the V-operators. The most specific absorption produces the rule C_2' : $p \leftarrow q, A, B$, instead of $C_2 : p \leftarrow q, B$, while the most specific identification produces the rule $C_1' : q \leftarrow A, B$, instead of $C_1 : q \leftarrow A$. The most specific absorption is also called *saturation* in [16]. Saturation alone does not generalize a program and is followed by *truncation*. Truncation drops the conjunction A from C_2', which results in C_2. Coupling saturation and truncation includes absorption as a special case, hence they have the same properties as those of absorption presented in this paper. It is easy to see that the properties of identification presented in this paper also hold for the most specific identification. The *W-operators* of [13] include the V-operators as a special case, hence they also inherit the properties of the V-operators.

There are few work which considers inverse resolution in normal logic programs. Bain and Muggleton [3,4] incorporate the *closed world specialization* technique into CIGOL, but they do not provide formal analysis of inverse resolution in nonmonotonic theories. Taylor [17] introduces *normal absorption* which is different from absorption in definite programs. Given the input rules $p \leftarrow q$ and $r \leftarrow q, \neg s$, normal absorption outputs the rule $p \leftarrow r, [q, \neg s]$ where $[q, \neg s]$ presents optional literals which can be dropped at the end. She shows that the output rule generalizes the input rule wrt the background theory under normal subsumption. However, she does not argue the effect of such normal V-operators in a whole theory.

---

[6] Any variable in a rule has an occurrence in a positive literal in the body of the rule.

6 Summary

This paper studied the effect of inverse resolution in normal logic programs. We posed several problems of the V-operators that may occur in the presence of negation as failure, and gave some sufficient conditions to avoid these problems. The results of this paper notice that care should be taken when using the V-operators as inductive operations in normal logic programs.

Acknowledgements

The author thanks Katsumi Inoue for comments on an earlier draft of this paper.

References

1. K. R. Apt, H. A. Blair, and A. Walker. Towards a theory of declarative knowledge. In: *Foundations of Deductive Databases and Logic Programming* (J. Minker ed.), Morgan Kaufmann, pp. 89–148, 1988.
2. K. R. Apt and M. Bezem. Acyclic programs. *New Generation Computing* 9:335–363, 1991.
3. M. Bain and S. Muggleton. Non-monotonic learning. In: [14], pp. 145–161.
4. M. Bain. Experiments in non-monotonic first-order induction. In: [14], pp. 423–436.
5. R. B. Banerji. Learning theoretical terms. In: [14], pp. 93–112.
6. C. Baral and M. Gelfond. Logic programming and knowledge representation. *Journal of Logic Programming* 19/20:73–148, 1994.
7. K. L. Clark. Negation as failure. In: H. Gallaire and J. Minker (eds.), *Logic and Data Bases*, Plenum Press, pp. 119–140, 1978.
8. M. Gelfond and V. Lifschitz. The stable model semantics for logic programming. In: *Proc. 5th Int'l Conf. and Symp. on Logic Programming*, MIT Press, pp. 1070–1080, 1988.
9. J. W. Lloyd. *Foundations of logic programming* (2nd edition), Springer-Verlag, 1987.
10. S. Muggleton. Duce, an oracle based approach to constructive induction. In: *Proc. IJCAI-87*, Morgan Kaufmann, pp. 287–292, 1987.
11. S. Muggleton. Inverting the resolution principle. In: *Machine Intelligence*, vol. 12, Oxford University Press, pp. 93–103, 1991.
12. S. Muggleton. Inductive Logic Programming. In [14], pp. 3–27, 1992.
13. S. Muggleton and W. Buntine. Machine invention of first-order predicate by inverting resolution. In: [14], pp. 261–280.
14. S. Muggleton (ed.). *Inductive Logic Programming*, Academic Press, 1992.
15. T. C. Przymusinski. On the declarative semantics of deductive databases and logic programs. In: J. Minker (ed.), *Foundations of Deductive Databases and Logic Programming*, Morgan Kaufmann, pp. 193–216, 1988.
16. C. Rouveirol. Extension of inversion of resolution applied to theory completion. In: [14], pp. 63–92.
17. K. Taylor. Inverse resolution of normal clauses. In: *Proc. ILP-93*, J. Stefan Institute, pp. 165–177, 1993.

An Assessment of ILP-Assisted Models for Toxicology and the PTE-3 Experiment *

Ashwin Srinivasan[1], Ross D. King[2] and Douglas W. Bristol[3]

[1] Oxford University Comp. Lab., Wolfson Bldg., Parks Rd, Oxford, UK
[2] Dept. of Comp. Sc., University of Wales Aberystwyth, Ceredigion, UK
[3] NIEHS, Lab. of Carcinogenesis and Mutagenesis, RTP, NC, USA

Abstract. The Predictive Toxicology Evaluation (or PTE) Challenge provided Machine Learning techniques with the opportunity to compete against specialised techniques for toxicology prediction. Toxicity models that used findings from ILP programs have performed creditably in the PTE-2 experiment proposed under this challenge. We report here on an assessment of such models along scales of: (1) quantitative performance, in comparison to models developed with expert collaboration; and (2) potential explanatory value for toxicology. Results appear to suggest the following: (a) across of range of class distributions and error costs, some explicit models constructed with ILP-assistance appear closer to optimal than most expert-assisted ones. Given the paucity of test-data, this is to be interpreted cautiously; (b) a combined use of propositional and ILP techniques appears to yield models that contain unusual combinations of structural and biological features; and (c) significant effort was required to interpret the output, strongly indicating the need to invest greater effort in transforming the output into a "toxicologist-friendly" form. Based on the lessons learnt from these results, we propose a new predictive toxicology evaluation experiment – PTE-3 – which will address some important shortcomings of the previous study.

1 Introduction

Hypothesing "good" models from data is at once one of the most routine and challenging of scientific activities. This task assumes a degree of urgency when the models are directly concerned with issues of public health and safety. The prediction of chemical toxicity provides a case in point. It is estimated that approximately 100,000 chemicals are in routine use daily, with 500–1000 new chemicals being introduced yearly [8]. Approximately 300 chemical studies (involving standardised bioassays for toxicity) are commenced world-wide each year, with each study taking at least five years to complete. The obvious gulf engendered between the rate of growth of chemical data and chemical knowledge has turned attention to machine-assisted methods of data analysis. The PTE

---

* Two figures in the paper and some of the discussion in Section 4 appear in part in a submission to a AAAI Spring Symposium on Predictive Toxicology [16] and to the Sixteenth International Conference on Artificial Intelligence (IJCAI-99, [17]).

Challenge [18] follows the lead of a comparative evaluation exercise undertaken earlier by the National Institute of Environmental Health Sciences (NIEHS, see: *dir.niehs.nih.gov/dirlecm/pte2.htm*[1] and [5]). The challenge described an experiment PTE-2, in which carcinogenesis predictions for 30 compounds were to be made by models constructed by Machine Learning programs[2]. This paper is concerned with these models. In particular, our focus is on "explicit" models – those capable of examination for toxicological insights – constructed with ILP assistance. We examine the quantitative performance of such ILP-assisted models and provide some assessment of their chemical value. We further provide details of a new experiment (PTE-3) that addresses many of the shortcomings of the PTE-2 experiment. The paper is organised as follows: Section 2 summarises submissions made to the challenge. Section 3 compares quantitatively the explicit ILP-assisted models against those developed under the guidance of expert toxicologists (this includes toxicology expert systems). Section 4 contains an appraisal of the explanatory value of the ILP-assisted models. Section 5 contains the proposal for PTE-3, and Section 6 concludes this paper.

2 Summary of submissions to the PTE Challenge

All submissions made to the challenge consisted of two parts: (1) *prediction:* "pos" and "neg" classification for the compounds in PTE-2 (standing for carcinogenic or otherwise: see [5] for a further description of the meaning of these classes); and (2) *description:* details of the materials and methods used, and results obtained with the technique. The former was needed to assess model accuracy, and the latter for replicability of results and evaluations of model comprehensibility by a toxicologist. Nine legal submissions[3] were received in the period between August 29, 1997 and November 15, 1998. These are summarised in Figure 1.

3 Quantitative Assessment of Models

At the time of writing this paper, the classification of 23 of the 30 compounds had become available. Figure 2 tabulates the predictive accuracies achieved by the models tabulated in Figure 1.

The primary focus of this paper precludes any further analysis of the models in OAI, and TA1. LRD also poses some concern, as it is still unclear whether any ILP assistance was required. No single model is presented as part of the description, although the developers appear confident that such a model can be obtained[4]. For comparative purposes, Benigni [2] provides a tabulation of the predictions made by several established toxicity prediction methods on a

---

[1] All Internet sites mentioned in this paper are to be prefixed with *http://*

[2] Submissions were received at: *www.comlab.ox.ac.uk/oucl/groups/machlearn/PTE*

[3] Those that contained both "prediction" and "description" parts.

[4] M. Sebag, private communication.

Model	Uses ILP	Description
LE1	√	*www.cs.kuleuven.ac.be/~hendrik/PTE/PTE1.html*
LE2	√	*www.cs.kuleuven.ac.be/~ldh/PTE/PTE2.html*
LE3	√	*www.cs.kuleuven.ac.be/~wimv/PTE/PTE2.html*
LRD	?	*www.lri.fr/~fabien/PTE/Distill/*
LRG	√	*www.lri.fr/~fabien/PTE/GloBo/*
OAI	×	*www.ai.univie.ac.at/~bernhard/pte2/pte2.html*
OU1	√	*www.comlab.ox.ac.uk/oucl/groups/machlearn/PTE/oucl1.html*
OU2	√	*www.comlab.ox.ac.uk/oucl/groups/machlearn/PTE/oucl2.html*
TA1	×	*ailab2.cs.nthu.edu.tw/pte*

Fig. 1. Models submitted to the PTE Challenge. An entry of √ under "Uses ILP" indicates that the model uses results from an ILP program; × that it does not use results from an ILP program; and ? that it is unclear whether ILP results are used. The models were constructed as follows: LE1 by the ILP program Tilde; LE2 by the maximum likelihood technique MACCENT using the results from the ILP program WARMR; LE3 by the ILP program ICL; LRD by a stochastic voting technique; LRG by a stochastic technique that uses amongst others, results from WARMR and and the ILP program P-Progol; OAI by voting with Naive Bayes and the decision-tree learner C4.5; OU1 by C4.5 and P-Progol; OU2 by C4.5 using amongst others, results from WARMR; and TA1 using a genetic search technique. In constructing LRD, the stochastic technique has access to results from WARMR and P-Progol. However, as there is no single model associated with the output, it is unclear whether the ILP results were used.

subset of the PTE-2 compounds. We concentrate here on those techniques that involve substantial input from experts. These include models devised directly by toxicologists or those that rely on the application of compilations of such specialist knowledge (that is, toxicity expert systems). In [2], there are 9 such "expert-derived" models due to: Huff et al. (HUF, [7]), OncoLogic (ONC, [20]), Bootman (BOT, [3]), Tennant et al. (TEN, [19]), Ashby (ASH, [1]), Benigni et al. (BEN, [14]), Purdy (PUR, [13]), DEREK (DER, [10]), and COMPACT (COM, [9]). Excluding missing entries, predictions are available from these methods for 18 PTE-2 compounds. A comparative tabulation on this subset against the ILP-assisted models is in Figure 3.

Comparisons based on predictive accuracy overlook two important practical concerns, namely (a) class distributions cannot be specified precisely. Distribution of classes in the training set are thus rarely matched exactly on new data; and (b) that the costs of different types of errors may be unequal. In toxicology modelling the cost of false negatives is usually higher than those of false positives. Using techniques developed in signal detection, the authors in [11] describe an elegant method for the comparative assessment of classifiers that takes these considerations into account In summary, they describe a technique for eliminating classifiers that could not possibly be "optimal" under any circumstances. The details relevant to the two-class problem addressed here are as follows:

Model	Accuracy
LRD	0.87 (0.07)
LRG	0.78 (0.09)
OU2	0.78 (0.09)
OAI	0.74 (0.09)
LE3	0.70 (0.10)
LE2	0.65 (0.10)
OU1	0.57 (0.10)
TA1	0.52 (0.10)
LE1	0.48 (0.10)
POS	0.74 (0.10)

Fig. 2. Estimated accuracies of submissions made to the PTE Challenge. Here, accuracy refers to the fraction of PTE-2 compounds correctly classified by the model. The quantity in parentheses next to the accuracy figure is the estimated standard error. The classifications are based on the outcome of 23 of the 30 PTE-2 bioassays. The classification of remaining 7 is yet to be decided. "POS" refers to the simple rule that states that all compounds will be carcinogenic. This was not an official submission to the challenge and is only included here for completeness.

1. Let the two classes be denoted $+$ and $-$ respectively. Let $\pi(+)$ and $\pi(-) = 1 - \pi(+)$ be the prior probabilities of the classes. Suppose we have unbiased estimates for the following: TP, the proportion of instances observed to be $+$ and classified as such; and FP, the proportion of instances observed to be $-$ and classified as $+$. Using the notation in [4], let the costs of false positives and false negatives be $C(+|-)$ and $C(-|+)$ respectively (that is, the cost of classifying an instance as $+$ when it is really a $-$, and vice versa).

2. The expected misclassification cost of a classifier is then given by $\pi(+) \cdot (1 - TP) \cdot C(-|+) + \pi(-) \cdot FP \cdot C(+|-)$. For brevity, "expected misclassification cost" will henceforth be simply called "cost". It is easy to see that two classifiers have the same cost if $\frac{TP_2 - TP_1}{FP_2 - FP_1} = \frac{\pi(-) \cdot C(+|-)}{\pi(+) \cdot C(-|+)} = m$.

3. The "operating characteristic" of a binary classifier can be represented as a point in the two-dimensional Cartesian space (called "Receiver Operating Characteristic" or ROC space) defined by FP on the X axis and TP on the Y axis. Classifiers with continuous output are represented by a set of points obtained by thresholding the output value (each threshold resulting in a classification of the instances into one of $+$ or $-$). A set of points may also be obtained by varying critical parameters in the binary classification technique, with each setting resulting in a binary classifier.

4. A specification of π and C defines a family of lines with slope m (as defined in item 2 above) in ROC-space. All classifiers on a given line have the same cost, and the lines are called *iso-performance* lines. Lines with a higher TP intercept represent classifiers with lower cost (follows from the cost formula

Model	Accuracy
LRD	0.89 (0.07)
LRG	0.84 (0.09)
HUF	0.78 (0.10)
LE3	0.78 (0.10)
ONC	0.78 (0.10)
OU2	0.78 (0.10)
LE2	0.72 (0.11)
BEN	0.67 (0.11)
OU1	0.67 (0.11)
ASH	0.56 (0.12)
LE1	0.56 (0.12)
TEN	0.56 (0.12)
BOT	0.50 (0.12)
COM	0.50 (0.12)
DER	0.50 (0.12)
PUR	0.28 (0.11)
POS	0.67 (0.11)

Fig. 3. Comparison of estimated accuracies of ILP-assisted models and expert-derived models. As before, estimates of standard errors are in parentheses. ILP-assisted models are in bold-face. Although unclear at this stage, we have included LRD in this list. The figures are based on the classification of 18 of the 30 PTE-2 compounds for which predictions are available from all models. Some expert-derived models include a third category of classification called "borderline carcinogen." These are simply taken as a "pos" classification here. As before POS predicts all outcomes as "pos".

      in item 2). Imprecise specifications of π and C will give rise to a range of possible m values.

5. Minimum cost classifiers lie on the edge of the convex hull of the set of points in item 3 above. For a given value of $m = m_1$, potentially optimal classifiers occur at points in ROC-space where the slope of the hull-edge is m_1 or at the intersection of edges whose slopes are less than and greater than m_1 respectively. (the proof of this is in [12]). If operating under a range of m values (say $[m_1, m_2]$), then potentially optimal classifiers will lie on a segment of the hull-edge (see Figure 4). Henceforth we will call such classifiers "FAPP-optimal" (to denote optimal for all practical purposes).

This procedure for obtaining FAPP-optimal classifiers has not be extended by the authors in [11] to classifiers that discriminate between more than 2 classes. In fact, the result that optimal classfiers are located on line segments joining vertices the convex hull holds for arbitrary number of classes for any cost function that is linear in the Euclidean space representing the classifiers (see [15]). With these preliminaries in place, we are in a position to examine the the ROC plot of the models in Figure 3. This is shown in Figure 5.

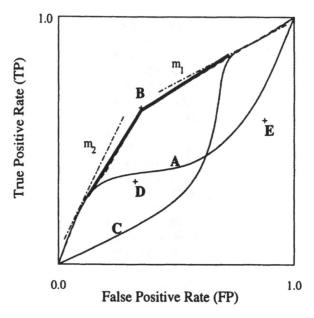

Fig. 4. Classifiers in ROC-space. Here A and C are continuous-output classifiers (represented by curves) and B, D, and E are binary classifiers (represented by points). The edge of the convex hull is the piecewise-linear curve separating the shaded area from the unshaded one. Potentially optimal classifiers lie on this edge and are found by comparing the slope of a linear segment comprising the edge, against the value m determined by the current specification of priors and costs. Thus for $m = m_1$, C is the only classifier that is potentially optimal. Imprecise specification of these will result in a range of values and potentially optimal classifiers then lie on a segment of the hull. Thus for $m \in [m_1, m_2]$ then potentially optimal classifiers lie along the thickened line segment (A, B, C are thus candidates). D and E can never be optimal for any value of m. A theoretically optimal classifier for any value of m would have a "step" ROC-curve joining the points $(0,0)$, $(0,1)$ and $(1,1)$.

The graph would appear to suggest that except for HUF, all other expert-assisted models are not FAPP-optimal. However, given that the plot is based on a very small sample of 18 points, we prefer to interpret these results as suggesting that the ILP-assisted models are closer to FAPP-optimal than their expert-assisted counterparts. This in itself is unexpected, and worthy of further investigation.

The authors of [11] provide a computer program ROCCH (www.croftj.net/ fawcett/ROCCH/) to calculate the hull and identify FAPP-optimal classifiers. The output of this program is summarised in Figure 6.

It is of interest to examine some representative values for the slope. The data available suggest that the prior probabilities on the "pos" class, $\pi(+)$, is approximately in the range $0.5 - 0.7$. Further, the cost of false negatives $C(-|+)$ distinctly outweighs that of false positives $C(+|-)$. Conventions vary, but a

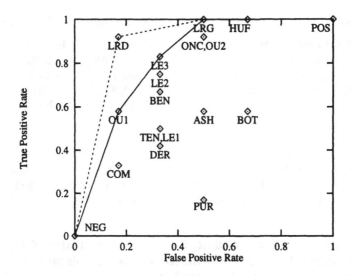

Fig. 5. ROC plot of ILP-assisted and expert models. It is unclear whether LRD should be included in this plot. The convex hull with LRD is given by the broken line, and without, by the unbroken line. NEG refers to a model that predicts all outcomes will be non-carcinogenic.

weighting factor between 10 and 20 would not be uncommon. This specifies the slope range $[0.02, 0.1]$. For this range LRG would appear to be FAPP-optimal.

4   Qualitative Assessment of Models

At the outset of this section, it is worth emphasising that as submitted, none of the ILP-assisted models would be considered toxicologically acceptable. This comment extends even to the most transparent submission like OU2, which presents a relatively simple decision-tree obtained from a well-known algorithm (C4.5). Much of this probably stems from a lack of toxicology expertise amongst the model developers. We intend to correct this partially by stipulating minimal requirements on output descriptions in the next round of experimentation (PTE-3: see Section 5). Nevertheless, the quantitative performance of the models have been sufficiently intriguing to foster further examination. It is not our intention to single out any one model as being the "best" – the toxicological shortcomings mentioned would make such statements meaningless. Rather, we provide an overall assessment of the type of constructs identified by the models.

Of considerable toxicological interest is the frequent appearance in all models of rules that consist of chemical structure and biological tests. For some time, there has been vigorous debate on how classical structure-activity modelling can be applied to toxicity problems. This form of modelling relates chemical features to activity, and works well *in-vitro*. The extent to which these ideas transfer to toxicity modelling – which deals with the interaction of chemical factors with

Slope Range	Best classifier(s)
[0.000, 0.000]	HUF,POS
(0.000, 0.242]	LRG
(0.242, 5.412]	LRD
(5.412, ∞)	NEG

(a)

Slope Range	Best Classifier(s)
[0.000, 0.000]	HUF,POS
(0.000, 1.000]	LRG
(1.000, 1.562]	LE3
(1.562, 3.412]	OU1
(3.412, ∞)	NEG

(b)

Fig. 6. Summary of the output of ROCCH. Recommendations of the best classifier are obtained by determining the ranges of slopes for which a classifier on the hull is on the optimal segment. The results are with (a) and without (b) LRD.

biological systems – is not evident. By using a combination of chemical features and biological test outcomes, the ILP-assisted models provide one possible method for dealing with the chemical effects in such "open" systems. If the accuracies obtained with such rules are borne out on larger datasets, then this would constitute a significant advance in structure-activity modelling for toxicology.

A number of aspects of some of the models are in line with what is currently known in toxicology. As an example, OU2 selects a combination of mouse lymphoma and Drosophilla tests as a strong indicator of carcinogenicity. Many toxicologists believe that relationships exist between genotoxicity and carcinogenicity. While the the only accepted correlation involves the Salmonella assay, this rule suggests a different combination of short-term tests could be equally, or more effective. Similar comments could be made on a number of other fronts: the presence of methoxy groups, sulphur compounds, and biphenyl groups are all identified in various ways as being related to toxicity. Far from being uninteresting, identification of these well-known aspects are essential, as they serve to reinforce a toxicologist's confidence in a model.

An interesting feature to arise is the re-use of ILP-constructed results by other prediction programs. Three ways of doing this are evident:

A. Incorporate other prediction methods as part of the background knowledge for an ILP program. None of the models here were developed in this manner.
B. Incorporate the results from an ILP program into an established prediction method. LRG, LE2 and OU2 were constructed in this manner, where the ILP results were incorporated as new features.
C. Use ILP to explain only those instances that are inadequately modelled by established techniques[5]. OU1 was constructed in this manner, with an ILP program constructing a "theory of exceptions" to a simple C4.5 rule model.

Based on results here, Method B appears to hold the greatest promise for toxicology modelling. The ILP program WARMR appears to be particularly well-suited to the task of identifying sub-structures that can constitute features for a propositional technique [6].

---

[5] This role for ILP was first brought to our attention by Donald Michie.

5 The PTE-3 Experiment

The experiment of predicting carcinogenicity outcome of compounds in PTE-2 contained the following shortcomings:

Classification. The simplistic classification into two classes gives the impression that toxicity is a property possessed by individual chemicals and that it is independent of the multi-factorial, dynamical systems that are used to conduct activity-classification experiments. Other classification schemes are both desirable and needed. For example, trans-species and gender-specific effects sometimes dominate the results obtained from an assay for carcinogenesis.

Data. The size of the PTE-2 data set is too small to obtain reliable statistics of performance. Further, the knowledge of chemicals in the test-set compromised the possibility of a true blind trial.

Evaluation. There were no specifications provided for the output descriptions. This led to model developers presenting their results in diverse ways, none of which were particularly meaningful to a toxicologist. This greatly impeded a careful assessment of explanatory value.

Dissemination. No clear directions were provided on methods of publicising the results obtained.

We have attempt to remedy each of these in the proposal of a new experiment, PTE-3. It is envisaged that PTE-3 will run from July 1999 to July 2000, and have the following attributes[6]:

Classification. Predictive models will be required for the following categories: (a) carcinogenicity outcome into 2 classes as before; and (b) gender (male or female) and species (rat or mouse) specific levels of evidence in 4 categories (clear evidence, some evidence, equivocal, and no evidence).

Data. It is our intention to increase the size of the test set to at least 50 chemicals. If feasible, we will also increase the size of the training set. The test set will not be advertised prior to closing date of submissions.

Evaluation. We intend to stipulate minimal requirements on output descriptions. These will contain at least the following: (a) contingency table from a 10-fold cross-validation on the training set; (b) estimates of accuracy, true and false positive rates using (a); (c) number and actual training cases covered by each component of the model (a "component" can be, for example, a rule in the model). Once the test set is released, these and the estimates in (b) have to be provided for this data as well; and (d) complete English translations of any special constructs used in the model (such constructs could be, for example, the substructure used in a rule). Models that do not meet the requirements will be discarded. Evaluation on the rest will proceed along quantitative and qualitative scales as before, and is expected to be completed by October, 2000.

---

[6] Complete details of Internet site etc., should be available by ILP'99.

Dissemination. If the results are sufficiently interesting, we intend to request space for a special issue from a toxicology journal. Model developers would then be encouraged to submit papers to such an issue.

6 Concluding Remarks

This paper has presented an assessment of ILP-assisted models submitted as part of a toxicology prediction experiment. The conclusions that can be drawn for toxicology modelling are these: (a) that ILP-assisted models have performed unexpectedly well on scales of quantitative performance; (b) the techniques certainly merit further investigation; and (c) greater attention must be paid to providing model-developers with toxicological requirements in order for the output of such techniques to be deemed "comprehensible". The new experiment proposed is designed to provide ILP techniques with an opportunity to build on the promising results here, and take the first steps towards a truly effective assistant to an expert toxicologist.

Acknowledgements

The authors would like to acknowledge the significant effort made by the Machine Learning community in responding to the PTE Challenge. In particular, sincere thanks are due to the groups whose models we have used in the analysis here, namely those at Leuven (Belgium), LRI (France), OFAI (Austria), and the AI Lab, Taiwan. At Oxford, the model OU1 was largely developed by Ngozi Dozie, a MSc student in Computation. A.S currently holds a Nuffield Trust Research Fellowship at Green College, Oxford. During the first six months of the PTE Challenge, he was supported by Smith-Kline Beecham. A.S. and R.D.K would also like to thank Donald Michie, Stephen Muggleton, and Michael Sternberg for interesting and useful discussions concerning the use of machine learning for predicting biological activity. We thank the support staff of the Computing Laboratory, Oxford – in particular, Ian Collier – for his help with the Web pages related to the PTE-2 Challenge.

References

1. J. Ashby. Predictions of rodent carcinogenicity for 30 compounds. *Environmental Health Perspectives*, pages 1101–1104, 1996.
2. R. Benigni. (Q)sar prediction of chemical carcinogenicity and the biological side of the structure activity relationship. In *Proceedings of The Eighth International Workshop on QSARs in the Environmental Sciences*, 1998. Held in Baltimore, May 16–20, 1998.
3. J. Bootman. Speculations on the carcinogenicity of 30 chemicals currently under review in rat and mouse bioassays organised by the us national toxicology program. *Mutagenesis*, 27:237–243, 1996.
4. L. Breiman, J.H. Friedman, R.A. Olshen, and C.J. Stone. *Classification and Regression Trees*. Wadsworth, Belmont, 1984.

5. D.W. Bristol, J.T. Wachsman, and A. Greenwell. The NIEHS Predictive-Toxicology Evaluation Project. *Environmental Health Perspectives*, pages 1001–1010, 1996. Supplement 3.

6. L. Dehaspe, H. Toivonen, and R.D. King. Finding frequent substructures in chemical compounds. In *Proceedings of the Fourth International Conference on Knowledge Discovery and Data Mining (KDD-98)*, pages 30–36. AAAI Press, 1998.

7. J. Huff, E. Weisburger, and V.A. Fung. Multicomponent criteria for predicting carcinogenicity: dataset of 30 ntp chemicals. *Environmental Health Perspectives*, 104:1105–1112, 1996.

8. J.E. Huff, J.K. Haseman, and D.P. Rall. Scientific concepts, value and significance of chemical carcinogenesis studies. *Ann Rev Pharmacol Toxicol*, 31:621–652, 1991.

9. D.F.V. Lewis, C. Ioannides, and D.V. Parke. COMPACT and molecular structure in toxicity assessment: a prospective evaluation of 30 chemicals currently being tested for rodent carcinogenicity by the NCI/NTP. *Environmental Health Perspectives*, pages 1011–1016, 1996.

10. C.A. Marchant. Prediction of rodent carcinogencity using the DEREK system for 30 chemicals currently being tested by the National Toxicology Program. *Environmental Health Perspectives*, pages 1065–1074, 1996.

11. F. Provost and T. Fawcett. Analysis and visualization of classifier performance: comparison under imprecise class and cost distributions. In *Proceedings of the Third International Conference on Knowledge Discovery and Data Mining (KDD-97)*, pages 43–48. AAAI Press, 1998.

12. F. Provost and T. Fawcett. Robust classification systems for imprecise environments. In *Proceedings of the Fifteenth National Conference on Artificial Intelligence (AAAI-98)*. AAAI Press, 1998.

13. R. Purdy. A mechanism-mediated model for carcinogenicity: model content a prediction of the outcome of rodent carcinogencity bioassays currently being conducted on 25 organic chemicals. *Environmental Health Perspectives*, pages 1085–1094, 1996.

14. R.Benigni, C. Andreoli, and R.Zito. Prediction of the carcinogenicity of further 30 chemicals bioassayed by the US National Toxicology Program. *Environmental Health Perspectives*, pages 1041–1044, 1996.

15. A. Srinivasan. Note on the location of optimal classifiers in n-dimensional ROC space. Technical Report PRG-TR-2-99, Oxford University Computing Laboratory, Oxford, 1999.

16. A. Srinivasan and R.D. King. Using Inductive Logic Programming to construct Structure-Activity Relationships. In *Proceedings of the AAAI Spring Symposium on Predictive Toxicology*. AAAI Press, Menlo Park, CA, 1999. (to appear).

17. A. Srinivasan, R.D. King, and D.W. Bristol. An assessment of submissions made to the Predictive Toxicology Evaluation Challenge. In *Proceedings of the Sixteenth International Conference on Artificial Intelligence (IJCAI-99)*. Morgan Kaufmann, Los Angeles, CA, 1999. (to appear).

18. A. Srinivasan, R.D. King, S.H. Muggleton, and M.J.E. Sternberg. The Predictive Toxicology Evaluation Challenge. In *Proceedings of the Fifteenth International Conference on Artificial Intelligence (IJCAI-97)*. Morgan Kaufmann, Los Angeles, CA, 1997.

19. R.W. Tennant and J. Spalding. Predictions for the outcome of rodent carcinogenicity bioassays: identification of trans-species carcinogens and non-carcinogens. *Environmental Health Perspectives*, pages 1095–1100, 1996.

20. Y.T. Woo, D.Y. Lai, J.C. Arcos, M.F. Argus, M.C. Cimino, S. DeVito, and L. Keifer. Mechanism-based structure-activity relationship (sar) analysis of 30 ntp test chemicals. *Environ. Carcino. Ecotox. Revs. C*, 15:139–160, 1997.

Author Index

Springer
and the
environment

At Springer we firmly believe that an international science publisher has a special obligation to the environment, and our corporate policies consistently reflect this conviction.
We also expect our business partners – paper mills, printers, packaging manufacturers, etc. – to commit themselves to using materials and production processes that do not harm the environment. The paper in this book is made from low- or no-chlorine pulp and is acid free, in conformance with international standards for paper permanency.

 Springer

Lecture Notes in Artificial Intelligence (LNAI)

Lecture Notes in Computer Science